THE SELECTED LETTERS OF
THOMAS BABINGTON MACAULAY

THE SELECTED LETTERS OF THOMAS BABINGTON
MACAULAY

EDITED BY

THOMAS PINNEY

PROFESSOR OF ENGLISH
POMONA COLLEGE, THE CLAREMONT COLLEGES
CLAREMONT, CALIFORNIA

DULCE · PERICULUM

CAMBRIDGE UNIVERSITY PRESS

CAMBRIDGE
LONDON · NEW YORK · NEW ROCHELLE
MELBOURNE · SYDNEY

Published by the Press Syndicate of the University of Cambridge
The Pitt Building, Trumpington Street, Cambridge CB2 1RP
32 East 57th Street, New York, NY 10022, USA
296 Beaconsfield Parade, Middle Park, Melbourne 3206, Australia

This collection first published 1982

Printed in Great Britain at the University Press, Cambridge

Library of Congress catalogue card number: 81–10016

British Library Cataloguing in Publication Data
Macaulay, Thomas Babington Macaulay, *Baron*
The selected letters of Thomas Babington Macaulay.
1. Macaulay, Thomas Babington, *Baron* – Biography
2. Authors, English – 19th century – Biography
I. Title   II. Pinney, Thomas
828'.809   PR4963

ISBN 0 521 24009 3

The title-page device is
the Macaulay coat of arms, taken from Macaulay's seal
on a letter of 17 December 1833;
it was later the basis of Macaulay's arms as Baron Macaulay.
Acknowledgement is made to the Master and Fellows of
Trinity College, Cambridge.

CONTENTS

INTRODUCTION

Thomas Babington Macaulay, first Baron Macaulay, was, in his own time, England's most notable man of letters, distinguished as an essayist for the *Edinburgh Review*, as the poet of the *Lays of Ancient Rome*, as an exciting parliamentary orator, and, most of all, as the author of a *History of England* which rendered the Glorious Revolution in fascinating detail and animated the story with the highest patriotic idealism. Macaulay's literary achievement is heightened by the fact that he had an active public life as well: he sat in Parliament for sixteen years, took a leading part in the Reform Bill contest, twice held cabinet office with the Whigs, and, for four years, sat on the Supreme Council of India in Calcutta. Like other great Victorians, he added to these claims on our interest a strongly marked personality. A lifelong bachelor, living at the center of London, he was a familiar figure in high Whig society, where he ranked as the most formidable talker of the day, knowing everything and able to produce everything he knew thanks to a photographic memory. His slashing reviews, his habit of violent rhetorical exaggeration in speech and writing, his fearless confidence in his opinions, made him seem strong, tough – perhaps a bit shallow and insensitive. Yet beneath this crust – as we know now from his letters – Macaulay concealed a sensibility so tender that he suffered almost debilitating agonies whenever his affections were touched.

Macaulay's letters would be interesting simply for their record of their writer's life and career. His life, which coincided with the first half of the nineteenth century, touched on a remarkable number of the significant events and movements of the age, and the letters have an added interest in their reflection of this larger historical scene. For the first fifteen years of his life England was engaged in the great drama of the Napoleonic wars; his undergraduate years and his young manhood were then spent in the period of reactionary politics that followed Waterloo. But he felt the strong counter-currents of reform sooner than most. He grew up in an Evangelical family, fully sharing in the Evangelical faith that reform in the morality of public life was both necessary and attainable. He had an almost hereditary interest in the great Evangelical cause of the abolition of slavery, a movement in which his father was one of the most active and important figures. His precocious literary tastes were, at least partly, determined by the works of the Romantic revolution, particularly those of Byron and Scott. At Cambridge, as an undergraduate, he lived in an atmosphere laden with the new ideas of Jeremy Bentham, ideas that to many idealistic young men seemed to open the way to a new society. If Macaulay did not go the whole way with them, he was nevertheless stirred by the Benthamite vision of reason and justice.

The post-Napoleonic system of reactionary politics was already breaking up at the moment when Macaulay, by a lucky chance, was brought into Parliament. He was privileged, then, while still a young man, to take an enthusiastic part in the exciting struggle to pass the English Reform Bill – a triumph of the orderly freedom of British constitutionalism, as Macaulay always saw it, and certainly the great symbolic event of his public life: he was always to remain, in outlook and loyalties, a Man of 1832. The Reform Bill was followed soon after by the success of the long campaign for the abolition of slavery in the British dominions. Macaulay then went out to India, as part of a newly reformed government, determined to bring to a subject country some, at least, of the benefits of reform; his part was to write a new penal code, according to Benthamite ideas, and to decree a new system of education, Western and English, to replace the old and traditional.

After these first victories of reform at home and in the British dominions, England had to endure a decade of difficulties and severe political anxieties – famine in Ireland, distress in the industrial cities, the agitations of Chartism, the fierce political struggles over the Corn Laws, made men doubtful and pessimistic. Macaulay's faith in the good work already done carried him through these troubled years. He did not think that progress was inevitable; but he did not doubt the value of what had been accomplished in his own life. The work of the Evangelicals in the reform of public morals, of politicians in the reform of laws, of men of science in providing new amenity and comfort and speed (it is fitting that Macaulay's sister married into the family that promoted the first railway in England) were matters of fact, achievements that had been made by active men working under the blessings of political freedom. Macaulay believed in the reality of heroism – not surprising, perhaps, in one whose first impressions had been formed at a time when the high romantic energies of such figures as Napoleon and Byron were astonishing the world. It was a belief that he shared with his age. As G. M. Young has observed in writing of Macaulay,

The patriotism of early Victorian England was at heart a pride in human capacity, which time had led to fruition in England; and in the great humanist, who brought all history to glorify the age of which he was the most honoured child, it heard its own voice speaking.

This conviction is most fully and memorably expressed in Macaulay's masterwork, the *History of England*. The book appeared, with symbolic fitness, in the portentous year of 1848, when all the thrones of Europe trembled. England's alone stood secure and exalted, on the basis of what Macaulay fervently believed to be a just combination of freedom and order, achieved through a long tradition of such political action as he had himself had a part in.

The last decade of Macaulay's life, the years of his unchallenged high standing as spokesman for the age, are the years that the historians have agreed to recognize as the Victorian climacteric – the struggles and agitations of reform are, for the moment, over; the terrors of the Hungry Forties have subsided, and England enjoys for a decade the blessings of political tranquillity and of prosperity (that such states are never perfect the Crimean War and the Indian Mutiny remind us). Macaulay's rather early death, in 1859, seems in retrospect to be rightly timed, for the names and ideas that begin to fill the air then are prophetic of different, newly problematic times: it was the year of Darwin's *Origin of Species*, of Marx's *Contribution to the Critique of Political Economy*, of Fitzgerald's *Rubáiyát*, all portents of a world very different from the one that had delighted to recognize itself in Macaulay's image of English achievement.

Directly or indirectly, Macaulay's letters tell us a great deal about the historical events of the first half of the nineteenth century. Their immediate interest does not lie in that, however, but in what they reveal of an interesting and attractive personality whose observations and activities are set down in a prose of great vigor, rapidity, and point. Macaulay is to me, and I cannot doubt that he is and will be to many others, a delightful letter-writer. Writing informally and rapidly, thinking of no public beyond the person addressed, he always manages to maintain the virtues of his formal and meditated works, virtues which include precision, economy, and vividness of language, pellucid clarity of arrangement, and strong rhetorical emphasis. In reading Macaulay, one moves easily from point to point in what seems a natural and obvious sequence, and one always knows what it is that Macaulay has said. At the same time, the letters, as befits the intimacy of the private form, are freer, more loose and expansive in their movement, more relaxed in tone, often more racy in their language. Consider this passage from a letter of 1833 (it is not included in this selected edition), written to his sister Margaret to explain why she found the report of a speech made in the House of Commons hard to understand:

As to Rice's speech which astonished you so much the explanation is quite simple. He had been dining with the Lord Mayor, and was as drunk as a fiddler. Lord Althorp called out to some of those who were sitting on the Treasury Bench to pull the poor Secretary down by his coat-tail. We are a very joyous assembly. The other day Colonel Torrens made a tipsy speech about rent and profits, and then staggered away, tumbled down a staircase, and was as sick as a dog in the Long Gallery.

The management of effect here is admirable; the passage, brief and seemingly unadorned, is yet filled with little expressive touches that tell. The comic contrast of dignified setting and office with clownish behavior permeates the language: Rice, we are reminded, is an official, a Secretary in the ministry, but in plain cliché he is simply 'drunk as a fiddler'. His formal 'coat-tail' becomes an appliance of farce, something to be pulled. The single instance of Rice's performance is quickly generalized by the laconic, ironic observation, 'We are a very joyous assembly'. There is no reaching after words – 'drunk', 'joyous', 'tipsy' convey no very heightened or melodramatic notion of the habits of the House, but establish a lightness of tone that is dramatized for us in the antics of Colonel Torrens, who undercuts the severe theme of 'rent and profits' by his staggerings and tumblings. But the final phrase leaves us in no doubt as to Macaulay's position – the unpleasant vulgarity of 'sick as a dog' side by side with the public decorum of 'Long Gallery' implies a clear enough judgment. The passage is a perfectly casual, even trivial, instance of Macaulay's habits as a writer of letters, but it is not the less representative for that, and much more analysis might be devoted to its praise.

Macaulay is at his very best and most characteristic when he is explaining, illustrating, making a point, or persuading. The clarity of his expression, the range and aptness of his illustrations, and the definiteness of his manner all combine to the best effect in this kind of writing; his own evident pleasure in it comes through strongly, and, reading it, we can form an idea of what it must have been like to hear his marvellous table-talk. See, to take only a few instances out of the many that clamor for notice, his explanation to his sister Fanny of the reasons why Bunyan has no memorial in Westminster Abbey (14 October 1854), or his presentation to Ellis of the case for choosing literature over politics (30 December 1835), or his illustration to Bulwer Lytton of the abuse of pronouns in English prose (30 December 1848), or, for an instance of rhetorical power on a controverted question, his letter to Tytler on Indian education (28 January 1835).

The letters also have a pleasing variety of tones. He can be urbane and easy, as in much of the correspondence with his friend Ellis; dignified and generous to opponents, as in his remarks on James Mill (21 January 1834), or unsparing in abuse, as in his account of Croker (3 January 1843); excited over political conflicts, as in the Reform Bill letters or that on the Edinburgh election (9 July 1846); thoughtful and kind to the unlucky, as in his delicate explanations to Leigh Hunt (29 October 1841); playful without condescension to a child, as in his letters to his niece (*e.g.*, 21 August 1847); amusing and detached, as in his sketches of Holland House (*e.g.*, 29 July 1833). The control of most of his letters makes all the more striking those moments when, as in certain of the letters to Margaret and to Hannah, he breaks down and cannot constrain his feelings (*e.g.*, 26 November 1832). Taken together, the letters show Macaulay as a most attractive person: loving in his family relations, eager and high-minded yet without pretense or pomposity in his public life, affectionate and good-natured with his colleagues and friends, kind to those who needed help. And running through them, as the ground-note of his life, is his deep, inexhaustible love of literature.

This selection of Macaulay's letters is drawn from the full edition published in six volumes by the Cambridge University Press between 1974 and 1981. Each letter is printed without abbreviation or omission but without the annotation which accompanies it in the six-volume edition. Readers who, from this sample, are moved to learn more about Macaulay and his letters are referred to that edition, which contains a full index as well as annotation. For this selection, a general context of information is provided by the headnotes to each section of the letters. Further aids are provided by a chronology of Macaulay's life, a family tree, and an index in which many of the more important persons figuring in the letters are identified.

MACAULAY'S FAMILY

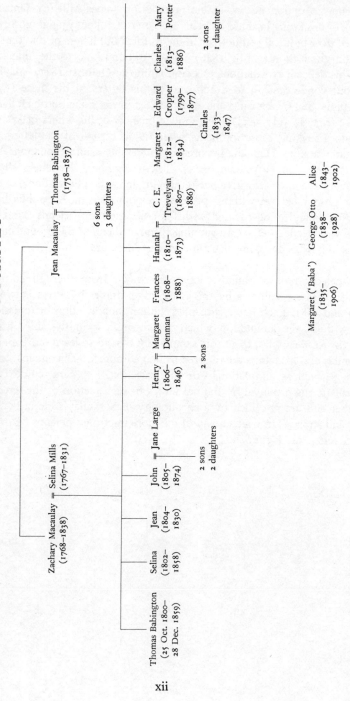

CHRONOLOGY

1800   October 25
        Macaulay born, Rothley Temple, Leicestershire
1802   Family moves from London to Clapham
1813   February
        Goes to school, Little Shelford, Cambridgeshire
1814   August
        School moves to Aspenden Hall, Hertfordshire
1818   October
        Enters Trinity College, Cambridge
1819   June
        Wins Chancellor's Prize for 'Pompeii'
1821   March
        Wins Craven University scholarship
        June
        Wins Chancellor's Prize for 'Evening'
        July–September
        On reading party, Llanrwst, North Wales
1822   January
        Takes B.A. without honors
        Admitted student of Lincoln's Inn
1823   June
        First contribution to *Knight's Quarterly Magazine*
        Autumn
        Family moves to 50 Great Ormond Street, Bloomsbury
1824   October
        Elected to Trinity fellowship
1825   January
        First contribution to *Westminster Review*
1826   February
        Called to the bar
        March
        Joins Northern Circuit

1846 July
Appointed Paymaster General in Russell's cabinet
1847 January
Appointed Trustee of British Museum
July
Defeated at Edinburgh
1848 December
Publishes *History of England*, vols. 1 and 2
1849 February
Begins second part of *History*
August–September
Trip to Ireland
1850 September
At Isle of Wight
1851 August–September
At Malvern
1852 July
Elected M.P. for Edinburgh
Suffers heart attack
August–September
Recuperates at Clifton
November
Speech at Edinburgh
1853 February
Elected to French Institute
June
Receives honorary D.C.L. from Oxford
July–August
At Tunbridge Wells
December
Publishes *Speeches*
1854 September
At Thames Ditton
December
Report on Indian Civil Service published
1855 June–September
At Richmond
December
Publishes *History*, vols. 3 and 4
1856 January
Retires from House of Commons

1856   May
            Leaves Albany for Holly Lodge
        August–September
            Italian tour with Ellis
        October
            Begins vol. 5 of *History*
1857   August
            Given peerage by Palmerston's government
1858   November
            Marriage of Margaret Trevelyan
1859   February
            C. E. Trevelyan returns to India
        October
            Learns that Hannah will leave for India
        December 28
            Dies

1 · FROM CLAPHAM TO WESTMINSTER, 1813–1833

These letters begin with the first moment of crisis in Macaulay's life, his departure at the age of twelve for Matthew Preston's school at Little Shelford, near Cambridge. Until that moment his life had been happily restricted to the circle of family and friends at the village of Clapham, near London. His father, Zachary, a London merchant engaged in trade with Sierra Leone, where he had once been governor, was a leader in the campaign to abolish the British slave trade and, later, to abolish slavery itself within the British dominions, campaigns whose most prominent name was William Wilberforce and whose unofficial headquarters was the circle of houses around Clapham Common where the Evangelical families of Wilberforce, Thornton, Venn, Stephen, and Macaulay made up the ranks of the 'Clapham Sect'. The Sect, which was extended to include such figures as Hannah More at Barley Wood, and the Evangelicals associated with Charles Simeon at Cambridge, determined the whole character and style of Macaulay's young years: domestic in its habits, strenuous in its religious practices, high-minded and public-spirited in its outlook. Balancing the austerity of this influence was a lively and happy family life in which Macaulay, despite the remarkable precocity which obviously set him apart from the ordinary, had no favored role beyond what belonged to his position as eldest son. By 1813 Zachary Macaulay and his wife Selina were the parents of nine children – in addition to their eldest, three other sons, and five daughters. Macaulay delighted in his family life and though as he grew older he came into some conflict with his father's strict views, he was always a dutiful and self-sacrificing son. Towards his mother, brothers, and sisters he was unfailingly loving and generous, always eager to be with them, whether at Clapham or at the Brighton house where they frequently stayed between 1814 and 1823.

Being sent off to school and separated from home was a cruel wrench to Macaulay, but he survived his homesickness at Little Shelford and at Aspenden, where the school later moved, to become a rather pedantic schoolboy (see, *e.g.*, [20? October 1817]). In October 1818 he entered Trinity College, Cambridge, a far happier move. Macaulay thoroughly enjoyed the freedom of undergraduate life, responded to the illustrious tradition of the college, and formed a lifelong pride in his connection with it. It is remarkable how high a proportion of Macaulay's friends and chosen counsellors were, to the end of his life and after all his varied associations, Trinity men whom he had known in his undergraduate days. He earned considerable literary distinction at Trinity, taking the Chancellor's Prize for English verse with 'Pompeii' in 1819 (see 5 February 1819) and again with 'Evening' in 1821. But the principal study of the place was mathematics, and for this, despite a summer devoted to the subject on a reading party in Wales (9 August 1821), Macaulay had neither taste nor aptitude. He attempted, but gave up on, the examination for an honors degree, to the scandal of Clapham. All was forgotten, however, when in 1824 he was elected to a Trinity fellowship.

Meantime, he had to think of a career, for his father's business was failing and it became clear while Macaulay was yet an undergraduate that he would have to take a large part of the care of his brothers and sisters. He chose to study law, was called to the bar from Lincoln's Inn in 1826, and in that year joined the Northern Circuit (2 April 1826). Macaulay's legal career hardly amounted to anything; he had few briefs, seems not to have made much effort to obtain practice, and quit the profession without regret as soon as he could. Yet for nearly four years the practice of law was his official business, and certainly contributed to his development. He was for some months in each of those years out of London, travelling over the roads of northern England in all weathers to such circuit towns as York, Appleby, Leeds, and Lancaster. There he would be in daily company with a crowd of judges, barristers, solicitors and their clients. Often, going to and from London, he would break his journey at the ancient estate of Rothley Temple, his birthplace in Leicestershire, the home of the uncle for whom he was named, Thomas Babington, and of a large cousinhood. It was on the Northern Circuit that Macaulay met his most intimate friend, Thomas Flower Ellis, and where he encountered the formidable Lord Brougham, maverick of the Whig party and for a time a rival of Macaulay within the literary and political world that both inhabited. Finally, such legal learning as Macaulay acquired in his barrister's career was his sole formal qualification for the appointment he received in 1833 as legal member of the Council of India; the crucial Indian episode in his career could not have come about otherwise.

As a lawyer based in London Macaulay was free for the first time since he had been sent off to school in 1813 to spend as much time as he liked with his family; he always looked back to these years when the family was still intact, and while he was yet a young man, as the happiest of his life. Something of the playfully affectionate style of the big brother appears in his letters to his brother Henry (26 May 1824) and his sister Hannah (20 March 1827 and 28 June 1830). It was during these years too that he discovered his special affection for his two youngest sisters, Hannah and Margaret. Both were infants when he left for school; in the years of his legal career they grew into young ladies, and by the time of his first parliamentary successes they had become the two whom he loved beyond all others, a relation ended only by death.

Macaulay's main ambition was to succeed in literature, and it was as a writer rather than a lawyer that he identified himself, even before leaving the university. Indeed, his publications went back to his schooldays, when he had contributed a defense of novel-reading to the severe pages of the *Christian Observer*, edited by his father (5 February 1819). While still at Cambridge he contributed essays and verses to *Knight's Quarterly Magazine* (7 and 20 June 1823), an enterprise directed by his Cambridge contemporary Praed. In 1825 he began contributing to the leading Whig journal, *The Edinburgh Review*, where, for the next twenty years, appeared the dazzling series of essays on history and literature that at once made his name and kept it before the public. The connection with the *Edinburgh Review* also brought him the friendship of literary Whigs like Sydney Smith (26 July 1826) and Francis Jeffrey (15 April 1828), for many years editor of the *Review* until succeeded by Macvey Napier.

Literature very soon led to politics; Lord Lansdowne offered him the seat for the pocket borough of Calne (10 February 1830), just on the eve of the conflict over the Reform Bill, and for most of the next quarter of a century Macaulay was an active Member of Parliament, several times holding office in Whig administrations, and, by his oratory, adding almost as much luster to his contemporary reputation as by his essays. His first, sensational, success came in the debates over the Reform Bill (7 March and 6 July 1831), marking him out at once as a rising hope of the liberal Whigs. It also put him in direct conflict with the Tory John Wilson Croker (7 March 1831), who became one of Macaulay's lifelong detestations. The atmosphere of reform in those days when Macaulay entered politics had been heavily charged by the French Revolution of 1830, and Macaulay, like other eager young men, was quick to make a visit of inspection to the scene itself (19 August and 14 September 1830).

Macaulay's ascent to the highest level of Whig society was made secure by his introduction to Holland House (30 May 1831), where the good-natured Lord Holland and the imperious Lady Holland brought together in their Kensington mansion all the lions on the Whig side of things, from Lord Grey, the prime minister, to Tom Moore, poet and diner-out. His experiences in the novel and exciting life of Holland House and its satellites in London society gave Macaulay a new set of scenes to describe

3

to his adoring sisters, and the letters of 1831 abound in some of his most amusing accounts of the great world at work and at play, rendered in the way most likely to interest two home-keeping sisters: in this way we see Lady Holland laying down the law on points of English usage (30 May 1831), Talleyrand telling stories in his inimitable manner (11 July 1831), the leaders of the Reform movement exchanging recipes for bedtime drinks (29 August 1831), and poor William IV behaving awkwardly at his coronation (9 September 1831). In the same letters we also see Macaulay's delight in his sisters' affection for him and his free and intimate relation to them, quizzing them over their taste in novel-reading, sharing in their concerns on their frequent visits to cousins and friends, and talking to them in Swift's 'little language' (6 July 1832, 17 June 1833).

Macaulay's political services were first rewarded by appointment to the Board of Control, the government body regulating the East India Company's management of India (6 July 1832); from this position he piloted through Parliament the important India Charter Act (30 July and 14 August 1832). Following the passage of the Reform Bill he was singled out as Whig candidate for the newly enfranchised borough of Leeds and triumphantly elected over his opponent, Michael Sadler, at the end of 1832. The triumph was mingled with bitterness, created by his sister Margaret's engagement and marriage to Edward Cropper, son of a Liverpool Quaker family. Macaulay objected not to Cropper but to what he took as the 'loss' of Margaret, strangely and unrestrainedly expressed in the letters of 26 November and 12 December 1832.

A fresh crisis arose through the struggles over the bill for the abolition of slavery in the British dominions, when Macaulay, out of loyalty to his father and to the Clapham Sect's long labor in the cause of abolition, repeatedly offered his resignation to the Whig ministers in protest against unsatisfactory provisions in the bill (11, 22, and 27 July 1833). At the end of this year came the culmination of the rapid climb that began in 1830; he was offered appointment as legal member of the Council of India – the supreme government – at the princely salary of £10,000 a year. Though acceptance meant long separation from England, an interruption – perhaps final – to his political career, and a considerable risk to his health in those unantiseptic days, Macaulay at once determined to take the chance. His reason was simple enough: he wanted the money. But not merely for himself, since his father, three of his sisters, and his youngest brother were all entirely dependent upon him. The opportunity of exercising power in a constructive way, according to the new currents of reform, was not lost on his imagination either. This section of the letters closes, then, with the prospect of a sharp turn in his fortunes, in an unknown direction, as the departure for India draws near.

MS: Trinity College.

Shelford February 3d. 1813

My dear Mamma

I do not remember being ever more gloomy in my life than when I first left Clapham. We got into the Cambridge Stage and at Chelmsford took a Post-Chaise which carried us on to Shelford where we arrived about 5 o'clock. Mr. Preston had put off the dinner hour till our arrival and here I met William Wilberforce who came but the day before; after dinner I got a little acquainted with the boys and after tea arranged my books in my shelves put my clothes in the drawers and began to shift for myself.

After prayers I went very sorrowfully to bed and in the morning went down expecting to be called instantly to work, but Papa was so kind as to take me with him to Cambridge on Mr. Preston's horses.

Of the boys only nine are come and there is but one more coming. William Wilberforce is as agreable and as mischievous. One boy at table was thought by Mr. Simeon who dined here to day to be a striking resemblance of Harry Venn upon which William as soon as dinner was over fastened the name of "Little master Wenn" upon him mimicking the boy's Cockney accent.

Added to the advantage of every boy's having a separate [room] is that Mr. Preston imposes a shilling fine upon every one who intrudes without leave into another boy's room. Give my kindest love to Selina Jane and John; tell Henry that I had rather be sitting by the fireside with him on my knee than seeing sights at Cambridge.

You cannot conceive with what pleasure I look forward to the holidays and in the mean time I ever remain

Your affectionate and dutiful Son
Thos. B Macaulay

TO ZACHARY MACAULAY, 22 [FEBRUARY] 1813

MS: Trinity College. Address: Mr. Macaulay / 26 Birchin Lane / London. Mostly published: Trevelyan, I, 40-1.

Shelford. Monday October 22nd. 1813

My dear Papa

As this is a Whole Holiday I cannot find a better time for answering your letter, and with respect to my health, I am very well, and tolerably cheerful, as Blundell the best and most clever of all the scholars is very kind and talks to me, and takes my part. He is quite a friend of Mr. Preston's. The other boys, especially Lyon, a Scotch boy, and Wilberforce are very goodnatured, and we might have gone on very well had not one Clayfield a Bristol fellow come here. He is unanimously allowed to be a queer fellow, and is generally characterized as a foolish boy, and by most of us as an ill-natured one.

In my learning I do Xenophon every day, and twice a week the Odyssey; in which I am classed with Wilberforce, whom all the boys allow to be very clever, very droll, and very impudent. We do Latin verses twice a week and I have not yet been laughed at, as Wilberforce is the only one who hears them being in my class. We are exercised also once a week in English compositions and once in Latin composition, as letters from persons renowned in history to each other. We get by heart Greek Grammar, or Virgil every evening. As for sermon writing, I have hitherto got off with credit, and I hope I shall keep up my reputation.

We have had the first meeting of our debating Society the other day, when a vote of censure was moved for, upon Wilberforce, but he getting up said, "Mr. President, I beg leave to second the motion" by this means he escaped. The kindness which Mr. Preston shows me is very great, he always assists me in what I cannot do, and takes me [to] walk out with him every now and then. Miss Preston is very kind: she comes now and then into my room to get me to read to her. My room is a delightful, snug, little chamber, which nobody can enter as there is a trick about opening the door. I sit like a king, with my writing desk before me, for (would you believe it) there is a writing desk in my chest of drawers, my books on one side my box of papers on the other with my armchair, and my candle for ev'ry boy has a candlestick snuffers and extinguisher of his own. Being press'd for room I will conclude what I have to say [to] morrow and ever remain my dear Papa,

your affectionate Son
Thomas B Macaulay

TO ZACHARY MACAULAY, 26 APRIL 1813

MS: Mr Gordon N. Ray. *Address:* Mr. Macaulay / Clapham. *Partly published:* Trevelyan, I, 42–3.

Little Shelford. April 26th. 1813.

My dear Papa,

I received yesterday a letter from Mamma, and an enclosed one from John, to whom I enclose an answer, with which I hope he will be satisfied; I am glad that Mamma is satisfied with my defence on the topic of exercise; and I assure her that though the current opinion here is that I shall grow tall there is not much suspicion of my being thin.

I am very much concerned to hear of the death of old Mrs. More; and I should be afraid it would put a stop to Miss H. More's intended journey. I am pleased however to hear of Mr. Venn's recovery; and I should be glad to know what illness he was labouring under.

Since I have given you a detail of my routine of weekly duties, I hope you will be pleased to be informed of my Sunday's occupations. It is quite a day of rest here, and I really look to it with pleasure through the whole of the week; after breakfast, we learn a chapter in the Greek Testament i.e. with the aid of our bibles, and without doing it with a dictionary etc. like other lessons. We then go to Church. We dine almost as soon as we come back, and we are left to ourselves till church-time; during this time I employ myself in reading; and Mr. Preston lends me any books for which I ask him, so that I am nearly as well off in this respect as at home, except for one thing; which though I believe it is useful is not very pleasant; I can only ask for one book at a time; therefore I am limited to one at a time; and cannot touch another till I have read it through; we then go to church, and after we come back I read as before till tea-time; after tea, we go in to sermon; and write it out as you were before told by Stainforth; I cannot help thinking that Mr. Preston uses all imaginable means to make us forget the sermon. For he gives us a glass of wine a-piece on Sunday, and on Sunday only, the very day when we want [to] have all our faculties awake; and some do literally go to sleep during the sermon, and look rather silly when they wake; I, however, have not fallen into this disaster.

My love to Mamma, and all at home. / I ever remain, My dear Papa
Your affectionate Son,
Thos. B. Macaulay

TO SELINA MILLS MACAULAY, [12 AUGUST 1813]

MS: Trinity College. *Address:* Mrs. Macaulay / 26 Birchin-Lane / London.

Shelford. Thursday

My dear Mamma.

I arrived here safe and sound, but as low-spirited as can well be imagined. I cannot bear the thoughts of remaining so long from home. I do not know how to comfort myself, or what to do. There is nobody here to pity me or to comfort me, and if I were to say I was sorry at being from home, I should be called a baby. When I am with the rest I am obliged to look pleasant, and to laugh at Wilberforce's jokes, when I can hardly hide the tears in my eyes. So I have nothing to do but to sit and cry in my room, and think of home and wish for the holidays. I am ten times more uneasy than I was last half year. I did not mean to complain, but indeed I cannot help it. Forgive my bad writing, for indeed, in the state in which I am it is a great deal for me to write at all. Pray write as soon as possible. I ever remain / my dear mamma

Your affectionate Son
T B Macaulay

P S My love to Papa and all at home.

TO SELINA MILLS, SELINA, AND JANE MACAULAY,
[29 APRIL 1814]

MS: Trinity College. *Address:* Mrs. Macaulay / No 26 Birchin / Lane / London.

[Little Shelford]

My dear Mamma,

I mean by this single letter to pay off all that I owe to Selina, Jane, etc. and shall therefore split it into 3 parts, one for each of you. What would I have given to see the King of France enter London. It was a day of triumph indeed, and crowned most gloriously the Events of the Year. What a scene for future Historians and Poets. It is a scene, however, I fear which we shall never see again.

I am much obliged to you for your kindness in offering me Lord Byron's Ode. Stainforth made me a present of it Yesterday; – this is only one of the many instances of Kindness I have received from him; – I hardly ever saw such Kindness united with such Talents and Knowledge.

The Ode pleases me exceedingly. The passages that please me most are

> "If thou hadst died as honour dies,
> Some new Napoleon might arise,
> But who would climb the Solar Height
> To set in such a starless night."

And again

> "The tumult and the Vanity,
> The rapture of the strife
> The EARTHQUAKE VOICE OF VICTORY
> To thee the breath of life."

What a grand metaphor is that "the Earthquake voice of Victory." The comparison between the late Emperor of the French, and Sylla I like. I cannot say I admire much that between him and Charles the Fifth. There is one couplet that strikes me

> "not till Thy fall could Mortal's guess
> ambition's less than littleness."

To take leave of Lord Byron and Napoleon the ci-devant Emperor, I was much concerned to hear of the Battle of Toulouse, and yet I think it was a glorious ending of the Contest too. Lord Wellington's military talents seem to sink into nothing when compared with the Magnanimity and Forbearance which he displayed. He is indeed a Hero.

After much talking and debating it has at length been all but decided that we shall go to Hayden. This is not the least among the many and great advantages flowing from the peace.

We are now reading Clarkson's History of the Slave-Trade. It interests me exceedingly. I am highly delighted with the character of Mr. Granville Sharpe. Such noble boldness and zeal! Such self-devotion in the cause of liberty and justice! I think without depreciating the merits of Mr. Wilberforce, he holds a most exalted station among the Abolitionists. Think of a man at a time of life when the habits are formed, and when he was professionally engaged, spending all the time he could in studying the law that he might forward this great cause!

I hear that Mr. Wilberforce is deeply engaged at present in business respecting the Slave-trade and I should be obliged to Papa to acquaint me with the nature of it. / I ever remain, my dear Mamma,

Your affectionate Son
T B Macaulay

To Selina Macaulay. One of the High and Mighty Triumvirate of girls, member of the most Honourable Committee for circulating "the Bride of Abydos," Greeting. I am much obliged unto thee for thy Epistles, unto me sent, and by me received. I am about to tell unto thee a story which however strange it may appear unto thee, and though thou mayest think it a terry-diddle, is a very true fact.

Mr. Preston hath a gardener, and his name is Jennings. This man hath a sister. This sister hath a friend. This friend had a law-suit. She gained it. The sister of Jennings happening to be telling this story to a Lady whose servant she was, the Lady asked her straitly of her Kinsfolk, and learning that she had a brother named Jennings, said unto her "There is an Estate in Suffolk of six thousand a year named Acton place, that hath been in

Chancery these 30 Years. The name of the late Proprietor was Jennings." The woman hereupon told her brother, and Jennings is now in a fair way of getting 6000 a year besides large property in the funds. The name of the Estate is Acton Hall. Jennings went to see it, and said that there were a Mort of Windows. Mr. Preston examined into it and thinks that Jennings hath hopes of getting the money.

Farewell. / I ever remain my dear Selina

your affectionate Brother
T B M

Unto Jane Macaulay Greeting

My dear Jane,

I received your letter and made it out with out much difficulty. I think it contains a fine description of my Uncle Colin's taking you to Town. It lays things b[efore] one in so forcible a light. Allow me to paraphrase it. "We had just sate down to lessons," to all that dull stuff [   ], and geography, and stuff-a-nonsense, "when" O [sur]prize of surprizes, "a coach stopped at the door and in came Uncle Colin;" to crown all this "he took Selina etc. to town in a coach drawn by eight cream coloured horses"! This error amused me a little. You and the rest seemed to have intruded yourself into the Coach of the Regent. I found however that you had only made a little mistake in the Order and stops. I have appropriated so much room to Buonaparte, and Jennings that I have very little more left. You must let me say however that I am much pleased at going to the Isle of Wight. Give my love to Papa etc. / I ever remain / My dear Jane

Your affectionate Brother,
T B Macaulay

TO ZACHARY MACAULAY, 11 JULY 1814

MS: Mr Gordon N. Ray. *Address:* Z. Macaulay Esqr. (in Selina Mills Macaulay's hand).

[Brighton] July 11. 1814

My dear Papa,

We are arrived at Brighton and comfortably settled there, as I suppose Mamma's letter has before now informed you. We are as well off as we can be without your company. When are we to expect you here? Can you accompany my Aunt Babington and Matthew?

Yesterday we went to Lady Huntingdon's Chapel, and heard two very good sermons from one Mr. Muffin, a travelling Minister, I believe, who now officiates at Brighton.

We bathed to day for the first time; the baby, I understand, put a very queer face upon the operation, and Fanny was actually petrified and overwhelmed by horror and amazement at finding herself precipitated from the tremendous height of the stairs of the machine (or, as Misery Beresford calls it) of the sea-hearse, into the raging deep. The bathing women, I am informed, animated and encouraged them to take the dreadful leap, by blandishments of a very remarkable kind. When Henry made his appearance upon the stairs they saluted him thus "Come my darling, come my pretty prince, come my King, Come, *defence of his country."*

I have not yet seen enough of this fashionable town to be able to give you any account of what is now going on in it. The Steine is a rare medley; – Generals, and Drummers, and Deserters, and bathing-women, and Peeresses, and Quakers, and masters, and misses, and Sailors, are taking the air perpetually in its walks. I have heard that there are from twenty to thirty thousand persons at Brighton who are not stated inhabitants. I suppose we may expect his royal Highness the Prince Regent, as the Pavilion is now being repaired and done up.

I was very sorry to hear of your tooth-ache. It is an additional reason however for coming to Brighton, and for taking the benefit of our fine sea-breezes, our ample beach, and our noble Cliffs.

I think I can venture to join with my own love the loves of Mamma, and all the youngsters who are at their favourite amusement of *shell*[*ing*] *pease*, which I dare not interrupt. / I ever remain, / my dear Papa,

Your affectionate Son,

Thos B Macaulay

TO SELINA MILLS MACAULAY, 26 OCTOBER 1814

MS: Trinity College. *Address:* Mrs. Macaulay / No 26. Birchin-Lane / London.

[Aspenden Hall] October 26th. 1814.

My dear Mamma,

I am both concerned and surprised that Papa should have found necessary to charge me with remissness in writing. I sent off a letter to you on Wednesday morning last, which would have reached you on Thursday. If it miscarried I most certainly am not to bear the blame.

Well then! – I am fourteen years old. The return of that memorable Æra brings with it many pleasant and many painful recollections. I cannot but smile when I remember my ninth birthday, upon which as I took a walk with you upon the Common I expressed my wonder, and actually doubted whether it could be really true that I was nine years old. The thoughts which struck me upon that reflection I cannot express better than in the Latin of my favourite Horace. Papa must construe it to you.

"Immortalia ne speras monet annus et almum
Quae rapit hora diem.
Frigora mitescunt Zephyris; – ver proterit æstas
Interitura simul
Pomifer Autumnus fructus effuderit, et mox
Bruma recurrit iners."

I like Smollett less and less the more I read of him. He has a ridiculous mixture of levity and anti-fanaticism whenever he mentions religion. He seems to use it and superstition as terms perfectly synonimous; – for instance in one of his Characters he says some such thing as this "He was ambitious, enterprising, and *religious*." He has a most furious invective against some misguided men who displeased him by carrying a bill in the house of Commons against "exercising the militia and volunteers on Sunday, which they gave the fanatical appellation of The Lord's day." Things of this sort are more disgusting, (to me at least), than even the broad and shameless Scepticism of Hume, who in his history of the great Rebellion puts religion at the head of the political engines which an able governor should employ, and honestly avows, at least by fair inference, that that is its only use.

England has certainly been unfortunate in her Historians. Till the appearance of Hume's history it was her reproach that the best account of her Kingdom was written by a foreigner Rapin-de-Thoyras. And now when one of her own children has produced a History equal to any of the Classical Models in elegance, and, except as far as regards religion, superior to them in authenticity, it is disgraced by the utter want of religious principle. This is a disadvantage, I think, not only as it tends to misrepresent those subjects in comparison of which history is unimportant, but as it takes away from the interest of the work. Livy and Herodotus believe [a]ll the stories of their Jupiters and [Minerva]s; – so that in reading their histori[es] we see that they enter into the spirit of the time, and yet can separate between what is true and what is false. Hume discards or omits every-thing about religion, except a very little which he distorts and misrepresents. I think that History should not only be pleasant and authentic, as Critics say, but that the Historian should not be entirely cold and incredulous upon the most important topic in every point of view that ever occupied the attention of man.

I did not perceive that I had filled 3 sides of a page with this stuff. To answer your interrogatories. I did not tell you how to send parcels when you asked last time, because when I wrote I expected to dine with Papa the next day; – The parcels are sent by the Cambridge coach which passes through Buntingford. There they are left, and transmitted to "the young gentlemen at the big Hall on the Hill."

Give my love to Papa, Kenneth, Selina, Jane, etc. Thank them in my name for the "many happy returns" which I am sure they wish me. / I ever remain, My dear Mamma

Your affectionate Son
T B Macaulay

TO ZACHARY MACAULAY, 14 MAY 1816

MS: Trinity College. *Address:* Z Macaulay Esq. / No 26. Birchin-Lane / Cornhill / London.

Aspenden Hall. May. 14. 1816.

My dear Father,

I now proceed to inform you of the subjects of an examination of which, to use a favourite military phrase, I have already paralysed a great part. For Latin verses. Moses on Mount Pisgah. Craniology: The monastery of Iona. An Heroic Epistle from Madame Bertrand to some friend in France. – For English Verses, the Runic superstitions. If a book happens to lie about the house on that subject I should be very much obliged to you to send it me. If not it would be useless trouble to procure any, as I am pretty well acquainted with the outline at least of the Creed of the Scalds. We have also to draw up a Synopsis of the notes of Porson, Professor Monk, and Bloomfield, to Euripides' plays; a very useful exercise, and approximating very nearly to my annual employment of index making. – As to the books in which we are to be examined, there is nothing either difficult or formidable in them, at least not to me. The Medea of Euripides, a pretty good play, not much worse than the worst of Racine's. Seriously, I think Euripides the vilest poet that ever put pen to paper. His three most famous plays are the Orestes, the Phœnissæ, and the Medea. There are ten good lines in the first, twenty in the second, and fifteen in the third. But I am digressing a little from the subject; we also read the 2nd Book of Thucydides (part of it rather), the Life of Agricola in Tacitus, and a few other trifling things not important enough to mention.

I was alarmed seriously at the account which the Times gave of the destruction of Sierra-Leone. But I did not believe it? And why? Because an American related it. What is the cause that that people wherever they go, do nothing but mischief and inspire nothing but aversion and disgust? Of all the hideous reptiles which the new world produces, boa-constrictors, Alligators, snakes of all shapes and sizes, I think none so full of venom, so dangerous, and so detestable, as a full-grown United-States viper. I did not see at first the extreme aptness of the metaphor. Vipers are said to devour their parents. The Americans have attempted to do this. But if I were John Bull, as I have the honour of being one of his members, I would drub our graceless offspring into reverence, if not into love.

My admiration of Sismondi is extreme. I rank him among the best writers of the age. He joins the profound research of an Italian, and the liberal independance which is the characteristic of Britons, with the light, gay, and amusing, liveliness of the French. There is one most splendid passage which concludes his Chapter on Arabian literature. Not having the book here, I will attempt to give you the words in English as nearly as I can; indeed I ought to remember it, for I have sate for hours considering and revolving it.

"Perhaps in the course of some centuries, Europe itself, which is now the Empire of the arts and sciences, of Civilization and of greatness, which judges so well of the ages that are past, and calculates so wisely on the events that are to come, may lose those advantages which are now its boast, and the power which it exercises over the most remote regions of the habitable Globe. Her cities may sleep in the dust. Her temples may fall as the Capitol and the Pantheon have fallen already; and nothing may remain of this happy region of the world, but the memory of what it once was, of the Genius which inspired, and the wisdom which instructed it. Some other people may arise, perhaps in the mountains from which the Orinoco rolls, perhaps in the forests of New Holland, a people of other languages, other manners, other religions, which will restore the human race again, and moralize like us upon the past which when it reflects that we have existed, that we have known what they know, that we have, like them, looked forward to an eternity of greatness, will pity the weak and unavailing efforts of man to obtain an immortality which fate has refused him; and will contemplate the names of a Newton, and a Tasso as instances of the fruitless struggle which genius maintains against the destiny which decrees that every thing human must perish." This paraphrase is very free. The passage defies translation.

With this passage which will very well supply the pl[ace of] a letter and with love to My Mother etc. and many congratulations on Mrs. Thatcher's convalescence.

Farewell.
T B Macaulay.

MS: Trinity College. *Address:* Z Macaulay Esq. / No 26 Birchin-Lane / Cornhill / London.

[Aspenden Hall]

My dear Father,

Mr. Preston returns to night to resume the delegated sceptre, and to morrow Mr. Scholfield leaves us. I like the deputy extremely upon the whole; He supplied the vacant chair admirably; but I think that he has contracted too much of the University style of literature. There seems to me to be the same difference between one of the accurate Cantabrigian Scholars who compares readings and collates Editions, and gives to every Greek particle its due honours and its definite significations, and an elegant scholar who tastes the beauties of the classics without condescending to those minutiæ, which there is between a mixer of colours and an amateur in painting, between a labourer who mends the roads on Malvern or Richmond Hill, and the tourist who admires the picturesque beauty of the scenery. The business of the one is to facilitate the enjoyment of the other. But to make that the end which ought only to be the means, and to consider the man who can give the best conjecture as to a corrupt passage in a nonsensical chorus, which no body can ever understand, and which no body would be wiser if he did, as a better scholar than him who can enjoy the beauties of the classics without digging into the rubbish which sometimes obscures and buries their meaning, is a truly deplorable perversion of judgement. "Words" said the greatest linguist that ever lived, "are the sons of earth; ideas are the daughters of heaven." Words bear to fine passages of writing, about the same relation which stones bear to the edifice which they compose; – and I think that the man who should neglect the magnificent architecture of St. Paul's in order to discuss the quality of its Portland stone, is not more destitute of taste than he who descends from the contemplation of the sublimity of Eschylus or the pathos of Euripides to settle the force of every μεν and δε which occurs in their pages.

I am indeed a little disposed to question that right of superiority which classical literature has so long claimed over that of other nations. Systems once believed impregnable, opinions once interwoven with the texture of all science, have been disputed, contested and overthrown, and consigned to oblivion; – Aristotle has fallen from the throne which he once shared with the inspired writers, unless indeed he may be said to have looked down upon them from a superior eminence of public estimation. The litterature of France has ceased to be the model of our belles-lettres; and writers who, like Cowley and Ben Jonson, flattered themselves with the hope of an immortality as durable as brilliant are hardly read or quoted.

Perhaps the time approaches when a more important revolution shall break the fetters which have so long entangled the litterature of Europe; – when some original thinker shall ask, why we spend the ten most important years of our life to enable ourselves to read odes and plays, about a tenth part as good as those in our mother tongue, or to understand histories of the quarrels of two little states like Athens and Lacedæmon, quarrels, about as important to the general system of the world as a lawsuit between two parishes. Àpropos of law-suits, – if anything on such a subject can be other than mal-àpropos, – so we must be content with our present abode – Amen. We have other and more powerful consolations against greater calamities. Against this let us use the prescription of the Roman Epicurean; – worthy of a better sect than Horace's.

> "Nunc domus Umbreni sub nomine; nuper Ofelli
> Dictus erit nulli proprius, sed cedet in usum
> Nunc mihi, nunc alii. – Quocirca vivite fortes
> Fortia que adversis opponite pectora rebus"

Loves to all. –

Farewell.

T B M.

TO ZACHARY MACAULAY, 23 OCTOBER 1818

MS: Harvard University. *Address:* Z Macaulay Esq. / No 20 Cadogan place / Chelsea / nr. London. *Mostly published:* Lady Knutsford, *Life and Letters of Zachary Macaulay,* 1900, pp. 342–3.

Cambridge. Oct. 23. 1818

My dear father,

I would have written earlier had I had any thing to communicate, which however is not even now the case; so that all my information must be that I am alive, and well, and comfortable, that Cambridge is a strict exemplification of the old maxim, Magna urbs, magna solitudo, and that I live among my small circle of friends as familiarly and as quietly as if we were in a desert island. I have resolved to have no second order of acquaintance, no deputy-friends who torment each other and themselves by ceremonies which only betray the coolness of their regard, and by a measured interchange of the dullest visits. I will be social and not gregarious.

George Stainforth makes a most excellent tutor, and indeed his instructions and preparation for them occupy so much of my time that I have not an overplus to spare for more private studies. The mathematical lectures are merely like learning my horn-book again, and will be so during the whole of this year.

I could not trust myself to say and can hardly venture to write all I feel upon entering on this world of hazard and danger and competition and honour. The evils of Cambridge, from all that I have been able to learn, are evils which must be *sought*, and from such a depth of moral degradation I trust that the goodness of God, my own education, and the connections which I have formed will preserve me. Its honourable distinctions are it seems the hard earned, but the certain, fruit of exertion and perseverance. If I would not willingly fail of attaining to some share in them, I trust it is not from selfish motives. I am sure I never valued any human applause so much as your quiet approbation, nor desired any human rewards so much as your pleasure in my success. And I am far less desirous to return loaded with medals or distinguished on the tripos-paper, than to acquire here those accomplishments and that information which may qualify me to inherit your public objects; and to succeed to your benevolent enterprises. There is an anecdote in Roman History which always affected me much. Fabius who when he was a child had been carried on his father's knee on his triumphal entry into Rome, insisted that when he himself came home with similar honours his father should enter his chariot, and share the honours of his son. I never had a higher ambition than that we might, if it please God, triumph together over the enemies of humanity, and I will do my utmost to obtain those weapons of assault and that armour of defence which literature furnishes for such contests, in this seat of its dominion.

My dear Mother, I send you my most affectionate love. My dear Jane are your tears dry? I kiss you with my "mind's lips." –

Farewell.

T B M

TO ZACHARY MACAULAY, 16 NOVEMBER 1818

MS: Harvard University. *Address:* To | Zachary Macaulay Esq. | No 20 Cadogan Place | Chelsea | Nr. London.

Cambridge Monday | 16 Nov. 1818

My dear Father,

You ask for the details of my days. These are not easily given. College which I had imagined the favourite abode of those powers of Method and Order the daughters of Mathesis and the Mighty Mother of the Dunciad, is alas! the place where I find myself least able to apportion certain hours to certain pursuits. Sometimes for a week together I never find it necessary to make the slightest preparation for lectures. At others I am employed for half-a-dozen hours in discovering the solution of some problem which is given out for the exercise of skill by our tutor. Sometimes George Stainforth finds me uninterrupted employment for a long course of time, and sometimes, while he is employed in collecting materials for me, I am left to my own devices.

I have not been idle, and I have not trifled. My veins have been like Maberley's strangers to the juice of the grape; I do not go to wine parties. And yet I do not find that I have done what I should have expected. I cannot accuse myself of having read any thing but grave Latin and Greek. But there is something desultory about an unaccustomed mode of life which renders, as I am told, the first few weeks of a man's residence here less useful than those which follow. Business with people to whom I am not accustomed and in forms of which I know nothing, interrupts and delays me. If I rise at four the chapel breaks in upon my morning studies. If I sit down after dinner it interrupts me immediately again. I suppose I shall soon get to calculate upon these interruptions better, and be enabled to measure out my time more accurately.

I have long been doubting how far it would be expedient for me to return at Christmas. The scholarship will not be contested till the last week of January, so that unless I paid you a visit before it, I shall not come home till Easter. I think, if you have no objection, of coming at the end of the term, about the 17th of December and staying over Christmas, and then returning to my preparations. I expect to do more in a day of the vacation when uninterrupted by lectures and chapel than in a week of the term. Francis of whom you know something is here. He took a high degree, but I believe allowed by the Exa[min]ers themselves to be below his Mathematical merits. He has paid me very kind attention [and] offered his assistance to me in any diffic[ulties] that may arise in my mathematical studies. Stainforth is all attention and kindness. His system is most rational, and costs me as much labour as it ought, and himself, I believe, rather more. He is assisting Malden, in the most friendly manner, in his classical preparations. –

I enclose a translation which I wrote the other day of Vincent Bourne's beautiful Latin Poem intended for an inscription on Milton's Statue in Westminster Abbey. It is rather a paraphrase, and that a pretty free one, than a translation, so that if the original is not at hand, it may be judged by its own demerits. I am without apology towards my dear Jane. But though I am compelled to defer my tardy epistle by the necessity of answering her queries, she is never out of my head or my heart.

My affectionate Love to my mother, to her, and all at home.

Farewell

T B M

MS: Trinity College. *Address:* Zachary Macaulay Esq. / No 16 George Street / Mansion House / London. *Partly published:* Trevelyan, 1, 89–91.

Cambridge Friday Feb. 5 1819

My dear Father,

Our contest, after a duration of nine days terminated yesterday at 3 o'clock. In a month its result will probably be known. Though I have been almost entirely debarred from exercise during its continuance I am in excellent health; and hope to be perfectly refreshed by a few days of idleness and amusement.

I have not of course had time to examine with attention all your criticisms on Pompeii. I certainly am much obliged to you for withdrawing so much time from other more important business to examine the effusions of a poetaster. Most of the remarks which I have examined are perfectly just. But I think that perhaps the use of the word barbarism in the sense in which I have employed it may be defended. This word and its cognates in both the classical languages is used to express anything foreign. By English writers it is often employed strictly in the ancient sense to express anything not Greek or Roman. Thus Milton in a line not very different from mine

"Show'rs on her Kings *barbaric* pearl and gold"

Par Lost Book 2.

And Bowdler in the best poem he ever wrote has this line. I quote from memory but I think accurately

"And Persia flaming with *barbaric* gold."

Even Gibbon, and the more severe Mitford frequently admit the word into their prose, where at all events it is more objectionable than in poetry.

As to introducing the theatrical spectacles at noonday, it is certainly in costume. Those of the Greeks were always celebrated in the morning; as also those of the Romans till the time of Nero. Tacitus mentions it as one of the disgraces of the reign of that monster that he changed the time of those exhibitions to the evening and thus rendered the theatre what it is in our country the centre of every thing that is vicious and disgusting. We may however suppose that this custom of the capital had not extended to the provincial towns, or at least an anachronism of a few years is scarcely of much importance.

As to the more momentous charge, the want of a moral, I think it might be a sufficient defence that, if a subject is given which admits of none, though the man who writes on it may be blamed, yet his writing without a moral is scarcely censurable. But is it the real fact that no literary employment is estimable or laudable which does not lead to the inculcation of moral truth or the excitement of virtuous feeling? Do we not think with pleasure rather than disapprobation of a man who delights to amuse little children, to play with them, to tell them agreable stories, and to give them fruit and play things. We do not put him on a level with him who teaches them to read, or instructs them in the first rudiments of religion. Yet we feel an approbation of his conduct. On what principle do we feel it? He effects no moral purpose. He teaches them nothing important. He rouses no laudable passion. – Simply, I conceive, because he *communicates pleasure innocently*. This then I take as an axiom which experience and the common sense of mankind demonstrate, and on which, as on every thing else which reason obviously inculcates, Christianity likewise places the seal of her sanction, – that it is an employment in itself laudable *to communicate pleasure innocently*.

Books of amusement are to men what toys and sugar plums are to children. They are the employment of the moments of leisure, the relief of hours of languor, they afford a refined, an elegant, and often an elevated enjoyment. They tend to polish the mind, to improve the style, to give variety to conversation, and to lend a grace to more important accomplishments. He who can effect this has surely done something. Is no useful end served by that writer whose works, though perhaps inculcating no direct moral information, have soothed weeks of languor and sickness, have relieved the mind exhausted from the pressure of employment, by an amusement which delights without enervating, which relaxes the tension of the powers without rendering them unfit for future exercise. That men should be eternally happy is doubtless the great object of benevolence. That they should be happy on earth as far as they innocently may, is surely an object not to be despised. And in this point of view the poet whose trifle amuses the reader for a spare hour may claim to be considered as an inferior labourer in the same field of benevolence with the liberators of Africa, the explorers of our prisons, and the surgeons of our hospitals.

I have been so used to see opinions which I tenaciously held subverted by arguments which though pretty obvious had never occurred to me, that I should not be surprised to see these observations refuted; and I shall not be sorry if they are so. I feel personally little interest in the Question. If my life be a life of literature, it shall certainly be one of literature directed to moral ends. But I write thus because I think the restrictions which some excellent persons now impose on writers too severe. Do we not allow various callings to be exercised in society? Are all our artificers and our tradesmen employed in providing for the necessaries or even for the comforts of life? Our butchers and bakers are surely not reputed a more respectable class of the community than our Goldsmith's and jewellers.

Then why should not some allowance be made to literary men. Is literature the only thing in which we are to be restricted from luxuries, and permitted to enjoy or manufacture nothing which does not come under the denomination of necessity. I can scarcely approve of this sumptuary law. 1 own I cannot see why the man who writes an amusing poem, the Lady of the Lake for instance, is not as well employed as the man who manufactures a pearl-broach. Which gives the more pleasure cannot be doubted. And certainly *I* cannot doubt which is of the more advantage to society. – "But the goldsmith lives upon his jewellery. He works for his subsistence." – And Southey has lived upon his poetry. So in a great measure has Scott. So has Campbell. So did Thomson, Pope, Johnson. – I cannot see why a useless book is worse than a useless necklace. And if it be an agreable book, I should not hesitate to pronounce it better.

At all events let us be consistent. I was amused in turning over an old volume of your kind present the Xtian Observer, to find a gentleman signed Excubitor, (one of my Antagonists in the Question of Novel-reading,) after a very pious argument on the hostility of Novels to a religious frame of mind, proceeding to observe that he was shocked to hear a young Lady who had displayed extraordinary knowledge of modern and ephemeral literature, own herself ignorant of Dryden's fables! – Consistency with a vengeance! – The reading of modern poetry and novels excites a worldly disposition and prevents ladies from reading Dryden's fables! – Excubitor who excludes Waverley from his library, who shudders at the sight of Roderick, who calls for salts at the name of Lord Byron, shocked at a Lady for not reading Dryden's fables!!! – This is only one out of ten thousand exemplifications of my meaning. There is a general disposition among the more literary part of the religious world to cry down the elegant literature of our own times, while they are not in the slightest degree shocked at atrocious profaneness or gross indelicacy when a hundred years have stamped them with the title of *Classical*. I pretend not to be right. But I am sure I am consistent. I say; "if you read Dryden you can have no reasonable objection to reading Scott." The strict antagonist of ephemeral reading exclaims, – "Not so. – Scott's poems are very pernicious. They call away the mind from spiritual religion and from Tancred and Sigismunda." "Do not expect perfection," says Hannah More, (herself, by the bye, not quite free from the fault which I censure) "but expect consistency." –

I intended to have added something upon the nature of the Ancient classic poets whom we are enjoined by all people to read, and to point out how much more exceptionable they frequently are than the very worst of the poets whose names excite the abhorrence of our modern critics. I plead for neither. I give no opinion. I merely demand a consistent sentence.

I merely demand with Horace and Pope, that a hundred or a thousand years should not be considered as purifying the licentious or canonizing the impious writer. – If mankind continue the same, it is not improbable that a couple of centuries hence future Excubitors will with similar zeal exclaim against ladies who read the poems which will then come from the shops of future booksellers, to the neglect of Parisina, and Lalla Rookh, those noble monuments of *Classical* genius. But I have far exceeded all ordinary limits. If these hasty remarks fatigue you, impute it to my desire of justifying myself from a charge which I should be sorry to incur with justice. Love to all at home.

Affectionately farewell.

T B M.

TO ZACHARY MACAULAY, [SEPTEMBER 1819]

MS: Trinity College. *Address:* Zachary Macaulay Esq / No 16. George Street / Mansion House / London. *Partly published:* Trevelyan, 1, 93–5.

[Cambridge]

My dear Father,

My mother's letter, which has just arrived, has given me much concern. The letter which has, I am most sorry to learn, given you and her uneasiness, was written rapidly and thoughtlessly enough, but can scarcely, I think, as far as I remember its tenour, justify some of the extraordinary inferences which it has occasioned. I can only assure you most solemnly that I am not initiated into any democratical societies here, that I know no people who make politics a common or frequent topic of conversation, except one man who is a determined Tory. It is true that this Manchester business has roused some indignation here, as at other places, and drawn philippics against the Powers that be from lips which I never heard opened before but to speak on University contests or University scandal. For myself I have long made it a rule never to talk on politics except in the most general manner; and I believe that my most intimate associates have no idea of my opinions on the general questions of party. I can scarcely be censured, I think, for imparting them to you; – which however I should scarcely have thought of doing, (so much is my mind occupied with other concerns,) had not your letter invited me to state my sentiments on the Manchester Business. Political questions must necessarily occupy some portion of every man's thoughts. There is scarcely a man in the country above the lowest classes who has not a chance and an expectation of being, at some period of his life, a wheel, more or less important, in the political machine. And, though it may be to be regretted that boys will form crude opinions on such subjects, it will scarcely be easy to prevent any person of reflection however young, who is engaged in studying the history and the politics of other nations from forming certain notions on such subjects and applying them to his own. All that can be expected is, I think, that he should do what I do, refrain from expressing them, from the knowledge that he may learn many facts and hear many arguments which will alter their whole character; and carefully keep from doing or saying any thing which he may repent, when time and experience have sobered his judgement. This has really been my course, and, if I have laid my crude ideas before you, (and it has been before you alone,) it has been by no means so much that you might approve as that you might correct them.

I hope that this explanation will remove some of your uneasiness. As to my opinions I have no particular desire to vindicate them. They are merely speculative, and therefore cannot partake of the nature of moral culpability. They are early formed, and I am not solicitous that you should think them superior to those of most people at eighteen. I will however say this in their defence. Whatever the affectionate alarm of my dear mother may lead her to apprehend, I am not one of the "sons of Anarchy and confusion," with whom she classes me. My opinions, good or bad, were learnt not from Hunt and Waithman, but from Cicero, from Tacitus, and from Milton. They are the opinions which have produced the greatest men that ever ornamented the world and redeemed human nature from the degradation of ages of superstition and slavery. I may be wrong as to the facts; – but if they be what I have seen them stated, I can never repent speaking of them with indignation. When I cease to feel the injuries of others, warmly detest wanton cruelty, and to feel my soul [rise] against oppression, I shall think myself unworthy to be your son, and to share, as I hope one day to do, the palm of the benevolent conquerors of West-Indian tyranny and inhumanity.

I could say a great deal more. Above all I might, I think, ask, with some reason, why a few democratical sentences in a letter, a private letter, of a collegian of eighteen, should be thought so alarming an indication of character, when Brougham and other people, who at an age which ought to have sobered them, talk with much more violence, are not thought particularly ill of? – But I have so little room left that I abstain and will only add thus much. Were my opinions as decisive as they are fluctuating, and were the elevation of a Cromwell or the renown of a Hampden the certain reward of my standing forth in the democratical cause, I would rather have my lips sealed on the subject, than give my mother and you one hour of uneasiness. There are not so many people in the world who love me, that I can afford to pain them for any object of ambition which it contains. If this assurance be not sufficiently strong, clothe it in what language you

23

please, and believe me to express myself in those words which you think the strongest and most solemn. Affectionate love to my Mother and sisters.

Farewell

T B M.

TO ZACHARY MACAULAY, 5 JANUARY 1820

MS: Trinity College. *Address:* Z Macaulay Esq. / No 16 George Street / Mansion House / London. *Partly published:* Trevelyan, 1, 95–7.

Cambridge Jany. 5th. 1820.

My dear Father,

Nothing that gives you disquietude can give me amusement. Otherwise I should have been excessively diverted by the dialogue which you have reported with so much vivacity. The accusation, the predictions, the elegant agnomen for which I am indebted to this incognito, (whom I shall designate, as algebraists do their unknown quantities by the letter (x)) are so gloriously absurd, so *utterly* and *absolutely false*, that I cannot help suspecting that the gentleman must be Marryatt of Trinity Hall, the son of your M P friend. He is at least endowed with some of the talents which distinguish the author of "Thoughts," and "more thoughts," and "more thoughts still."

I went in some amazement to Malden, Romilly, and Barlow. Their acquaintance comprehends, I will venture to say, almost every man worth knowing in the University in every field of study. They had never heard the appellation or the slightest allusion to any such propensity in me, from any man. Their intimacy with me would of course prevent any person from speaking to them on the subject in an insulting manner. For it is not usual here, whatever (x) may do, for a gentleman who does not wish to be kicked down stairs to reply to a man who mentions another as his particular friend, "Do you mean the blackguard or the novel-reader?" But the habit of novel reading is too frequently indulged to excess to be considered as a subject of reproach; and I am fully convinced that had the charge prevailed to any extent it must have reached the ears of one of those whom I interrogated. At all events I have the consolation of not being thought a novel-reader by the three or four who are entitled to judge on the subject, and whether their opinion be of equal value with that of this John-a-Nokes against whom I have to plead I leave you to decide.

It is absurd to suppose that I should have acquired this name, had my voracity been even extreme, considering how many scores of undergraduates might dispute the title with me. I cannot conceive how I should have gained it even if I had deserved it. The charge of having deserved it

I shall not condescend to deny, until you tell me that you give it credit.

But stronger evidence, it seems, is behind. This gentleman was in company with me. Alas! that I should never have found out how accurate an observer was measuring my sentiments, numbering the novels which I criticised, and speculating on the probability of my being plucked. "I was familiar with all the novels whose names he had ever heard." – If so frightful an accusation did not stun me at once, I might perhaps hint at the possibility that this was to be attributed almost as much to the narrowness of his reading on this subject as to the extent of mine. If my conjectures as to the gentleman are right, every man who has studied Milton is familiar with a book which *he* has never read, and probably never heard of. – Yet to accuse the poor man on that account of being immoderately addicted to poetry would be scarcely just. A man may be familiar with all the novels whose names are known to some people without being much of a novel reader. Probably the conversation turned on some popular works of that nature; and I joined in discussing the merits of Miss Edgeworth or of the Scotch novels, or very likely of some tragedy of Shakespeare's or poem of Lord Byron's, or tale of Dryden's, whose title he had heard and fancied it that of a novel. I have heard of such things, and seen such men, – mere mathematical blocks, whom the Tripos serves for a graduated scale of intellect, who plod on their eight hours a day to the honours of the Senate House, who leave the groves which witnessed the musings of Milton of Bacon and of Gray, without one liberal idea or elegant image, and carry with them into the world minds contracted by unmingled attention to one part of science, and memories stored only with technicalities. How often have I seen such men go forth into society for people to stare at them, and ask each other how it comes that beings so stupid in conversation, so uninformed on every subject of history, of letters, and of taste, could gain such distinctions at Cambridge. It is in such circles, which, I am happy to say, I hardly know but by report, that knowledge of modern literature is called novel-reading – a commodious name, invented by ignorance, and applied by envy, in the same manner as men without learning call a scholar a pedant, and men without principle call a Christian a methodist. To me the attacks of such men are valuable as compliments. The man whose friend tells him that he is known to be extensively acquainted with elegant literature may suspect that he is flattering him. He may feel real satisfaction when some Johnian, who plods on day after day at the pace of a tortoise, and with the insensibility of one, sneers at him for a novel reader.

I will attempt to make up my mind as well as possible to the fate with which this gentleman menaces me. "I am to lose ground," it seems. "My friends told him so." My friends *did not* tell him so. They could not tell him so. Calumny is not *every body's* trade. No person could estimate my progress or declension but Malden and Stainforth. Malden did not tell him so. Stainforth could not – for he thinks the direct contrary. –

As to the main question, I shall leave that for time to answer. I cannot afford to sacrifice a day every week in defence and explanation as to my habits of reading. Next June will come, and then – "Nous verrons."

I saw John and his mother to day. They think of setting out on Monday.

My Uncle wished to procure a book for Baptist Noel. I cannot of course learn exactly what he would like. A Newton was what I thought of; but he has one. I think a Cicero would do. He sent to borrow mine the other day; – and a good Edition is at once a handsome and an appropriate part of the library of every scholar.

My most affectionate love to My Mother and all at home.

In about three weeks I shall come into college, I hope finally. Barlow is going to leave Cambridge, after taking his degree, for a few months, and very kindly insisted on my occupying them till his return, by which time I shall probably have procured a Scholarship and become entitled to a set of my own.

I think I have said all that I have to say. I hope so at least. For my paper approaches its ter[mi]nation. You allude to my having said, that [I] spent two days with Malden in reading novels. It is but fair to remember that it was at the end of a *vacation* spent in hard work, and of a trying examination of ten days. I value, most deeply value, that sollicitude which arises from your affection for me – but let it not debar me from justice and candour. / Believe me ever, my dear Father,

Your most affectionate Son
T B M.

TO ZACHARY MACAULAY, 9 AUGUST 1821

MS: Trinity College. *Address:* Zachary Macaulay Esq. / No 16 George Street / Mansion House / London.

Llanrwst Denbighshire. August 9. / 1821

My dear Father,

I have received the letter and am much obliged to you both for the money and the directions. I thought that I had given an account in a former letter of the nature of the sprain. It was in the ancle. I am going for a few hours to Bangor to execute your directions. It gives me no pain in general, but is uneasy and weak when I get up in the morning, and the slightest false step brings on a renewal of the pain for some time. At Bangor, I doubt not, I shall get all necessary assistance.

A report has just reached me of the Queen's death; – left, it is said, by one of the coaches that passed Bettws last night. A similar report was afloat last week but turned out false; This however comes with circumstance, and though the last bulletin which I have seen, that in the Courier of Monday, was favourable, her state appeared precarious. What an event, if it be true! His Majesty, I presume, must return. He has left Plassomething or other, the Marquis of Anglesea's seat, for Ireland. But he cannot in decency spend in pageantry and revels the interval between the death and burial of his wife. Her vices and their enmity would only make the event more shocking to a well regulated mind. It remains to be seen whether his be so. The ceremonies of the Coronation have not raised my opinion of his sense. As a pageant, it seems, nothing could be more perfect, and the King's taste is said to have contributed to the elegance of the dresses and decorations. Such is the language of all the courtly writers on the subject. – High praise to a sovereign of sixty years of age that he is a good upholsterer and man-milliner! I am not, in truth, a great enthusiast about the Coronation, perhaps from envy. It is a magnificent but I think an unmeaning, and, I am sure, an expensive ceremony. Its principal value is that it preserves some of our ancient national garbs, rites, and usages. But that 100000 pounds should be squandered, that the courts of law should be pulled down to make room for a pageant of a few hours, and all this boyish folly committed by a man for whom the archbishop may very likely be required in a few months to perform the burial service within those very walls – this strikes me as most frivolous and contemptible and m[akes] me think that our country is suffering u[n]der the woe denounced against those whose ruler is a child. –

Many thanks to Jenny for her letter. Poor dear girl! I am still anxious to hear more about her health.

I want very much to write to Henry; but I suppose he will be at School now. If so my letter will be stopped by Mr. Elwell, who is in that, as in every thing else that I can learn about him, the most absurd and illiberal of school-masters. Tell him that that is my reason for not writing to him; – he is immensely solicitous that my letter should be kept extremely secret.

My love to Hannah and Madge. I am delighted with their pretty letters. I hope to hear from my mother. My affectionate love to her and everybody else.

T B M.

MS: Harvard University. *Address:* Zachary Macaulay Esq / No 16 George Street / Mansion House / London. *Extracts published:* Trevelyan, I, 114–15.

[Rothley Temple]

My dear Father,

I have seen the two last letters which you have sent to my mother. They have given me deep pain; – but pain without remorse. I am conscious of no misconduct – and whatever uneasiness I may feel arises solely from sympathy for your distress.

You seem to imagine that the book is edited or principally written by friends of mine. I thought that you had been aware that the work is conducted in London, – that my friends and myself are merely contributors, and form a very small proportion of the contributors. I believe that not one third part of the volume is written by persons whom I ever saw. I have not yet seen the work. To the very few papers which I saw I am sure that no moral objection could exist, – with the exception of one in which I earnestly recommended alteration. The manners of almost all of my acquaintances who have contributed to it are so utterly alien from coarseness, and their morals from libertinism, that I feel assured that no objection of that nature can exist to their works. As to my own contributions I can only say that the Roman Story was read to my mother before it was published and would have been read to you if you had happened to be at home. Not one syllable of censure was uttered.

The Essay on the Royal Society of Literature was read to you. I made the alterations which I conceived that you desired, and submitted them afterwards to my mother. As to the poem which you parallel with Little's, I am utterly unable to conceive what poem you mean.

If any thing vulgar or licentious have been written by myself, I am willing to bear the consequences. If any thing of that cast have been written by my friends, I allow that a certain degree of blame attaches to me for having chosen them at least indiscreetly. If however a bookseller of whom we knew nothing have coupled improper productions with ours in a work over which we had no controul, I cannot plead guilty to any thing more than misfortune – a misfortune in which some of the most rigidly moral and religious men of my acquaintance have participated in the present instance.

Can it be supposed that I could have thought of introducing an immoral book into our family? Could it be conceived, on any principle of worldly prudence, that I should have invited your attention and that of my mother to a work in which I could expect that any thing exceptionable would find a place? – This would have been gratuitously to insult your feelings, and to throw away your regard. The more charitable interpretation would be that I had no cause to expect that any such articles would be admitted, and that I had not voluntarily transgressed in my own contributions.

I am pleading at random for a book which I never saw. I am defending the works of people most of whose names I never heard. I am therefore writing under great disadvantages. I write also in great haste. I am unable even to read over what I have written. I have only to say that I await your arrival with great anxiety; unmingled, however, with shame, remorse, or fear. / Ever my dear Father

affectionately yours
T B M

to Charles Knight, 20 June 1823

MS: Mr F. R. Cowell. *Address:* Mr. Charles Knight / No 7 Pall-Mall East / London. *Published:* Charles Knight, *Passages of a Working Life,* 1 (1864), 304–5.

Rothley Temple Leicestershire June 20. 1823

My dear Sir,

As I fear that it will be impossible for me to contribute to your Magazine for the future, I think it due to you and to myself to acquaint you, without reserve, of the circumstances which have influenced me.

You are probably aware that there are among my family connections several persons of rigidly religious sentiments. My father, in particular, is, I believe, generally known to entertain, in their utmost extent, what are denominated evangelical opinions. Several articles in our first number, one or two of my own in particular, appeared to give him great uneasiness. I need not say that I do not in the slightest degree partake his scruples. Nor have I at all dissembled the complete discrepancy which exists between his opinions and mine. At the same time, gratitude, duty, and prudence, alike compel me to respect prejudices which I do not in the slightest degree share. And, for the present, I must desist from taking any part in the Quarterly Magazine.

The sacrifice gives me considerable pain. The Magazine formed a connecting tie between me and some very dear friends from whom I am now separated, probably for a very long time; – and I should feel still more concerned if I could imagine that any inconvenience could result from my [compulsory] conduct.

I shall probably be in London in about a month. I will then explain my motives to you more fully. In the mean time, I can only say that all that has passed between us increases my regrets for the termination of our con-

nection, and my wishes that it may be renewed under more favourable
circumstances.

Let me beg that you will communicate what I have said to nobody
excepting Coleridge, Moultrie, Praed or Malden; and to them under the
injunction of secrecy. / Believe me, my dear Sir,

Yours Sincerely
T B Macaulay

TO HENRY MACAULAY, 26 MAY 1824

MS: University of Texas. *Address:* H. W. Macaulay (in another hand).

Great Ormond Street / May 26th. 1824

My dear Hal,

I am waiting here for my dinner with nothing to do. Says Meg, "Now
do just spend these two minutes in writing to Hal. He will be so delighted
to hear from you." "You simpleton," said I, "what have I to tell him?
I never can write without something to say." Says our revered parent –
my mother I mean, "Say anything. He will be glad to hear from you." So
my vanity was flattered. And I was ashamed moreover of not having
written you a line for so long a time. And as members of parliament are
always very complaisant to the people just on the eve of an election, I was
inclined to give you a letter just before you came home – lest I should be
exposed to your reproaches. "So," said I, "bring the pen and ink." In it
came. Down I sate. And here you have the fruits. Never imagine, my dear
Hal, that, because I do not write to you as often as the young ladies who
have nothing to do, and who, moreover, have no objection to write when
they have nothing to say, I have forgotten you. None of them, you may
depend upon it, is more anxious to see you. We are all delighted to learn
that you are so useful to the old Quaker. Stick by that, my boy. If you
are inclined to turn Quaker yourself, I am sure, I have no objection. The
drab will become you. And you have already the demure look – the sharp
eye to the main-chance, and the coolness – aye, Hal, and, if I remember
right, the obstinacy too, necessary for supporting the character. The whine
of the meeting thou hast not yet acquired. But what of that? The Spirit
can impart gifts even more miraculous. And even if thou shouldst never
become a public friend, thou mayest still be a conspicuous member of the
body.

However, Quaker or not, whether in drab or in blue, with a dandy hat
or a broad-brim, come home to us, Hal, as fast as thou canst. – How indeed canst thou reconcile it to thy conscience to be from London at the
Season of the yearly meeting, when the friends are gathered together like

30

many waters, and the godly ones like the sands of the sea? Behold thy sisters, that is to say Margaret and Hannah and Fanny, went unto their worship meeting, and were moved to laugh, as though they had been full of new wine. Come then thou and admonish the sinful damsels and delight the eyes of

Thy brother after the flesh
T B M

TO ZACHARY MACAULAY, 2 APRIL 1826

MS: Trinity College. *Address:* Zachary Macaulay Esq / 16 George Street / Mansion House / London. *Partly published:* Trevelyan, I, 140–1.

York April 2nd. 1826

My dear Father,

I am sorry that I have been unable to avail myself of the letters of introduction which you forwarded to me. Since I received them I have been confined to the house with a cold; and now that I am pretty well recovered, I must take my departure for Pontefract. But if it had been otherwise I could not have presented these recommendations. Letters of this sort may be of great service to a barrister. But the barrister himself must not be the bearer of them. On this subject the rule is most strict – at least on this circuit. The huggery of the Bar, like the Simony of the Church, must be altogether carried on by the intervention of third persons. We are sensible of our dependance on the attorneys, and proportioned to that sense of dependance is our affectation of superiority. Even to take a meal with an Attorney is a high misdemeanour. One of the most eminent men among us, Frederic Pollock, brought himself into a serious scrape by doing so. But to carry a letter of introduction, to wait in the outer-room while it is being read, to be then ushered into the presence, to receive courtesies which can only be considered as the condescensions of a patron, to return courtesies which are little else than the blessings of a beggar, would be an infinitely more terrible violation of our professional code. If Mr. Pearson had written, for instance to Mr. Thorpe, without sending his letter to me, Mr. Thorpe might, if he had been inclined to pay any attention to the recommendation, have looked at the bar-list which lies open to public inspection, and which, of course, he must perpetually have to consult. He would there have seen where I lodged, and might have sent me briefs, if such had been his good pleasure. This would have been the regular and decorous course. As it is, every barrister to whom I have applied for advice, has most earnestly exhorted me on no account whatever to present the letters myself – I should perhaps add that my advisers have been persons who cannot by any possibility feel jealous of me.

31

It is not indeed of much consequence, since, as I have said, my cold has prevented me from stirring abroad, and to morrow I leave York. But the intimation may be useful in case you should have it in your power to make interest among the attorneys of the West Riding.

One W[ord] more. Do not mention w[hat] I have said about Pollock. These are awkward stories; and, in some sense, circuit secrets. He has been very kind and civil to me, and the error is now of old date. I should be sorry therefore if any hint of it should get abroad by my means. Love to my Mother and Sisters.

Ever yours most affectionately

T B M.

TO ZACHARY MACAULAY, 26 JULY 1826

MS: Trinity College. *Address:* Zachary Macaulay Esq / 16 George Street / Mansion House / London. *Partly published:* Trevelyan, 1, 142–4.

Bradford. July 26. 1826.

My dear Father,

The idle people at the Temple are such indifferent correspondents that, until they improve, I shall send all my letters to you, and leave them to pick up such information of my movements as you may chuse to vouchsafe to them at second hand.

On Saturday I went to Sydney Smith's. His parish lies three or four miles out of any frequented road. He is, however, most pleasantly situated. "Fifteen years ago," said he to me when I alighted at the gate of his shrubbery, "I was taken up in Piccadilly and set down here. There was no house, and no garden, nothing but a bare field." One service this eccentric divine has certainly rendered to the Church. He has built the very neatest, most commodious, and most appropriate rectory that I ever saw. All its decorations are in a peculiarly clerical style, grave, simple, and Gothic. The bed chambers are excellent, and excellently fitted up, the sitting rooms handsome, and the grounds sufficiently pretty. Tindal and Parke, not the judge of course, two of the best lawyers, best scholars, and best men in England, were there. We passed an extremely pleasant evening, had a very good dinner, and many amusing anecdotes. Mrs. Sydney Smith was very hospitable, and seems to be very accomplished. Their daughters are two very pleasant girls, one of them very handsome, in my judgment, though dark enough for a Queen of the Gypsies.

After breakfast the next morning I walked to Church with Sydney Smith. The ladies came in the Carriage. The edifice is not at all in keeping with the rectory, a miserable little hovel with a wooden belfry. It was however very well filled and with very decent people, who seemed to take very much to their pastor. I understand that he is a very respectable apothecary; and most liberal of his skill, his medecine, his soup, and his wine, among the sick. He preached a very queer sermon – the former half too familiar and the latter half too florid, but not without some ingenuity both of thought and expression. It was on the duty of good will to our neighbours, and, for aught I know, may have been the same that opened Beaumont's eyes to the depravity of Lady Swinburne. For it certainly was open to the same charge with that.

He drove me through the magnificent woods of Castle Howard. Lord Carlisle, whom he knows very well, was at Paris; but I caught a glimpse of this celebrated structure, one of the finest works of Vanbrugh, and contrived to see the three Maries, the most renowned ornament of the Orleans Gallery, and the glory of Caracci. It is indeed a wonderful picture. The Magdalene, the Virgin, and the dead body of Christ are superior to any thing which I remember to have seen.

Sydney Smith brought me to York on Monday Morning in time for the stage-coach which runs to Skipton. We parted with many assurances of good will. I have really taken a great liking to him. He is full of wit, humour, and shrewdness. He is not one of those shew-talkers who keep all their good things for great occasions. It seems to be his greatest luxury to keep his wife and daughters laughing two or three hours every day. His notions of law, government, and [   ] are surprisingly clear and just. His misfo[rtune] is to have chosen a profession at once above and below him. Zeal would have made him a prodigy. Formality and bigotry would have made him a bishop. But he could neither rise to the duties of his order, nor stoop to its degradations.

He praised my articles in the Edinburgh Review with a warmth which I am willing to believe sincere, because he qualified his compliments with several very sensible cautions. My great danger, he said, was that of taking a tone of too much asperity and contempt in controversy. I believe that he is right, and I shall try to mend.

I reached Skipton on Monday evening late. Yesterday the Sessions took place and closed at eleven in the evening. This morning I came in a chaise with two other barristers to the filthiest and most inconvenient town in the West-Riding. I am, however, tolerably lodged by comparison; and I expect to escape to Leeds by Saturday.

Ever affectionately yours
T B M

P.S. Of course nothing that I have said about Sydney Smith must get abroad.

MS: Trinity College.

Lancaster March 20. 1827

My dear Hannah,

I cannot in gratitude delay to answer your very pleasant letter, which, for a large school hand, is not ill written, and really deserves good penmanship. I heard from my mother by the same frank; and am much obliged to her for her epistle. But as she is an older correspondent and does not require encouragement, I think it best to inscribe my reply to you. From my mother's letter I infer, though she does not actually say so, that her eyes are quite recovered. I hope that it is so.

On Thursday Wakefield is to be tried. On Friday Ellis and I leave Lancaster in a chaise, and sleep at Bolton, the most beautiful spot on the road and the scene of a silly poem of Wordsworth's, the White Doe. I caught a glance at it last year. It is indeed a place in which nature and art strive for the mastery, a beautiful ruin in a beautiful situation, not equal to Tintern, but superior to anything else of the kind that ever I saw. On Saturday we shall proceed to York. All your letters therefore from the time that you receive this ought to be directed thither.

I always thought your hero Sibthorpe a goose. But the excellent story you tell me of him puts the matter out of all doubt. I hope that Miss Edgeworth's Harrington will never fall in his way. If it should he will infallibly turn Jew, nourish his beard, and eat the Passover while his congregation is waiting for a Good Friday Sermon. Mr. Lewis Way and Wolfe will have to reconvert him. By bribing him with a pipe of the real Hockheimer, and taking him to see the Merchant of Venice acted he may perhaps be reclaimed.

I wish that I knew where my old friend Mrs. Meeke · lives. I would certainly send her intelligence of the blessed effects of her writings. I grieve to think how carelessly I have read them, and how little I have considered them in a theological light. Mr. Elliott, you know, boasts that he read St Paul's Epistles over in a geographical point of view, and found them very useful in that respect. I shall read over Mrs. Meeke's hundred and one novels in a theological point of view; I hope with equal benefit.

A new edition of Laughton Priory ought certainly to be published cheap for distribution among the poor Irish. It would aid Lord Farnham in the mighty work which he is performing in Cavan. He would be the very person to preside over the British and Foreign Laughton Priory Association. I will certainly attend Freemasons hall, and perhaps favour the Ladies and Gentlemen with a speech.

So the Jesuits kept Sibthorpe in hiding. Alas, my dear Carolina Wilhelmina Amelia, I must like Sir William Thornhill, pronounce your anecdote in that respect fudge. I suspect that, having experienced the good effects of fictitious narrative in his own case, he intends to try the same experiment on other people and to pass himself off for Juliano Algernon, I suppose. If he really were, like Juliano, confined as insane, I cannot much blame his keepers. – But enough of Mr. Sibthorpe.

I am rather pleased than otherwise at the event of the Leicester petition. Success was not to be expected; and, considering the strong and, indeed, discreditable tone which Peel adopted, I was agreably surprised to find the minority so respectable.

But I must stop and go back to court. There is a highwayman to be tried for his life who interests the ladies very much; a stout handsome swaggering fellow, the very image of Macheath. He has been twice tried since we came hither and has got off by alibi both times. If he is convicted the Lancashire witches will be inconsolable – "such a nice gentleman; – and if he did rob the folks, why, it is hard to hang such a pretty young man for that. It is a shame, so it is, to hang a fellow-creature for a few sovereigns. They would not have such a thing to answer for, not if you would give them the whole world." Pretty creatures! But in spite of their prettiness and of their pity I would not give two pence for the life of this Adonis if he should be convicted. Love to every body at home.

Ever your affectionate Brother

T B M

TO SELINA MILLS MACAULAY, 15 APRIL 1828

MS: Trinity College. *Address:* Mrs. Macaulay. / 50 Gt. Ormond St. / London. *Frank:* Pontefract April fifteen 1828. / John Wood. *Partly published:* Trevelyan, 1, 146–50.

Court House Pomfret April 15. 1828

My dear Mother,

My father is, I suppose, on his way to Bristol by this time; or at least will be so before this epistle reaches London. I therefore address it to you as the least undeserving of a very undeserving family. You, I think, have sent me one letter since I left London; My sisters none at all. My father has sometimes favoured me with two or three in the day when franks were plentiful.

I have nothing here to do but to write letters, and, what is not very often the case, I have members of parliament in abundance to frank them, and abundance of matter to fill them with. My Edinburgh expedition has given me so much to say that, unless I write off some of it before I come home, I shall talk you all to death, and be voted a bore in every house which I visit. Oh for the indefatigable pens of Richardson's heroes and

heroines! – Oh for the accurate memory of Belford and Miss Byron!
Then would I relate word for word all my dialogue with Mr. Macculloch
about the poor laws, and my dispute with Macvey Napier about Porson,
and the talk in which Jeffrey and I lingered every night till between two
and three. Which will you have? Or shall I begin as Richardson's heroine
does, by full length characters of every body – and describe my companions as she describes Miss Allestree and Miss Cantillon. Well then.
I will commence with Jeffrey himself. I had almost forgotten his person:
and indeed I should not wonder if even now I were to forget it again. He
has twenty faces almost as unlike to each other as my father's to Mr. Wilberforce's, and infinitely more unlike to each other than those of near
relatives often are, infinitely more unlike for example than those of the two
Grants or of Matthew and John Preston. When absolutely quiescent,
reading a paper for example, or hearing a conversation in which he takes
no interest, he looks very much like my old master Preston, – with rather
more colour to be sure, and not quite so grey. There is no indication whatever of intellectual superiority of any kind. But as soon as he is interested,
and opens his eyes upon you, the change is like magic. There is a flash in
his glance, a violent contortion in his frown, an exquisite humour in his
sneer, and a sweetness and brilliancy in his smile beyond any thing that
ever I saw. A person who had seen him in only one state would not know
him if he saw him in another. For he has not, like Brougham, marked
features which in all moods of mind remain unaltered. The mere outline
of his face is insignificant – much like that of the Prestons, as I said before.
The expression is every thing; and such power and variety of expression I
never saw in any human countenance, not even in that of the most celebrated actors. I can conceive that Garrick may have been like him. I have
seen several pictures of Garrick – none resembling another; and I have
heard Hannah More speak of the extraordinary variety of countenance by
which he was distinguished, and of the unequalled radiance and penetra-
tion of his eye. The voice and delivery of Jeffrey resemble his face. He
possesses considerable power of mimicry; and rarely tells a story without
imitating several different accents. His familiar tone, his declamatory tone,
and his pathetic tone are quite different things. Sometimes Scotch pre-
dominates in his pronunciation, sometimes it is imperceptible. Sometimes
his utterance is snappish and quick to the last degree – sometimes it is
remarkable for rotundity and mellowness. I can easily conceive that two
people who had seen him on different days might dispute about him as the
travellers in the fa[ble] disputed about the cameleon; and both, if they
were to see him again, would probably find themselves equally deceived.

In one thing, as far as I observed, he is always the same; and that is the
warmth of his domestic affections. Neither Mr. Wilberforce nor my uncle

Babington, come up to him in this respect. The flow of his kindness is quite inexhaustible. Not five minutes pass without some fond expression or caressing gesture to his wife or his daughter. He has fitted up a study for himself: but he never goes into it. Law-papers, reviews, whatever he has to write, he writes in the drawing-room or in his wife's boudoir. When he goes to other parts of the country on a retainer he takes them in the carriage with him. I do not wonder that he should be a good husband: for his wife, bating her unfortunate nervous malady, which by the bye is by no means so bad as it was, is a very amiable woman. But I was surprised to see a man so keen and sarcastic, so much of a scoffer, pouring himself out with such simplicity and tenderness in all sorts of affectionate nonsense. Through our whole journey to Perth he kept up a sort of mock quarrel, like mine with Hannah and Margaret; attacked his daughter about novel-reading, laughed her into a pet, kissed her out of it, and laughed her into it again. She and her mother absolutely idolise him: and I do not wonder at it.

His conversation is very much like his countenance and his voice – of immense variety, sometimes plain and unpretending even to flatness, sometimes whimsically brilliant and rhetorical almost beyond the license of private discourse. He has many very interesting anecdotes, and tells them very well. He is a very shrewd observer; and so fastidious that I am not surprised at the awe in which many people seem to stand when in his company. Though not altogether free from affectation himself – as indeed nobody seems to be when very closely watched, he has a peculiar loathing for it in other people, and a great talent for discovering and exposing it. He has a particular contempt, in which I most heartily concur with him, for the *fadaises* of bluestocking literature, for the mutual flatteries of coteries, the handing about of vers de societé, the albums, the conversaziones, and all the other nauseous trickeries of the Sewards, Hayleys, and Sothebys. Such people as Professor Smyth, Chancy Townsend, and my poor old hostess Lydia White, are objects of his especial aversion. I am not quite sure that he has escaped the opposite extreme, and that he is not a little too desirous to appear rather a man of the world, an active lawyer, or an easy careless gentleman, than a distinguished writer. Congreve, you probably know, was devoured by this affectation. He could not bear the least allusion to his plays: and liked to be considered as an independant man of fashion who had never dirtied his fingers with ink. When Voltaire called on him and complimented him on the excellence of his comedies he said, with some pettishness, that he wished to be treated merely as a gentleman like his neighbours. Voltaire told him that if he had been merely a gentleman like his neighbours, he would not have been troubled with the visits of a literary foreigner.

I rather suspect myself of unfairness, I must own, in this critique. For when Jeffrey and I were by ourselves, he talked much and very well on literary topics. His kindness and hospitality to me were, indeed, beyond description: and his wife was as pleasant and friendly as possible. I liked everything but the hours. We were never up till ten and never retired till two hours at least after midnight. Jeffrey indeed never goes to bed till sleep comes on him overpoweringly, and never rises till forced up by business or hunger. He is extremely well in health, so well that I could not help suspecting him of being very hypochondriac: for all his late letters to me have been filled with lamentations about his various maladies. His wife told me when I congratulated her on his recovery that I must not absolutely rely on all his accounts of his own diseases. I really think that he is, on the whole, the youngest looking man of fifty that I know, at least when he is animated.

I have little more at present to tell you about him. Small traits of his conversation will come out, one by one, as I talk over this visit with you. I will only add that his table is very elegant, his wine remarkably choice and old, and his whiskey so good that I drank a glass of it every day. One circumstance struck me as odd; though in Scotland I suppose it is common. While I was with him he had two large parties, of rather high people. The dinners were even splendid, the wines of the best sort and of the best quality, champagne, hock, Constantia. But there was no dessert whatever – not so much as an orange or a spunge-cake.

His house in Edinburgh is most magnificent. He has just taken it; and several rooms are still unfurnished. It is in Moray place – the newest pile of buildings in the town; looking out to the Forth on one side and to a green garden on the other. It is really equal to the houses in Grosvenor Square – superior to any in Portman Square that I have seen. There is a very fine dining room, three large drawing rooms and a library; and all this not mere fillagree work like the new habitations which are run up at Brighton or in the Regent's Park, but of massive stone – the masonry and the wood-work of extraordinary stability. When I told Jeffrey of the condition into which the occupants of the new houses about Russell Square are compelled to enter, that they will have no dancing on the upper floor, he laughed and said that if the Elephant who danced at Covent Garden-Theatre could be got up to caper in his drawing room he should have no objection. I understand however that the furniture of these fine houses is by no means suited to the spaciousness and elegance of the rooms. The fact is that instead of wondering at the extent of the town-houses of the Scotch gentry, we ought rather to wonder at the smallness of those in which the aristocracy of London box themselves up. An Italian noble with an annual income of perhaps 800 or 1000 pounds sterling a year lives in a palace as large as Northumberland House. A writer in India, I understand, has four or five rooms fifty feet long each. The materials for building are cheap. Very little furniture is wanted, and the principal article of expense is the mere skeleton of the house itself. In London the case is quite different. A nobleman like Lord Fitzwilliam or Lord Carlisle who in the country has a mansion six-hundred feet in length, when he comes to London, shuts himself up in a house three or four windows wide, – in a house which he might put into one of the pavilions of his seat.

Fine as these new buildings are in some respects, I decidedly prefer the High Street in the Old Town. There is nothing like it in the island. The ancient parts of London were consumed by the great fire; and, even if that fire had never happened, would probably have perished of themselves. They were of wood or, at best, of brick. There is such a profusion of the best stone about Edinburgh that from the earliest times all the streets have been built of that material in a very solid manner; they therefore remain such as they were centuries ago. Conceive walking between huge masses of dark smoky stone, eight or nine windows high, down the ridge of a hill, with the Castle on its summit, and the venerable, though irregular palace of Holyrood at its foot. You have been there. But you have not seen the town – and no lady ever sees a town. It is only by walking on foot through all sorts of crowded streets at all hours that a town can be really studied to good purpose.

There is a new pillar to the memory of Lord Melville – very elegant and much better than the man deserved. His statue is at the top with a wreath on the head very like a nightcap drawn over the eyes. It is impossible to look on it without being reminded of the fate which the original most richly deserved. There is an imitation of the Temple at Pæstum fitted up for an exhibition of pictures. The pictures are poor – not much worse than those at Somerset House to be sure. The building is handsome, though very ill placed. The observatory I think detestable. These are the most remarkable public edifices which have been erected at Edinburgh since we were there last. But there are several handsome streets and squares. Moray Place is well built but its shape is strangely irregular. Sir Walter Scott calls it a circle in hysterics.

But my letter will overflow even the ample limits of a frank, if I do not conclude. I hope that you will be properly penitent for neglecting such a correspondent when you receive so long a dispatch written amidst the bellowing of justices, lawyers, criers, witnesses, prisoners, prisoners' wives and mothers, and spectators. If you write after the receipt of this, direct to Leeds. I shall be there, probably on Saturday, at the latest on Monday. Love to my Father, if he is at home – to my sisters – and to yourself.

Ever yours affectionately
T B M.

Text: Trevelyan, I, 152–3.

Bowood: February 10, 1830.

My dear Father, –

I am here in a very nice room, with perfect liberty, and a splendid library at my command. It seems to be thought desirable that I should stay in the neighbourhood and pay my compliments to my future constituents every other day.

The house is splendid and elegant, yet more remarkable for comfort than for either elegance or splendour. I never saw any great place so thoroughly desirable for a residence. Lord Kerry tells me that his uncle left everything in ruin, – trees cut down, and rooms unfurnished, – and sold the library, which was extremely fine. Every book and picture in Bowood has been bought by the present Lord, and certainly the collection does him great honour.

I am glad that I stayed here. A burgess of some influence, who, at the last election, attempted to get up an opposition to the Lansdowne interest, has just arrived. I called on him this morning, and, though he was a little ungracious at first, succeeded in obtaining his promise. Without him, indeed, my return would have been secure; but both from motives of interest and from a sense of gratitude I think it best to leave nothing undone which may tend to keep Lord Lansdowne's influence here unimpaired against future elections.

Lord Kerry seems to me to be going on well. He has been in very good condition, he says, this week; and hopes to be at the election, and at the subsequent dinner. I do not know when I have taken so much to so young a man. In general my intimacies have been with my seniors: but Lord Kerry is really quite a favourite of mine, – kind, lively, intelligent, modest, with the gentle manners which indicate a long intimacy with the best society, and yet without the least affectation. We have oceans of beer and mountains of potatoes for dinner. Indeed, Lady Lansdowne drank beer most heartily on the only day which she passed with us, and, when I told her laughing that she set me at ease on a point which had given me much trouble, she said that she would never suffer any dandy novelist to rob her of her beer or her cheese.

The question between law and politics is a momentous one. As far as I am myself concerned, I should not hesitate: but the interest of my family is also to be considered. We shall see, however, before long what my chance of success as a public man may prove to be. At present it would clearly be wrong in me to show any disposition to quit my profession.

I hope that you will be on your guard as to what you may say to

Brougham about this business. He is so angry at it that he cannot keep his anger to himself. I know that he has blamed Lord Lansdowne in the robing-room of the Court of King's Bench. The seat ought, he says, to have been given to another man. If he means Denman, I can forgive, and even respect him, for the feeling which he entertains.

Believe me ever yours most affectionately

T. B. M.

TO HANNAH MACAULAY, 28 JUNE 1830

MS: Mrs Humphry Trevelyan.

London June 28. 1830

My dear Hannah,

I will tell you a story. There was a naughty girl who was always grumbling and honing and moaning for letters. And it was from morning to night – "Write to me. Only write. I am letter-sick. Nobody cares for me. I will never write again." This young lady had a brother who, in the midst of many literary, professional, and political, engagements, contrived to find time to write an affectionate and simple epistle to her. Immediately Miss Shrew – for that was her name – began to murmur again. "Such letters are only fit for a footman to write. You must ask pardon on your bended knees." – So her brother never wrote to her again.

Moral –

Young ladies who wish for letters very much should receive them when they come very civilly.

So the King is dead. And all London is in a stir with the business of proclaiming William the fourth. The members of parliament are being sworn in again. I vowed all sorts of things and smacked the calf-skin 6 or 7 times. Peel was there in a dress not much unlike my Uncle Babington's liveries. They call it the Windsor Uniform – a great deal of gilding and lace. He looked like a good boy's beau ideal of human happiness – the reward of doing as you are bid and shutting the door after you. We are to go to court soon in a body. I shall not go unless I can go without a sword and a fool's coat.

A word of consolation, and I have done. Pray, my dear, do not take on so about the poor old King. Exert your excellent sense, and bear up against this calamity. I know how you feel it. So do I. The paper is blistered with my tears – to say nothing of Fanny's and Selina's which are falling fast on each side.

Ever yours most affectionately

T B M.

MS: Trinity College. *Address:* Miss H M Macaulay.

London July 21. 1830

My darling Hannah,

We are to be prorogued the day after to-morrow – and my franks will be of no more value than so much waste paper – a sermon of Mr. Erskine's for example. But only think – I shall go to the House of Lords, and there the King will sit on his throne – so grand – with his crown of gold on his head, and his sceptre in his hand, and all his royal robes. And he will make a speech to us – and he will call us his faithful Commons, and say "Gentlemen of the House of Commons, I thank you for voting me such handsome supplies." Only think of a brother of yours being thanked for his munificence by a King in all his glory. And there will be the Lords – bless their hearts – all in their best – red velvet, gold, ermine and so forth. And we of the Commons shall not be so shabby neither as you may think, Miss – pursing up your quality mouth at us as you always do – a proud stuck-up swan! – No. Not so bad as all that comes to, neither. The speaker will have his long black gown all flowered with gold; and the members who are officers will have their uniforms – the soldiers red – the sailors blue – as it is written

"Some men get coats of red and blue
To shew their Sovereign honour due."

And the ministers who are not in the army or the navy will wear the Windsor Uniform – a very dashing costume I can tell you. So don't you wish to be there? – What would you give? A ring worth five shillings? Or would you tell me what it was that Madge and you talked about, if I would take you? Lauk o' me – what a little sheet of paper. Quite big enough for you though.

T B M

TO MACVEY NAPIER, 19 AUGUST 1830

MS: British Museum. *Address:* Macvey Napier Esq / Edinburgh. *Frank:* London August nineteen 1830 / T B Macaulay. *Mostly published: Selection from the Correspondence of the Late Macvey Napier,* 1879, pp. 82–3.

London August 19. 1830

My dear Sir,

The new number appeared this morning in the shop windows. It is certainly respectable; but I do not think that it is eminently good. The article on Niebuhr contains much that is very sensible; but it is not such an article as so noble a subject required. I am not like Ellis Niebuhr-mad; and I agree with many of the remarks which the reviewer has made both on this work and on the school of German critics and historians. But surely the Reviewer ought to have given an account of the system of exposition which Niebuhr has adopted and of the theory which he advances respecting the institutions of Rome. Some of the notions of the German are I think extremely just – some false and extravagant. But true or false they all indicate a vigourous and cultivated mind and will all find favourable acceptance with a large party in the literary world. The appearance of the book is really an æra in the intellectual history of Europe; and I think that the Edinburgh Review ought at least to have given a luminous abstract of it. The very circumstance that Niebuhr's own arrangement and style are obscure, and that his translators have need of translators to make them intelligible to the multitude, rendered it more desirable that a clear and neat statement of the points in controversy should be laid before the public. But it is useless to talk of what cannot be mended. The best editors cannot always have good writers, and the best writers cannot always write their best.

Brougham must be out of his wits. I heard that his triumph in Yorkshire had turned his brains or something very near it. I have no notion on what ground he imagines that I am going to review his speech. He never said a word to me on the subject. Nor did I ever say either to him or to any one else a single syllable to that effect. I do remember, indeed, what till to day I had quite forgotten, that a friend of mine begged me, some time ago, to write an article on slavery. I said that I thought it impossible that parliament could do any thing on the subject before Christmas, and that the beginning of next year would be a fitter time than the autumn of this. At all events I shall not make Brougham's speech my text. We have had quite enough of puffing and flattering each other in the E[dinburgh] R[eview]. It is in vile taste for men united in one literary undertaking to exchange these favours.

I have a plan of which I wish to know your opinion. In ten days or thereabouts I set off for France where I hope to pass six weeks. I shall be in the best society, that of the Duc de Broglie, Guizot, and so on. I think of writing an article on the politics of France since the Restoration, with characters of the principal public men, and a parallel between the present state of France and that of England. I think that this might be made an article of extraordinary interest. I do not say that I could make it so. It must, you will perceive, be a long paper, however concise I may try to be. But as the subject is important, and I am not generally diffuse, you must not stint me. If you like this scheme let me know as soon as possible. The Italian poets must stand over, – that is if you approve of my plan. I am

43

glad to hear that Ellis found so good a Cicerone, or, as Mr. Shepherd of Liverpool always calls it in his travels, – so good a *Cicisbeo*. John Mill is gone to France on a mission to preach up the republic and the physical check, I suppose.

Ever yours truly

T B Macaulay

JOURNAL LETTER, 14 SEPTEMBER 1830

MS: Trinity College. *Extracts published:* Trevelyan, 1, 164–5.

Paris Septr. 14. 1830. Tuesday.

Sir R Inglis does not I find go till to morrow. So that I have time to carry my story further. But where shall I begin or leave off. Though I have been ten days in this great city there are large districts and interesting sights which I have not yet visited. Take however the best account which I can give of the impression which Paris has produced on me.

As to public buildings, I doubt whether the advantage be with Paris or London. On the whole I lean to London. The Pantheon is fine, but immeasurably inferior to St Paul's. Notre Dame is pretty well – but not to be compared with Westminster abbey. St Roch is well enough. But not equal to several of Sir Christopher Wren's Churches. The Hotel des Invalides is very magnificent – but hardly, I think, so fine as Greenwich Hospital, either within or without. As to bridges it would be absurd to institute a comparison. Three arches of the Waterloo Bridge would span the Seine in the broadest part of its course through Paris. And there is nothing like those gigantic masses of warehouses and those vast docks which line the Thames at the East of London.

On the other hand we have not, I think, in London any architectural compositions so beautiful – so correct and at the same time so magnificent – as the Palace of the Deputies, – the Place Louis Seize, – and, above all, the Eastern facade of the Louvre. The monument, though a fine pillar and twice as large, I should think, in every dimension, as the column of Austerlitz, is by no means equal to that column in beauty. None of our public offices – not even the Post Office, is equal to the Bourse: and though the architecture of the Thuilleries and of the galleries which run between the Thuilleries and the Louvre, is by no means pure, there is certainly great splendour in the general effect. When the whole plan is completed the circumference of this vast palace will be, I should think, considerably upwards of a mile.

Above all we have nothing in London like the Palais Royal. If I were to select the spot in all the earth in which the good and evil of civilisation are most strikingly exhibited, in which the arts of life are carried to the highest perfection, in which all pleasures, high and low, intellectual and sensual, are collected in the smallest space, I should certainly chuse the Palais Royal. It is the Covent Garden Piazza, the Pater-Noster Row, the Vauxhall, the Albion Tavern, the Burlington Arcade, the Crockford's, the Finish, the Athenæum, of Paris, all in one. Even now, when the first dazzling effect has passed by, I never pass through it without feeling bewildered by its magnificent variety.

I will try to give you an idea of it. My father can illustrate, if my description is obscure. Fronting the Rue St Honoré is a modest looking building – not much unlike the front of Somerset House towards the Strand, but far inferior. This is the part of the Palais Royal inhabited by the present King. He will probably soon remove. The ground floor, as you can see through glass doors, is constantly occupied by national guards. Above is a suite of apartments, which seems to be splendidly furnished, where his majesty resides. Behind this residence, – a splendid one for the Duke of Orléans, but hardly fit for the King of the French, lies a small but brilliant square of shops. After traversing this square you reach the great court of the Palais Royal.

Imagine a space as large as Portman square, planted with trees, a fountain in the centre, and a continued range of lofty buildings, of the most florid architecture, running round it. The whole ground-floor consists of the most brilliant shops, cafés, and taverns, that you can conceive. Books, jewellery, millinery, fruit, pastry, china, glass, prints, all in the most rapid succession. An arcade runs along all these shops, and this arcade is full from morning to night of all the gayest people – as far as dress at least is a sign of gaiety, in Paris. I have passed at eight in the morning. I have passed at eleven at night, and always found it swarming with people, and in a constant buz of voices. At night it is gorgeously lighted up with lamps. Among the trees in the middle of the court are cabinets, neatly painted, where newspapers are to be seen, and where ices and lemonade are sold. Pedlars run about from morning to night with their boxes, flower-women with baskets of nosegays, little Italian boys with squirrels and monkeys, national guards hurrying to and from the palace; – singing in one cabinet, smoking in another – women staring at the shops, dandies staring at the women, and Englishmen staring at every thing.

Here are the restaurateurs of the greatest fame. Here are Vefour and Very. Here is the Café des Mille Colonnes. Of a French Café you can have no conception. A splendidly dressed and often a handsome woman presides instead of a dirty servile waiter. You take off your hat and make your bow on entering. During the morning dejeuners à la fourchette are going on, – during the middle of the day people are drinking lemonade and eating grapes and peaches, at night they are playing cards. The newspapers attract many people to these places. It is not the fashion to take in a paper here. You go to a café – call for a cup of coffee – a glass of liqueur or lemonade, and dawdle over the Constitutionel. I have not adopted this course much, as I subscribe to Galignani's.

But not only are there these brilliant shops and coffee-houses in the Palais Royal. Low flash-houses are intermingled with them. While you are dining above with ladies of the highest character, – for Ladies dine here at the respectable Restaurateurs, – underneath in the cellarage there is a dance of the lowest thieves and blackguards in Paris at the Café des Aveugles – or du Sauvage. A man dressed in skins beats a drum and yells in a frightful manner for the diversion of these gentry; – above your head is probably a gaming house; – and still higher in the attics of this vast building sharpers, swindlers, and all the wretched creatures who live on the follies and vices of a great metropolis have their lodgings. The Palais Royal is perhaps the spot in all the world in which the extremes of the social system are brought together within the smallest compass. As a great capital is a country in miniature, the Palais Royal is a capital in miniature, an abstract and epitome of a vast civilised community, exhibiting at one glance the politeness which adorns its higher ranks, – the coarseness of its populace – the arts which embellish, the wealth which enriches, the knowledge which enlightens it, the vices and the misery which lie underneath its brilliant exterior. – Every thing is there – and every body – Statesmen, wits, philosophers, beauties, dandies, blacklegs, adventurers, artists, idlers, King Louis Philippe and his court, beggars with matches crying for charity, wretched creatures dying of disease and want in garrets. There is no condition of life, I believe, which is not to be found in this gorgeous and fantastic Fairy land.

The general aspect of Paris is certainly superior to what I had expected – yet by no means equal to that of London. London is larger than Paris in still greater proportion than I should have expected from the difference of population. Set out in what direction you will in Paris, a vigorous walk of three quarters of an hour brings you to green trees and open country. The streets are much higher and much narrower than ours; few of them have pavements for the walkers and a gutter runs foaming down the middle, so deep that children have been drowned there. To compensate the want of accommodation for walkers in the streets they have numerous arcades. This fashion is recent; but has been carried very far. There are now probably twelve or fifteen arcades in different parts of Paris the poorest of which is far broader – and more brilliant – than our only arcades – that by Burlington House and that behind the Opera House. The principal shops are in these places – the shops at the Palais Royal which are the finest in Paris always excepted. I do not mind walking even through their worst streets. Thames Street is worse than the worst, and I have many a time fought my way through the carts of Thames Street.

There is scarcely a square or open Place in Paris. The most remarkable is the Place Vendôme. It is as like one of the Bath circuses and Hexagons as possible – the stone of the same colour – the architecture in the same style. You might fancy yourself at Bath, but for the pillar in the middle, cast of brass from the cannon taken in the war against Austria and Russia in 1805. I went up to the top of this pillar by a winding staircase in utter darkness, and had a view of Paris. No cloud of smoke as in London. The view was as clear as that from Richmond hill. An honest labouring man in a smock frock had climbed just before me – for nothing is paid at the sights here. We entered into chat. "Ah Monsieur il avoit du génie – le garçon qui a bâti ceci." "Et di qui donc parlez-vous?" said I. I thought he meant the architect. "Eh, mais c'étoit Napoleon," said he. He pointed out the Pantheon and told me that it was by Soufflot. I wonder how many English carters know that St Paul's was built by Wren.

But I must stop. I have a great deal more to say – The Fauxbourg St Germain – the Chamber of Deputies – the Duke and Duchess de Broglie etc. etc.

Ever yours affectionately
T B M.

TO WILLIAM WHEWELL, 5 FEBRUARY 1831

MS: Trinity College. *Address:* Rev W Whewell / Trinity College / Cambridge. *Frank:* London February five 1831 / T B Macaulay. *Partly published:* Trevelyan, I, 173–4.

London Feby. 5. 1831

Dear Whewell,

I received your letter and the inclosure this morning. You will see what I have to say about Sadler, or part of it, in the new Number of the Edinburgh. I am fully resolved to come and take up my quarters for a month or two in College as soon as I can. I love it the more, the more I see the men whom it sends out. They beat the world before them. But I cannot say much for our recent appearance on the Tripos.

I suppose Malden is regular in settling with you. We think highly in London of his Roman History. Tell him, when you see him, that Hallam, the most fastidious and one of the most competent judges that I know, praises it to the skies.

We are admiring another production of a great Cambridge man –

Herschel's Treatise in Lardner's Cyclopædia. A very little physical science would make me admire. But the vigour and propriety of the style, of which I can judge better, are very remarkable. Herschel must be a man of letters as well as a man of science.

I am impatient for Praed's debut. The House of Commons is a place in which I would not promise success to any man. I have great doubts even about Jeffrey. It is the most peculiar audience in the world. I should say that a man's being a good writer, a good orator at the bar, a good mob-orator, or a good orator in debating-clubs, was rather a reason for expecting him to fail than for expecting him to succeed in the House of Commons. A place where Walpole succeeded and Addison failed, – where Dundas succeeded and Burke failed, – where Peel now succeeds and where Macintosh fails – where Erskine and Scarlet were dinner-bells, where Lawrence and Jekyll – the two witti[est] men or nearly so of their time, were thought bores, – is surely a very strange place. And yet I feel the whole character of the place growing upon me. I begin to like what others about me like, and to disapprove what they disapprove. –

Canning used to say that the House, as a Body, had better taste than the man of best taste in it; and I am very much inclined to think that Canning was in the right.

Ever yours
T B Macaulay

TO THOMAS FLOWER ELLIS, 7 MARCH 1831

MS: Trinity College. *Address:* T F Ellis Esq / Northern Circuit / Lancaster. *Frank:* London March seven 1831 / T B Macaulay. *Published:* John Clive and Thomas Pinney, eds., *Selected Writings of Macaulay*, Chicago, 1972, pp. 425–7.

London March 7 – 1831

Dear Ellis,

I have been so busy during the last few days that I have not been able to spare a moment. The H[ouse] of Commons lasts from 3 in the afternoon to 2 in the morning – and the rest of my time has been spent in preparing for the press the speech which I made on Wednesday night and which has had a great success. I will send a copy to you under franked covers when it is published.

London is thoroughly well disposed towards us; and the country will, I hope, follow the lead of London. Give me news from Lancashire. What say the manufacturers? What say the Squires? What say the lawyers? And of the lawyers what say, in especial, Milner, Holinshed, – (or how does the brute spell his name?) – Adolphus, Henderson, – and the

48

Devil? – By the bye is not Holt's nickname an excellent illustration of the title of Ben Jonson's play – The Devil is an Ass.

How things will go seems a little doubtful. But I have a good hope.– Lord Duncannon, who knows the House of Commons better than any other man in it – Billy Holmes excepted who maketh a lie and loveth it – is quite confident of success. He is sure, he says, of a majority. Peel is evidently trimming. Croker would trim, if his infernal impudence and spite were not beyond even his own controul. By the bye, you never saw such a scene as Croker's oration on Friday night. He abused Lord J Russell. He abused Lord Althorpe. He abused the Lord Advocate – and we took no notice – never once groaned or cried – no! – But he began to praise Lord Fitzwilliam – "a venerable nobleman, – an excellent and amiable nobleman, –" and so forth: – and we all broke out together – "Question – no – no – this is too bad – don't – don't –" and such other exclamations. He then called Canning his right honourable friend. "Your friend! damn your impudent face!" said the member who sate next me.

Croker is now beyond all comparison the most impudent man in the house. I always thought him so. But some of us gave the palm to O'Gorman Mahon. O'Gorman fell greatly. Cæsar in the senate did not die with more attention to the proprieties of character. He came to hear, what few people care to hear, his own sentence read at the bar by the chairman of the Committee. To make the matter better he was expelled for bribery by his agents. The fellow sate on the Treasury bench – heard the report, – and never stirred. "Sir" – said the Speaker – "you must withdraw." Up he got and swaggered off as fast as he could with his acre of ruff and his three bushels of dirty hair. Sorrow such another we will be having any how plaze God – or be wishing to have; and no great blame to us for that same – the craturs.

I will not tell you the compliments that I have received on my speech, lest you should think that I am telling lies –.

Ever yours truly
T B Macaulay

TO THOMAS FLOWER ELLIS, 30 MARCH 1831

MS: Trinity College. *Address:* T F Ellis Esq / Northern Circuit / York. *Frank:* London March thirty 1831 / T B Macaulay. *Published:* Clive and Pinney, *Selected Writings of Macaulay*, pp. 427–30.

London March 30. 1831

Dear Ellis,

I have little news for you, except what you will learn from the papers as well as from me. It is clear that the Reform Bill must pass, either in this or in another Parliament. The majority of one does not appear to me, as it does to you, by any means inauspicious. We should perhaps have had a better plea for a dissolution if the majority had been the other way. But surely a dissolution under such circumstances would have been a most alarming thing. If there should be a dissolution now there will not be that ferocity in the public mind which there would have been if the House of Commons had refused to entertain the Bill at all. – I confess that, till we had a majority, I was half inclined to tremble at the storm which we had raised. At present I think that we are absolutely certain of victory, and of victory without commotion.

Such a scene as the division of last Tuesday I never saw, and never expect to see again. If I should live fifty years the impression of it will be as fresh and sharp in my mind as if it had just taken place. It was like seeing Cæsar stabbed in the Senate House, or seeing Oliver taking the mace from the table, a sight to be seen only once and never to be forgotten. The crowd overflowed the House in every part. When the strangers were cleared out and the doors locked we had six hundred and eight members present, more by fifty five than ever were at a division before. The Ayes and Noes were like two vollies of cannon from opposite sides of a field of battle. When the opposition went out into the lobby, – an operation by the bye which took up twenty minutes or more, – we spread ourselves over the benches on both sides of the House. For there were many of us who had not been able to find a seat during the evening. When the doors were shut we began to speculate on our numbers. Every body was desponding. "We have lost it. We are only two hundred and eighty at most. I do not think we are two hundred and fifty. They are three hundred. Alderman Thompson has counted them. He says they are two hundred and ninety nine." This was the talk on our benches. I wonder that men who have been long in parliament do not acquire a better coup d'œil for numbers. The House when only the Ayes were in it looked to me a very fair house, – much fuller than it generally is even on debates of considerable interest. I had no hope however of three hundred. As the tellers passed along our lowest row on the left hand side the interest was insupportable, – two hundred and ninety one: – two hundred and ninety two: – we were all standing up and stretching forward, telling with the tellers. At three hundred there was a short cry of joy, at three hundred and two another – suppressed however in a moment. For we did not yet know what the hostile force might be. We knew however that we could not be severely beaten. The doors were thrown open and in they came. Each of them as he entered brought some different report of their numbers. It must have been impossible, as you may conceive, in the lobby, crowded as they must have been, to form any exact estimate. First we heard that they were three hundred and three – then the number rose to three hundred and ten, then went down to three hundred and seven. Alexander Baring told me that he had counted and that they were three hundred and four. We were all breathless with anxiety, when Charles Wood who stood near the door jumped on a bench and cried out, "They are only three hundred and one." We set up a shout that you might have heard to Charing Cross – waving our hats – stamping against the floor and clapping our hands. The tellers scarcely got through the crowd: – for the house was thronged up to the table, and all the floor was fluctuating with heads like the pit of a theatre. But you might have heard a pin drop as Duncannon read the numbers. Then again the shouts broke out – and many of us shed tears – I could scarcely refrain. And the jaw of Peel fell; and the face of Twiss was as the face of a damned soul; and Herries looked like Judas taking his neck-cloth off for the last operation. We shook hands and clapped each other on the back, and went out laughing, crying, and huzzaing into the lobby. And no sooner were the outer doors opened than another shout answered that within the house. All the passages and the stairs into the waiting rooms were thronged by people who had waited till four in the morning to know the issue. We passed through a narrow lane between two thick masses of them; and all the way down they were shouting and waving their hats; till we got into the open air. I called a cabriolet – and the first thing the driver asked was, "Is the Bill carried?" – "Yes, by one." "Thank God for it, Sir." And away I rode to Grey's Inn – and so ended a scene which will probably never be equalled till the reformed Parliament wants reforming; and that I hope will not be till the days of our grand-children – till that truly orthodox and apostolical person Dr. Francis Ellis is an archbishop of eighty.

What are your movements? Mine are not absolutely determined. Have you had many briefs? At any rate you have, I suppose, been employed against the coiners. However the weightier matters of the law may fare, the tithe of mint, I hope, goes on.

As for me, I am for the present a sort of lion. My speech has set me in the front rank, if I can keep there; and it has not been my luck hitherto to lose ground when I have once got it. Shiel and I are on very civil terms. He talks largely concerning Demosthenes and Burke. He made, I must say, an excellent speech – too florid and queer; but decidedly successful.

Why did not the great Samuel Grove Price speak? He often came to the front rows, and sate making notes. Every body expected him to rise, and prepared night-caps accordingly. But he always sneaked away. On my soul, I believe that he is a craven with all his bluster. Indeed if he is afraid, it is the best thing that I ever knew of him. For a more terrible audience there is not in the world. I wish that Praed had known to whom he was speaking. But with all his talent, he has no tact, no perception of the character of his audience; and he has fared accordingly. Tierney used to say that he never rose in the House without feeling his knees tremble under him: and I am sure that no man who has not some of that feeling will ever succeed there.

Ever yours
T B Macaulay

TO HANNAH MACAULAY, 30 MAY 1831

MS: Trinity College. *Address:* Miss H M Macaulay. *Mostly published:* Trevelyan, I, 207–9.

London May 30. 1831

My dearest girl, –

Thank you for your letter. But I must begin with criticism. You say that Fanny is quite *épris* of Miss Mortlock. Now Fanny is surely a feminine noun – and can only be *éprise* of Miss Mortlock. If Miss Mortlock were the loveliest creature on earth, I defy Fanny to be *épris* of her. I remark this because it is a bad habit to use foreign words even in the most familiar chat or writing with inaccuracy.

Well, I have been to Holland House. They sent to ask me for an earlier day, I believe because Charles, my Colleague, is just on the point of going to Paris. He starts this afternoon. I took a glass coach and arrived, through a fine avenue of elms at the great entrance, towards seven o'clock. The house is delightful, – the very perfection of the old Elizabethan style, – a considerable number of very large and very comfortable rooms, rich with antique carving and gilding, but carpeted and furnished with all the skill of the best modern upholsterers. The library is a very long room, as long, I should think, as the gallery at the Temple, with little cabinets for study branching out of it, warmly and snugly fitted up, and looking out on very beautiful grounds. The collection of books is not, like Lord Spenser's, curious; but it contains almost every thing that one ever wished to read. Round the library hang some very interesting portraits, Addison – who, you know, lived at Holland house after his marriage with Lady Warwick, Crabbe the poet, Moore the poet, and many other distinguished men. The famous bust of Mr. Fox by Nollekens stands on a table. I found nobody there when I arrived but Lord Russell – the son of the Marquess of Tavistock. We are old House of Commons friends: so we had some very pleasant talk, and, in a little while in came Allen, who is warden of Dulwich College, and who lives almost entirely at Holland House. There are several stories against

52

him. He is certainly a man of vast information and great conversational powers. Some other gentlemen dropped in, and we chatted till Lady Holland made her appearance. Lord Holland dined by himself on account of his gout.

We sate down to dinner in a fine long room the wainscot of which is rich with gilded coronets, roses, and portcullises. There were Lord Albemarle, Lord Alvanley, Lord Russell, Lord Mahon, – a violent Tory, but a very agreable companion, and a very good scholar. There was Cradock, a fine fellow who was the Duke of Wellington's Aide de Camp in 1815, and some other people whose names I did not catch. Oh! I cry you mercy. There was my friend Boddington, Sharp's relation and quondam partner.

What however is more to the purpose, there was a most excellent dinner. I have always heard that Holland House is famous for its good cheer, and certainly the reputation is not unmerited.

During dinner I had some chat with Allen and Lord Mahon about the great European libraries, and particularly that at the Escurial, about the Jesuits, about Macintosh's new volume, and about the Collection of old State Papers which has lately been published by the Government. After dinner Lord Holland was wheeled in; and placed very near me. He was extremely amusing and good-natured.

In the drawing-room I had a long talk with Lady Holland about the antiquities of the House and about the purity of the English language – wherein she thinks herself a most exquisite critic. I happened in speaking about the Reform bill to say, that I wished that it had been possible to form a few commercial constituencies, if the word constituency were admissible. "I am glad you put that in," said her Ladyship, "I was just going to give it you. It is an odious word. Then there is *talented*, and *influential*, and *gentlemanly*. I never could break Sheridan of *gentlemanly*, though he allowed it to be wrong." I joined in abusing *talented* and *influential*; but *gentlemanly*, I said, had analogy in its favour, as we say *manly* and *womanly*. But her ladyship was perverse. She said truly enough that analogy was not a safe guide. "As to the word *womanly*," said she, "I hate it. You men never use it but as a term of reproach." – It is a reproach, thought I, which I shall scarcely bring against your ladyship. We talked about the word *talents* and its history. I said that it had first appeared in theological writing – that it was a metaphor taken from the parable in the new testament, and that it had gradually passed from the vocabulary of divinity into common use. I challenged her to find it in any classical writer in general subjects before the restoration or even before the year 1700. I believe that I might safely have gone down later. She seemed surprised and amused by this theory, never having, as far as I could judge, heard of the parable of the talents, or at all events having no distinct remembrance of it. I did not tell her, though I might have done so, that a person who professed to be a critic in the delicacies of the English language ought to have the Bible at his finger's ends.

She is certainly a woman of considerable talents and great literary acquirements. To me she was excessively gracious; yet there is a haughtiness in her courtesy which, even after all that I had heard of her, surprised me. The Centurion did not keep his soldiers in better order than she keeps her guests. It is to one "Go," and he goeth, and to another "Do this" and it is done. "Ring the bell, Mr. Macaulay." "Lay down that screen, Lord Russell; – you will spoil it." "Mr. Allen, take a candle and shew Mr. Cradock the picture of Buonaparte."

Lord Holland is, on the other hand, all kindness, simplicity, and vivacity. He talked very well both on politics and on literature. He asked me in a very friendly manner about my father's health and begged to be remembered to him.

When my coach came Lady Holland made me promise that I would, on the first fine morning, walk out to breakfast with them, and see the grounds; – and, after drinking a glass of very good iced lemonade, I took my leave, much amused and pleased. The house certainly deserves its reputation for pleasantness and her Ladyship used me, I believe, as well as it is her way to use any body.

Love to Selina and Fanny. I see Margaret every day. She seems to be very comfortable.

Ever, my darling, yours
T B M.

TO HANNAH MACAULAY, I JUNE 1831

MS: Trinity College. Address: Miss H M Macaulay / Post Office / Leamington / Warwick. Frank: London June one 1831 / T B Macaulay. Mostly published: Trevelyan, I, 211–14.

London June 1 1831

My dearest Sister,

My last letter was a dull one. I mean this to be very amusing. My last was about Basinghall Street, attorneys and bankrupts. But for this – take it dramatically in the German style.

Time morning. Scene the great entrance of Holland House. Enter Macaulay and two Footmen in livery.

First Footman.

Sir may I venture to demand your name?

Macaulay.

Macaulay, and thereto I add M.P.
And that addition even in these proud halls
May well insure the bearer some respect.
Second Footman.
And art thou come to breakfast with our Lord?
Macaulay.
I am: for so his hospitable will
And hers – the peerless dame ye serve – hath bade.
First Footman.
Ascend the stair, and thou above shalt find,
On snow-white linen spread, the luscious meal.
(Exit Macaulay up stairs.)

In plain English prose – I went this morning to breakfast at Holland
House. The day was fine, and I arrived at twenty minutes after ten. After
I had lounged a short time in the dining-room, I heard a gruff good-
natured voice asking, "Where is Mr. Macaulay. Where have you put
him;" and in his arm-chair Lord Holland was wheeled in. He took me
round the apartments, he riding and I walking. He gave me the history
of the most remarkable portraits in the library – where there is by the
bye, one of the few bad pieces of Lawrence that I have seen – a head of
Charles James Fox, – an ignominious failure: Lord Holland said that it
was the worst ever painted of so eminent a man by so eminent an artist.
There is a very fine head of Machiavelli – another of Earl Grey, a very
different sort of man. I observed a portrait of Lady Holland painted some
thirty years ago. I could have cried to see the change. She must have been
a most beautiful woman. She is now, I suppose, very near sixty, very
large, and with a double chin. She still looks however as if she had been
handsome; – and shews in one respect great taste and sense. She does not
rouge at all; or at least not in any manner which I could detect; and her
costume is not youthful, so that she looks as well in the morning as in
the evening.

We came back to the dining room. Our breakfast party consisted of
My Lord and Lady – myself – Lord Russell, – Luttrell – and another
person whose name I could not catch. You must have heard of Luttrell.
I met him once at Rogers's; and I have seen him, I think, in other places.
He is a famous wit – the most popular, I think, of all the professed wits, –
a man who has lived in the highest circles, – a scholar, and no contemptible
poet. He wrote a little volume of verse entitled "Advice to Julia," – not
first-rate, but neat, lively, piquant, and shewing the most consummate
knowledge of fashionable life.

Well, we breakfasted on very good coffee and very good tea and very good eggs, – butter kept in the midst of ice and hot rolls. Lady Holland told us her dreams; how she had dreamed that a mad dog bit her foot, and how she set off to Brodie, and lost her way in St Martin's lane and could not find him; – she hoped, she said, the dream would not come true. I said that I had had a dream which admitted of no such hope. For I had dreamed that I heard Pollock speak in the House of Commons, that the speech was very long, and that he was coughed down. This dream of mine diverted them much, and we talked of Pollock, of law and lawyers, of the art of decyphering, and of the art of acoustics. Lord Holland told us that there was formerly something in the structure of his library which conveyed the voice from one recess to another at a great distance. He had opened a bow window between them and this had removed the evil. An evil it was indeed by his account. "Why, Sir," said he, "a friend of mine asked another friend of mine in one of those recesses whether he should propose to a girl – and the adviser dissuaded him most strongly. The lady was in the other recess, and heard every word." – A pretty business indeed!

After breakfast Lady Holland offered to conduct me to her own drawing-room; – or rather commanded my attendance. A very beautiful room it is, opening on a terrace, and wainscotted with miniature paintings interesting from their merit, and interesting from their history. Among them I remarked a great many, thirty I should think, which even I, who am no great connoisseur, saw at once could come from no hand but Stothard's. They were all on subjects from Lord Byron's poems. "Yes," said she; "poor Lord Byron sent them to me a short time before the separation. I sent them back, and told him that if he gave them away, he ought to give them to Lady Byron. But he said that he would not – and that, if I did not take them, the bailiffs would, and that they would be lost in the wreck." Her ladyship then honoured me so far as to conduct me through her dressing room into the great family-bedchamber to shew me a very fine picture by Reynolds of Fox when a boy bird's-nesting. I had seen it at the British Gallery. She then consigned me to Luttrell, asking him to shew me the grounds.

Through the grounds we went and very pretty I thought them. Much more, however, might be done at little cost. But Lady Holland, has not, I find, paid much attention to gardening. In the Dutch garden – a very appropriate and pretty appendage to such an antique building as the house, – there is an interesting object – a very fine bronze bust of Napoleon, which Lord Holland put up in 1817, while Napoleon was a prisoner at St Helena. The inscription was selected by his Lordship, and is remarkably happy. It is from Homer's Odyssey. I will translate it as well as I can extempore into a measure which gives a better idea of Homer's manner than Pope's sing-song couplet.

"For not, be sure, within the grave
Is hid that prince, the wise, the brave, –
But in an islet's narrow bound,
With the great Ocean roaring round,
The captive of a foeman base,
He pineth for his native place." –

There is a seat near the spot which is called Rogers's seat. The poet loves, it seems, to sit there. A very elegant inscription by Lord Holland is placed over it.

"Here Rogers sate; and here forever dwell
With me those pleasures which he sang so well."

Very neat and condensed, I think. Another inscription by Luttrell hangs there. Luttrell adjured me with mock pathos to spare his blushes; but I am author enough to know what the blushes of authors mean. So I read the lines; and very pretty and polished they were – but too many to be remembered from one reading.

Having gone round the grounds I took my leave, very much pleased with the place. Lord Holland is extremely kind. But that is of course; for he is kindness itself. Her Ladyship too, which is by no means of course, is all graciousness and civility. But, for all this, I would much rather be quietly walking with you, my darling. And the great use of going to these fine places is to learn how happy it is possible to be without them. Indeed I care so little for them that I certainly should not have gone to day, but that I thought that I should be able to find materials for a letter which you might like. Farewell – my sweet sister. Give my love to Selina and Fanny. I am delighted to hear that Selina has placed herself under Dr. Jephson with good hopes. I believe that the hope, in her case, is half the cure. Love to my father.

Ever yours, dearest,
T B M

TO HANNAH MACAULAY, 7 JUNE 1831

MS: Trinity College. *Mostly published:* Trevelyan, I, 205; 216–19.

London June 7. 1831

My dearest girl,

Yesterday I dined at Marshall's; and was almost consoled for [not] meeting Ramohun Roy, by a very pleasant party. There were Protheroe the member for Bristol, and Colonel Davies the member for Worcester, and Lady Henry Howard, and many other unknown gentlemen and ladies. But the great sight was the two great wits, Rogers and Sydney

Smith. Singly I have often seen them. But to see them both together was a novelty – and a novelty not the less curious because their mutual hostility is well known, and the hard hits which they have given to each other are in every body's mouth. They were very civil however. But I was struck by the truth of what Matthew Bramble, – a person of whom you probably never heard, – says in Smollett's Humphrey Clinker. One wit in a company, like a knuckle of ham in soup, gives a flavour. But two are too many. Rogers and Sydney Smith would not come into conflict. If one had possession of the company the other was silent, and, as you may conceive, the one who had possession of the company was always Sydney Smith, and the one who was silent was always Rogers. Sometimes however the company divided, and each of them had a small congregation. I had a good deal of talk with both of them; for, in whatever they may disagree, they agree in always treating me with very marked kindness.

I had a good deal of pleasant conversation with Rogers. He was telling me of the curiosity and interest which attached to the persons of Sir W Scott and Lord Byron. When Sir Walter Scott dined at a gentleman's in London some time ago, all the servant-maids in the House asked leave to stand in the passage and see him pass. He was, as you may conceive, greatly flattered.

About Lord Byron whom he knew well, he told me some curious anecdotes. When Lord Byron passed through Florence Rogers was there. They had a good deal of conversation, and Rogers accompanied him to his carriage. The inn had fifty windows in front. All the windows were crowded with women, mostly English women, to catch a glance at their favourite poet. Among them were some at whose houses he had often been in England, and with whom he had been on friendly terms. He would not notice them or return their salutations. Rogers was the only person that he spoke to.

The worst thing that I know about Lord Byron is the very unfavourable impression which he made on men, who certainly were not inclined to judge him harshly, and who, as far as I know, were never personally ill used by him. Sharp and Rogers both speak of him as an unpleasant, affected, splenetic, person. I have heard hundreds and thousands of people who never saw him rant about him. But I never heard a single expression of fondness for him fall from the lips of any of those who knew him well. Yet, even now, after the lapse of five and twenty years there are those who cannot talk for a quarter of an hour about Charles Fox without tears. What strongly attached friends Canning made every body knows.

Sydney Smith leaves London on the 20th – the day before parliament meets for business. I advised him to stay and see something of his friends who would be crowding to London. "My flock," said this good shepherd. "My dear Sir, remember my flock.

'The hungry sheep look up and are not fed.'"

I could say nothing to such an argument – but I could not help thinking that if Mr. Daniel Wilson had said such a thing it would infallibly have appeared in his funeral sermon and in his Life by Baptist Noel. But in poor Sydney's mouth it sounded like a joke. He begged me to come and see him at Combe Flory. "There I am, Sir, – the priest of the Flowery Valley – a delightful parsonage about which I care a good deal – and a delightful country, about which I do not care a straw." I told him that my meeting with him was some compensation for missing Ramohun Roy. Sydney broke forth. "Compensation! Do you mean to insult me – a beneficed clergyman – an orthodox clergyman – a nobleman's chaplain – to be no more than compensation for a Brahmin – and a heretic Brahmin too – a fellow who has lost his own religion and can't find another – a vile heterodox dog who, as I am credibly informed, eats beef-steaks in private – a man who has lost his caste – who ought to have melted lead poured down his nostrils, if the good old Vedas were in force as they ought to be." He then told me that he had dined with Scarlet. "Oh, Macaulay! – A fallen angel! – And a complete Pandæmonium of his brethren he had assembled to dinner – all the powers and dominations who are out of place. There was Mammon Herries, and there was Beelzebub Twiss." These are some Boswelleana of Sydney – not very clerical, you will say, – but indescribably amusing to the hearers whatever the readers may think of them. Nothing can present a more striking contrast to his rapid, loud, laughing utterance, and his rector-like amplitude and rubicundity than the low, slow, emphatic tone and the corpse-like face of Rogers. There is as great a difference in what they say as in the voice and look with which they say it. The conversation of Rogers is remarkably polished and artificial. What he says seems to have been long meditated, and might be published with little correction. Sydney talks from the impulse of the moment, and his fun is quite inexhaustible.

The Miss Marshalls were full of Paganini and his violin. The man seems to be a miracle. The newspapers say that long streamy flakes of music fall from his string interspersed with luminous points of sound which ascend the air and appear like stars. Fanny probably understands this eloquence. But it is quite beyond me. Love to her, to Selina, and to my father. Write to me, my sweet darling.

Ever yours, dearest,

T B M.

MS: Trinity College. *Address:* Miss H M Macaulay / Post Office / Leamington / Warwick. *Frank:* London June fourteen 1831 / T B Macaulay.

London June 14. 1831 –

My dearest girl,

I have looked at the Morning Chronicle. But I have not been able to procure a copy for you. The thing is set right; – and indeed it was never worth caring about. They spoke civilly of my father even while they considered him as responsible for the passage which they were reprobating. My father is in high favour with the liberals on account of his conduct at the London University. All the members of the Council whom I see tell me that they can do nothing without him, and that he was the most valuable of their members.

I dined yesterday evening at Philips's – the son of Sir George, and member of Parliament for Steyning. Philips lives in Hill Street. Sir George must be a very rich man to keep up two such handsome town establishments. I should judge that he can hardly allow his son less than five thousand a year. The house is large, handsomely furnished, and fashionably situated, and the display of plate and of every other ornament quite equal to what I have seen at Sir George's own house in Mount Street.

Philips married a Miss Cavendish – a sister of Lord Waterpark. The company consisted of Sir George and Lady P[hilips], Rice and Rice's wife and daughter, – Sydney Smith, – George Lamb, – Tom Moore, – Whishaw or Wishaw, – I forget how he spells his name, – and myself. Rice came looking as fine as if he had been going to a Jew's fancy ball. There was a great party and dancing at the Palace yesterday night – and all the official men were invited with their families. Rice had on his official dress – a superb brown coat covered with rich gold embroidery, looking something between an uniform and a livery. He told me that it cost at least a hundred pounds, and that some of his friends threatened that he would not have less than a hundred and twenty to pay for the coat alone. He had also a sword and a gorgeous cocked hat. George Lamb had to leave us early in order to attire himself in a similar fool's coat.

We had a pleasant evening. Moore was very silent, – Sydney very loud and George Lamb very diverting. I heard one good story. Lord Dudley – I do not know whether you ever heard of his habit – has an inveterate trick of talking to himself. He cannot help doing it, – and it sometimes brings him into scrapes. Many people think that it is all affectation. But his friends say that he struggles against it and laments it. He was in a carriage with the late Chancellor – when only Sir John Copley;

and began to murmur in an audible tone. "Shall I ask Sir John to dinner? Hum – Ha – Hum. Shall I ask Sir John to dinner? Hey. Shall I ask Sir John to dinner? – No. I won't. Not to day." Sir John who was excessively diverted began to mutter in the other corner of the chariot. "Shall I dine with Dudley if he asks me? Hey. Shall I? No. I'll see him hanged first. No. Not to day." This recalled Lord Dudley to his recollection and half killed him with laughing.

We talked about prosecutions for blasphemy, – and about Taylor, and Carlisle, and the Rotunda. I was surprised at the way in which we divided on the matter. Sydney, Tom Moore, and Lamb, were for prosecution, – at least in extreme cases, – Rice and I against prosecuting in any case. I somewhat doubtingly – Rice quite warmly and decidedly.

We talked of statesmen and great parliamentary orators. They all agreed that Tierney was the clearest speaker that ever they heard. Fox, they said, was sometimes too refined in his arguments. "I have never heard," said Sir G[eorge], "any thing that reminded me of Fox in the House of Commons except now and then a burst of Whitbread's." But none of the company would allow this. "I know," said George Lamb, "that people who dined at Whitbread's brew house used to butter him by telling him that he spoke like Fox. I dare say, Rice, when you eat beef-steaks at Buxton's brewery, you tell him that he speaks like Fox." We talked about Percival. Sydney described him with great cleverness and bitterness. "The most mischievous little man that ever lived, – just every thing that John Bull likes, – moral, and religious, with a wife and ten children, quiet and meek, with the heart of a lion, – and always in the wrong, – always flattering some rascally prejudice, always oppressing and humbugging and, – hang the fellow! – making oppression and humbug respectable by his decent character and his admirable demeanour, and his skill in debating." I believe this to be very near the truth. Sir Robert Inglis, I remember, once told me that England never had but one government quite after his own heart and that government was Mr. Percival's. My notion of Perceval is that he was Inglis with great talents for debate, – the same opinions both religious and political, – the same rectitude of principle, the same sweetness of temper, and the same bigotry and narrowness.

The day after to-morrow I dine at Sir G Philips's – on Friday at Rice's, and on Sunday *en famille* at Mackintosh's, to meet nobody but Empson and Malthus.

Write to me, my love. I had a short note from you yesterday enclosed in a letter to Margaret the length of which made me quite envious. I shall be angry, not with you, but with my self, if I think that you cannot write to me with as much ease and freedom as to her. You never need want a subject. A book, a walk, a friend, a bore, – any th[ing or] any body will do. Remember that [I have] never been at Leamington. Write a Leamington guide for me with a fine description of scenery. Tell me what sort of Pump room there is, how the town is built – whether of brick or stone, to how many circulating libraries you subscribe, whether you ride on donkies – whether you have yet been to Warwick castle and how you liked it. I am more and more pleased by what I hear of Selina. Kindest love to her and Fanny. I enclose a paper for my father, which has just been sent to me by Margaret. George, I suppose, is in London again by this time.

Ever, my darling, yours

T B M

TO HANNAH MACAULAY, 24 JUNE 1831

MS: Trinity College. *Address:* Miss H M Macaulay / Post Office / Leamington / Warwick. *Frank:* London June twenty four 1831 / T B Macaulay. *Mostly published:* Gordon S. Haight, ed., *The Portable Victorian Reader*, New York, 1972, pp. 3–6.

London June 24. 1831

My love,

I am to breakfast with Rogers this morning; and here I am in my dressing gown writing to you at seven o'clock – which we Members of Parliament call the Middle of the night – because I shall be so busy all the day that, if I do not write now, you have no chance of a letter. And I have such a subject! – such a noble subject! – If Margaret gave you a hint of it yesterday evening, I never will forgive her. It would be like telling the catastrophe of a novel, just at the moment when the Hero and Heroine have been parted – never – as it should seem – to meet again. Suppose that I had told you that Lord St Orville was Lady Storamont – or that Frank Yates was Lord Caerleon – before the proper time – would you ever have forgiven me? –

This morning, as I was sitting at breakfast in my dressing-gown – the Times before me – sipping a full bason of tea and eating between whiles of a well-baked loaf, the accompanying note was delivered at my door. Read here enclosure marked A, as the Diplomatists say. I send it, because I love accuracy; and because I wish to teach you to love it. File this note – (it is from Lord Althorp) with your papers. A hundred years hence people will give ten pounds for it. It will then be a relique of famous times.

Well, – having received this note, I was not disobedient to the summons. I attired myself in my drawing-room dress; – and at half after twelve was in the house of Commons. We mustered, gradually, about a hundred and eighty members – all of us ministerial. There were a few court-dresses – many official uniforms; – and some members in the uniforms of the regular army or of the local militia. There were many in boots. But the majority were dressed, like me, as for an evening party. Admire, I pray you, for a moment the tact which I showed, in dressing myself quite comme-il-faut, without the least instruction. Burdett, who never went up with an address before in his life, was in full court dress. So was Sir Richard Price and Bernal. Admire, again, I beseech you, these little touches of narrative. Lord Althorpe came in court mourning – Rice – Stanley – Graham – Tennyson – Howick, Baring and Macdonald – were blazing with gold lace and white satin. We nicknamed my late colleague Marshal Macdonald.

In came Mr. Speaker with a gown flowered with gold and a long lace ruff. We had prayers; and then Lord Althorpe moved that we should adjourn till four, and go to the King with our address. The motion was, of course, carried, and we set forth in a train of carriages which reached from Westminster Hall to the Horse Guards, if you know – which I much doubt – where those two places are. Shiel gave me a place in his carriage together with Mr. Perrin and Sir Robert Harty the successful candidates for Dublin at the late election. We went on at a foot's pace, – the Speaker preceding us in a huge old-fashioned, painted, gilded, coach, drawn by two immense black horses. The Serjeant, with the mace, and the Chaplain, went in the Speaker's coach.

At half after one we reached St James's Palace. The coaches set down their inmates, one by one, and we were among the last. In we went – and I was in the inside of a real King's Palace for the first time in my life.

I have seen finer houses. We passed first through a long matted passage with wooden benches, bearing the royal arms, set on both sides. Beef-eaters with their red coats and gold lace stood here and there; and now and then we met a magnificent looking person in a blue suit loaded with dazzling embroidery. At the end of this matted passage was a staircase of stone – not by any means very fine – I have seen finer at several country-seats, and those at the London Club houses beat it all to nothing. Up this staircase we went and were ushered by two tall yeomen of the guard into a large antiroom. – A few fine pictures hung round the walls. I caught a glimpse of one of Vandyke's Henrietta-Marias as we passed through. The room was however comfortless. The only furniture consisted of two or three large scarlet benches. The floor was covered with red cloth which looked as if his Majesty was in the habit of riding over it with the whole Royal Hunt. From this Anti-room we passed into a reception room – smaller than the Anti-room – but still of noble size – with pictures round the walls and a general air of great magnificence in the furniture. We had scarcely assembled here when a large pair of folding-doors at the further end was thrown open, and we advanced, pushing as hard as we could without making a disturbance; – and thus we squeezed ourselves into the presence-chamber. – The room is handsome – the walls and cieling covered with gilding and scarlet hangings. – On the walls is a picture of the battle of Vittoria – another of the battle of Waterloo – a full-length of George IV by Lawrence – and two or three older pictures which I could not examine on account of the crowd. Fronting us was the throne under a gorgeous canopy. We marched up to it between two rows of officers, in scarlet and gold, bearing halberts. His Majesty was seated in all his glory – wearing an admiral's uniform. Lord Wellesley – in a state of fine preservation looking as if he had just been taken out of a band box – held the white staff at the King's elbow. What a sublime dandy that Marquess Wellesley is! I could see little of the other attendants of the King – by reason of the crowd. The Speaker read our address. The King bowed at the end of every sentence and at all the peculiarly emphatic words. When the Speaker had done the King turned to one of the Lords in waiting who handed him a paper containing what he was to say in answer to us. Another presented a pair of spectacles. His majesty placed them on his royal nose – read a short answer which you will see in the paper – and bowed us out. The Speaker stept forward and kissed the Sacred hand of our Gracious Sovereign. Then came the worst part of the show. For we had to walk out backwards – bowing all the way down the presence chamber. You may conceive how two hundred people cooped pretty close in a room performed this ceremony. We came out with broken shins and broken toes in abundance – vowing – many of us – that we would never do Ko-tou more.

I went only because I wanted to find something to tell you – and if you like to hear about these fine doings, I am satisfied. Kindest love to my father – Selina – and Fanny. Fanny sends me some very kind lines now and then. I do not answer them particularly only because I know that she sees all that I write to you. Selina will, I hope, soon be brought by Dr. Jephson into condition to be an equally good correspondent.

Ever yours, dearest,

T B M.

MS: Trinity College. *Address:* Miss H M Macaulay / Post Office / Leamington / Warwick. *Frank:* London July six 1831 / T B Macaulay. *Published:* Clive and Pinney, *Selected Writings of Macaulay*, pp. 430–1.

London July 6. 1831

My love,

I have been so busy during the last two or three days that I have found no time to write to you. I have now good news for you. I spoke yesterday night with a success beyond my utmost expectations. I am half ashamed to tell you the compliments which I have received. But you well know that it is not from vanity, but to give you pleasure, that I tell you what is said about me. Lord Althorpe told me twice that it was the best speech he had ever heard. Graham and Stanley and Lord John Russell spoke of it in the same way. Grahame told me that I had surpassed myself out and out. Robert Grant said that he liked this speech far better than my speech of last Parliament. O'Connell followed me out of the house to pay me the most enthusiastic compliments, and old John Smith cried as he talked to me. But what flattered me most was to come on a knot of old members whom I did not know, and who did not see me, who were disputing whether Plunket or I were the better speaker. I delivered my speech much more slowly than any that I had before made – and it is in consequence better reported than its predecessors – though not well. I send you several papers. You will see some civil things in the leading articles of some of them. My greatest pleasure in the midst of all this praise is to think of the pleasure which my success will give to my father and my sisters. It is happy for me that ambition – the fiercest and most devouring of all passions – has in my mind been softened into a kind of domestic feeling – and that affection has at least as much to do as vanity with my wish to distinguish myself. This I owe to my dear mother and to the interest which she always took in my childish successes. From my earliest years the gratification of those whom I love has been associated with the gratification of my own thirst of fame, until the two have become inseparably joined in my mind.

Do not, – my love, – but of course you will not – shew this letter to anybody but my father and sisters, or talk to any body else about the compliments which I repeat to you. I should appear ridiculously conceited to people who do not understand the feeling which induces me to repeat them. Kindest love to my father, Selina, and Fanny.

Ever yours my darling

T B M

MS: Trinity College. *Address:* Miss H M Macaulay / Rothley Temple / Mountsorrel / Leicestershire. *Frank:* London July eleven 1831 / T B Macaulay. *Mostly published:* Trevelyan, I, 230–2.

London July 11. 1831

My darling,

Since I wrote to you I have been out to dine and sleep at Holland House. We had a very agreable and splendid party – the Duke and Duchess of Richmond, – the Marquess and Marchioness of Clanricarde, – Lord Duncannon, Denison the Member for Nottinghamshire, – and Allen the common goer on errands and fetcher and carrier of trifles. Lady Holland sent him, five or six times, out of the room on footman's messages, and called him once from the other end of the drawing-room where he was talking to pick up her fan. The Duchess of Richmond is not so handsome as her charming portrait by Lawrence would have led me to expect. But Lady Clanricarde is very beautiful, and very like her father, with eyes full of fire and great expression in all her features. She and I had a great deal of talk. She shewed great cleverness and information – but, I thought, a little more of political virulence than is quite beseeming in a pretty woman. However she has been placed in peculiar circumstances. The daughter of a statesman who was a martyr to the rage of faction may be pardoned for speaking sharply of the enemies of her parent – and she did speak sharply. With knitted brows, and flashing eyes, and a look of feminine vengeance about her beautiful mouth, she gave me such a character of Peel as he would certainly have had no pleasure in hearing. Her husband is a poor creature, – a great gawky schoolboy who grins at every thing that is said in such a way as to shew an enormous row of tusks and the whole cavity of a most capacious mouth. The Marchioness should have said to him, as Lady G said to her poor Lord, who was not, I believe, more henpecked than Lord Clanricarde, – "And why must thou show all thy teeth man."

In the evening Lord John Russell came; and soon after old Talleyrand. I had seen Talleyrand in very large parties, but had never been near enough to him to hear a word that he said. I now had the pleasure of listening for an hour and a half to his conversation. He is certainly the greatest curiosity that I ever fell in with. His head is sunk down between two high shoulders. One of his feet is hideously distorted. His face is as pale as that of a corpse, and wrinkled to a frightful degree. His eyes have an odd glassy stare quite peculiar to them. His hair thickly powdered and pomatumed hangs down his shoulders on each side as straight as a pound of tallow-candles. His conversation however soon makes you

66

forget his ugliness and infirmities. There is a poignancy without effort in all that he says, which reminded me a little of the character which the wits of Johnson's circle give of Beauclerk. For example – we talked about Metternich – Talleyrand said – "L'on a voulu faire un parallèle de M. de Metternich au Cardinal Mazarin. J'y trouve beaucoup à redire. Le Cardinal trompoit; mais il ne mentoit pas. Or M. de Metternich ment toujours, et ne trompe jamais." He mentioned M. de St Aulaire, – now one of the most distinguished public men of France. I said – "M. de St Aulaire est beau-père de M. le Duc de Cazes; – n'est-ce pas?" "Non, Monsieur," said Talleyrand, "l'on disoit, il y a douze ans, que M. de St Aulaire étoit beau-père de M. de Cazes. L'on dit maintenant que M. Decazes est gendre de M. de St Aulaire." It was not easy to describe the change in the relative positions of two men more tersely and sharply; – and these remarks were made in the lowest tone, and without the slightest change of muscle, – just as if he had been remarking that the day was fine. He added – "M. de St Aulaire a beaucoup d'esprit. Mais il est devot, – et, ce qui pis est, devot honteux. – Il va se cacher dans quelque hameau pour faire ses Pâques." This was a curious remark from a Bishop. He told several stories about the political men of France – not of any great value in themselves. But his way of telling the[m is] beyond all praise, concise, pointed, and delica[tely] satirical. When he had departed, I could not help breaking out into praise of his talent for relating anecdotes. Lady Holland said that he had been considered for nearly forty years as the best teller of a story in Europe, – and that there was certainly nobody like him in that respect.

When the Prince was gone we went to bed. In the morning Lord John Russell drove me back to London in his cabriolet, much amused with what I had seen and heard. – But I must stop. Thank you for your kind little note. Love to my father, sisters, uncle, aunt, and cousins. I forgot to tell my clerk to change the direction of the newspapers. Farewell, – my dearest, – and write to me when you have a few minutes to spare. You cannot think how much I love to see your handwriting on a letter.

Ever yours my love
T B M

Where is Mr. Wilberforce? Some blockhead sends me letters for him without a direc[tion.]

MS: Trinity College.

London August 3. 1831

My love,

I do not think that, since you left London, I have suffered so long a time to pass without writing to you. I have been very busy, and still am so. But I steal a few minutes during an examination in Quality Court to write a line or two. I breakfasted with Rogers the other day. Nobody was there but Sharp, Lord Plunkett, a stupid silent nephew of our host, – and Luttrell, who was extremely amusing. I liked Lord Plunkett. He is, to be sure, very ugly – but with a strong expression of intellect in his strong coarse features and massy forehead. We had much pleasant talk – and several good stories. One in particular amused me a good deal. An inquisitive lady was boring Canning with questions. – 'And why have they shut one of the gates into the Park at Spring Gardens. The passage is only half as wide now as it used to be. Why is that, Mr. Canning." Canning answered with the gravest face. "It had really become necessary. Such very fat people used to go through."

Rogers has added some fresh curiosities to his collection – a good Claude, and a Guido of the very highest merit. He has two very remarkable reliques – the original deed by which Milton sold the copyright of the Paradise Lost signed by the poet himself – and the original deed by which Dryden contracted to translate the Eneid – signed by Dryden himself and witnessed by Congreve.

On Monday Empson sent to tell me that, if I had any ladies to oblige, he could give them room to see the procession on the Thames from his chambers. I took Margaret and Sarah Anne. We mounted his leads which overlook the Temple Gardens and the river. The sight was really noble. The whole Waterloo Bridge on the West – the whole of Blackfriar's Bridge on the East was one solid mass of human beings. The Southwark Bridge beyond Blackfriar's Bridge was equally crowded. The whole shore was one mass of people. The whole terrace before Somerset House was a sea of heads. The river looked like a street. Two lines of barges and large boats were drawn at the distance of about two hundred feet from each other through the middle of the stream – all blazing with flags – all covered with men and women – decks, masts, shrouds, and all. Through this street the train of royal barges past – the people on each side cheering as the King went by, and bridge after bridge sending up a great shout as he passed under them in succession. All the bells from all the hundred spires and towers of the city were pealing together. The roar of guns was almost incessant. Our prospect extended as far as the balloon on London

Bridge and we remained till it went up in signal of the King's arrival. Then down we went to Empson's cold collation – he flirting with Margaret all the way down stairs and through the whole repast. The room was filled with damsels eating peaches, grapes, and ices, and of gentlemen indulging their more masculine appetites with pigeon pye and Moselle. Margaret will give you a more copious narrative of our proceedings. Tell me whether it is a better. So I have now lost her too. I think, as I told her, that you and she have treated me as the birds in the nursery song treated the stone

> "There were two birds that sate on a stone
> One flew away, and then there was but one.
> The other flew away and then there was none
> And the poor stone was left all alone."

You ought to write oftener to me now. I am up till three every morning – hallooing, crying *question*, and dividing. Kindest love to all.

Ever yours, my dearest,

T B Macaulay

TO HANNAH MACAULAY, 29 AUGUST 1831

MS: Trinity College. *Address:* Miss H M Macaulay / M Babington's Esq / Rothley / Mountsorrel / Leicestershire. *Frank:* London August twenty nine 1831 / T B Macaulay. *Published* Clive and Pinney, *Selected Writings of Macaulay*, pp. 439–42.

London August 29. 1831

My darling,

Here I am again settled, sitting up in the House of Commons till three o'clock five days in the week, and getting an indigestion of great dinners on the remaining two. I dined on Saturday with Lord Althorpe and yesterday with Sir James Graham. Both of them gave me exactly the same dinner; – and, though I am not generally copious on the repasts which my hosts provide for me, I must tell you, for the honour of official hospitality, how our ministers regale their supporters. Turtle, turbot, venison, and grouse, formed the principal part of both entertainments – the effect of which is that I had the heartburn all last night, and have solemnly vowed never to eat of such a variety of good things again.

Lord Althorp was extremely pleasant at the head of his own table. We were a small party – Lord Ebrington, Hawkins, Captain Spencer, Stanley, and two or three more. We all of us congratulated Lord Althorpe on his good health and spirits. He told us that he never took exercise now, that from his getting up till four o'clock he was engaged in the business of his office – that at four he dined, went down to the house at five, and never stirred till the house rose, which is always after midnight, – that he then went home, took a basin of arrow-root with a glass of sherry in it, and went to bed – where he always dropped asleep in three minutes. "During the week," said he, "which followed my taking office I did not close my eyes for anxiety. Since that time I have never been awake a quarter of an hour after taking off my clothes."

Stanley laughed at Lord Althorp's arrow-root and recommended his own supper – cold meat and warm negus – a supper which I will certainly begin to take when I feel a desire to pass the night with a sensation as if I was swallowing a nutmeg-grater every third minute.

We talked about timidity in speaking. Lord Althorp said that he had only just got over his apprehensions. "I was as much afraid," he said, "last year as when first I came into parliament. But now I am forced to speak so often that I am quite hardened. Last Thursday I was up forty times." I was not much surprised at this in Lord Althorp – as he is certainly one of the most modest men in existence. But I was surprised to hear Stanley say that he never rose without great uneasiness. "My throat and lips," he said, "when I am going to speak are as dry as those of a man who is going to be hanged." Nothing can be more composed and cool than Stanley's manner. His fault is on that side. A little hesitation at the beginning of a speech is graceful; and many eminent speakers have practised it merely in order to give the appearance of unpremeditated reply to prepared speeches. Stanley speaks like a man who never knew what fear or even modesty was. Tierney, it is remarkable, who was the most ready and fluent debater almost ever known, made a confession similar to Stanley's. He never spoke, he said, without feeling his knees knock together when he rose.

Sir James Graham's official house is much finer than Lord Althorp's, and indeed than Lord Grey's. It is really a palace. The rooms in which we dined and took coffee look out on St James's park. They are very handsome and are hung round with paintings from which the prints in Cook's Voyages were taken – of scenes in Otaheite and New Zealand. Cook's Voyages, you are aware, were undertaken under the direction of the Admiralty.

Lord Althorp was at Graham's. James the member for Carlisle, the Attorney and Solicitor General, and the Lord Advocate were also there. There was a little more constraint than at Lord Althorp's, who is simplicity itself. I came away with Jeffrey who brought me in his carriage to the entrance of Gray's Inn.

My opinion of Lord Althorp is extremely high. In fact his character is the only stay of the ministry. I doubt whether any person has ever lived in England who, with no eloquence, no brilliant talents, no profound information, – with nothing in short but plain good sense and an excellent heart, possessed as much influence both in and out of Parliament. His temper is an absolute miracle. He has been worse used than any minister ever was in debate; and he has never said one thing inconsistent, I do not say with gentlemanlike courtesy, but with real benevolence. His candour is absolutely a vice in debate. He is perpetually shewing excuses and ways of escape to his adversaries which they would never find of themselves. Lord North perhaps was his equal in suavity and good nature. But Lord North was not a man of strict principles. His administration was not only an administration hostile to liberty; but it was supported by vile and corrupt means – by direct bribery, I fear, in many cases. Lord Althorp has the temper of Lord North with the principles of Romilly. If he had the oratorical powers of either of those men, he might do any thing. But his understanding, though just, is slow; and his elocution painfully defective. It is however only justice to him to say that he has done more service to the Reform Bill even as a debater than all the other ministers together, Stanley excepted. Graham is either afraid or idle. Grant and Palmerston are idle, and, I suspect, not very hearty. Lord John Russell gives all that he has – to wit two mites which make a farthing. I must in fairness say, however, that Lord John made a better speech on Saturday than any that I have heard from him for a long time.

We are going, – by *we* I mean the Members of Parliament who are for reform – , as soon as the Bill is through the Commons, to give a grand dinner to Lord Althorp and Lord John Russell as a mark of our respect. Some people wished to have the other Cabinet Ministers included. But Grant and Palmerston are not in sufficiently high esteem among the Whigs to be honoured with such a compliment. Where we [are to] hold our festivities – whether at the Albion or the City of London Tavern, or whether we shall go to Greenwich to eat white-bait is undecided.

But I must stop. Kindest love to all at the Temple.

Ever yours, my love
T B M

TO HANNAH MACAULAY, 9 SEPTEMBER 1831

MS: Trinity College. *Address:* Miss H M Macaulay / Rothley Temple / Mountsorrel / Leicestershire. *Frank:* London September nine 1831 / T B Macaulay. *Mostly published:* Trevelyan, I, 243–5.

London September 9. 1831

My love,

I scarcely know where to begin or where to end my story of the magnificence of yesterday. No pageant can be conceived more splendid. The newspapers will happily save me the trouble of relating minute particulars. I will therefore give you an account of my own proceedings, and mention what struck me most. I rose at six. The cannon awaked me, and as soon as I got up, I heard the bells pealing on every side from all the steeples in London. I put on my court-dress and looked a perfect Lovelace in it. At seven the glass coach which I had ordered for myself and some of my friends came to the door. I called in Hill Street for William Marshall, M P for Beverley, and in Cork Street for Strutt the member for Derby and Hawkins the member for Tavistock. Our party being complete we drove through crowds of people and ranks of horse-guards in cuirasses and helmets to Westminster Hall, which we reached as the clock struck eight.

The House of Commons was crowded. There must have been four hundred members present, and the aspect of the assembly was very striking. The great majority were in military or naval uniforms. All officers in the militia or the yeomanry, and all the Deputy-Lieutenants of Counties wore their military garb. The ministers were in their official suits of purple and gold. There were three or four Highland Chiefs in Kilts, plaids and philibegs with eagle's plumes in their hats, dirks and pistols at their sides, and claymores in their hands. The Speaker came at nine in his robes of State, covered with gold embroidery. After prayers we went out in order by lot, the Speaker going last. My county, Wiltshire, was among the first drawn so I got an excellent place, next to Lord Mahon, who is a very great favourite of mine, and a very amusing companion, though a bitter Tory.

Our gallery was immediately over the great altar. The whole vast avenue of lofty arches was directly in front of us. In the centre of the Abbey, where the nave and transept cross each other, were several raised steps, covered with a Brussels carpet. On these steps a footcloth of yellow silk was spread, and the throne and footstool for the king were in the centre of this cloth. The Queen's throne was a few steps lower. The Chair in which the Kings are crowned is different from the Throne. They are not enthroned till after they have been crowned. The Coronation Chair I have seen a hundred times. It is one of the shews of the Abbey, six hundred years old at least; and quite mouldering. The seat is placed on a stone which Edward the First brought from Scotland as a trophy. Stone and wood however were now completely covered with cloth of gold and satin. All the pavement of the Abbey was covered – with blue cloth and red cloth in the less conspicuous parts, – with rich carpeting in the place where the ceremony was to be performed. Vast galleries hung with red cloth were extended between the pillars, and some were hung at a dizzy height far above our heads.

72

Gradually the body of the Abbey filled with Peers, Peeresses, and Judges, and Bishops, all in full robes, the Peers and Peeresses with coronets in their hands. Our gallery was quite full, and was, I understand, one of the most brilliant objects in the Abbey. On our right hand was a gallery filled with the foreign Ambassadors and their ladies. There were Talleyrand, Washington Irving, the Duchess de Dino – the Princess Lieven, and a crowd of others. All the uniforms and orders of Europe might be seen there. Other galleries in our neighborhood were occupied by charming English women, who outbloomed the ladies of the Corps Diplomatique most indisputably.

At eleven the guns fired, the organ struck up, and the procession entered. I never saw so magnificent a scene. All down that immense vista of gloomy arches there was one blaze of scarlet and gold. First came heralds in coats stiff with embroidered Lions, Unicorns and harps, then nobles dressed in Ermine and velvet bearing the Regalia – with pages in rich dresses carrying their coronets on cushions – then the Dean and Prebendaries of Westminster in rich Copes of Cloth of gold, – then a crowd of beautiful girls and women – or at least of girls and women who at a distance looked altogether very beautiful attending on the queen. Her train of purple velvet and ermine was borne by six of these fair creatures. All the great officers of state in full robes. The Duke of Wellington with his marshal's staff – the Duke of Devonshire with his white rod, Lord Grey with the Sword of State – and the Chancellor with his seals came in procession. Then all the Royal Dukes with their trains borne behind them, and last the King leaning on two Bishops. – I do not, I dare say, give you the precise order. In fact it was impossible to discern any order. The whole Abbey was one blaze of gorgeous dresses, mingled with lovely necks and faces.

The Queen behaved admirably, with wonderful grace and dignity – the King very ill and awkwardly. The Duke of Devonshire looked as if he came to be crowned instead of his master – I never saw so princely a manner and air. The Chancellor looked like Mephostopheles behind Margaret in the Church.

The ceremony was much too long, and some parts of it were carelessly performed. The Archbishop mumbled. The Bishop of London preached, well enough indeed, but not so effectively as the occasion required; and, above all, the low, clumsy bearing of the King made the foolish parts of the ritual appear monstrously ridiculous, and deprived many of the better parts of their proper effect. Persons who were at a distance perhaps did not feel this. But I was near enough to see every turn of his finger and every glance of his eye. The moment of the crowning was extremely fine. When the Archbishop placed the crown on the head of the King, the trumpets sounded, – the whole audience cried out God save the King. All the Peers and Peeresses put on their coronets, and the blaze of splendour through the Abbey seemed to be doubled.

The King was then conducted to the raised Throne, where the Peers successively did him homage, – each of them kissing his cheek and touching the Crown. Some of them were cheered which I thought indecorous in such a place and on such an occasion. The Tories cheered the Duke of Wellington, and our people, in revenge, cheered Lord Grey and Brougham.

You will think this a very dull letter for so great a subject. But I have only had time to scrawl these lines in order to catch the post. I have not a minute to read them over. I lost yesterday and have been forced to work to day. If I find time I will tell you more to morrow.

Ever yours

T B M

TO HANNAH AND MARGARET MACAULAY, 13 JUNE 1832

MS: Morgan Library. *Address:* Miss Macaulay / J Cropper's Esq / Dingle Bank / Liverpool. *Frank:* Calne June thirteen 1832 / T B Macaulay.

Calne June 13 – 1832

My dearest girls, –

This is the day of election, and in three or four hours I shall again be M P. I snatch the only minutes which I shall have to myself till midnight, to prattle with you on paper. When shall we prattle again face to face, and make puns on the names of the shopkeepers along the streets? My own dear sisters, my heart becomes quite heavy when I think for how long a time we are to be separated.

But this is no day for being heavy. The bells are ringing. Flags are flying on the housetops. Music is playing in front of the Inn – Macaulay for ever! Huzza! – Read the inclosed handbill, and you will see how much honor a prophet may have out of his own country who has none in it. I shall have I understand to dine with all the élite of all the surrounding towns. From Chippenham, from Marlborough, yea even from Devizes, I am told, people are coming to gaze upon and listen to the great patriot. And I am wishing all the time that I were two hundred miles away, gazing upon and listening to my own little girls.

But I have been at Bath. I have seen all the spots made classical by Miss Austen, – the pump-room and the identical bench whereon Miss Thorpe and Miss Morland discussed the merits of novels, – the nasty buildings wherein Mrs. Smith lodged, – the street where Captain Wentworth made his proposals to Anne. The assembly room, I own, I did not see. But I climbed the hill whereon the Revd Henry Tilney M A,

Miss Tilney, and Catherine held their conversation; – and I did not agree, I must say, with their opinion that the city of Bath might with advantage have been struck out of the landscape. I went to the Abbey where, as you may remember, Mrs. Macmaurice heard so good a sermon that she exclaimed "What a mercy it is that one can go home and forget it all." I heard a very bad sermon; and have most certainly forgotten it all.

I saw Russell Street and the outside of Tom Babington's house: but having a hundred and twenty pounds or so in bank-notes about me, I did not venture in. – But here come the Guild-Stewards and the Burgesses in their best. Here comes the music. Here come the beadles with fine coats and gold-headed staves: and here comes – is it? no – yes – it is Lord Kerry. I had no notion that he was here. I must go and shake hands with him. God bless you, my own dearest girls.

T B M

TO HANNAH AND MARGARET MACAULAY, 27 JUNE 1832

MS: Morgan Library. *Address:* Miss Macaulay / J Cropper's Esq / Dingle Bank / Liverpool. *Frank:* London June twenty seven / 1832 / T B Macaulay.

London June 27 – 1832

My darlings,

> Wherefore come ye not to Court?
> Certie, 'tis the bravest sport

As old Sir David Lindsay sings. Oh if you but knew the pleasure of being admitted to the Royal presence! I cannot keep my elation to myself. I cannot describe my feelings in dull creeping prose. I burst forth in unpremeditated verse, worthy of the judicious poet whom I so often quote.

> I passed in adorning
> The whole of the morning
>   When the hand of the King must be kissed,
>   must be kissed.
> I put on my back
> A fine suit of black
> And twelve ells of lace on my wrist
>   on my wrist.
> I went to the levee
> And squeezed through the bevy
> Till I made good my way to his fist
>   to his fist.

But my wing fails me. I must creep in prose for a few lines. At one we assembled in the House of Commons. For this was the day appointed for taking up our address to the King on his escape from the beggar who threw a stone at him the other day. The House looked like a parterre of tulips – all red and blue – like certain Heathen Gods of whom you may have heard. Much gold lace was there and much silver lace – many military uniforms – yeomanry uniforms – navy uniforms, official uniforms, – and so forth. Then the Speaker rose and walked majestically down stairs to his state carriage, – an old thing covered with painting and gilding of the days of Queen Anne. In this huge conveyance he drove away with the Serjeant at Arms carrying the mace, and the Chaplain carrying his own fat rotundity – quite load enough, I assure you. We came behind in about a hundred carriages. I was in Littleton's, and away we went, at hearse pace, forming a string from Westminster Hall to St James's palace. The carriage stopped. We alighted at the door of a long passage, matted, and furnished only with large wooden benches. Along this passage we went to a stone staircase. On the landing places guards with their swords and carbines were in attendance to slay us if we behaved improperly. At the top of the staircase we passed through two ranks of beef-eaters, blazing in scarlet and gold, to a table, where we wrote our names, each on two cards. One card we left on the table with the page. The other we took with us to give to the Lord in Waiting.

As a member of the House of Commons, I had peculiar advantages. For before the levee we were admitted to present our address. The throne room was however so crowded that while we were going through the ceremony I heard little, and saw nothing. But I mistake – one thing I saw – a great fool with a cocked hat and a coat like that of the fifer of a band, Mr. Edwin Pearson, who was performing his duties as Exon. He condescended to quiz me through his glass, and then to extend his hand and congratulate me on my appointment. "Such instances of elegant breeding," – as Sir William Lucas says, "are not uncommon at the Court." When we had walked out backward, trampling on each other's toes and kicking the skin off each other's shins, the levee began, and we were re-admitted singly to the apartment which we had just left in a body. The King stood near a door. We marched before him and out at a door on the other side, bowing and scraping the whole way. When I came to him, I gave my card to the Lord in Waiting who notified the name to the King. His Majesty put forth his hand. I kneeled, or rather curtseyed, and kissed the sacred object most reverently. Then I walked away backwards bowing down my head like a bulrush, and made my way through the rooms into the street with all expedition.

This is a levee: and a stupid affair it is. I had a thousand times rather have one of the quiet walks which I used to have this time year with Margery than cuff and kick my way through these fine people – and I would a thousand times rather kiss my Nancy's lips than all the hands of all the Kin[gs in] heaven.

Given from the library of the House of Commons at five in the afternoon. Present Lord Lowther, writing, James Brougham, reading, Pendarves yawning, Sir Ronald Fergusson sealing letters, and Billy Holmes telling lies. / Farewell and farewell

my own darlings

T B M

TO HANNAH AND MARGARET MACAULAY, 6 JULY 1832

MS: Trinity College. Address: Miss Macaulay / J Cropper's Esq / Dingle Bank / Liverpool. Frank: London July six 1832 / T B Macaulay. Partly published: Trevelyan, I, 258.

London July 6. 1832

My loves, –

Be you Lords or be you Earls
You must write [to] naughty girls
Be you Foxes, be you Pitts,
You must write to silly chits
Be you Tories, be you Whigs,
You must write to sad young gigs.
Of whatever board you are –
Treasury, Admiralty, War,
Customs, Stamps, Excise, Controul,
Write you must, upon my soul.

So sings the judicious poet. And here I sit in my parlour looking out on the Thames and divided, like Garrick in Sir Joshua's picture, between Tragedy and Comedy – a letter to you and a bundle of papers about Hydrabad, my sweet sisters and the firm of Palmer and Co. late bankers to the Nizam. It is like the choice of Hercules. Indeed I resemble Hercules in another point. My labour of to day is the same with one of his labours. Guess the joke. Can you? No – Adad – Adad – Adad – poor Stellakins, not you. Why, did not Hercules deal with a bad Hydra, and I have to deal with Hydrabad.

What news? This morning I broke my fast again with Sam Rogers. Sydney and Luttrell were there, and Sydney said one or two good things. By the bye Ellis has written a most capital squib on me in imitation of my style. I will send it to you when the new Edinburgh Review is out. You will hardly understand it fully till then. –

77

Poor Sir Walter is going back to Scotland by sea to morrow. All hope is over; and he has a restless wish to die at home. He is many thousand pounds worse than nothing. Last week he was thought to be so near his end that some people went, I understand, to sound Lord Althorp about a public funeral. Lord Althorp said, very like himself, that if public money was to be laid out, it would be better to give it to the family than to spend it in one day's shew. The family, I hear, however, are not so ill off. The land is entailed on the eldest son. The daughter is married. And the other children have 5000 £ a piece, the bequest of some relation who died in India.

But what do you care for this stuff? I hardly know why I go on writing – except for writing's sake, and that I may feel a little as if you were near me. Come back – come back to me, my own little darlings; and let the world go as it likes. Let the Whigs sta[y] in or be turned out. Let m[oney] be abundant or scarce. I do not know how love in a cottage may do with a wife. But I am sure that it would suit me with a sister.

Farewell – dear girls,

T B M.

So here is Nancy's letter. What travellers you are! As the judicious poet sings

> "Pray, Miss, what may you be *ar'ter?*"
> Seeing trees and stones and water.
> Up and down, through all the day,
> On the hills of Wales I stray.
> And at night it is my habit
> For to sup on a Welch rabbit.

TO HANNAH AND MARGARET MACAULAY, 30 JULY 1832

MS: Morgan Library. *Address:* Miss Macaulay / J Cropper's Esq / Dingle Bank / Liverpool. *Frank:* London July thirty one 1832 / T B Macaulay. *Partly published:* Trevelyan, 1, 264–6.

Library of the House of Commons
July 30 – 1832 – 11 o'clock at night –

My darlings,

Here I am. – Daniel Whittle Hervey is speaking. The house is thin. The subject is dull. And I have stolen away to write to you. Lushington is scribbling at my side. Alderman Thompson, as fat as butter, is reading letters at the next table. No sound is heard but the scratching of our pens and the ticking of the clock. We are in a far better atmosphere than in the smoking room whence I wrote to you last week; and the company is more decent, inasmuch as that beast Gordon, whom Nancy blames me for describing in just terms, is not present.

By the bye, you know doubtless the lines which are in the mouth of every member of parliament, describing the comparative merits of the two rooms. They are, I think, very happy.

> If thou goest into the smoking-room
> Three plagues will thee befall, –
> The chlorate of lime, and the bacco-smoke
> And the captain who's worst of all, –
>   The canting sea captain,
>   The lying sea captain
> The captain who's worst of all.

> If thou goest into the library
> Three good things will thee befall, –
> Very good books, and very good air,
> And M+c++l+y, who's best of all.
>   The virtuous M+c++l+y
>   The prudent M+c++l+y,
> M+c++l+y who's best of all.

Oh! how I am worked. I never see Fanny from Sunday to Sunday. All my civilities wait for that blessed day; and I have so many scores of visits to pay that I can scarcely find time for any of that Sunday reading in which, like my Nancy, I am in the habit of indulging. Yesterday, as soon as I was fixed in my best and had breakfasted, I paid a round of calls to all my friends who had the cholera. Then I walked to all the clubs of which I am a member, to see the newspapers. The first of these two works you will admit to be a work of mercy; – the second, in a political man, one of necessity. Then, like a good brother, I walked, under a burning sun, to Kensington, to ask Fanny how she did, and staid there two hours. It was very kind of James Stephen to lend Sarah Anne and George his garden and house; but, as the poet says,

> For me, I would not gi'e a fard'en
> For such a house and such a garden.

Then I went to Knightsbridge to call on Mrs. Lister, and chatted with her till it was time to go and dine at the Athenæum. There I dined, and, after dinner, like a good young man, I sate and read Bishop Heber's journal till bed-time. There is a Sunday for you. I think that I excel in the diary line. I will keep a journal like the Bishop, that [my] memory may

Smell sweet and blossom in the dust.

Next Sunday I am to go to Lord Lansdowne's at Richmond, and to sleep there; so that I hope to have something to tell you. But, on second thought, I will tell you nothing – nor ever write to you again – nor ever speak to you again. I have no pleasure in writing to undutiful sisters. Why do you not send me longer letters? When you know that I love the very sight of your handwriting, why do you put me off with little notes, – one to every three letters of mine? But I am at the end of my paper. So that I have no room to scold.

Ever yours, my darlings,

T B M.

TO HANNAH AND MARGARET MACAULAY, 14 AUGUST 1832

MS: Trinity College. *Address:* Miss Macaulay / J Cropper's Esq / Dingle Bank / Liverpool. *Frank:* London August fourteen 1832 / T B Macaulay. *Partly published:* Trevelyan, I, 266–7.

London August 14. 1832

My dearest girls,

Our work is over at last, not, however, till it has half killed us all. On Saturday we met for the last time, I hope, on business. When the House rose, I set off for Holland House. We had a small party, but a very distinguished one. – Lord Grey, the Chancellor, Lord Palmerston, Luttrell and myself were the only guests. Allen was of course at the end of the table, carving the dinner and sparring with my Lady. The dinner was not so good as usual – for the French Cook was ill; and her Ladyship kept up a continued lamentation during the whole repast. I should never have found out that everything was not as good as usual but for her criticisms. The soup was too salt; the cutlets were not exactly comme il faut; and the pudding was hardly enough boiled. I was amused to hear from the splendid mistress of such a house the same sort of apologies which Mary Parker made when her cook forgot the joint and sent up too small a dinner to table. I told Luttrell that it was a comfort to me to find that no rank was exempted from these afflictions.

I learned two things at this dinner which I repeat to all my unfashionable friends for their guidance, and which you will do well to teach to friends at Liverpool. The time for eating melon is at the beginning of dinner – before the soup. It is handed round with ginger, pepper, and salt. The time for eating maccaroni is between the fish and the meat, – just as you would eat patties. Treasure up these instructions, my darlings, that, if you ever preside over banquets, you may do the genteel thing.

They talked about Lord Abercorn's approaching marriage. He is to be married to Lady Louisa Russell. All the noble persons present are very intimate friends of the Bedford family. They, however, treated the whole thing as a take-in, and laughed at the Duchess for pouncing on so rich a youth before he knew what he was about. Lady Holland vehemently defended the match; and when Allen said that Lord Abercorn had caught a Tartar, she quite went off into one of her tantrums – "Lady Louisa a Tartar! – such a charming girl a Tartar! – He is a very happy man, and your language is insufferable – insufferable, Mr. Allen." Lord Grey had all the trouble in the world to appease her. His influence however is very great. He prevailed on her to receive Allen again into favour, and to let Lord Holland have a slice of melon, for which he had been petitioning most piteously, but which she had steadily refused on account of his gout. Lord Holland thanked Lord Grey for his intercession. "Ah, Lord Grey, I wish you were always here. It is a fine thing to be prime minister." This tattle is worth nothing – absolutely nothing, except to shew how much the people whose names will fill the history of our times resemble in all essential matters the quiet folks who live in Mecklenburgh Square and Brunswick Square.

I slept in the room which was poor Mackintosh's. The next day – Sunday, – I walked over to James Stephen's, and sate there two hours. Fanny was well and seemed very comfortable. In the afternoon I walked back to Holland House and found her ladyship in her poney cart, being wheeled up and down the pretty lawn behind the house. I walked beside her for half-an-hour. She shewed me the beauties of the gardens, and read me some letters which Lord Grey had just sent to Lord Holland, giving a more favourable account of the state of things in Portugal than I had at all expected. Henry Fox, Miss Fox, Lord Holland's sister, and Tom Duncombe, came to dinner. Henry Fox I had before seen – but I had never heard his voice. He scarcely ever speaks in the society of Holland House. Rogers, who is the bitterest and most cynical observer of little traits of character that ever I knew, once said to me of him, "Observe that man. He never talks to men. He never talks to girls. But, when he can get into a circle of old tabbies, he is just in his element. He will sit clacking with an old woman for h[ours] together. That always settles my opinion of a young fellow." This description is quite correct. Yet Fox's address is extremely polished, his person agreable, and his mind, I believe, not uncultivated. He was, on this occasion, very courteous to me. But I despise his shallowness and instability; and I hate him for his conduct to Mrs. Lister. Labouchere told me some circumstances about that affair which made me think much worse of it than I had ever before thought. But my paper is nearly full; and this letter will weigh an ounce or very nearly so. I therefore must stop for the present.

Ever yours, dear girls
T B M

TO MARGARET MACAULAY, 26 NOVEMBER 1832

MS: Mrs Lancelot Errington. *Extracts published:* Trevelyan, 1, 286–7.

London Nov 26. 1832

My dearest Margaret,

When you receive this letter, I shall be on the road to Leeds; and I shall not see you again till the separation of which I cannot think without losing all my firmness shall have taken place. I have not taken leave of you. For I wished to spare you the pain of witnessing distress which you would, I know, feel acutely, but which you would not be able to relieve. I purpose to bear my affliction, as I have borne it hitherto, that is to say, alone. Mine is no case for sympathy or consolation. The heart knows its own bitterness.

My sufferings, like the sufferings of most other men, are the natural consequences of my own weakness. The attachment between brothers and sisters, blameless, amiable, and delightful as it is, is so liable to be superseded by other attachments that no wise man ought to suffer it to become indispensable to his happiness. Very few, even of those who are called good brothers, do suffer it to become indispensable. But to me it has been in the place of a first love. During the years when the imagination is most vivid and the heart most susceptible, my affection for my sisters has prevented me from forming any serious attachment. But for them I should be quite alone in the world. I have nothing else to love. Yet I knew, or ought to have known, that what was every day becoming more and more necessary to me might be withdrawn in a moment. That women shall leave the home of their birth and contract ties dearer than those of consanguinity is a law as ancient as the first records of the history of our race, and as unchangeable as the constitution of the human body and mind. To repine against the nature of things, – against the great fundamental law of all society, because, in consequence of my own want of foresight, it happens to bear heavily on me, would be the basest and most absurd selfishness. And I do not repine. You can bear me witness that I have suffered with fortitude; and, if I now break silence for the first and last time, it is only that you may not attribute my sudden departure to any want of affection for you.

I have still one more stake to lose. There remains one event for which, when it arrives, I shall, I hope, be prepared. I have another sister, no less dear to me than my Margaret, from whom I may be separated in the same manner. From that moment, with a heart formed, if ever any man's heart was formed for domestic happiness, I shall have nothing left in this world but ambition.

There is no wound, however, which time and necessity do not render endurable. And, after all, what am I more than my fathers, – than the millions and tens of millions who have been weak enough to pay double price for some favourite number in the lottery of life, and who have suffered double disappointment when their ticket came up a blank? All life is a system of compensations. My reason tells me that, but for the strong attachment which is at this moment a cause of pain to me, I might, like my friend Charles Grant, have been crossed in love, or, what is much worse, might, like his brother, have married a fool. I am glad too, in the midst of my sorrow, that I shall not be at the wedding, that I shall pass the next fortnight in a constant storm, that I shall have no time to be sad, and that, at the worst, I shall be able to wreak all the bitterness of my heart on Michael Sadler.

When we meet I shall, I hope, be reconciled to what is inevitable. But I cannot think, without a flood of tears, of that meeting. Once so much to each other – and henceforth to be so little.

Farewell, dearest. From my soul I thank you for the many happy days which I have owed to you, and for the innumerable proofs which I have received of your affection. May he to whom you are about to entrust the care of your happiness love you as much as you deserve, – as much as I have loved you. And, at this parting, – for it is a parting scarcely less solemn than that of a death bed, – forgive me, my own Margaret, if I have ever neglected you, if I have ever, from thoughtlessness or in a moment of irritation, wounded your feelings. God knows that it must have been by inadvertence, and that I never in my life did or said anything intended to give you pain.

Lastly, shew this letter to no person, – not even to my dear Nancy. I do not wish her to know how deeply this separation has affected me, lest, on some future occasion, she should take my feelings into the account in forming a decision which she ought to form with a view to her own happiness alone.

Again and again, dearest, farewell.
T B Macaulay.

MS: Trinity College. *Address:* Miss H M Macaulay / 44 Bernard Street / Russell Square / London. *Partly published:* Trevelyan, 1, 287–8.

Leeds Decr. – 12 – 1832

My darling,

The election here is going on as well as possible. To day the poll stands thus

Marshall	Macaulay	Sadler
1804	1792	1353

The probability is that Sadler will give up the contest. If he persists he will be completely beaten. The voters are under 4000 in number. Those who have already polled are 3100, and about five hundred will not poll at all. If we were not to bring up another man; the probability is that we should win.

On Sunday morning early I hope to be in London; and I shall see you in the course of that day.

I had written thus far when your letter was delivered to me. I am sitting in the midst of two hundred friends, all mad with exultation and party-spirit, all glorying over the Tories, and thinking me the happiest man in the world. And it is all that I can do to hide my tears and to command my voice when it is necessary for me to reply to their congratulations. Dearest, dearest, girl, you alone are now left to me. – Whom have I on *earth* but thee – and what is there in *heaven* that I desire in comparison of thee? But for you, in the midst of all these successes, I should wish that I were lying by poor Hyde Villiers. But I cannot go on. I am wanted to write an address to the electors: and I shall lay it on Sadler pretty heavily. By what strange fascination is it that ambition and resentment exercise such power over minds which ought to be superior to them? – I despise myself for feeling so bitterly towards this fellow as I do. Yet I must own to you dearest, to whom I own almost every thing, that I enjoy my victory over him and his impotent, envious, fury, more than any thing else in this contest. But this separation from dear Margaret has jarred my whole temper. I am cried up here to the skies as the most affable and kind hearted of men, while I feel a fierceness and restlessness within me quite new and almost inexplicable. When shall I be with you, my darling, and be soothed by your sweet tenderness, and amused by your kind womanly vivacity. I see some pleasing women here, some who have pretty faces, and some who wear my orange ribbands, and some who quote Latin to me; – but none who is worthy to tie the shoe-latchet of my two darling sisters.

I shall send you a second Edition of the Leeds Mercury Extraordinary to night. It will contain my address. Kindest love to all. Thank my father for his letter and for his congratulations.

Ever yours, dear, dear, girl,
T B M

TO MRS EDWARD CROPPER, 8 FEBRUARY 1833

MS: Morgan Library.

House of Commons Feby. 8. 1833

Dearest Margaret,

You will think that I write to you seldom. Think so, if you will; but attribute it to any thing but want of affection for you. Indeed, my dear girl, I love you very much. I am sitting in our library, crowded by Members of parliament. A fierce debate is going on. Yet I cannot begin a letter to you without being quite blinded with tears. We are engaged in most agitating discussions. We are on the verge of great events. I do not know what a week may bring forth. But my fears are stronger than my hopes. Yet of this I am sure, that if the worst come I shall meet the worst with unalterable philosophy. To be in or out – popular or unpopular – is a small matter. I shall bear the most adverse turn of political fortune in a manner very different from that in which I bore the loss of you.

But why should a man be sad in a world so full of things to laugh at? To day your Quaker – Mr. Joseph Pease – tried to take his seat. The matter is not decided. We have appointed a Committee to examine the Journals and the Statute Book. I have very little doubt that he has a right to sit: and I have no doubt at all that, if he has not a right, a law must be made to admit him. But how I was astonished! He called on me at the India Board a day or two ago to solicit my assistance. The porter brought in his name on a card – "Joseph Pease." "Shew him in." The card ought to have awakened my suspicions. For would a truly simple Christian have had his name engraved in copperplate on paste board? I am sure you will feel with me how inconsistent such a luxury was with such a profession. This, however, escaped me. I imaged Joseph to my self as a tall, stiff, elder, – a public friend, – with grey hair hanging down his shoulders, a hat like an umbrella, and a vocabulary full of third days and twelfth months. Alas! Alas! [   ] male friends abstained from worldly dress, manners, and conversation? I know of one sad exception. In came a smart, slender, dapper, grinning young gentleman, or rather gemman, with a sort of overstrained civility and alacrity in his manner, – bowing, skipping, smirking, – and flourishing his hands, instead of contenting himself with

85

the Christian pastime of twirling his thumbs. Nothing was wanting to make a very good third rate dandy of him but to have taken away two inches from the brim of his hat and added them to the collar of his coat. Then his talk. Not – as it should have been – "Behold, Thomas, hum! I pray thee to be good unto our people, hum! that they may sit among the elders without swearing, hum! and be judges in the gate without kissing the skin of calves – hum! hum!" Instead of that he talked as the carnal man talketh. But this is not the worst. To day he did hat-worship to the Speaker. He stood bare headed – bowed over and over again. I grieve to write these. One of our Irish members has also written a beautiful stanza on the subject, if you can allow for the Hibernian brogue in the last line.

> "There was a sturdy quaker –
> His hat-brim measured an acre
> But he took it off
> While the Churchmen did scoff,
> In honour of Sutton our *Spaker*.

But I must have done with this rambling nonsense.

Ever yours, my darling
T B M

TO HANNAH MACAULAY, 1 JUNE 1833

MS: Trinity College. *Address:* Miss Macaulay / E Cropper's Esq / Dingle Bank / Liverpool. *Frank:* London June one 1833 / T B Macaulay. *Partly published:* Trevelyan, 1, 294–5; 296.

London June 1. 1833

My love,

You have public news of course. What say the Liverpool abolitionists, specially they of the drab coat and the broad brim, to the modifications introduced into Stanley's bill. I am very nearly satisfied; and so Buxton seems to be. The papers will scarcely contain any account of what passed yesterday in the House of Commons at 12 o'clock in the middle of the day. Grant and I fought a battle with Fool Briscoe and Rogue O'Conel in defence of the Indian people, and won it by 38 to 6. It was a rascally claim of a dishonest agent of the Company against the employers whom he had cheated and sold to their own tributaries. The nephew of the original claimant has been pressing his case on the Board most vehemently. He is an attorney living in Russell Square and very likely hears the word at St John's Chapel. He hears it however to very little purpose: for he lies as much as if he went to hear a "cauld clatter of morality" at the parish

Church. He wanted 50000 £ or thereabouts out of the Indian revenues, and thought himself sure of pouching that sum. Indeed he would have succeeded but for me: for Grant at one time wavered much. It was by our uncle when he was Resident at Travancore that the rascality of the transaction was originally exposed twenty five or twenty six years ago. It was by me that the coup-de-grace was given. Mr. Hutchinson must love the name of Macaulay. Do you know him? Is he a Johnian?

Apropos of Johnians – what differences of taste and feeling there are in this world! The day before yesterday I found Selina and Fanny in ecstasies over a note which they had received from Baptist Noel – the sweetest note – oh such a sweet note – they must shew it me – and they shewed it me. This sweet note set forth that Baptist had seen his sister Augusta – but that, as other people were by, he had not had an opportunity of talking with her and ascertaining the state of her mind; but that he very much feared that she was – and then came the usual cant. How sweet that a brother should write to all his acquaintance the glad tidings that his sister is dying in a state of reprobation. I stormed till I think I made both Selina and Fanny a little ashamed of themselves and of their spiritual pastor and master. I hope that your confidential communications to Noel are not of this kind. I always hated confessors – protestant or Catholic. But this is enough of theology for one letter. I have written these edifying remarks because you may possibly receive my letter on Sunday evening and I wish you to employ your Sunday more Agnewishly than you did when you read my speech about the Jews.

I remember that when you were at Leamington two years ago I used to fill my letters with accounts of the people with whom I dined. High life was new to me then; and now it is so familiar to me that I should not, I fear, be able, as I formerly was, to select the striking circumstances. I have dined with sundry great folks since you left London. Yesterday night I went to a very splendid rout at Lord Grey's – the last party which he or more properly speaking my Lady gives this season. I stole thither at about eleven from the House of Commons with Stewart Mackenzie. I do not mean to describe the beauty of the ladies – who, excepting always Lady Seymour, were all of them as ugly as sin – nor the brilliancy of stars and uniforms. I mean only to tell you one circumstance which struck and even affected me. I was talking to Lady Charlotte Lindsay, a great favourite of mine, about the apartments and the furniture, when she said with a good deal of emotion, "This is an interesting visit to me. I have never been in this House for fifty years. It was here that I was born. I left it a child when my father fell from power in 1782, and I have never crossed the threshold since." Then she told me how the rooms seemed dwindled to her – how the stair case which seemed to her in recollection to be the most spacious and magnificent that she had ever seen had disappointed her. She longed, she said, to go over the garrets and rummage her old nursery. She told me how in the riots of 1780 – the No Popery riots – she was taken out of bed at two o'clock in the morning. The mob threatened Lord North's house. There were soldiers at the windows, and an immense and furious crowd in Downing Street. She saw, she said, from her nursery the fires in different parts of London. But she did not understand the danger; and only exulted in being up at midnight. Then she was conveyed through the Park to the Horseguards as the safest place; and was laid, wrapped up in blankets, on the table of the guard-room in the midst of the officers. "And it was such fun," she said, "that I have ever since had rather a liking for insurrections."

I must stop here. I dine to day with Ellis – and Napier is to be of the party. His name reminds me that I have some gossip for you about the Edinburgh Review but that must wait for another day. I am delighted to learn, dearest, that you are better and that you are comfortable, though I never doubted that with country air you would soon be better and that with Margaret and Edward you would be perfectly comfortable. Dear Margaret! I love her as much as ever. But I shall not write to her for the same reason for which Frank gave the extra piece of cake to poor James who had no pudding at dinner. She has a husband to look after her; and you have only a brother; so I shall continue to correspond with you. She has only herself to thank for my not writing to her. If she will only separate from Edward I will send her the most delightful letters that she ever read. In the meantime give her and Edward my love.

Ever yours dearest girl,
T B M

TO HANNAH MACAULAY, 6 JUNE 1833

MS: Trinity College. *Address:* Miss Macaulay / E Cropper's Esq / Dingle Bank / Liverpool. *Frank:* London June seven 1833 / T B Macaulay. *Partly published:* Trevelyan, 1, 297–8.

London June 6. 1833

My darling,

The House is sitting. Peel is just down. Lord Palmerston is speaking. The heat is tremendous, – the crowd stifling: so here I am in the smoking room – three filthy repealers making chimneys of their mouths under my very nose – writing to Nancy in the midst of stench and noise. I dare say my letter will bear to my Anna the exquisite scent of O'Connor's Havannah. Did you find out the rhyme?

Well but what news? – Public news you have. You know that the

Lords have been foolish enough to pass a vote implying censure on the Ministers. The ministers do not seem inclined to take it of them. The King has snubbed their Lordships properly: and in about an hour as I guess (for it is near eleven,) we shall have come to a resolution in direct opposition to that agreed to by the Upper House. Nobody seems to care one straw for what the Peers say about any public matter. A resolution of the Court of Common Council or of a meeting at Freemason's Hall has often made a greater sensation than this declaration of a branch of the legislature against the Executive Government. The institution of the peerage is evidently dying a natural death.

One of their Lordships has been taken away from the evil to come – and indeed he was one of whom their House was not worthy – poor Lord King. Bless my soul! here are three more fellows with cigars. I shall smell like a tobacconist's foreman when I go out of this dusky atmosphere. That interruption has spoiled the funeral oration in which I was just about to celebrate my poor friend Lord King.

I dined yesterday – where and on what and for what I am ashamed to tell you. Such base scandalous gluttony and extravagance I will not commit to writing. I blush when I think of it. When we meet I will breathe my low confession in your ear; and receive absolution.

You however are not wholly guiltless in this matter. My nameless offence was partly occasioned by Napier. And I have a very strong reason for wishing to keep Napier in good humour. He has promised to be at Edinburgh when I take a certain damsel thither, – to look out for very nice lodgings for us in Queen Street, to shew us every thing and every body, and to see us as far as Dunkeld on our way northward, if we do go northward. In general I abhor friends. But at Edinburgh we must see the people as well as the walls and windows; and Napier will be a capital guide.

I dine to morrow with the Duchess of Kent and the Princess Victoria at Kensington Palace. – So I shall have something to tell you when I write next. What sad stuff my letters are! Kindest love to Margaret and Edward. London is swarming with quakers – there they are like troops of the shining ones, as Charles Lamb would say. As the poet says

> "Come hither, my little foot page,
> And tell the truth to me –
> Look out into Bishopsgate Street
> And say what dost thou see."

> "Behold, Sir Knight, a cab
> With a brace of Quakers comes
> The wife in a bonnet of drab
> The husband a twirling his thumbs."

"Come hither my little foot page
I charge thee come hither to me
Look forth into Grace Church Street
And tell me what thou dost see."

"I see a public friend, Sir Knight,
Repeating an oration
Which is to be given him half an hour hence
By sudden inspiration."

Don't shew these atrocious lampoons to Edward, or he will perhaps slay me as he slew Canning's voter long ago.

Good bye my darling
T B M

TO HANNAH MACAULAY, 10 JUNE 1833

MS: Trinity College. *Address:* Miss Macaulay / E Cropper's Esq / Dingle Bank / Liverpool. *Frank:* London June eleven 1833 / T B Macaulay. *Extract published:* Trevelyan, II, 193n.

London June 10. 1833

My darling,

You have certainly done me about the seal – I acknowledge it. Imagine my feelings when I saw on the letter inclosed to me my own impression. I felt like Othello when the story of the handkerchief was explained away. I saw at a glance that I had been wronging celestial innocence. Oh Nancy, can you forgive me? I feel that I never can forgive my self. How pathetic! Almost as pathetic as Miss Austin's Persuasion which I have just been reading. A charming novel. And Northanger Abbey too is excellent. A little less pure in manner than her later works. Yet much of the pleasantry on the romances of the Udolpho school is worthy of Addison himself, – and, I own, I think it a better, because a less unnatural satire on the appetite of young ladies for novel-reading than the Female Quixote or Barrett's Heroine. The publisher of the last volume of poor Miss Austin has succeeded in procuring two pictures decidedly worse than the worst that I ever saw before. Get a sight of the Book next time you go to a circulating library at Liverpool; and tell me whether Henry Tilney be not the most offensive Varmint man that ever you saw. The artist must have read the book carelessly and must have confounded the adorable young parson with John Thorp. As to Miss Anne, sitting under a hedge, her appearance at once vindicates all Captain Wentworth's doubts as to her identity with the pretty girl whom he had known, and renders the final triumph of his constancy so admirable as to be almost incredible.

I dined at Holland House yesterday.

Dramatis Personæ

Men

The Lord Holland /	a fine old gentleman very gouty and good-natured.
The Earl Grey /	Prime Minister, a proud, and majestic, yet polite and affable person.
The Revd. Sydney Smith /	A holy and venerable Ecclesiastic, director of the consciences of the above named Lords.
Edward Ellice Esq M P /	Brother in law to the Earl Grey, – a great jobber, liar, and rhodomontader.
Lord Russell /	A meek God-fearing young gentleman.
John Allen Esq /	Atheist in ordinary to the household of My Lady Holland.
T B Macaulay Esq M P /	A virtuous and most accomplished man – the flower of the party.

Women

Lady Holland /	A great lady – fanciful, hysterical, and hypochondriacal, ill-natured and good natured, sceptical and superstitious, afraid of ghosts and not of God, – would not for the world begin a journey on a Friday morning, and thought nothing of running away from her husband.
Lady Dover /	A charming woman, like all the Howards of Carlisle.
Lady Grey /	A pattern wife and mother – has outlived her beauty if she ever had any.

Servants, Humble companions, My Lady's Page, Mr. Macaulay's Cab-driver etc. etc. etc.

I have occupied so much paper with the Dramatis Personæ that it will be impossible for me to give you the dialogue. Some parts of it however deserve to be remembered. But I may perhaps tell them to you when we meet. Lord Grey was very amusing. It was curious to see how he winced and kicked when Ellice tried to lead him by the nose.

As to your questions about the duties – I shall preserve the strict taciturnity which becomes a gentleman in office. A very few days will make all clear.

[Our?] India Bill comes on next Thursday. Till then I shall be very busy. So you must not be surprised if you should not hear from me till Sunday next. Kindest love to Margaret and Edward. Have you read the Parson's Daughter? – I have. And very poor stuff it is.

Ever yours, my own darling,

T B M

TO HANNAH MACAULAY, 17 JUNE 1833

MS: Trinity College. *Address:* Miss Macaulay / E Cropper's Esq / Dingle Bank / Liverpool. *Frank:* London June eighteen 1833 / T B Macaulay. *Mostly published:* Trevelyan, I, 300–3.

London June 17. 1833

Dearest Nancy,

All is still anxiety here. Whether the House of Lords will throw out the Irish Church Bill, – whether the King will consent to create new Peers, – whether the Tories will venture to form a ministry, – are matters about which we are all in complete doubt. If the ministry should really be changed the Parliament will, I feel quite sure, be dissolved. Whether I shall have a seat in the next Parliament I neither know nor care. I shall regret nothing for myself but the loss of our Scotch tour. For the public I shall, if this Parliament is dissolved, entertain scarcely any hopes. I see nothing before us but a frantic conflict between extreme opinions, – a short period of oppression, then a convulsive reaction, and then a tremendous crash of the funds, the Church, the peerage, and the Throne. It is enough to make the most strenuous royalist lean a little to republicanism to think that the whole question between safety and general destruction may probably, at this most fearful conjuncture, depend on a single man whom the accident of his birth has placed in a situation to which certainly his own virtues or abilities would never have raised him.

The question must come to a decision, I think, within the fortnight. In the meantime the funds are going down. The newspapers are storming, – and the faces of men on both sides are growing day by day more gloomy and anxious. Even during the most violent part of the contest for the reform-bill I do not remember to have seen so much agitation in the political circles. I have some odd anecdotes for you which I will tell you when we meet.

If the parliament should be dissolved the West Indian and East Indian Bills are of course dropped. What is to become of the slaves? What is to become of the Tea-trade? Will the negroes, after receiving the resolutions of the House of Commons promising them liberty, submit to the cart-whip? Will our merchants consent to have the Trade with China, which has just been offered to them, snatched away? The Bank Charter too is suspended. But that is comparatively a trifle.

Smoke Presto writing politics to little M D. After all what is it to me who is in or out, and whether those fools of Lords are resolved to perish and drag the King to perish with them in the ruin which they have themselves made? I begin to wonder what the fascination is which attracts men who could sit over their tea and their books in their own cool quiet room to breathe bad air, hear bad speeches, lounge up and down the long gallery and doze uneasily on the green benches till three in the morning. Thank God, these luxuries are not necessary to me. My pen is sufficient for my support, and my Nancy is sufficient for my happiness. Only let me see her well and cheerful; and let offices in government and seats in parliament go to those who care for them. Indeed, indeed, dearest, if I know my own heart, there is not the very smallest affectation or dis-guise in what I am now writing. If I were to leave public life to morrow, I declare that, except for the vexation which it might give you and one or two others, the event would not be in the slightest degree painful to me. As you boast of having a greater insight into character, you know, than I allow to you, let me know how you explain this philosophical disposition of mine, and how you reconcile it with my ambitious inclinations. That is a problem for a young lady who professes knowledge of human nature.

Did I tell you – I forget – that I dined at the Duchess of Kent's and sate next that loveliest of women – of women above forty, mind – Mrs. Littleton? She is the natural daughter of Lord Wellesley; and her husband, our new Secretary for Ireland, told me this evening that Lord Wellesley, who sate near us at the Duchess's, asked Mrs. Littleton after-wards who it was that was talking to her. "Mr. Macaulay." "Oh," said the Marquess, "I am very sorry I did not know it. I have a most particular desire to be acquainted with that man." Accordingly Littleton has engaged me to dine with him, in order to introduce me to the Marquess. I am particularly curious, and always was, to know him. He has made a great and splendid figure in history, and his weaknesses and vices, though they make his character less respectable, make it more interesting as a study. Such a blooming old swain I never saw, – cheeks as brilliant as his handsome daughter's who has the highest colour of any beauty in London, – hair combed with exquisite nicety, – a waistcoat of driven snow, and a star and garter put on with rare skill.

To day we took up our resolutions about India to the House of Lords. The two houses had a conference on the subject in an old Gothic room called the painted chamber. The painting consists in an old mildewed daub of a woman in the niche of one of the windows. The Lords sate in little cocked hats along a table; and we stood uncovered on the other side, and delivered in our resolutions. I thought that before long it may be our turn to sit and theirs to stand. But I must stop. I write from the smoking room of the House of Commons. Halcomb is speaking, and every soul has gone out in order to avoid hearing him. I have not read Godolphin; and I do not hear such an account of it as is likely to tempt me to read it. Kindest love to Margaret and Edward.

Ever yours my love
T B M

TO HANNAH MACAULAY, 11 JULY 1833

MS: Mrs Humphry Trevelyan. *Address:* Miss Macaulay / E Cropper's Esq / Dingle Bank / Liverpool. *Frank:* London July eleven 1833 / T B Macaulay. *Mostly published:* Trevelyan, I, 310–11.

London July 11. 1833

Dearest Nancy,

I have been so completely overwhelmed with business for some days that I have not been able to find time for writing a line. Yesterday night we read the India Bill a second time. It was a Wednesday, and the reporters gave hardly any account of what passed. They always resent being forced to attend on that day, which is their holiday. I made the best speech, by general agreement, and in my own opinion, that I ever made in my life. I was an hour and three quarters up. And such compliments as I had from Lord Althorp, Lord Palmerston, Lord John Russell, Wynne, O'Connel, Grant, the Speaker, and twenty other people you never heard. As there is no report of the speech, I have been persuaded, rather against my will, to correct it for publication.

I will tell you one compliment that was paid me and which delighted me more than any other. An old member said to me "Sir, having heard that speech may console the young people for never having heard Mr. Burke."

The slavery bill is miserably bad. I am fully resolved not to be dragged through the mire, but to oppose, by speaking and voting, the clauses which I think objectionable. I have told Althorp this, and have again tendered my resignation. He hinted that he thought that the government would leave me at liberty to take my own line, but that he must consult his colleagues. I told him that I asked for no favour; that I knew what inconvenience would result if official men were allowed to dissent from ministerial measures and yet to keep their places, and that I should not think myself in the smallest degree ill used if the cabinet accepted my resignation. This is the present posture of affairs. In the meantime the two houses are at daggers drawn. Whether the government will last to the end of the Session I neither know nor care. I am sick of boards and of the House of Commons, and pine for a few quiet days, a cool country breeze, and a little chatting and fondling with my own Nancy.

As to money matters, my love, I do intreat you to ask me for whatever you want without scruple. If we stay in place, I will try to arrange some plan for making you quite easy about your little expenses. Kindest love to Meg and Ned.

Ever yours
T B M

P S No news of the picture.

TO HANNAH MACAULAY, 22 JULY 1833

MS: Trinity College. *Address:* Miss Macaulay / Dingle Bank / Liverpool. *Frank:* London July twenty two / 1833 / T B Macaulay. *Extract published:* Trevelyan, 1, 312.

London July 22. 1833

My darling,

Things are still as dark as ever. The Lords have read the Church Bill a second time. But we fear that they will mutilate it in the Committee, and that the ministers will be forced to resign before the end of his week. I am placed in a situation of peculiar embarrassment. The discussions on the West India Bill commence to day. I do not like to oppose the government at such a moment – both from fear of increasing their difficulties, and still more from fear that I may be suspected of ratting from them when their places are insecure. I have, however, fully made up my mind to vote and speak against some parts of the Bill. I shall do nothing however hastily. I shall defer taking part in the discussion as long as I can. And I hope that, before it becomes absolutely necessary for me to take part in it, the fate of the Irish Church Bill will be decided one way or the other. Which way it will be settled I do not know, and, in truth, do not very much care. I am much more desirous to come to an end of this interminable session and to see my dear girls again than to stay either in office or in parliament. The Tories are quite welcome to take every thing, if they will only leave me my pen and my books, a warm fire side, and my Nancy chattering beside it. This sort of philosophy, an odd kind of cross between Stoicism and Epicureanism, I have learned where most people unlearn all their philosophy, in crowded senates and fine drawing-rooms. I will say for myself that I am the only *parvenu* l ever heard of, who, after being courted into splendid circles, and after having succeeded beyond expectation in political life, acquired in a few months a profound contempt for rank, fashion, power, popularity, and money, – for all pleasures in short but those which arise from the exercise of the intellect and of the affections.

I have no dinner parties to tell you of. Lord Robert Grosvenor and Lady Holland invited me for Saturday. Lord Palmerston and Strutt the Member for Derby invited me for yesterday. I was so tired that I refused all four, and had two quiet evenings over my tea and my books; – the first that I have had for a month.

I must stop here, my darling. Kindest love to Meg and Edward.

Ever yours, my love

T B M

TO HANNAH MACAULAY, 27 JULY 1833

MS: Trinity College. *Address:* Miss Macaulay / E Cropper's Esq / Dingle Bank / Liverpool. *Frank:* London July twenty seven / 1833 / T B Macaulay. *Mostly published:* Trevelyan, I, 315–16.

London July 27. 1833

My darling,

Here I am safe and well at the end of one of the most stormy weeks that the oldest man remembers in parliamentary affairs. I have resigned my office, and my resignation has been refused. I have spoken and voted against the ministry under which I hold my place. The ministry has been so hard run in the Commons as to be forced to modify its plan, and has received a defeat in the Lords – a slight one to be sure and on a slight matter – yet such that I and many others fully believed twenty four hours ago that they would have resigned. In fact some of the cabinet – Grant, among the rest, to my certain knowledge, were for resigning. At last Saturday has arrived. The ministry is as strong as ever. I am as good friends with the ministers as ever. The East India Bill is carried through our House. The West India Bill is so far modified that, I believe, it will be carried. The Irish Church Bill has got through the Committee in the Lords: and we are all beginning to look forward to a prorogation in about three weeks.

To day I went to Haydon's to be painted into his great picture of the Reform Banquet. Ellis was with me, and declares that Haydon has touched me off to a nicety. I am sick of pictures of my own face. I have seen within the last few days one drawing of it – one engraving – and three paintings. They all make me a very handsome fellow. Haydon pronounces my profile a gem of art – perfectly antique. And, what is worth the praise of ten Haydons, I was told yesterday that Mrs. Littleton, the handsomest woman in London, at least the handsomest woman of forty in London, had paid me exactly the same compliment. She pronounced Mr. Macaulay's profile to be a study for an artist. What say you to that –you who always denied my claims to beauty? Let me tell you that I have bought a new looking glass and razor case on the strength of these compliments, and am meditating on the expediency of having my hair cut in the Burlington Arcade rather than in Lamb's Conduit Street. As Richard says,

> "Since I am crept in favour with myself
> I will maintain it with some little cost."

I begin, like Sir Walter Elliot, to rate all my acquaintance according to their beauty. I hope I shall find my darling in good looks. Have you been using Gowland? But what nonsense I write, – and in times that make many merry men look grave. Kindest love to Margaret and Edward.

Ever yours, my love,

T B M

TO HANNAH MACAULAY, 29 JULY 1833

MS: Trinity College. *Address:* Miss Macaulay / E Cropper's Esq / Dingle Bank / Liverpool. *Frank:* London July twenty nine 1833 / T B Macaulay. *Partly published:* Trevelyan, I, 317–18.

London July 29. 1833

Dearest Nancy,

As I was shaving my self this morning, I was informed that a gentleman wished to see me. As this announcement is generally followed by the appearance of a beggar – specially of three beggars – old discarded servants of ours who spunge on me without mercy, I put on my dressing-gown and went very sulkily into my sitting-room, fearing that I should not get off under half-a-crown. But behold! there was Edward. So I gave him the newspaper to read while I dressed, and then breakfasted before him, and was so hospitable as to regale him with seeing me devour two eggs and half a loaf, and swallow a bason of tea. We talked about many things – the East Indies, the West Indies, the House of Lords, the Liverpool freemen, and two foolish girls whom nobody else cares a straw about. And, after an hour's chat, he went his way to call on that personage who is designated in the Fifth Commandment as one's father, but in the conversation of the ingenuous youth of this generation as the Governor.

He told me that on Monday morning he expected to find me earlier up. Alas poor, dear, good, young man! How little he knows of us town rakes! I dined yesterday at Holland House. There was a very pleasant party. My Lady was very courteous, and my Lord extravagantly entertaining – telling some capital stories about old Bishop Horsley which were set off with some of the drollest mimicry that I ever saw. There was Lord Melbourne, and Lord Essex, and Lord Lilford, and Sir James Graham, and Dr. Holland who is a good scholar as well as a good physician, and Wilkie who is a modest, pleasing, companion as well as an excellent artist, and Allen, and my self for gentlemen. For ladies we had her Grace of Bedford, and her daughter Lady Georgiana, a fine, buxom, sonsy lass, with more colour and firmer flesh than, I am sorry to say, are often seen among fine ladies, and that paragon of old aunts Miss Fox, and that lovely woman Lady Lilford. So our dinner and our soirée were very agreable.

We narrowly escaped a scene at one time. One of the Russells – Lord Edward, – is in the navy and is now on duty in the fleet at the Tagus. We got into a conversation about Portuguese politics. His name was mentioned, and Graham, who is first Lord of the Admiralty, complimented the Duchess on her son's merit, to which he said every dispatch bore witness. The Duchess forthwith began to intreat that he might be recalled. He was very ill – she said. If he staid longer on that station she was sure that he would die; – and then she began to cry. I cannot bear to see women cry, and the matter became serious, for her pretty daughter began to bear her company. That hard-hearted Lord Melbourne seemed to be diverted by the scene. He, by all accounts, has been doing little else than making women cry during the last five and twenty years. However we all were as still as death while the wiping of eyes and the blowing of noses proceeded. At last Lord Holland contrived to restore our spirits. But before the Duchess went away she managed to have a tête à tête with Graham, and, I have no doubt, begged and blubbered to some purpose. I could not help thinking how many honest stout-hearted fellows are left to die on the most unhealthy stations for want of being related to some Duchess who has been handsome or to some Lady Georgiana who still is so.

The Duchess said one thing that amused us. We were talking about Lady Morgan. "When she first came to London," said Lord Holland, "I remember that she carried a little Irish harp about with her wherever she went." Others denied this. I mentioned what she says in her Book of the Boudoir. There she relates how she went one evening to Lady Cork's with her little Irish harp, and how strange every body thought it. "I see nothing very strange," said the Duchess, "in her taking her harp to Lady Cork's. If she took it safe away with her, that would have been strange indeed." On this, as a friend of yours says, we la-a-a-a-a-a-ft.

While Edward was sitting with me the letters came – yours among the rest; but none for him. I shewed him his wife's epistle with great ostentation. But he did not seem jealous. As jealousy is a proof of love, I would have a quarrel with him, if I were Margaret.

I am glad to find that you approve of my conduct about the Niggers. I expect, and indeed wish, to be abused by the fools of the Agency Society. My father is quite satisfied, and so are the best part of my Leeds friends.

Had I any thing more to say? Whole volumes. But I have not time to go on gossiping. To day I sent my Indian Speech to the Press. To morrow I am to have the proofs. Perhaps I may send you a proof-sheet. I do not suppose that you know enough about the question to enter into all the reasonings of the speech. It is certainly, I think and those who heard it think, the best that I ever made.

I amuse myself as I walk back from the House at two in the morning with translating Virgil. I am at work on one of the most beautiful episodes, and I think, am succeeding pretty well. You shall hear what I have done when I come to Liverpool, which will be, I hope, in three weeks or thereanent.

I agree with you and Meg in liking the article on Goethe. I do not yet know who wrote it. But I think it out and out the best in the Number.

A pun! A pun! – The other day Holt Mackenzie – Stewart Mackenzie – and I were talking over Indian politics. I said, "Pray why is our board the most fashionable place in London?" They could not think. "Why," said I, "because we're all Macs." *Almacks*. There is for you. Conceive their raptures of delight and admiration, mixed however with a deep and bitter feeling of envy.

But I must and will stop. Kindest love to Margery.

Ever yours my darling
T B M

TO HANNAH MACAULAY, 17 AUGUST 1833

MS: Trinity College. *Address:* Miss Macaulay / E Cropper's Esq / Dingle Bank / Liverpool. *Frank:* London August seventeen 1833 / T B Macaulay. *Mostly published:* Trevelyan, I, 323–7.

London August 17. 1833

Dearest Nancy,

I am about to write to you on a subject which to you and Margaret will be one of the most agitating interest; and which, on that account chiefly, is so to me.

By the new India Bill it is provided that one of the members of the Supreme Council which is to govern our Eastern empire is to be chosen from among persons who are not servants of the Company. It is probable, indeed nearly certain, that the situation will be offered to me.

The advantages of the situation are very great. It is a post of the highest dignity and consideration. The salary is ten thousand pounds a year. I am assured by persons who know Calcutta intimately, and who have themselves mixed in the highest circles and held the highest offices at that presidency, that I may live in splendour there for five thousand a year, and may save the rest of the salary with the accruing interest. I may therefore hope to return to England at only thirty nine, in the full vigour of life, with a fortune of thirty thousand pounds. A large fortune I never desired.

I am not fond of money or anxious about it. But though every day makes me less and less eager for wealth, every day shews me more and more strongly how necessary a competence is to a man who desires to be either great or useful. At present the plain fact is that I can continue to be a public man only while I can continue in office. If I left my place in the government, I must leave my seat in parliament too. For I must live. I can live only by my pen. And it is absolutely impossible for any man to write enough to procure him a decent subsistence, and at the same time to take an active part in politics. I have not during this Session been able to send a single line to the Edinburgh Review: and, if I had been out of office, I should have been able to do very little. Edward Bulwer has just given up the New Monthly magazine on the ground that he cannot conduct it and attend to his parliamentary duties. Cobbett has been compelled to neglect his Register so much that its sale has fallen almost to nothing. Now in order to live like a gentleman, it would be necessary for me to write, not as I have done hitherto, but regularly, and even daily. I have never made more than two hundred a year by my pen. I could not support my self in comfort on less than five hundred. And I shall in all probability have many others to support. The prospects of our family are, if possible, darker than ever. My father and my uncle are absolutely at the mercy of William Wilberforce. He will have scarcely any thing but what he can wring out of them. He is, I hear, violently incensed at the state in which he finds himself; and I can hardly blame him. What is to be expected from his forbearance and generosity in a case in which both his avarice and his resentment are excited you may guess: for you know him. I have seen a letter to George from James Stephen, who seems to anticipate the worst. And George tells me plainly that he shall not be surprised if my father should be arrested and my uncle turned out of Rothley Temple.

In the meantime my political prospects are very gloomy. A schism in the ministry is approaching. It requires only that common knowledge of public affairs which any reader of the newspapers may possess to see this. I have more, much more, than common knowledge on the subject.

They cannot hold together. I tell you in perfect seriousness that my chance of keeping my present situation for six months is so small that I would willingly sell it for fifty pounds down. If I remain in office I shall, I fear, lose my political character. If I go out and engage in opposition, I shall break most of the private ties which I have formed during the last three years. In England I see nothing before me, for some time to come, but poverty, unpopularity, and the breaking up of old connections.

If there were no way out of these difficulties, I would encounter them with courage. A man can always act honourably and uprightly; and, if I were in the Fleet Prison or the rules of the King's Bench, I believe that I could find in my own mind ressources which would preserve me from being positively unhappy. But if I could escape from these impending disasters I should wish to do so. By accepting the post which is likely to be offered to me, I escape for a short time from the contests of faction here. When I return I find things settled, – parties formed into new combinations, – new questions under discussion. I shall then be able, without the scandal of a violent separation, and without exposing myself to the charge of inconsistency, to take my own line. In the meantime I shall save my family from distress. I shall return with a competence honestly earned, – as rich as if I were Duke of Northumberland or Marquess of Westminster, – and able to act on all public questions without even a temptation to deviate from the strict line of duty. While in India, I shall have to discharge duties not painfully laborious, and of the highest and most honorable kind. While there I shall have whatever that country affords of comfort or splendour; nor will my absence be so long that my friends or the public here will be likely to lose sight of me.

The only persons who know what I have written to you are Lord Grey, the Grants, Stewart Mackenzie, and George Babington. Charles Grant and Stewart Mackenzie, who know better than most men the state of the political world, and George, who knows better than any body all the peculiarities of my constitution, think that I should act unwisely in refusing this post: and this though they assure me, and I really believe sincerely, that they shall feel the loss of my society very acutely. But what shall I feel? And with what emotions, loving as I do my country and my family, can I look forward to such a separation, enjoined, as I think it is, by prudence and by duty? Whether the period of my exile shall be one of misery, or of comfort, and, after the first shock, even of happiness, depends on you, my dear, dear Nancy. I can scarcely see the words which I am writing through the tears that force themselves into my eyes. Will you, my own darling, if, as I expect, this offer shall be made to me, will you go with me? Will you entrust to me for a few years the care of your happiness? I call God to witness that it is as dear to me as my own – that

I love the very ground that you tread on – that, if I shrink from poverty, it is more for your sake than for my own. I know what a sacrifice I ask of you. I know how many dear and precious ties you must, for a time, sunder. I know that the splendour of the Indian court and the gaieties of that brilliant society of which you would be one of the most conspicuous ornaments have no temptation for you. I can bribe you only by telling you that, if you will go with me, I will love you better than I love you now, if I can.

I have asked George about your health and mine. He says that he has very little apprehension for me and none at all for you. Indeed he seemed to think that the climate would be quite as likely to do you good as harm.

All this, my love, is most strictly secret. You may of course shew the letter to Margaret – dear, dear Margaret – if I could take you both with me, I should hardly care to return: – and yet I should: for I love my country dearly. Margaret may tell Edward: for I never cabal against the lawful authority of husbands. But further the thing must not go. It would hurt my father, and very justly, to hear of it from any body before he hears it from myself: and if the least hint of it were to get abroad I should be placed in a very awkward position with regard to the people at Leeds. It is possible, though not probable, that difficulties may arise at the India House; and I do not mean to say any thing to any person who is not already in the secret till the Directors have made their choice, and till the King's pleasure has been taken.

And now, my dear, dear love, think calmly over what I have written. I would not have written on the subject even to you, till the matter was quite settled, if I had not thought that you ought to have full time to make up your mind. If you feel an insurmountable aversion to India, I will do all in my power to make your residence in England comfortable during my absence, and to enable you to confer instead of receiving benefits. But if my darling would consent to give me, at this great crisis of my life, that proof, that painful and arduous proof of her affection which I beg of her with tears running down my cheeks, I think that she will not repent of it. She shall not, if the unbounded confidence and the tenderest fondness of one to whom she is dearer than life can compensate her for a few years' absence from much that she justly loves. I do not tell her that my fortune shall be hers. It will be hers, decide as she may. I have only one inducement to offer to her, that she is necessary to my happiness, and that the sacrifice which I intreat of her, painful as I know it will be to her, cannot [be as] painful to her as parting from her would be [to me.]

[If my] dearest Nancy consents to what I ask, the [most] acutely painful circumstance attending this matter [will] be the separation from

102

Margaret. Dearest Margaret! She will feel this much. Consult her, my love, and let us both have the advantage of such advice as her excellent understanding and her warm affection for us may furnish. On Monday next, at the latest, I expect to be with you. Our Scotch tour, under these circumstances, must be short. Indeed if I did not feel that my health required a little travelling, I should hardly be inclined to leave the Dingle. By Christmas it will be fit that the new Councillor should leave England. His functions in India commence next April. We shall leave our dear Margaret, I hope, a happy mother.

Farewell, my dear, dear Nancy. You cannot tell how impatiently I shall wait for your answer.

TBM

TO HANNAH MACAULAY, 17 OCTOBER 1833

MS: Trinity College. *Partly published:* Trevelyan, 1, 330–2.

London October 17. 1833

Dearest Nancy,

It is the 17th, and no news of Grant. He promised to be here a week ago. The Directors are foaming. The Chairs are sending daily to ask after him. The business is of the most pressing importance. A frigate is ordered to be ready to sail for India on the first of November with dispatches of the highest consequence; and he neither comes, nor writes. This is one of those cases in which we become sensible of the relief derived from swearing. At such seasons I cease to wonder at the maledictory propensities which are thought so vulgar by the ladies. He is at Dieppe, as somebody in London has heard from somebody there: but he himself does not take the trouble to send us any intelligence. Of all the Ministers he is most wanted: and he is almost the only one of them who is not in town.

Charles made some strange miscalculation of his wants: for when the expenses for which he required money were drawn out the whole amounted only to sixteen pounds, which I shall pay with a very good will. I have told my father not to trouble himself about the hundred pounds that I lent, or rather gave him: and, in truth, I would as soon give him another hundred as be pestered to provide for Pate Robertson. He is at me on that subject. What on earth have I to do with Pate Robertson? The relationship is one which none but Scotchmen would recognize. The lad is such a fool that he would utterly disgrace my recommendation. And, as if to make the thing more provoking, his sisters say that he must be provided for in England; for that they cannot think of parting with him. This to be sure matters little: for there is at present just as little chance of getting any thing in India as in England.

But what strange folly this is which meets me in every quarter. People wanting posts in the army – the navy – the public offices – and saying that, if they cannot find such posts, they must starve. How do all the rest of mankind live? If I had not happened to be engaged in politics, and if my father had not been connected, by very extraordinary circumstances, with public men, we should never have dreamed of having places. Why cannot Pate be apprenticed to some hatter or tailor? He may do well in such a business. He will do detestably ill as a clerk in my office. He may come to make good coats. He will never, I am sure, write good dispatches. There is nothing truer than poor Richard's saw. We are taxed twice as heavily by our pride as by the state. The curse of England is the obstinate determination of the middle classes to make their sons what they call gentlemen. So we are over-run with clergymen without livings, lawyers without briefs, physicians without patients, authors without readers, clerks soliciting employment, who might have thriven and been above the world as bakers, watch-makers or inn-keepers. The next time my father speaks to me about Pate, I will offer to subscribe twenty guineas towards making a pastry-cook of him. He had a sweet tooth when he was a child; – a child indeed he is and will always be; – and I shall not be surprised if he should succeed as well as Birch in tarts with custard.

So you are reading Burnet. Did you begin from the beginning? What do you think of the old fellow? He was always a great favourite of mine – honest, though careless; a strong party-man on the right side, yet with much kind feeling towards his opponents and even towards his personal enemies. He is to me a most entertaining writer; – far superior to Clarendon in the art of amusing – though of course far Clarendon's inferior in discernment, dignity, and correctness of style. Do you know by the bye Clarendon's life of himself. I like it, – the part after the Restoration at least, – better than his great History. I hear that Lister is writing a life of Clarendon. The Villierses could of course furnish him with ample materials: and, if I am not mistaken, Lister would succeed in history. His novels are, to my thinking, the novels of a man who would shine more in working up and arranging a story furnished to him than in constructing one of his own.

I am very quiet, rise at seven or half past, read Spanish till ten, breakfast, walk to my office, stay there till four, take a long walk, dine towards seven, and am in bed before eleven. I am going through Don Quixote again, and admire it more than ever. It is certainly the best novel in the world, beyond all comparison.

In a few days I suppose we shall have the Edinburgh Review. I am impatient to know what you think of my article.

104

Kindest love to Margaret and Edward. We shall have Fanny soon, I suppose.

Ever yours, my love

T B M

I managed to get a place in the Ordnance at Sierra Leone for a friend of Henry's – a great raff in appearance, but apparently a good sort of fellow of the name of Graham, and I have had a most fervid letter of thanks from him.

TO HANNAH MACAULAY, 2 NOVEMBER 1833

MS: Trinity College. *Address:* Miss Macaulay / E Cropper's Esq / Dingle Bank / Liverpool. *Frank:* London November two 1833 / T B Macaulay. *Extract published:* Knutsford, *Zachary Macaulay,* p. 472.

London Novr. 2. 1833

Dearest love,

I have not much to add to what I wrote yesterday. The India House is on excellent terms with us. We receive assurances every day of the willingness of the Court to comply with any proposition of the Board which may not be very unreasonable. But my appointment has not yet been formally discussed. The Chairman is gone into the country; Grant set off to day for Winchester to pass Sunday with Dealtry; and till they return to town nothing can be done.

In the meantime reports are getting abroad. Yesterday at a large party where three directors were present it was asserted that I was going out to India. Some officious person carried the rumour to my father who came to my office this morning in considerable agitation – agitation rather, as I found, of hope than of fear. When I told him exactly how things stood he seemed greatly pleased, – and quite approved of your going with me. The fact is, as I had rather expected, that the pressure of pecuniary distress, the dread of leaving his children quite unprovided for, and the prospect of complete and immediate relief by honorable means and without any obligation to strangers, affected him more strongly than the thought of parting with us. He has of late felt so acutely the constant humiliation and the constant anxieties of poverty, that any mode of relief was welcome. He said, and, I dare say, very correctly, that he had himself been so much tossed about the world, had traversed the ocean so often, and had resided so long in tropical climates, that the separation did not shock him as it would shock other people; and he added that he had fully made up his mind to such a separation; for that he had himself entertained thoughts of soliciting an appointment abroad. You who profess to be a student of human nature – (you remember how we argued that matter on our tour,) may explain, if you can, why the most affectionate of fathers, as he certainly is, shewed less emotion at the thought of parting with me than Sharp or Charles Grant. My own explanation is that people like a fat sorrow better than a lean one, to use the words of the vulgar proverb. I believe that there are very few sentimental sorrows which pinch like the daily and hourly sense of penury. My laundress has a son dying of a consumption. I send him trifling presents now and then. The other day I gave her a dressing gown for him. She complains more of the protraction of his malady than of its certain termination. "It's a hard thing for a poor woman like me to have a poor boy six months a dying." But there is love, I believe, which, as the Bible says, many waters cannot quench nor the floods drown, and for which if a man should give his whole substance it would be utterly contemned. And such love is mine for my Nancy, and, I think, hers for me.

I spoke to Fanny to the same effect with what I wrote to you yesterday. She almost anticipated me. She says that, in my father's present state of health, she should think it wrong to leave him. I fully agree with her. I have another objection to her going which I did not hint to her. My taking out one sister to preside over my establishment is a step which every body must approve. Grant and Sharp were both delighted with it. But to take two unmarried sisters, leaving an infirm father and many other relations in England, is another thing. It looks like a matrimonial venture – a thing from the thought of which you would shrink.

I write, you see, as if all were settled. I believe that all will be settled before long, and settled for our going. I find within myself a firmness and composure of which I did not think myself capable. The anxieties of this week have not cost me three extra beatings of the pulse, not one moment of sleep, not one mouthful of food. It would be thus, I suppose, with a general before a battle. It is thus, I imagine, with those who suffer death on great occasions, – your Russells and Sidneys. I wonder whether I should be as tranquil as they on the scaffold. Very likely I should. I have often thought that in minds not altogether weak and abject the emergency itself produces the qualities which it demands.

I go to Leeds by the mail of Monday night. On Wednesday I dine with my constituents. OnThursday, I am sorry to say, I am forced to attend a meeting for founding a Mechanic's Institute. I shall not be in London till late on Friday night. Your letters of Monday and Tuesday should be directed to me at Leeds. Let me hear from you, my love. It is long since I have had a letter. Kindest love to my dear Margaret and Edward.

Ever yours, darling

T B M

Tom Babington comes to town to day. I shall try to avoid seeing him. The girls are afraid of a scene between him and my father. Sarah Anne predicts a scene between him and George. George cannot speak of him with temper.

TO HANNAH MACAULAY, 5 DECEMBER 1833

MS: Trinity College.

London Decr. 5. 1833

Dearest love,

I was appointed yesterday. Twenty two directors were present at the Court. Nineteen voted for me; three against me. So complete a victory was beyond our hopes. It is, I hope, an augury of a future good understanding between the two branches of the Indian government.

The news was brought to me at the Admiralty where I dined with Sir James Graham and a party of the ministers. Many kind expressions of regret were employed. But all seemed to think that I had done wisely. Labouchere is most strongly of that opinion.

Labouchere and I mean to go down to Bowood for a few days next week. Lord Lansdowne has sent me a very kind and pressing invitation. After my return I shall be fixed in London till Christmas when I am to resign my secretaryship.

To morrow I shall probably be able to give you some information on the subject of the ships which are about to sail. I shall not fix absolutely without a reference to you. Indeed, indeed, my darling, I never think of your kindness to me and of the sacrifices which you are making for me without feeling the tears well into my eyes. But I will not write thus lest I should infect you with my weakness. My part is to set an example of firmness: and I have never failed in it for a moment except when I have thought of the Dingle.

I had the kindest letter possible from Edward the other day. He insists on being allowed to take some share of the expence of supporting those whom we shall leave behind. Considering the relation in which he stands to us, and still more the real friendship which we have for him, I should think that it would be unjustifiable in me altogether to refuse his assistance. We must take care however that he shall not be allowed to do too much.

107

I have so much to do, and so many letters to write this morning, as you may imagine, that I must delay what I have further to say till to morrow.

My father has just been with me. He is very calm and did not touch on any unpleasant topic. To morrow he goes into the country.

Kindest love to dear Margaret and Edward.

Ever yours, my darling,

T B M

TO MACVEY NAPIER, 5 DECEMBER 1833

MS: British Museum. *Mostly published*: Trevelyan, 1, 348–9.

London Decr. 5. 1833

Dear Napier,

You are probably not unprepared for what I am about to tell you. Yesterday evening the Directors of the East India Company elected me one of the members of the Supreme Council. It will therefore be necessary that in a few weeks, – ten weeks at furthest, I should leave this country for a few years.

I may on some future occasion explain to you all the circumstances which have actuated me on this occasion. You would, I am sure, from friendly feeling to me, take a warm interest in them. But I have much to write and much to do this morning. I will therefore proceed to business.

It would be mere affectation in me to pretend not to know that my support is of some importance to the Edinburgh Review. In the situation in which I shall now be placed, a connection with the Review will be of considerable importance to me. I know well how dangerous it is for a public man wholly to withdraw himself from the public eye. During an absence of six years I run some risk of losing most of the distinction, literary and political, which I have acquired. As a means of keeping myself in the recollection of my countrymen during my sojourn abroad the Review will be invaluable to me. Nor do I foresee that there will be the slightest difficulty in my continuing to write for you at least as much as ever. I have thought over my late articles; and I really can scarcely call to mind a single sentence in any one of them which might not have been written at Calcutta as easily as in London. Perhaps in India I might not have had the means of detecting two or three of the false dates in Croker's Boswell. But that would have been all. Very little, if any, of the effect of my most popular articles is produced by minute research into rare books, or by allusions to the mere topics of the day.

I think therefore that we might easily establish a commerce mutually beneficial. I shall wish to be supplied with all the good books which come out in this part of the world. Indeed many books which in themselves are of little value, and which, if I were in England, I should not think it worth while to read, will be interesting to me in India, just as the commonest daubs and the rudest vessels at Pompeii attract the minute attention of people who would not move their eyes to see a modern signpost or a modern kettle. Distance of place like distance of time makes trifles valuable.

What I propose then is that you should pay me for the articles which I may send to you from India, not in money, but in books. As to the amount I make no stipulations. You know that I have never haggled about such matters. As to the choice of books, the mode of transmission, and other matters, we shall have ample time to discuss them before my departure. Let me know whether you are willing to make an arrangement on this basis.

I heartily wish that I could see you again before I go. But that is out of the question, I fear. My sister is to accompany me and to preside over the seventy or eighty Hindoos and Mahometans who will compose my houshold.

I have not forgotten Chatham in the midst of my avocations. I hope to send you an article on him early next month.

Ever yours sincerely
T B Macaulay

How does Howick's paper turn out?

TO HANNAH MACAULAY, 18 DECEMBER 1833

MS: Trinity College. *Partly published:* Trevelyan, I, 351–2.

London Decr. 18. 1833

Dearest love,

I went with George to the Asia yesterday. We saw her to every disadvantage, – all litter and confusion. But she is a very fine ship; and our two cabins will be very good. Some inconveniences we must of course put up with: but every experienced person says that such inconveniences are inevitable. The worst of them is that every thing that we say in our cabins will be heard by our next neighbours. But so it is in all ships.

The Captain I like much. He is an agreable, intelligent, polished man of forty, – very good looking considering what storms and changes of climate he has gone through. He advised me strongly to put very little furniture into our cabins. A good sofa bed in each – an easy chair, a comfortable table, and a wash-hand-stand, was all that he advised – a carpet of course. I told him to have your cabin made as neat as possible, without regard to expense. He has promised to have it furnished according to his own notions, that is simply, – but prettily; and when you see it, if any addition occurs to you, it shall be made. He assures me that he can make it all that a lady's cabin can be for a small sum.

I find that I shall have more money in hand after paying for our passage than I had reckoned upon. Brownrigg most earnestly advises me to lay out some of it in providing china and glass. I mean to take his counsel. We must have a very large and very fine dinner set and tea set. We must also have less splendid articles for daily use. I intend to defer my purchases till you come to London, as China is peculiarly a lady's article. I dare say that you will have no objection to go a shopping to Mr. Mortlock's. Who knows, munificent as he is, but that he may insist on supplying us *gratis*?

If I have money enough I may perhaps buy plate in England. I am delighted to learn that it will not be so expensive as I thought. To a person accustomed to Lansdowne house and Holland house the quantity of forks and spoons necessary for a dinner of thirty people would seem to be enormous. But I find that two dinner-forks to a guest is the Calcutta allowance. As every guest brings at least one servant to stand behind his chair, the forks are cleaned in an instant. It is the same with spoons. As for other articles Brownrigg advises me to use plated goods instead of silver, and assures me that I may do so without incurring the charge of shabbiness.

To day I breakfasted with Sharp whose kindness is as warm as possible. Indeed all my friends seem to be in the most amiable mood. I have twice as many invitations as I can accept: and I have been begged to name my own party. Empty as London is I never was so much beset with invitations. Sharp asked me about you. I told him how much I regretted my never having had any opportunity of shewing you the best part of London Society. He said that he would take care that you should see what was best worth seeing before your departure. He promises to give us a few breakfast parties and dinner parties where you will meet as many as he can muster of the best set in town – Rogers, Luttrell, Rice, Tom Moore, Sydney Smith, Grant, and other great wits and politicians. I am quite delighted at this – both because you will, I am sure, be amused and pleased at a time when you ought to have your mind occupied, and because even to have mixed a little in a circle so brilliant will be of advantage to you in India. You have neglected, and very rightly and sensibly, frivolous accomplishments. You have not been at places of fashionable diversion: and it is therefore, I think, the more desirable that you should appear among the dancing, piano-forte playing, opera-going, damsels at Calcutta as one who has seen society better than any that they ever approached.

I hope, my love, that you will not disapprove of what I have done. I accepted Sharp's offer for you eagerly, and even with tears, and he was as much affected as I.

I am delighted at your news about Margaret and the baby. And now, my love, I want some advice from you as to my movements. When ought I to go to the Dingle. My stay will be very short. I hate chewing and ruminating on the bitterness of separation – beating out the pain of a moment till it covers weeks. What must be done will be best done quickly. Shall I escort you back from the Dingle – call with you at the Temple – and so bring you home? After Christmas I shall be quite at liberty: and this plan, if you do not object to it, would, I think, be the best. But, if you have any reason against it, – or even if you fancy that you should like to part from Margaret and Jane without my being near, – you shall chuse for yourself. My first wish is, as it ought to be, to consult your tastes in every thing.

Do not let your woman be extravagant in outfit. I shall keep a tight hand in that respect over my clerk.

Kindest love to dear Margaret and Edward. Is Jane with you yet. If she is give her my love.

Ever yours, darling,
T B M.

11 · FROM INDIA TO THE *HISTORY OF ENGLAND*, 1834–1848

The India to which Macaulay, accompanied by his sister Hannah, sailed in February of 1834 was just beginning to be touched by the spirit of reform at work in England; one of its first results was Macaulay's appointment itself, for the post of legal member of council had just been created by the Charter Renewal Act of 1833. Macaulay's task was to advise on and prepare legislation in order to bring the best current principles of law-making to the procedures of the government of India; luckily for his comfort in this new and untested position, he had the warm support of the Governor-General, Lord William Bentinck. Macaulay took on various other duties as well, though they did not necessarily belong to the job. Two were of special importance: first, the work of preparing a new penal code for India, a work that he did largely by himself (24 August 1835) despite the slenderness of his legal studies; secondly, the reform of the program of state-supported education. On this matter there was a long-standing dispute between the side comitted to Western learning and the English language and the side committed to Oriental traditions and languages. Arriving in India at a time when the two sides had reached stalemate Macaulay quickly made his choice and, by his authority and persuasiveness, settled the question in favor of English, making it the language of Indian education (28 January 1835). He also had good commonsensical notions about methods of instruction ([May? 1835?]), but here he was less successful in imposing himself.

Macaulay's first excited interest in the Indian scene is brought out in his letters home in 1834, only a small sample of which can be represented in this selection (*e.g.*, 3 October 1834). Two severe blows to his happiness and mental balance seem to have driven him back on himself for the rest of his years in India. The first was the marriage of Hannah to the young and rising civil servant Charles Trevelyan, an event, like Margaret's marriage before it, that overwhelmed Macaulay in grief and self-pity (7 December 1834). The second, more devastating, blow was the news he received at the beginning of 1835 of his sister Margaret's death from typhoid fever some five months earlier. Macaulay was able to hold up under the misery of these losses only by distracting himself, both by taking on extra work in his office and by immersing himself in classical literature. He had always been bookish, but his reading now became obsessive in quantity and range (8 February 1835). He was able, too, to keep up the *Edinburgh Review* connection, contributing the long article on Mackintosh's *History* and the very long one on Lord Bacon (26 November 1836). The changes in his life during the Indian years led him to a choice between literature and politics, eloquently expressed in his letter to Ellis of 30 November 1835. The idea of the *History of England* was already at work in his mind, and growing more and more attractive to a man who had lost much of his political ambition but who, as he said, 'need not despair of equalling Gibbon' (19 June 1837).

On his return to England in 1838 Macaulay faced a fresh set of changes; his father had died just shortly before his arrival back in England, all of the family were now scattered, two sisters were dead, Hannah married, and he himself out of public life. He was now, for the first time ever, free, with money enough to make him independent for life. At the same time, he was taking on a new domesticity as uncle to Hannah's children, particularly the eldest, Margaret, always called after her Indian nursery name, 'Baba' (20 March 1839, 21 August 1847). The first use he made of his freedom was a tour to Italy, especially to Rome, at the end of 1838. The wish to see the classic places had been much intensified by his extraordinary reading in India; whether he also thought that such an exposure to classical air would help him to fix the subject of his historical work no one can say. But he was shaping his plan soon after (3 May 1839).

At first, while the pleasure of his freedom was yet fresh, he refused all offers and inducements to return to politics (19 December 1838), but he was tempted back by an offer to stand for Edinburgh (29 May 1839). In the next year he took office in Lord Melbourne's rapidly weakening ministry as Secretary at War and was sworn of the Privy Council. In this position he could at least continue to be useful to his family by asking for such things as a living for his brother John from Lord Melbourne (2 November 1840); he was also privileged to have such things as the earliest news of the birth of Queen Victoria's first child (21 November 1840). And he could improve the leisure of his not very demanding office by preparing the *Lays of Ancient Rome* for publication (12 July 1841).

The defeat of the Whigs put Macaulay out of office (27 July 1841) and sent him happily back to his *History* (5 November 1841). It had not been a terribly important episode in his life, but as his experience as Captain of the Hampshire Volunteers was useful to Gibbon the historian, so the experience of being Secretary at War taught Macaulay the historian. He still remained M.P. for Edinburgh, and had much vicissitude to endure from that quarter. Questions of church government raised loud passions in the city (28 June 1841); anti-Catholic fervor, especially against state subsidy to the Catholic college of Maynooth in Ireland, repeatedly swept through his constituents (9 July 1846); he was slow to satisfy them on the great question of the Corn Laws (22 February 1843), and his high resolve to remain an independent representative, not to be a 'slave' (as he put it) to the electors, roused many of them to fury at what they saw as arrogance and stubbornness. In the end, not surprisingly, he was defeated at the polls (30 July 1847).

The rudeness of the Edinburgh electors made a scandal much enjoyed by the English, for by that time Macaulay's literary reputation stood very high, and it seemed a good joke on the Modern Athens that it did no honor to an artist in its midst. The modest venture of the *Lays of Ancient Rome* in 1842 had succeeded beyond all expectation, and was followed in 1843 by the even greater success of the collected *Essays*, which Macaulay had been genuinely reluctant to republish at all (24 June 1842). Macaulay's reputation as a parliamentary speaker had been maintained by a series of brilliant performances after his return to the House of Commons; the whisper through the corridors of the House that 'Macaulay is up' still sent members running to hear him. This formidable reputation – both critical and popular – was soon to be crowned by the publication of the *History*. By the end of the 1840s it is safe to say that Macaulay was, by common consent, the first literary name in England.

In his enjoyment of seemingly unbroken success, Macaulay did not forget the poor devils of literature like Leigh Hunt (27 March 1841) and many other, less notable, toilers in the literary marketplace; he used his authority to get all possible help for them from the public purse and was steadily generous with his own.

The form of Macaulay's social life grew quite settled in the 1840s, following his move to chambers in the Albany (12 July 1841), where he was to remain for the next fifteen years. He had his clubs – the Athenaeum, Brooks's, the Reform – his intimate friend Ellis, his breakfast parties for a familiar circle, including Henry Hallam, Samuel Rogers, Dean Milman, Lord Mahon, and other successful men of Whiggish cast and literary or historical tastes. He visited Hannah and her family regularly, often to dine and sometimes to stay the night with them at Clapham, where the Trevelyans first settled, and later in London. Hannah's residence at Clapham kept Macaulay in touch with the old community, to which he showed his loyalty in his defense of James Stephen's essay on the Clapham Sect (6 July 1844). Macaulay had an increasing number of committees and public responsibilities to attend to apart from his political life: he was, for example, a trustee of the British Museum, a founding trustee of the

National Portrait Gallery, and a member of the committee supervising the decoration of the new Houses of Parliament. Such duties and amusements were the routine of his life in the prosperous decade from his return from India in 1838 to the publication of the *History* in 1848. His main work, throughout, was the composition of that *History*, for which his trips to Europe were partly undertaken, including that to Holland (9 October 1844), and for the sake of which he gave up the connection with the *Edinburgh Review*, after nearly twenty years (6 December 1844).

A fresh flurry of political activity arose in 1846, when Peel's defeat following the Corn Laws crisis brought the Whigs back and put Macaulay into office again, this time as Paymaster General. His defeat at Edinburgh in 1847, however, restored him to leisure and had the good effect of allowing him at last to concentrate on bringing the first part of the *History* to publication. A year's labor took him to the stage of struggling with the proofs and anxiously speculating about the book's reception ([Late October 1848]). Early in December volumes one and two were published, to be received with praise and delight.

MS: Trinity College. *Address:* Miss Macaulay / Rothley Temple / Leicester. *Frank:* London January two 1834 / T B Macaulay. *Partly published:* Trevelyan, 1, 352–3.

London Jan 2. 1834

Dearest love,

I have not much to tell you: but I love to have a two minute's gossip with you whether what I have to tell be much or little. I called at Cockerell's house to day and saw Larpent and Brownrigg. I imagine, by what I learn, that we shall stop for a day or two at Madeira to take on board a cargo of wine to be roasted, as it is called, in India. I shall like to see Funchal. I wonder whether we shall be invited to meet Mr. Hanningham Junr.

Brownrigg earnestly advises me to buy carriages here and take them out with me. It seems that we must have two – a close chariot, and an open landau. The price at Calcutta is enormous – four hundred pounds a piece. Yet I doubt whether I shall be able to afford to make this purchase. I have 1600 £ in Henry Thornton's hands. Five hundred will go for our passage. My outfit and that of our servants will come to more than 250 £ – perhaps 300 £. Then I have some Christmas bills to pay here. And we are to lay in china and glass. I must also have some money when I arrive in India. If it should be necessary for me to chuse whether I will buy carriages or plate in England, I shall decide for the carriages. For the price of plate is much the same in Bengal that it is here.

Brownrigg tells me to my great joy that house rent has fallen at Calcutta, and that we may procure a very handsome house at Garden Reach, as it is called, for less than 500 £ a year.

I am busy with an article for Napier. I cannot in the least tell at present whether I shall like it or not. I proceed with great ease; and in general I have found that the success of my writings has been in proportion to the ease with which they have been written.

I had a most extraordinary scene with Lady Holland. If she had been as young and handsome as she was thirty years ago she would have turned my head. She was quite hysterical about my going, paid me such compliments as I cannot repeat, cried, raved, called me dear dear Macaulay. "You are sacrificed to your family. I see it all. You are too good to them. They are always making a tool of you – last session about the slaves – now sending you to India to make money for them. Your sister is to go with you I hear. Is she pretty? – " "I think her so – " I said. "But I am a great deal too fond of her to be a judge. I have watched her face ever since she was a month old." "Well" – cried my lady – "She will marry some rich Nabob within six months after she reaches Bengal – six months – no – three – I won't allow more than three. That's what you are taking her out for." I very calmly assured her ladyship that neither you nor I had any such plan and that no girl could make a greater sacrifice. I was not allowed to finish. "Sacrifice – dear Macaulay – don't – don't – sacrifice. Oh what dupes you men are. How women turn you round their fingers. Make me believe that any girl who has no fortune would not jump at visiting Calcutta as the sister of such a man and in such a situation." I always do my best to keep my temper with Lady Holland for three reasons – because she is a woman – because she is very unhappy in her situation and in her health – and because she has a real kindness for me. But I could not stand this, and I was beginning to answer her in a voice trembling with anger when she broke out again. "I beg your pardon. Pray forgive me, dear Macaulay. I was very impertinent. I know you will forgive me. Nobody has such a temper as you. I have said so a hundred times. I said so to Allen only this morning. I am sure you will bear with my weakness. I shall never see you again:" – and she cried; and I cooled. For it would have been to very little purpose to be angry with her. I hear that it is not to me alone that she runs on in this way. She storms at the ministers for letting me go. Labouchere says that at one dinner where he was – I think it was Labouchere who told me – she became so violent that even Lord Holland, whose temper, whatever his wife may say, is much [cooler?] than mine, could not command [himself?] and broke out – "Don't talk such nonsense my lady. What the d[evil!] Can we tell a gentleman who has a claim upon us that he must lose his only chance of getting an independence, that he may come and talk to you in an evening?" –

Good bye, darling, and take care not to become such a woman as my Lady. It is now my duty to omit no opportunity of giving you wholesome advice. I am your papa now. I have bought Gisborne's duties of women, Moore's fables for the female sex, Mrs. King's Female Scripture Characters, and Fordyce's sermons. With the help of these books I hope to keep my responsibility in order on our voyage and in India. Love to all at the Temple.

Ever yours, my darling
T B M

MS: Morgan Library. *Address*: Mrs. E Cropper / Dingle Bank / Liverpool. *Frank:* London January two 1834 / T B Macaulay. *Extract published:* John Clive, *Macaulay: The Shaping of the Historian*, 1973, p. 281.

London Jan 2. 1834

Dearest Margaret,

While Nancy was at the Dingle I thought it unnecessary to write separate letters to you. But now I must resume my character of correspondent. Dear dear Margaret – you cannot know and I do not wish you to know all the feelings which rise in my mind when I sit down to write to you. They are, I fear, very wrong and very selfish feelings. You are happy: and you still love me: and that ought to be enough for me. And why is it not enough? Why is it that I cannot trust myself to finish this letter without locking my door lest I should be found crying like a child? It is not because I am going to India. I am as far from you here as there. The additional distance looks great on a globe. It is nothing in reality. It is not the separation which is to take place six weeks hence that makes me weep, but the separation which took place last year. I shall sustain no new loss. Half of my happiness I lost then. The other half I carry with me.

The wound is still fresh. I expected more from time. But time passes in vain. No successor comes to occupy your place. You are as necessary to me as when I used to call for you every day in Golden Square, as when I walked with you that fine Sunday afternoon through the streets of the city. But you have forgotten that walk and those calls, and ten thousand little circumstances that I must remember as long as I live, and which even now crowd upon me so that I cannot see the lines which I trace. And it is right that this should be so. It is the ordinance of nature and of society. And as new ties multiply around you, as new affections and hopes arise, the more will the past seem to you like a dream. It is not so with me. My loss is all pure loss. Nothing springs up to fill the void. All that I can do is to cling to that which is still left to me. I do not know how I got this train of thought. I had no intention of bestowing any of my sadness on you when I took up my pen. – My sadness will steal, I hope, only a few moments from the serenity of a happy wife and a happy mother. Tell me all a[bou]t your little boy, dearest Margaret, and whom he is like, an[d] what he is to be called, and whether he sucks his thumb, and whether he has yet given any of those wonderful proofs of wit and wisdom which babies, in the opinion of their mammas, generally begin to exhibit before they are a month old. And tell me when you shall be well enough to bear a short visit from me. It shall be very short. One day is enough for pain.

A man should bolt a pill of aloes down at once, and not stay to chew it. My kindest love to Edward, and a kiss to baby.

Yours ever, dearest Margaret,
T B M

TO JAMES STEPHEN, 21 JANUARY 1834

MS: Mr F. R. Cowell.

Gray's Inn Jany. 21. / 1834

Dear Stephen,

I had not heard that Mill was reputed to be the author of the attack on me in Tait; nor indeed had I heard that such an attack had been made. I have now read the article: and certainly Mill's disclaimer was not necessary to satisfy me that it could not be his. A more helpless attempt at mischief I never saw.

Mill has some reason to complain of me. For, though I still think myself quite in the right on all the main points of what I formerly wrote in the Edinburgh Review about his book, I certainly used language about him personally which I now feel to have been neither just nor decorous. The truth is that I had not read his history of India, which, when the difficulties of such an undertaking are considered, must be allowed to be a very extraordinary performance: nor had I read his metaphysical work: indeed it had not been published. I judged of him by the Essays in the Encyclopædia, and by the absurd rants of some foolish young men who talked as if all human knowledge were included in those Essays, and would have burned every other book in the world on the same principle on which Omar is said to have burned the Alexandrian library. I did great injustice to him, though I think that I only did justice to the Essay on Government. Whenever he is inclined to retaliate, I have not the least doubt that he will do it like a man and like an able man, – not in the wretched style of Mr. Tait's correspondent.

I leave London for a few days on Saturday morning. I fear that I shall not be able to complete my round of country visits in less than a week: so that I cannot engage to dine with you on Friday night. I have no engagements as yet for the following week: and if you will fix a day, I shall have the greatest pleasure in accepting your invitation. / Ever, dear Stephen,

Yours most truly,
T B Macaulay

MS: British Museum. *Mostly published:* Napier, *Correspondence*, pp. 144–6.

London Feby. 13. 1834

Dear Napier,

It is true that I have been severely tried by ill health during the last few weeks. But I am now rapidly recovering, and am assured by all my medical advisers that a week of the sea will make me better than ever I was in my life. Ill as I have been, and busy as I have been, I ought to have answered your letter earlier. But I will lose no time in apologies, or in thanks for your kind expressions, or in assurances of good will for which you, I well know, will give me credit. Time flies. In forty eight hours I shall be under sail; and we must go at once to business.

I have several subjects in my head. One is Mackintosh's History – I mean the fragment of the large work. Empson advised me to ask Longman for the sheets and take them with me. But, as there would not have been time for a reference to you, and as you may have engaged some other writer, I have not thought it right to do this. If you approve of the plan, you can send the book after me by the earliest conveyance.

Another plan which I have is a vèry fine one, if it could be well executed. I think that the time is come when a fair estimate may be formed of the intellectual and moral character of Voltaire. The extreme veneration with which he was regarded during his life time has passed away. The violent reaction which followed has spent its force; and the world can now, I think, bear to hear the truth and to see the man exhibited as he was, – a strange mixture of greatness and littleness, virtues and vices. I have all his works, and shall take them in my cabin on the voyage. But my library is not particularly rich in those books which illustrate the literary history of his times. I have Rousseau and Marmontel's memoirs, and Madame du Deffand's letters, and perhaps a few other works which would be of use. But Grimm's correspondence and several other volumes of memoirs and letters would be necessary. If you would make a small collection of the works which would be most useful in this point of view, and send it after me as soon as possible, I will do my best to draw a good Voltaire. I fear that the article must be enormously long – seventy pages perhaps. But you know that I do not run into unnecessary length.

I may perhaps try my hand on Miss Austin's novels. That is a subject on which I shall require no assistance from books.

Whatever books you may send me ought to be half bound; or the white ants will devour them before they have been three days on shore.

You will of course set off any books which you may send against what you may consider as due to me. If there should be a balance in my favour, it had better be paid to Mr. George Gisborne Babington, Number 26 Golden Square, London. From him you will at any time learn any particulars about me which you may be desirous to know.

Besides the books which may be necessary for the Review, I should like to have any work of very striking merit which may appear during my absence. The particular department of literature which interests me most is history, above all English history. Any valuable book on that subject I should wish to possess. Sharp, Miss Berry, and some of my other friends, will perhaps, now and then, suggest a book to you. But it is principally on your own judgment that I must rely to keep me well supplied.

Any letters for me you can send under cover to Grant, or, after the 22d of April next, to Stewart Mackenzie, who will then become Secretary of the India Board. They will be franked to me whatever their size may be.

I have now, I think, said all that I had to say about business. The day after to morrow, as I told you, is the day of my departure. There is much that is sad in this separation. But the prospect of honor, usefulness, and independence, – the consciousness that I mean well and am endeavouring well – has supported me and will support me through it. Many thanks for all your kindness. May we meet again with undiminished regard. If we live, I have no doubt that we shall so meet. – Believe that I entertain every friendly feeling towards you, and that it will give me the greatest pleasure to find that it is in my power in any way to be of use to you or to those in whom you are interested. / Ever, dear Napier,

Yours most truly

T B Macaulay

TO THOMAS FLOWER ELLIS, 1 JULY 1834

MS: Trinity College. *Address:* T F Ellis Esq / 15 Bedford Place / Russell Square. *Subscription:* T B Macaulay. *Partly published:* Trevelyan, 1, 369–73; 374.

Ootacamund July 1. 1834

Dear Ellis,

You need not get your map to see where Ootacamund is: for it has not found its way into the maps. It is a new discovery, a place to which Europeans resort for their health, or, as it is called by the Company's servants – blessings on their learning! – a sanaterion. I always spell the word σανατηρίον. It is indeed a very remarkable place. It lies at the height of 7000 feet above the level of the sea amidst the mountains which separate Mysore from Malabar. While London is a perfect gridiron, here

121

am I at 13° North from the Equator by a blazing wood-fire, with my windows closed. My bed is heaped with blankets, and my black servants are coughing round me in all directions. One poor fellow in particular looks so miserably cold that, unless the Sun comes out more, I am likely soon to see under my own roof the spectacle which according to Shakspeare is so interesting to the English, – a dead Indian.

I came to this sanatήριον not from want of any sanifying process, but on public duty. When we reached Madras, I found a letter waiting for me from Lord William. He told me that he was in these hills, that he was not well enough to leave them at present, that he wished to hold the Council of India here, and that without me a Council could not well be formed. This summons left me no choice. To take my sister was impossible. It would have been as much as her life was worth. The medical men at the Presidency told me that even for me it was a desperate undertaking to travel four hundred miles up the country immediately after landing. The Bishop had earnestly invited us to be his guests at Calcutta. There could be no more creditable protection for my sister. So we parted very reluctantly. She went on to Bengal by sea, and I came up to my Lord by land.

I travelled the whole four hundred miles on men's shoulders. I went in one palanquin, my native servant in another. Each palanquin required twelve bearers who were changed every fifteen miles or so. My baggage, though I brought no more than was absolutely necessary, required ten porters. Two police officers with swords and badges ran by my side, and when I crossed the Mysore frontier I was honored by the attendance of some of the Rajah's horse-soldiers, the most miserable ragamuffins that I ever saw, except indeed his Highness's infantry. I had an agreable journey on the whole. On the third day I got fairly on the table-land, and was afterwards little molested by the heat. I stopped for some time at Bangalore, where I found many interesting sights and much pleasant society. I saw Seringapatem, and went over all the decaying monuments of Hyder's and Tippoo's greatness. I was honored with an interview by the Rajah of Mysore who insisted on shewing me all his wardrobe and his picture-gallery. He has six or seven coloured English prints not much inferior to those which I have seen in the sanded parlour of a country inn, – "Going to cover" – "The death of the Fox," – and so forth. But the *bijou* of his gallery, of which he is as vain as the Grand Duke can be of the Venus or Lord Carlisle of the Three Maries is a head of the Duke of Wellington which has, most certainly, been on a sign-post in England. Yet after all the Rajah was by no means the greatest fool whom I found at Mysore. I alighted at a bungalow appertaining to the British Residency. There I found an Englishman who, without any preface, accosted me thus.

"Pray, Mr. Macaulay, do not you think that Buonaparte was the Beast?"
"No, Sir, I cannot say that I do." "Sir, he was the Beast. I can prove it.
I have found the number 666 in his name. Why, Sir, if he was not the
Beast, who was?" This was a puzzling question, and I am not a little vain
of my answer. "Sir," said I, "the House of Commons is the Beast. There
are 658 members of the House, and these, with their Chief Officers, the
three clerks, the Serjeant and his Deputy, the Chaplain, the Doorkeeper,
and the Librarian, make 666." "Well, Sir, that is strange. But I can assure
you that if you write Napoleon Buonaparte in Arabic leaving out only
two letters, it will give 666." "And pray, Sir, what right have you to
leave out two letters? And as St John was writing Greek and to Greeks,
is it not likely that he would use the Greek rather than the Arabic nota-
tion?" "But, Sir," said this learned divine, "every body knows that the
Greek letters were never used to mark numbers." I answered with the
meekest look and voice possible. "I do not think that every body knows
that. Indeed I have reason to believe that a different opinion, – erroneous
no doubt, – is universally embraced by all the small minority who happen
to know any Greek." So ended the controversy. The man looked at me
as if he thought me a very wicked fellow, and, I dare say, has by this time
discovered that if you write my name in Tamul, leaving out T in Thomas,
B in Babington, and M in Macaulay, it will give the number of this unfortunate beast.

When I left Mysore I proceeded through a jungle where a traveller
runs a great chance of catching a bad fever, and some chance of being
breakfasted on by a tiger or trode out into the shape of a half-crown by a
wild elephant. However, I escaped fever, tigers and elephants, and came
hither in safety through the finest scenery that I ever saw. Imagine
Windsor forest spread over the highest and boldest of the Cumberland
mountains and you will have some idea of it.

I am very comfortable here. I am the Governor General's guest. But I
am in a pretty little cottage buried in laburnums, or something very like
them, and geraniums which grow here in the open air, at the distance of
a two minute's walk from the large house in which his Lordship and his
suite are lodged. He is the frankest and best natured of men. Sir Frederic
Adam is also a very pleasing companion. The chief functionaries who
have attended the Governor General hither are clever people, but not
exactly on a par as to general attainments with the society to which I
belonged in London. I thought however that, even at Madras, I could
have found a very agreable circle of acquaintance. I am assured that at
Calcutta I shall find things far better. After all the best rule in all parts of
the world, even in London itself, is to be independent of other men's
minds – Ne te quæsiveris extra.

My power of finding amusement without help from companions was pretty well tried on my voyage. I read insatiably – the Iliad and Odyssey – Virgil, Horace, Cæsar's Commentaries, Bacon de Augmentis, Dante, Petrarch, Ariosto, Tasso, Don Quixote, Gibbon's Rome, Mill's India, all the seventy volumes of Voltaire, Sismondi's history of France, and the seven thick folios of the Biographia Britannica. I found my Greek and Latin in good condition enough. I liked the Iliad a little less and the Odyssey a great deal more than formerly. Horace charmed me more than ever, – Virgil not quite so much as he used to do. The want of human character, the poverty of his supernatural machinery, struck me very strongly. Was ever any thing duller and poorer than the third Book? Compare it with the *speciosa miracula* of the Odyssey. Can any thing be so bad as the living bush which bleeds and talks, or the Harpies who befoul Æneas's dinner? It is as extravagant as Ariosto, and as dull as Wilkie's Epigoniad. The poem contains, to be sure, some magnificent speeches and descriptions. But they are a little too much like the purple patches which Horace censures. The last six Books which Virgil had not fully corrected pleased me better than the first six. I like him best on Italian ground. I like his localities, his national enthusiasm, his frequent allusions to his country, its history, its antiquities, and its greatness. In this respect he often reminded me of Sir Walter Scott, with whom, in the general character of his mind, he had very little affinity. The Georgics pleased me better, – the Eclogues best, the second and tenth above all. But I think that the finest lines in the Latin language are those five which begin
    "Sepibus in nostris parvam te roscida mala"
I cannot tell you how they struck me. I was amused to find that Voltaire pronounces that passage to be the finest in Virgil.

I liked the Jerusalem better than I used to do. I was enraptured with Ariosto; and I still think of Dante, as I thought when I first read him, that he is a superior poet to Milton, that he runs neck and neck and neck with Homer, and that none but Shakspeare has gone decidedly beyond him.

As soon as I reach Calcutta I intend to read Herodotus again. By the bye why do not you translate him? You would do it excellently; and a translation of Herodotus well executed would rank with original compositions. A quarter of an hour a day would finish the work in five years. The notes might be made the most amusing in the world. I wish you would think of it. At all events I hope you will do something which may interest more than seven or eight people. Your talents are too great and your leisure-time too small to be wasted in inquiries so frivolous, I must call them, as those in which you have of late been too much engaged, – Whether the Cherokees are of the same race with the Chickasaws, – whether Van Dieman's land was peopled from New Holland or New

Holland from Van Dieman's land, – what is the precise mode of appointing a headman in a village in Tombuctoo. I would not give the worst page in Clarendon or Fra Paolo for all that ever was or ever will be written about the migrations of the Leleges and the laws of the Oscans.

I have already entered on my public functions, and I hope to do some good. The very wigs of the judges in the Court of King's Bench would stand on end if they knew how short a chapter my law of evidence will form. I am not without many advisers. A native of some fortune at Madras has sent me a paper on legislation which is almost as good as if Sir Gregory himself had written it. "Your honor must know," says this judicious person, "that the great evil is that men swear falsely in this country. No judge knows what to believe and what not to believe. For every man swears falsely when he can gain any thing. So innocent men are punished and offenders are cleared, whereby laws are of no use. Surely if your honor can make men to swear truly your honor's fame will be great and the Company will flourish. Now I know how men may be made to swear truly: and I will tell your honor for your fame and for the profit of the Company. Let your honor cut off the great toe of the right foot of every man who swears falsely, whereby your honor's fame will be extended." Is not this an exquisite specimen of legislative wisdom?

I must stop. When I begin to write to England, my pen runs as if it would run on for ever. You shall soon hear from me again and pray let me hear often from you. Malkin, I hear, is very well. I shall press him to pay me a visit at Calcutta in the cold season.

Remember me most kindly to Mrs. Ellis. Tell me when you write how all your household are going on. Remember me to Adolphus – Drinky – and our other circuit friends.

Ever yours affectionately
T B M

TO MRS EDWARD CROPPER, 3 OCTOBER 1834

MS: Mrs Lancelot Errington. *Address:* Mrs. E Cropper / Messrs. Cropper Benson and Co / Liverpool. *Subscription:* T B Macaulay. *Extracts published:* Trevelyan, I, 376; 378–81.

Calcutta October 3. 1834

Dearest Margaret,

I mean this for a general epistle to all the venerable circle, as Miss Byron would have called it. Before it reaches you, you will, I hope, have received the letters which I wrote to you from Ootacamund. The last was sent by a ship which sailed from Madras, if I remember right, on the

19th of August. Since that time I have had no opportunity of writing. I have travelled a good deal by land and sea, and have seen very much more than I shall be able to find time to relate.

I staid on the hills of Malabar till the end of August. Nothing could be duller. The rain streamed down in floods. It was very seldom that I could see a hundred yards before me. There were no books in the place except those which I had brought up with me. As to my companions, their faces reflected only each other's ennui. They pined for Calcutta, just as a town-beauty married to a country curate, would pine for Almack's and the Opera. I really thought that we should have had to cut Macnaghten down from the beam of his ceiling, and to fish Colonel Casement out of the tank. I bore the dulness of the place better than any of the party; and yet I never was so dull in my life.

At length Lord William gave me leave of absence. My bearers were posted along the road. My baggage was sent off. My palanquins were packed. My debts were paid. Every thing was ready. I was to start next day, when an event took place which may give you some insight into the state of laws, morals, and manners among the natives.

I told you that my servant Peter died after I had been on the hills about a month. He was succeeded by a man from Bangalore – a Christian – such a Christian as the missionaries make in this part of the world, – that is to say a man who superadds drunkenness to the other vices of the natives. I should hardly have ventured to say this formerly. But late events have cleared up truths which had long been concealed: and I believe that the missionaries and the Bishop himself will now acknowledge that their converts are among the most worthless members of society in India.

My servant had been persecuted most unmercifully by the servants of some other gentlemen on the hills for his religion. At last they contrived to excite against him, – whether justly or unjustly I am quite unable to say, – the jealousy of one of Lord William's under-cooks. We had accordingly a most glorious tragicomedy – the part of black Othello by the cook aforesaid, – Desdemona by an ugly impudent Pariah girl, his wife, – Iago by Colonel Casement's servant, – Michael Cassio by my rascal. The place of the handkerchief was supplied by a small piece of sugar-candy which Desdemona was detected in the act of sucking, and which had found its way from my canisters to her fingers. If I had my part in the piece, it was, I am afraid, that of Rodrigo, whom Shakspeare describes as "a foolish gentleman," and who also appears to have had "money in his purse."

On the evening before my departure my bungalow was besieged by a mob of blackguards. The native judge whose business it is to try cases of this kind, under the controul of the English authorities, came with them. After a most prodigious quantity of jabbering of which I could not understand one word, I called the judge, who spoke tolerable English, into my room, and learned from him the nature of the case. I was, and still am, in utter doubt as to the truth of the charge. I have a very poor opinion of my man's morals, and a very poor opinion also of the veracity of the accusers. It was however so very inconvenient for me, at setting out on a journey of four hundred miles through countries of which I did not know the language, to be deprived of my servant, that I offered to settle the business at my own expence. This would, under ordinary circumstances, have been easy enough. For the Hindoos of the lower castes have no delicacy on these subjects. The husband would gladly have taken a few rupees and walked away. But the persecutors of my servant interfered, and insisted that he should be brought to trial, in order that they might have the pleasure of smearing him with filth, beating kettles before him, carrying him round the town on an ass with his face to the tail, and giving him a good flogging. As I found that the matter could not be accommodated, I begged the judge to try the cause instantly. He would gladly have done so. But the rabble insisted that the trial could not take place for some days. I argued the matter with them very mildly. I told them that judge, parties, witnesses, were all present, – that there could be no reason for not deciding the matter immediately, – that I must go the next day, – and that, if my servant was detained, he would lose his situation, which would be very hard upon him, if, on investigation, he appeared to be innocent. They were obstinate. They returned no answer to my reasons, but threatened the judge, and repeated that my servant should not be tried for three days, and that he should be imprisoned in the meantime. I now saw that their object was to deprive him of his bread, whether he turned out to be guilty or innocent. I saw also that the gentle and reasoning tone of my expostulations made them impudent. They are in truth a race so much accustomed to be trampled on by the strong, that they always consider humanity as a sign of weakness. The judge told me that he never heard any gentleman speak such sweet words to the people in his life. But I was now at the end of my sweet words. My blood was beginning to boil at the undisguised display of rancorous hatred and shameless injustice. I sate down and wrote a line to the Commandant of the station, under whose controul the administration of justice is placed. I begged him to give orders that the case might be tried that very evening. He instantly sent the necessary directions. The court assembled; and continued all night in violent contention. At last the judge pronounced my servant not guilty. I did not then know, what I learned some days after, that this respectable magistrate received twenty rupees as a bribe on the occasion.

The beaten party were furious, as you may imagine. The husband would gladly have taken the money which he had refused the day before. But I would not give him a farthing. The rascals who had raised the whole disturbance were furious at being disappointed of their revenge. I had no notion however that they would have gone such lengths as they did go.

My servant was to set out at eleven in the morning. I was to follow at two. We had made this arrangement in order that he might arrive before me at the bungalow where I was to sleep, and might make every thing ready. His palanquin had scarcely left the door when I heard a noise. I looked out. And I saw that the gang of blackguards who had pestered me the day before had attacked him, pulled him out, torn off his turban, stripped him almost naked, and were, as it seemed, about to pull him to pieces. I snatched up a sword-stick, and ran into the middle of them. It was all that I could do to force my way to him: and really, for a moment, I thought my own person in danger as well as his. But this was a mistake. Even in their rage, they retained a great respect for my race and station. I supported the poor wretch in my arms. For, like most of his country-men, he is a chicken-hearted fellow, and was almost fainting away. They surrounded us storming, and shaking their fists, and would not suffer me to replace him in his palanquin. But my honest barber, a fine old soldier in the Company's army, and a great admirer of me, as soon as he saw me in this scrape, ran to the Governor General's and soon returned with some police officers. I ordered the bearers to turn round, and to proceed instantly to the house of Colonel Crewe, the Commandant.

I was not long detained here. Nothing can be well imagined more expeditious than the administration of justice in this country when the judge is a Colonel and the plaintiff a Councillor. I told my story in three words. In three minutes the rioters were marched off to prison, and my servant with a sepoy to guard him was fairly on his road and out of danger. Though he is, I fear, a very worthless fellow, he seemed deeply affected by my exertions in his defence. He cried, prostrated himself on the ground, and put his turban into my hands. I had and have great doubts about his innocence on this occasion. But I am sure that the persecution which he underwent was prompted by religious malignity, and that the last attack on him, after he had been legally acquitted, was a gross and intolerable outrage. I did not then know that the judge had been corrupted: and even if I had known it, such is the state of Indian morality that there would have been nothing uncommon or disgraceful in the transaction.

I had acted through this whole business without assistance or advice from any person. Indeed the emergency came so suddenly that I could not send for any body. When I went up to the Governor General's to take my leave, Lord William and all the party were surprised and indignant at the outrage which had taken place. It is very seldom that such a thing happens in this country when an European functionary of high rank is concerned. But the rabble of Ootacamund is remarkable for profligacy, ferocity and impudence.

I took leave of all my friends on the hills with many expressions of good-will. There are two for whom I have really a very great regard, Lord William and Macnaghten the Secretary of Government. Lord William absolutely insisted on my making the Government House my residence at Calcutta, till I could find a convenient place of abode.

I had forgotten, oddly enough, to mention that Henry Babington and his wife arrived on the hills some days before my departure. I liked them both much and saw much of them. She is a woman of agreable manners, and, in spite of ill health, of agreable person. He seems to make her a very good husband. He has a fair – indeed a high – character for ability and attention to his public duties. I desired him to let me know when any situation fell vacant which he might desire to have. If I can, I will serve him. His relationship to me has already, I hope, been of use to him. I have just learned with great pleasure that Lord William has selected him to be one of three civil servants who have been commissioned to report on the internal customs and transit duties of India. It is not improbable that in the discharge of his functions he may find it necessary to visit Calcutta and to become our guest. The office itself is not permanent, and may not be very lucrative. But it is a noble opportunity. The subject is of prodigious importance. And if Henry acquits himself well, he will be quite on the high road to preferment. In justice to Henry I ought to tell you that he owes the notice of Lord William chiefly to his own good character, and that, unless he had been a man of merit, his connection with me would not, I am quite certain, have been of the smallest use to him. Whether he comes to Bengal or not, Nancy hopes that his wife will pay her a visit during the approaching cold season.

Now to my journey. At twelve on the 31st of August my servant set out from Ootacamund to Needobutta – , a distance of eighteen miles. I followed at two. I was six hours in running this stage. I think that, in a former letter, I described to you the mode of travelling. There are twelve bearers to each palanquin – six at a time. They walk or trot relieving each other. On a good road they go from four to five miles an hour. But the road along the ridge of the Neilgherries is very indifferent: and two months of incessant rain had marred it most fearfully. We had to cross ten or twelve mountain streams which rose above the girdles of the men. The fog was thick round us. The rain poured down in torrents. I had a new publication of Theodore Hook's with me – Love and Pride, – which I had picked up at a sale of some deceased officer's effects on the hills. This amused me while the day light lasted. But we had to light torches long before we arrived at the bungalow where I was to sleep. I had slept here before in going up from Madras. I knew therefore how miserable the accommodations were: and I would gladly have gone on. But it is thought very dangerous to pass through the great jungle at night. And therefore I submitted to my fate. That fate might have been worse. A very honest friend of mine who has passed a year or more on the hills, Mr. Ironside, Member of the Council of Bombay, had very kindly, without telling me his intentions, sent a servant forward with provisions to cook me a dinner. I found a miserable barn with stone floor and naked walls. But I found also a heap of logs blazing, a beef-steak smoking, a bottle of ale bubbling and another of Sherry by its side. I made a hearty dinner, finished a volume of my novel, and lay down in this wilderness. My bearers and my servant's bearers, twenty four in number altogether, slept round me without any partition between them and me.

The next day rose, like almost all the days that I had seen on the mountains, dark and misty. I breakfasted very tolerably on milk, eggs, bread and butter, and set out at about half after eight. I was now to descend from the tops of the Neilgherries to the table land of Mysore. You can form no conception of the change. After going down for about half an hour, we emerged from the immense mass of cloud and moisture in which I had been buried for two months, and the immense plain of Mysore lay before us, – a vast ocean of foliage on which the sun was shining gloriously. I am very little given to rant about the beauties of scenery. But I really was moved almost to tears. I jumped out of my palanquin, and walked in front of it down the immense declivity. In about two hours we descended about three thousand feet – the height of Helvellyn or thereabouts. Every turning of the road shewed the boundless forest below in some new point of view. I was greatly struck by the resemblance which this prodigious jungle, – as old as the world, and planted by nature, – bears to the fine works of the great English land-scape-gardeners. It was exactly a Wentworth Park or a Bradgate Park as large as Devonshire.

When we got to the foot of the hill, we entered on the jungle. We had to run thirty six miles through this vast forest, which has a very bad name for tigers and elephants. I know several people who have been in danger there. But I met with no molestation. The jungles of India are dreadfully unhealthy. It is necessary to run through them by day, and with all speed. Even a native who passes a night in them is in great danger of catching a bad fever. But though they are by no means salubrious, the scenery is gloriously beautiful. I was for several hours passing through a succession of spots which might have been parts of the garden of Eden. – Such gigantic trees I never saw. In a quarter of an hour I passed hundreds the smallest of which would bear a comparison with any of those oaks which are shewn as prodigies in England. The grass, the weeds, and the wild flowers grew as high as my head. The sun, almost a stranger to me for two months, was shining brightly. When, in the afternoon, I got out of my palanquin and looked back, I saw the huge mountain ridge from which I had descended about twenty miles behind me, still buried in the same mass of fog and rain in which I had been living for weeks.

It was late in the evening before we got out of the jungle, and entered the inhabited country of Mysore. I stopped to dine, after a sort, at a bungalow, – a much neater place than that which I had slept in the preceding night. I procured a few mutton chops. I had brought bread with me, and I drank a bottle of pale ale. Having thus refreshed myself I entered my palanquin again. It was now quite dark. I soon fell fast asleep: and did not wake till day-break when I found myself in the streets of the town of Mysore.

There had been some mistake about the posting of my bearers; and I was forced accordingly to stay here about two hours. I had a very comfortable breakfast with an officer who was in command of the Company's troops at the station, and with his wife – a very civil lady, who asked me repeatedly whether my tea was agreable. I told you in a former letter the adventures that befel me at Mysore on my journey up to the hills, – how I had an interview with the Rajah, – how I saw all the finery of his court, – and, as Mrs. Meeke would say, every etc. etc. I had no mind to undergo the court ceremonial again, and I hoped that I might have been able to go through the capital incognito. But the princes and courtiers of the dependent states have a quick scent for a great European functionary. I had not been at Mysore ten minutes when I received a message from the Rajah begging to see me. I excused myself on the ground of haste: and he was pleased to accept my apologies graciously. He sent one of the princes of the blood, who speaks English very decently, to attend me during my short stay, and honoured me with presents of flowers, fruit, and atar of roses, after the fashion of the country.

The illustrious person who was in attendance on me amused me very much. He had never been out of Mysore, and his questions about England were very diverting. He said that he had heard that the English roads were very good. I confirmed this. "Who makes the roads? – " he asked. "Is it the King's Majesty." – No – I said – the King has nothing to do with our roads. "Oh then," said he, "I suppose it is the Company." I tried – but quite in vain, I suspect, to explain to him that the Company – a power which in India seems to be irresistible – which put his kinsman on the throne of Mysore and pulled him down from it – has in England just as little power as the Grocer's Company or the Merchant Tailors' Company.

At about ten in the morning of the 2nd of September I started again. My palanquin had been sent forward to Seringapatam, which is the next stage, and the Rajah of Mysore, – the Highness as his cousin called him, – furnished me with one of his own English made barouches for that part of the journey. The road between Mysore and Seringapatam is one of the few roads in India which are suited for wheel-carriages on springs. I sent you a full account of Seringapatam in a former letter. I saw nothing new this time. But I was, if possible, more struck than before by the contrast which the extent and strength of the fortification and the magnificence of some of the buildings present to the miserable state of the crumbling and uninhabited streets. Forty years ago the town contained probably a hundred and fifty thousand inhabitants. There are not now five thousand.

We ran on all day and all the following night, stopping only once for half an hour at a bungalow where I made an excellent dinner on a biscuit, half a dozen fresh eggs, and a bottle of ale. I slept sound during the night. Indeed the motion of the palanquin and the peculiar chaunt of the bearers always have a very lulling effect on me. What they sang I could not imagine. There is a great difference in their note in different provinces. In the Mysore, I have since learned, they generally chaunt extemporaneous eulogies on the person whom they carry, interspersed at intervals with sounds between grunting and howling. Sir John Malcolm who was unusually well acquainted with the native languages, made out the burden of one song which they sang while they carried him. "There is a fat hog – a great fat hog – how heavy is is – hum – shake him – hum – shake him well – hum – shake the fat hog – hum." Whether they paid a similar compliment to me I cannot say./They might have done so, I fear, without any breach of veracity.

At eight o'clock in the morning of the 3d of September I was comfortably seated in Colonel Cubbon's house at Bangalore. With him I passed three or four very pleasant days. I described him to you in a letter from the hills. I think him one of the ablest and most pleasing men that I have found in India.

If I had to chuse my place of residence in this part of the world it should, I think, be Bangalore. The place stands three thousand feet or more above the level of the sea. It is therefore agreably cool during the greater part of the year. I have been there both in June and September, and found that even in those months, which are very hot in most parts of India, I was able to take exercise at all times except in the very middle of the day. The situation is central. In forty eight hours you may be on the tops of the Neilgherries for health. In forty eight hours you may be at

Madras for business. So ready is the communication from Bangalore to every other part of Southern India that in one of our discussions in Council, Lord William, Sir Frederic Adam, and Colonel Morison, all distinguished military men, agreed that whoever holds Bangalore holds India south of the Kistna from sea to sea. The society is, I suppose, better than at any other place in the Presidency of Madras – Madras itself excepted. There is a large military cantonment and an important civil establishment. Many invalids also go up from the sea-coast for their health. I do not find however that the mortality is smaller here than in other parts of India. Indeed in this country caution is everything. The care which people take of themselves in unhealthy places and seasons compensates for the superior salubrity of other places and seasons. Every body at Calcutta leads the life of a valetudinarian, eats, drinks, and sleeps by rule, notes all the smallest variations in the state of his body, and would as soon cut his throat as expose himself to the heat of the sun at noon. At Bangalore a man feels himself as healthful and active as in England. He takes liberties. He drinks his two bottles at night, walks two miles at twelve o'clock in the day, has a coup-de-soleil, – and is in the churchyard in twenty four hours.

I left Bangalore late in the evening of the 7th of September, and ran to Madras without stopping except for a few hours in the heat of the day, after I got into the Carnatic. I reached Madras as the sun was rising on the morning of Wednesday the 10th of September. A carriage of the Governor's met me a few miles from the town and carried me to the Government House. Here I found my old friends Captain Barron and his wife, who, in Sir Frederic's absence, superintend the household. They were as kind as possible. I was soon comfortably lodged in my old rooms: and, after breakfast, I made inquiries about the ships which were then lying in the roads bound for Calcutta.

The largest and best was the Broxbournebury, under the command of a Captain Chapman, a brother-in-law of my friend Macnaghten, the Chief Secretary to the Government. Macnaghten had begged me to go with his relation, if I could contrive it. I therefore sent for the Captain, and engaged a passage in a very good cabin, which had been vacated by a lady whom he had brought to Madras. The cabin was part of the poop. I furnished it, – not as I furnished my little room in the Asia, – but in the very simplest manner. One strong table served for dressing and for writing. A large brass basin which I had used on my journey and two jars of the same metal contained water for my ablutions. The couch of my palanquin sufficed for a bed. We were not likely to be many days on the water, and at this season of the year carpeting and curtaining would have been mere annoyance.

133

I passed my time at Madras very pleasantly till the 16th of September, when I went on board. I heard, just before embarking, that a schism had taken place in the ministry at home – that several resignations had been sent in – and that more were expected. I did not obtain full information as to the particulars. But the general nature of the event could not be mistaken. I had foreseen it many months ago: and it was quite clear to me, from Lord John Russell's speech on the Irish Church, delivered early in May, that the crisis was at hand. I have even now very imperfect information as to particulars. But it seems to me that the new arrangements are very far indeed from being what they ought to have been. Indeed, with the exception of Rice's appointment, nothing that has been done pleases me. Abercromby ought to have been brought into the cabinet, and perhaps Sir Henry Parnell. I have very little hope that the ministry as now composed will be able to stand a year: and I shall be much surprised if Lord Lansdowne and some others do not leave it before long.

I think I described Madras fully to you in my first letters. I have little or nothing to add. I kept very quiet during the week which I passed there on my return from the interior, and saw hardly any body except the Governor's household, and the Archdeacon who is a great favourite of mine.

On the evening of Tuesday the 16th I went on board the Broxbourne-bury. I was carried through the surf in a native boat. But I think I have already described all that to you. I was honoured with a farewell salute of fifteen guns from Fort St George, and greeted by as many from the Broxbournebury. I found my cabin tolerably comfortable. I had laid in two dozen bottles of soda water, a little sherry, a little sugar, and a few limes; – so that I was able to bid defiance to thirst. Captain Barron sent on board a large supply of fruit and fresh vegetables from the Governor's garden.

I amused myself during this short voyage with learning Portuguese; and made myself as well or almost as well acquainted with it as I care to be. I read the Lusiad, and am now reading it a second time. I own that I am disappointed in it. But I have so often found my first impressions wrong on such subjects that I still hope to be able to join my voice to that of the great body of critics. I never read any famous book which did not, on the first perusal, fall below my expectations, except Dante's poem and Don Quixote, which were prodigiously superior to what I had imagined. Yet in those cases I had not pitched my expectations low.

I did not like Captain Chapman quite so well as Captain Bathie. By the bye poor Bathie is dead. He died of fever here more than a month ago. He has left a wife and children, all whose fortunes, I am afraid, are afloat in the Asia. I feel most acutely for them. He was an excellent officer, and a kind and honorable man. Nancy speaks in the warmest terms of his attention to her after our separation at Madras.

But to return to Captain Chapman. He is a very good navigator, and manages to have the business of his ship done very well, with less noise and scolding than I ever heard even in much smaller vessels. He seems to be very humane and conscientious. But he is a shallow, fanatical, fellow, a believer in the tongues, and in all similar fooleries. He brought out a missionary to Madras with whom he had long and fierce theological contests. He is famous for the care which he takes to prevent flirtations among the young ladies and gentlemen whom he carries out. They sate separate at table; and I was told at Madras that, in order to prevent them from giving any signs of partiality under the table, he had buckets, painted alternately white and green, into which all his passengers were forced to put their legs. This was a lie, as you may suppose. It is true, however, that he would not allow dancing and that psalm-singing was the only amusement of the poor girls on board. He is, in short, a good sort of man who understands his profession, but who is not overburdened with brains. In person he is very like Sir Robert Inglis.

We had a remarkably fine passage up the Bay of Bengal – at least for the time of year. The voyage in September is often more than a fortnight. We performed it within a week. At two in the morning of Tuesday the 23d we saw the floating light which marks the entrance of the Hoogley. At break of day we procured a pilot. At noon we saw the island of Saugur; and by dinner time we anchored for the night at Kedgeree.

The following morning we weighed anchor, and proceeded up the river with wind and tide in our favour. We had a most unusually good run. The day was fine and not oppressively hot. The banks of the Hoogley were far prettier than I had expected. Indeed I think that justice has never been done to them. They are low. But they are of the richest green, well wooded, and sprinkled with pretty little villages. They are far superior, I am sure, to the banks of the Thames or the Humber. I was a little surprised to find Bengal more verdant than Leicestershire in a moist April. But I came at the end of the rains; and the bright, cheerful, silky, green of the rice-fields was in all its beauty. The least agreable part of the scenery was the river itself. It comes down black and turbid with the mud collected in the course of fifteen hundred miles. For many leagues out to sea the water of the Ocean is discoloured by the filth which the innumerable mouths of the Ganges pour into it. The Hoogley often brings down with it great masses of jungle, whole trees, and acres of shrubs and brambles. We passed several of these floating islands. But this is not the worst. The boiling coffee-coloured river swept several naked corpses along close to our ship. This ghastly sight would once have shocked me very much. But in India death and everything connected with it become familiar subjects of contemplation. And habit is a much better strengthener of the nerves than philosophy. Six months ago I could not have believed that I should look on with composure while the crows were feasting on a dead man within twenty yards of me. If we had taken one of the fine houses at Garden Reach which are close to the river, we should have been forced to keep a man whose only business would have been to push away the corpses from our garden into the stream.

We had so quick a run up the river that by dinner time – that is at five or a little later – we were within fifteen or sixteen miles of Calcutta. Here we met a steam vessel going down. It had been sent to meet me, as soon as the telegraph had announced that I was in the river. I dined on board the Broxbournebury and when she anchored for the night, I went on board the steamer. I invited two or three passengers who were very desirous to reach Calcutta immediately, to accompany me. We found however that the tide was strong against us, and that little could be done till midnight. I took a comfortable nap of two hours; and at twelve went on deck. Soon after we began to move. The moon was past the full, but was very bright, and the night was calm and beautiful. At about two we came in sight of the villas of Garden Reach, which looked, I dare say, the prettier for being seen indistinctly peeping from amidst groves of trees. It was about half past three when the steam vessel reached the landing place. A boat was in waiting to land me. A palanquin was instantly sent down from the government house: and before four o'clock I was again with dear Nancy. I found her in excellent health and spirits, looking well and pretty, and bearing the climate as well as I: – for nobody can possibly bear it better.

I may as well say a little here about my health. I shall this week have been in India four months. Two of those months I passed on the Neilgherries, where the climate is the same with that of the Scotch Highlands or nearly so. The rest has been spent almost entirely travelling, or at Madras, or here at Calcutta. The time at which I arrived in Bengal is generally considered as the most unhealthy in the whole year. Indeed Nancy wrote to press me not to leave Madras so soon. But I did not think it right to remain at a distance from her, after the public duties which called me to the hills had been performed, merely in order to avoid a danger to which she was exposed. I came hither accordingly: and I never was better in my life. I have not swallowed five pills since I reached India. My appetite is good; my sleep is sound; I can do anything here that I could do in England, except taking strong exercise in the heat of the day. This season has been, I hear, a very favourable one. I hear also that new comers often get on better during their first year than afterwards. But as yet the climate agrees perfectly with me. I do not think that I ever had better health in England than I have here. I am sure that during the Session of Parliament I was never so well as I am at present.

And now that I have brought you to Calcutta I will close this long letter. In my next I will give you an account of the place and of our way of life. I will only add that nothing can exceed the kindness of Lady William Bentinck both to Nancy and to me.

With love to everybody believe me, dearest, ever yours

T B Macaulay

TO MRS EDWARD CROPPER, 7 DECEMBER 1834

MS: Mrs Lancelot Errington. *Partly published:* Trevelyan, 1, 383–7; G. M. Trevelyan, *George Otto Trevelyan,* 1932, pp. 5; 8–9; Clive, *Macaulay,* pp. 285–7; 301.

Calcutta Decr. 7. 1834

Dearest Margaret,

I rather suppose that some late letters from Nancy may have prepared you to learn what I am now about to communicate. She is going to be married, and with my fullest and warmest approbation, to Trevelyan, the Deputy Secretary to the Supreme Government in the political, or what we should call at home the Foreign Department. 1 can truly say that if I had to search India for a husband for her, I could have found no man to whom I could with equal confidence have intrusted her happiness.

Trevelyan is about eight and twenty. He was at the Charter House, and was there a great crony of Charles Babington. So intimate were they that, when Charles was left to himself to shew him what a poor creature he was, he called Trevelyan to prove that the stolen money was his own. Trevelyan however refused to tell a lie for him. I remember to have heard at the time of the distress of George and Tom when their brother's own friend, being called to prove his innocence, stood silent and agitated before Dr. Russell. Trevelyan then went to Haileybury and came out hither. In this country he has distinguished himself far beyond any man of his standing by his great talents for business, by his liberal and enlarged views of policy, and by literary merit which, for his opportunities, is considerable. He was at first placed at Delhi under Sir Edward Colebrook – a very powerful and a very popular man, but extremely corrupt. This man tried to initiate Trevelyan in his own infamous practices. But the young fellow's spirit was too noble for such things. At only twenty one he publicly accused Sir Edward, then almost at the head of the service, of receiving bribes from the natives. A perfect storm was raised against

137

the accuser. He was almost everywhere abused, and very generally cut. But, with a firmness and ability scarcely ever seen in any man so young, he brought his proofs forward, and after an inquiry of some weeks, fully made out his case. Sir Edward was dismissed in disgrace, and is now living obscurely in England. The Government here and the Directors at home applauded Trevelyan in the highest terms: – and from that time he has been considered as a man certain to rise to the very top of the service. When Lord William went up the country Trevelyan attended him. Lord William then told him to ask for any thing that he wished for. Trevelyan begged that something might be done for his elder brother who is in the Company's army. Lord W. told him that he had richly earned that or any thing else, and gave Lieutenant Trevelyan a very good diplomatic appointment. Indeed Lord William, – a man who makes no favourites, – has always given to Trevelyan the strongest marks, not of a blind partiality, but of a thoroughly well-grounded and discriminating esteem. Not long ago Trevelyan was appointed by him to the under-secretaryship for foreign affairs, an office of a very important and confidential nature. While holding this place he was commissioned to report to Government on the operation of the internal transit-duties of India. About a year ago his report was completed. I shall send to England a copy or two of it by the first safe conveyance: for nothing that I can say of his abilities or of his public spirit will be half so satisfactory. I have no hesitation in saying that it is a perfect masterpiece in its kind. Accustomed as I have been to public affairs, I never read an abler state-paper: and I do not believe that there is, – I will not say in India, – but in England, – another man of twenty-seven who could have written it.

Trevelyan is a most stirring reformer. He is indeed quite at the head of that active party among the younger servants of the company who take the side of improvement. In particular he is the soul of every scheme for diffusing education among the natives of this country. His reading has been very confined. But to the little that he has read he has brought a mind as active and restless as Lord Brougham's, and much more judicious and honest. His principles I believe to be excellent, and his temper very sweet. His own religious feelings are ardent, like all his feelings, even to enthusiasm: but he is by no means intolerant with regard to others.

He has faults, certainly; but they are for the most part faults which time, society, domestic life, and a visit which in a very few years he will pay to England, are almost certain to correct. He is rash and uncompromising in public matters. If he were a wrongheaded and narrow minded man, he would be a perfect nuisance. But he has so strong an understanding that, though he often goes too fast, he scarcely ever goes in a wrong direction. Lord William said to me, before anybody had observed

Trevelyan's attentions to Nancy, "That man is almost always on the right side in every question: and it is well that he is so: for he gives a most confounded deal of trouble when he happens to take the wrong one." This is a fault which experience will do much to remove, and which, after all, has a great affinity to his good qualities.

His manners are odd, – blunt almost to roughness at times, and at other times awkward even to sheepishness. But when you consider that during the important years of his life from twenty to twenty five or thereabouts, he was in a remote province of India, where his whole time was divided between public business and field-sports, and where he seldom saw an European gentleman, and never an European lady, you will not wonder at this. Every body says that he has been greatly improved since he came down to Calcutta. Under Nancy's tuition he is improving fast. His voice, his face, and all his gestures, express a softness quite new to him. There is nothing vulgar about him. Even in his oddities and *brusqueries* he is always the gentleman: and those oddities and *brusqueries*, I have no doubt, will speedily disappear. He has no great tact or knowledge of the world. You may judge of this by what passed on the very first day on which I met him. He asked me whether I was not related to Charles Babington, and, as soon as he was satisfied of the connexion, he proceeded to relate at full length the whole story of the Sovereign, – or, as he for Charles's greater degradation insisted that it was, the half-Sovereign. A man less accustomed to have rascals for cousins than I have been would have been grievously affronted.

But these drawbacks, were they ten times more serious, would be trifling when compared with the excellencies of his character. He is a man of genius, a man of honor, a man of rigid integrity, and of a very kind heart.

As to his person, nobody can think him handsome; and Nancy, I suppose in order to anticipate the verdict of others, pronounces him ugly. He has however a very good figure, and looks like a gentleman everywhere, but particularly on horse-back. He is very active and athletic, and is renowned as a great master in the most exciting and perilous of field-sports, the spearing of wild boars. His face is not unlike George Babington's in general character, but is more youthful, and, in spite of the Indian sun, much more blooming. Besides George's look of thought and resolution, Trevelyan's face has a most characteristic expression of ardour and impetuousity which make his countenance very interesting to me, and, if she would own it, to Nancy too.

Birth is a thing that I care nothing about. But his family is one of the oldest and best in England. Money is a more important matter: and there I think that Nancy is fortunate. He has five thousand pounds in

England. His salary here is at present about 2000 £ sterling a year, and will, in all probability, be soon increased. If he lives there can be no doubt of his rising rapidly to the most lucrative places in the Indian Government.

He was struck with Nancy at her first arrival: but she could not bear him. His manners as I told you are at once shy and rough, and his conversation is not likely to attract a young lady who does not know him well. He has not only no small talk, but he has very little English literature, and – what surprises me greatly – does not know a word of French. His mind is full of schemes of moral and political improvement, and his zeal boils over in all his talk. His topics, even in courtship, are steam-navigation, the education of the natives, the equalization of the sugar duties, the substitution of the Roman for the Arabic alphabet in the oriental languages. Nancy was so cold to him that he studiously avoided her, for fear, he says, of falling in love hopelessly. When I came, things were in this state. I had formed a very high opinion of him from his political correspondence, of which I had read whole reams at Ootacamund. Lord William, though quick-sighted to his faults, had always spoken to me of him as a most distinguished young man. His report on the internal transit-duties was extolled by every body in the South of India. I found it on Colonel Cubbon's table at Bangalore: and Cubbon, one of the ablest and most enlightened men in the Service, praised it in terms so high that, till I read it, I thought them hyperbolical. I came to Calcutta therefore prepossessed in Trevelyan's favour. I found him engaged in a furious contest against half a dozen of the oldest and most powerful men in India on the subject of native education. I thought him a little rash in his expressions; but in essentials, quite right. I joined him, threw all my influence into his scale, brought over Lord William, – or rather induced Lord William to declare himself, – and thus I have, I hope, been the means of effecting some real good. The question was whether the twenty thousand pounds a year which Government appropriates to native education should be employed in teaching the natives Sanscrit and Arabic, as heretofore, or in teaching them English and thus opening to them the whole knowledge of the western world. You will not doubt on which side Trevelyan and I were found. We now consider the victory as gained. Lord William has made me President of the Education Committee, and intends, very speedily, to pronounce a decision in our favour on the points at issue. While this was going on I was constantly in communication with Trevelyan: and he was constantly becoming more and more in love with Nancy. At first I saw that she disliked him: but soon she began to listen to his political disquisitions with more interest. Then I found her reading an account of the inquiry into the conduct of Sir Edward Colebrook. The minutes of the Education Committee had been sent to me. I missed them; and found that Nancy had stolen them, and was pouring over some very powerful, but rather too vehement, papers which Trevelyan had placed on record. Then she began to talk with him about the oriental alphabets. Then she engaged a Moonshee from among his followers to teach her Hindostanee after his new fashion with the Roman character. Her eyes looked bright whenever we met him on the Course, and her cheeks extremely red whenever he spoke to her. In short she became as much in love as he.

I saw the feeling growing from the very first, for, though I generally pay not the smallest attention to such matters, I had far too deep an interest in Nancy's happiness not to watch her behaviour to everybody who saw much of her. I knew it, I believe, before she knew it herself: and I could most easily have prevented it by merely treating Trevelyan with a little coldness. For he is a man whom the smallest rebuff would completely discourage. But you will believe, my dearest Margaret, that no thought of such base selfishness ever passed through my mind. I knew how painful a sacrifice I should have to make. But I knew that I had no right to enjoy her society at the expense of her happiness. Whatever prudes may chuse to say, nature made the two sexes for each other. It is the fundamental law on which the whole universe rests that they shall mutually attract each other. The celibacy of women has always been to me an object of more pity than I can express. I never see an amiable girl passing the prime of life unmarried without concern. And as to my dear Nancy, I would as soon have locked her up in a nunnery as have put the smallest obstacle in the way of her having a good husband. I therefore gave every facility and encouragement to both of them. What I have myself suffered it is unnecessary to say. My parting from you almost broke my heart. But when I parted from you I had Nancy – I had all my other relations – I had my friends – I had my country. Now I have nothing except the resources of my own mind, the consciousness of having acted not ungenerously, and the contemplation of the happiness of others.

This it is to make war on nature. This it is to form a scheme of happiness inconsistent with the general rules which govern the world. My Margaret and my Nancy were so dear to me and so fond of me that I found in their society all the quiet social happiness of domestic life. I never formed any serious attachment – any attachment which could possibly end in marriage. I was under a strange delusion. I could not see that all the qualities which made them so dear to me would probably make them dear to others. I could not see that others might wish to marry girls whose society was so powerfully attaching as to keep me from marrying. I did not reflect – and yet I well knew – that there are ties between man and woman dearer and closer than those of blood; – that I was suffering an indulgence to become necessary to me which I might lose in a moment – that I was giving up my whole soul to objects the very excellence of which was likely to deprive me of them. I have reaped as I sowed. At thirty four I am alone in the world. I have lost everything – and I have only myself to blame. The work of more than twenty years has vanished in a single month. She was always most dear to me. Since you left me she was everything to me. I loved her – I adored her. For her sake more than for my own I valued wealth, station, political and literary fame. For her sake far more than for my own I became an exile from my own country. In her society and affection I found an ample compensation for all that brilliant society which I had left. She was everything to me: and I am to be henceforth nothing to her – the first place in her affections is gone. Every year some new object of love will push me lower and lower in the scale of her regard till I am to her what our uncles and aunts were to our father and mother.

I do not repine. Whatever I suffer I have brought on myself. I have neglected the plainest lessons of reason and experience. I have staked my happiness without calculating the chances of the dice. I have hewn out broken cisterns. I have leant on a reed. I have built on the sand. And I have fared accordingly. I must bear my punishment as I can: and above all I must take care that the punishment does not extend beyond myself. I am proud to say that, in all this affair, amidst the most acute suffering, I cannot accuse myself of one selfish proceeding, and that I have done everything in my power to secure Nancy's happiness at the expense of my own.

Nothing can be kinder than her conduct has been: and Trevelyan evidently feels much for me: though neither of them, I believe, know what my feelings are. Nancy proposed that we should form one family: and Trevelyan, though, like most other lovers, he would, I imagine, prefer having his goddess to himself, consented with strong expressions of pleasure. The arrangement is not so strange as it might seem at home. The thing is often done here: and those quarrels between servants which would inevitably mar any such plan in England are not to be apprehended in an Indian Establishment. I feel the kindness of their intentions: and I cling too much to Nancy's society not to be desirous to defer the separation as long as I can. Yet I hardly know whether I judge rightly in taking this course, and whether it would not be wiser in me to bear the pain of separation once for all than to see the gradual growth of new feelings, the multiplication of new objects of attachment, the progress of that inevitable estrangement which it will not be in the dear girl's power to avert. But I have not fortitude enough to relinquish her society at once in this strange country. One advantage there will be in our living together of a most incontestable sort. We shall both be able to save more money. Trevelyan will soon be entitled to his furlough, but he proposes not to take it till I go home. Thus he has done all that he can do to alleviate this great blow. He will return to India with Nancy for ten years more; and it matters little whether we meet again or no.

I have gone on, I scarcely know how, pouring out to you all my thoughts. My grief is not without a mixture of mirth. The world is a tragi-comedy, and the scene now acting in this house is no bad instance of it. I have never seen a more amusing specimen of human – I might say of female nature – than dear Nancy is now exhibiting. It nearly broke her heart to come to India. She pined for nothing but home. Whenever I asked her jokingly whether if I should ever hereafter be made Governor General she would come out with me again, she screamed with horror at the bare idea. And here is a young fellow who, six weeks ago, was positively disagreable to her, for whose sake she is not only ready, but happy, to stay here in all probability fourteen or fifteen years. Nevertheless she is frightened out of her wits at the thought of being married; and will, I apprehend, go into fits before every thing is over. But as I never heard of any young lady dying in such fits, I am not very uneasy about her.

As to Trevelyan he is by no means so good a wooer as a financier or a diplomatist. He has had no practice: and he never read, I believe, a novel in all his life – so that his love-making, though very ardent and sincere, is as awkward and odd as you would wish to see. He will not however be the worse husband on that account.

The match is loudly applauded by the most intimate friends on both sides. Intimate friends, indeed, we can hardly be said to have here. But there are some whose kindness to us has been very great – particularly Lord and Lady William. Lord W has taken the warmest interest in the business. My lady came here immediately after she heard of the declaration, – a rare compliment from her I assure you, – kissed Nancy over and over, and seemed transported with joy. They take a warm interest both in her and in Trevelyan.

When the ceremony will take place I do not know: but probably about the middle of January. I heartily wish that it were over: for poor Nancy is in a most dreadful flutter of spirits, and will continue so, I suspect, till she knows the worst. I do what I can to enliven her: but it is hard for the miserable to find spirits for the happy.

This letter is of course private, and meant only for yourself. But you can communicate parts of it to our family and friends. Whatever you divulge, keep secret what I have said about my own feelings. I would gladly conceal from Nancy that I suffer at all. I hope that she does not know the whole extent of what I suffer. Yet sometimes within the last few days I have been unable, even at Church or in the Council-room to command my voice or to restrain my tears. I have known poverty. I have known exile. But I never knew unhappiness before.

So there you have my heart before you with all its inconsistency and weakness. I have half a mind not to send the letter; and yet I will: for there is a pleasure in reposing confidence somewhere, in exciting sympathy somewhere. I shall write in a very different style to my father, and to George. To them I shall represent the marriage, as what it is in every respect except its effect on my own dreams of happiness, [a] most honorable and happy event, prudent in a worldly point of view, and promising all the felicity which strong mutual affection, excellent principles on both sides, good temper, youth, health, and the general approbation of friends, can afford. As to myself it is the tragical denouement of an absurd plot. I remember quoting some nursery rhymes to you years ago when you left me in London to join Nancy at Rothley Temple or Leamington – I forget which. Those foolish lines contain the history of my life –

> There were two birds that sate on a stone:
> One flew away, and then there was but one
> The other flew away and then there was none
> And the poor stone was left all alone.

I shall soon write again, and tell you about a thousand other matters. At present I will only say that our climate is at present agreeably cool – that my health, though it has suffered a little during the last week from mental agitation, is in the main very good – certainly better than in England, – and that, in all external matters, I am going on as well as possible.

Give my kindest love to Edward. The necessity of paying ready money for furniture, china, plate, glass, and table linen has prevented me hitherto from discharging my debt to him. But by the end of this month I shall be able to remit fifteen hundred pounds home without the smallest inconvenience. My love to the baby. Pray when are we to have another? I presume that Master Charles will be destined by you to be a match for Miss Trevelyan – heiress of the great Indian Trevelyan just returned from the Government of Agra with a hundred thousand pounds. Kiss him for me at anyrate. / Ever, my dearest Margaret,

Yours most tenderly
T B Macaulay

MS: Trinity College. *Address:* T F Ellis Esq / 15 Bedford Place. *Subscription:* T B Macaulay. *Mostly published:* Trevelyan, 1, 426–30.

Calcutta Dec 15. 1834

Dear Ellis,

Many thanks for your letter. It is delightful in this strange land to see the handwriting of such a friend. I can truly say that England contains very few people indeed, not more than three or four, whether in my own family or out of it, who are so dear to me as you. We must keep up our spirits. We shall meet, I trust, in little more than four years at the outside, with feelings of regard only strengthened by our separation.

My spirits are not bad; and they ought not to be bad. I have at present health, affluence, consideration, great power to do good, functions which, while they are honorable and useful, are not painfully burdensome, leisure for study, good books, an unclouded and active mind, warm affections, and a very dear sister. There will soon be a change in my domestic arrangements. My sister is to be married next week. She came hither on no matrimonial speculation: and indeed the match is, in a temporal point of view, no very good speculation. As mistress of my house, she was second only to Lady William Bentinck in Indian society; and, while she remained unmarried, no house of mine, either in England or in India, would ever have had another mistress. She marries from attachment, and from very honorable and well-placed attachment. Her lover, who is lover enough to be a knight of the Round Table, is one of the most distinguished of our young civilians. I have the very highest opinion of his talents both for action and for discussion. Indeed I should call him a man of real genius. He is also, what is even more important, a man of the utmost purity of honor, of a sweet temper, and of strong principle. He is very fervently religious, – perhaps too much so for my taste: but this is, at all events, a fault on the right side in the man to whom I am about to give away a girl whose happiness is quite as dear to me as my own. His public virtue has gone through very severe trials, and has come out resplendent. Lord William, in congratulating me the other day, said that he thought my destined brother in law the ablest young man in the service, and the most noble-minded man that he had ever seen. His name is Trevelyan. He is a nephew of a Sir John Trevelyan, a baronet, in Cornwall, I suppose, by the name; for I never took the trouble to ask.

He and my sister will live with me during my stay here. I have a house about as large as Lord Dudley's in Park Lane, or rather larger, so that I shall accommodate them without the smallest difficulty. This arrangement is acceptable to me, because it saves me from the misery of parting with my sister in this strange land; and is, I believe, equally gratifying to Trevelyan, whose education, like that of other Indian servants, was huddled up hastily at home, who has an insatiable thirst for knowledge of every sort, and who looks on me as little less than an oracle of wisdom. He came to me the other morning to know whether I would advise him to keep up his Greek, which he feared he had nearly lost. I gave him Homer, and asked him to read a page; and I found that like most boys of any talent who have been at the Charter-House, he was very well grounded in the language. He read with perfect rapture, and has marched off with the book, declaring that he shall never be content till he has finished the whole. He is now set most vehemently on a scheme for our reading Mitford's History of Greece together, referring, as we go on, to the poets, historians, philosophers, and orators, whose works throw light on the narrative. This, you will think, is not a bad brother-in-law for a man to pick up in 22 degrees of North Latitude and 100 degrees of East Longitude.

I read much – and particularly Greek; and I find that I am, in all essentials, still not a bad scholar. I could, I think, with a year's hard study, qualify myself to fight a good battle for a Craven's Scholarship. I read however, not as I read at College, but like a man of the world. If I do not know a word, I pass it by, unless it be important to the sense. If I find, as I have of late often found, a passage which refuses to give up its meaning at the second reading, I let it alone. I have read during the last fortnight, before breakfast, three books of Herodotus, and four plays of Æschylus. I began the Χοηφοροι* this morning. I now and then give up particular passages. But I thoroughly enter into the spirit, not only of the iambics, but of most of the chorusses. My admiration of Æschylus has been prodigiously increased by this reperusal. I cannot conceive how any person of the smallest pretensions to taste should doubt about his immeasurable superiority to every poet of antiquity, Homer only excepted. Even Milton, I think, must yield to him. It is quite unintelligible to me that the ancient critics should have placed him so low. Horace's notice of him in the Ars Poetica is quite ridiculous. There is to be sure the "magnum loqui." But the great topic insisted on is the skill of Æschylus as a manager, as a property-man – , the judicious way in which he boarded the stage, the masks, the buskins, and the dresses. And, after all, the *magnum loqui,* though the most obvious characteristic of Æschylus, is by no means his highest or his best. Nor can I explain this by saying that Horace had too tame and unimaginative a mind to appreciate Æschylus. I think that Horace's taste was excellent. He knew what he could himself do, and, with admirable wisdom, he confined himself to that. But he seems to have had a perfectly clear comprehension of the merit of those

* *Choephori.*

great masters whom he never attempted to rival. He praised Pindar most enthusiastically. It seems incomprehensible to me that a critic who admired Pindar should not admire Æschylus far more.

Greek reminds me of Cambridge and of Thirlwall, and of Wordsworth's unutterable baseness and dirtiness. When you see Thirlwall tell him that I congratulate him from my soul on having suffered in so good a cause: and that I would rather have been treated as he has been treated on such an account than have the Mastership of Trinity. There would be some chance for the Church, if we had more Churchmen of the same breed – worthy successors of Leighton and Tillotson.

From one Trinity Fellow I pass to another – (This letter is quite a study to a metaphysician who wishes to illustrate the law of association). We have no official tidings yet of Malkin's appointment to the vacant seat on the Bench at Calcutta. But private letters represent it as certain; and we are assured that another fellow of our College, Gambier, has actually kissed hands on being appointed to Penang. I cannot tell you how delighted I am at the prospect of having Malkin here. An honest enlightened Judge, without professional narrowness, is the very man whom we want on public grounds. And as to my private feelings nothing could be more agreable to me than to have an old friend and so estimable a friend brought so near to me in this distant country.

I heartily wish that your letter had contained better news about your eldest boy. I will say no more on that painful subject. It is not a subject on which consolation can be of the smallest avail. Even with this terrible drawback, I think you one of the happiest men in domestic life that I have ever known. I hope from the bottom of my soul that, when I return, I shall find you as happy in your home and as deserving to be so as I left you. My kindest regards to Mrs. Ellis. Tell Frank that if he is not a better Greek scholar than I when I come back, I shall hold him in great contempt. Love to all the children. / Ever dear Ellis

Your affectionate friend
T B Macaulay

TO JOHN TYTLER, 28 JANUARY 1835

Text: Copy, India Office Library. *Published:* Gerald and Natalie Sirkin, 'The Battle of Indian Education,' *Victorian Studies*, 14 (June 1971), 426–7.

[Calcutta] Janry. 28th 1835
Dear Sir

Our difference of opinion is quite fundamental, nor do I conceive that discussion is likely to bring us nearer to each other. I deny every one of your premises without exception. I deny that no nation was ever educated by means of foreign languages. I say that all the progress which knowledge has made in Russia has been altogether through the medium of languages as remote from the Russian as English is from the Bengali.

I deny that no derivative language can be well understood without a knowledge of the original language[;] the best and most idiomatic English has been written by men who knew neither Anglo-Saxon or Norman French. I deny that there is the smallest use in making the vernacular dialects of India at the present time, precise, regular, or eloquent. These things come without fail in their proper season. They are conveniences or luxuries. What we now want are necessaries. We must provide the people with something to say, before we trouble ourselves about the style which they say it in. Does it matter in what Grammar a man talks nonsense? with what purity of diction he tells us that the World is surrounded by a Sea of butter? in what neat phrases he maintains that Mount Meru is the centre of the world?

I deny that it is necessary to teach absurdities either to a man* or to a native for the purpose of afterwards refuting those absurdities. It is very well for a few studious men to pass their lives in tracing the history of opinions. But the great mass of students have not a life to give to such researches. If they are taught errors while their education is going on, they will never learn truth afterwards. Nor is it necessary to the rational belief of truth that men should be acquainted with all the forms which error has taken. The same reasoning which establishes truth does ipso facto refute all possible errors which are opposed to that truth. If I prove that the earth is a sphere, I prove at the same time that it is not a cube, a cylinder, or a cone; – nor is it necessary for me to go through all possible figures one after another, and to direct a separate argument against each.

I deny that there is the smallest analogy between our attempt to teach sound science to people who are desirous to learn it, and the attempts of the Spanish Government to bring up Jewish Children in the Christian faith. I do not propose to bribe any body to learn English as the pupils of the Sanscrit College are now bribed to learn Sanscrit. I would merely provide the means of wholesome instruction for those who desire it. I have no doubt that there are many such.

I deny that we wish to conceal both sides of any scientific question from our students. But life is too short to study every thing. You cannot teach your pupils truth and all the various forms of error in the short time which is allotted to education. I cannot see the wisdom of making a boy, for example, a great astrologer, of keeping him several years employed in casting nativities – and then telling him that the whole of the Science

* Thus in the copy, but Macaulay probably wrote 'Englishman'.

which he has painfully mastered is good for nothing. I think myself entitled to laugh at astrology though I do not know its very rudiments – to laugh at alchemy though I have no knowledge of it but what I have picked up from Ben Jonson. Would you teach your children astrology? And would you not think it strange if any body were to tell you that it was cowardly in you not to teach them astrology? that you shewed great distrust in the force of truth – that truth could not be defended unless its defenders were thoroughly acquainted with all the details of the errors which they rejected?

You say that there is some truth in the Oriental systems. So there is in the Systems held by the rudest and most barbarous tribes of Caffraria and New Holland. The question is why we are to teach any falsehood at all. You say it is necessary in order to make the truth palatable to the Natives. I am not convinced of this. I know that your Sanscrit and Arabic Books do not sell. I know that the English books of the School book Society do sell. I know that you cannot find a single person at your Colleges who will learn Sanscrit and Arabic without being paid for it. I know that the Students who learn English are willing to pay. I believe therefore that the native population if left to itself would prefer our mode of education to yours. At all events the *onus probandi* lies upon you.

You see how unlikely it is that we should come to the same opinion on this subject. I am greatly obliged to you for taking the trouble to place your sentiments before me in so clear and precise a manner – and I wish you most heartily a pleasant voyage with a speedy restoration to health. We will finish our dispute when we return. / Believe me, Dear Sir

Your faithful Servant

T B Macaulay.

TO THOMAS FLOWER ELLIS, 8 FEBRUARY 1835

MS: Trinity College. *Address:* T F Ellis Esq / 15 Bedford Place. *Subscription:* T B Macaulay. *Partly published:* Trevelyan, I, 430–4.

Calcutta Feby. 8. 1835

Dear Ellis,

The last month has been the most painful that I ever went through. Indeed I never knew before what it was to be miserable. Early in January letters from England brought me news of the death of my youngest sister. What she was to me no words can express. I will not say that she was dearer to me than any thing in the world: for my sister who is with me was equally dear. But she was as dear to me as one human being can be to another. Even now, when time has begun to do its healing office, I cannot write about her without being altogether unmanned. That I have not utterly sunk under this blow I owe chiefly to literature. What a blessing it is to love books as I love them, – to be able to converse with the dead and to live amidst the unreal. Many times during the last few weeks I have repeated to myself those fine lines of old Hesiod.

ει γαρ τις πενθος εχων νεοκηδει θυμῳ
αζηται κραδιην ακαχημενος, αυταρ αοιδος
μουσαων θεραπων κλεια προτερων ανθρωπων
ὑμνησῃ, μακαρας τε θεους οἱ Ολυμπον εχουσι
αιψ ὁγε δυσφρονεων επιληθεται, ουδε τι κηδεων
μεμνηται, ταχεως δε παρετραπε δωρα θεαων. *

I have gone back to Greek literature with a passion quite astonishing to myself. I have never felt any thing like it. I was enraptured with Italian during the six months which I gave up to it. I was little less pleased with Spanish. But, when I went back to the Greek, I felt as if I had never known before what intellectual enjoyment was. Oh that wonderful people. There is not one art, not one science, about which we may not use the same expression which Lucretius has employed about the victory over superstition – "Primum Graius homo."

I think myself very fortunate in having been able to return to these great masters while still in the full vigour of life, and when my taste and judgment are mature. Most people read all the Greek that they ever read before they are five and twenty. They never find time for such studies afterwards till they are in the decline of life. Then their knowledge of the language is in a great measure lost, and cannot easily be recovered. Accordingly almost all the ideas that people have of Greek literature are ideas formed while they were still very young. A young man, whatever his genius may be, is no judge of such a writer as Thucydides. I had no high opinion of him ten years ago. I have now been reading him with a mind accustomed to historical researches and to political affairs; and I am astonished at my own former blindness, and at his greatness. I could not bear Euripides at college. I now read my recantation. He has faults undoubtedly. His extraordinary talent for declamation and debate, and perhaps the taste of a public accustomed to a war of tongues on all speculative and practical questions, sometimes led him to indulge his talent at the expense of all the probabilities of character and situation. But what a poet! – The Medea – the Alcestis – the Troades – the Bacchæ – are alone sufficient to place him in the very first rank. Instead of depreciating him, as I have done, I may, for aught I know, end by editing him.

* 'For if to one whose grief is fresh, as he sits silent with sorrow-stricken heart, a minstrel, the henchman of the Muses, celebrates the men of old and the gods who possess Olympus; straightway he forgets his melancholy, and remembers not at all his grief, beguiled by the blessed gift of the goddesses of song' (G. O. Trevelyan's translation).

I have read Pindar, – with less pleasure than I feel in reading the great Attic poets, but still with admiration. Two things occurred to me in reading him, which may very likely have been noticed by a hundred people before, but I mention them as they are quite new to me, and I should like to have your opinion about them.

I was always puzzled to understand the reason for the extremely abrupt transitions in those Odes of Horace which are meant to be particularly fine. The "justem et tenacem" is an instance. All at once you find yourself in heaven – heaven only knows how. What the firmness of just men in times of tyranny or of tumult has to do with Juno's oration about Troy it is hardly possible to conceive. Then again how strangely the fight between the Gods and Giants is tacked on to the fine hymn to the muses in that noble ode "Descende Cœlo, et dic age tibia." This always struck me as a great fault, and an inexplicable one. For it is peculiarly alien from the calm good sense and good taste which distinguish Horace.

My explanation of it is this. The Odes of Pindar were the acknowledged models of lyric poetry. Lyric poets imitated his manner as closely as they could; and nothing was more remarkable in his compositions than the extreme violence and abruptness of the transitions. This in Pindar was quite natural and defensible. He had to write an immense number of poems on subjects extremely barren and extremely monotonous. There could be little difference between one boxing-match and another. Accordingly he made all possible haste to escape from the immediate subject, and to bring in, by hook or by crook, some local description, some old legend, something or other which might be more susceptible of poetical embellishment and less utterly threadbare than the circumstances of a race or a wrestling-match. This was not the practice of Pindar alone. There is an old story which proves that Simonides did the same, and that sometimes the hero of the day was nettled at finding how little was said about him in the Ode for which he was to pay. This abruptness of transition was therefore in the Greek lyric poets a fault rendered inevitable by the peculiarly barren and uniform nature of the subjects which they had to treat. But, like many other faults of great masters, it appeared to their imitators a beauty, and a beauty almost essential to the grander ode. Horace was perfectly at liberty to chuse his own subjects and to treat them after his own fashion. But he confounded what was merely accidental in Pindar's manner with what was essential. And because Pindar, when he had to celebrate a foolish lad from Ægina who had tripped up another's heels at the Isthmus, made all possible haste to get away from so paltry a topic to the ancient heroes of the race of Æacus, Horace took [it] into his head that he ought always to begin as far from the subject as possible, and then to arrive at it by some strange and sudden bound. This is my solution. At least I can find no better.

The other remark that occurred to me in reading Pindar is that the political feelings of a Theban have, in a most extraordinary degree, tinged his poetry, though he scarcely says a word about contemporary politics. He has only two odes to Athenians. They are two of his shortest. One of them, – that to Megacles, though complimentary to the individual, contains a reflection on the Athenian people. The other is to Timodemus. He goes back to Ajax for a theme. He mentions the island of Salamis. But he has nothing to say about the great battle which was fought there in his own time. On the other hand no less than eleven of his forty five odes are addressed to citizens of the little island of Ægina, the deadliest enemy of Athens. When these thirteen odes are taken out, thirty two remain: and of those thirty-two only two are to the citizens of states which opposed the Persian invasion. The remaining thirty are all addressed to men whose cities had either *medized*, as Mitford would say, or remained neuter.

But I shall run on for ever, if I get into this vein. One word however in answer to a question in your last letter. You ask whether I think that the Shield of Hercules is Hesiod's. Most certainly not. You ask whether it is not a mere cento of a late age. I think not. I rather suspect that it is an old poem – older than the time when the Iliad and Odyssey were edited in their present form. In the first place I do not think that a sophist of the later ages would have borrowed from Homer in so impudent a manner. In the undoubted forgeries of later times – the Epistles of Phalaris for example, – you do not find whole passages of Plato and Xenophon stolen. This is not the way in which an imitator proceeds in a literary age. But it is exactly the way in which a minstrel would borrow verses of a brother-minstrel in an age when books were very rare. There are several different versions of Chevy Chase, the history of which is I suppose much the same.

I have another reason for thinking the poem, bad as it is, an old one. An imitator of a late period would have dressed up Hercules in the lion's skin and armed him with the club. The author of the Shield makes him fight in the panoply and with the spear – just like Hector or Diomede in the Iliad. Now this is exactly like the Hercules of Homer, and quite unlike the Hercules of the later writers.

You must excuse all this. For I labour at present, under a suppression of Greek; and am likely to do so for at least three years to come. Malkin might be some relief. But I am quite unable to guess what he means to do. I should think that Calcutta would be in every respect the most agreable place of abode that he could find in this part of the world. But he is very unwilling to change. He is protracting his stay at Penang as long as he can: and, if any thing should happen to Gambier, may remain there permanently. Every body that I see speaks highly of him. The bishop writes in the warmest terms of gratitude and respect both about Sir Benjamin and his lady.

I am in excellent bodily health: and I am recovering my mental health: but I have been cruelly tried. Money-matters look well. My new brother-in-law and I are brothers in more than law. I am more comfortable than I expected to be in this country: and as to the climate I think it beyond all comparison better than that of the House of Commons.

My kindest remembrances to Mrs. Ellis. You are a happy man. Yet I thought of you as well as of myself when I read over and over again the other day, not without many tears, these exquisite lines

πολλὰ διδασκει μ' ὁ πολυς βιοτος.
χρῆν γὰρ μετριας εις αλληλους
φιλιας θνατους ανακιρνασθαι,
και μη προς ακρον μυελον ψυχας,
ευλυτα δ' ειναι στεργηθρα φρενων,
απο τ' ωσασθαι και ξυντεῖναι.
το δ' ὑπερ δισσων μιαν ωδινειν
ψυχαν χαλεπον βαρος, ὡς κἀγω
τησδ' ὑπεραλγω.*

I hope Frank gets on well, and is becoming a better scholar than either of us. With all kind wishes for you and yours believe me ever, / Dear Ellis,

Yours affectionately
T B Macaulay

PS. By the bye it has crossed my mind that the most obscure passage – at least the strangest passage – in all Horace may be explained, as I said above, by supposing that he was misled by Pindar's example – I mean that odd parenthesis in the "Qualem ministrum" –

Quibus
Quos unde deductus per omne
etc.

This passage, taken by itself, always struck me as the harshest, queerest, most preposterous digression in the world. But there are several things in Pindar very like it.

*   '– with many a lesson stern
      The years have brought, this too I learn –
      Be links of mortal friendship frail!

Let heart-strings ne'er together cling,
     Nor be indissolubly twined
     The chords of love, but lightly joined
For knitting close or severing.

Ah weary burden, where one soul
     Travails for twain, as mine for thee!'
(Euripides, *Hippolytus*: Loeb translation.)

153

MS: National Library of Scotland. *Extract published:* W. F. Gray, 'A Budget of Literary Letters,' *Fortnightly*, CXXIII (1928), 349.

[Calcutta]

Dear Sir,

I meant to have joined you this morning. But I have just received several boxes which I must go through before breakfast, as they are to be brought before Council this morning. You must therefore go on without me.

Will you have the goodness to send me any papers which may contain an account of Dr. Wise's relation to the Hoogley College and of the reasons which led to his dismissal. I think that we want some efficient and able superintendant there; and, from my short personal acquaintance with him, I should say that it would be impossible to find a better.

I have made some objections to your indent. I am convinced that we are all on a wrong tack. – To think of teaching boys a language by means of grammars of logic and grammars of rhetoric! – Give them Jack the Giant Killer and Tom Thumb; – and then let them have Robinson Crusoe and Gulliver. – That is what I would do: and I will bet ten thousand to one that my pupils would beat yours hollow.

Ever yours truly

T B Macaulay

TO JAMES MILL, 24 AUGUST 1835

MS: Mr Gordon N. Ray. *Address:* James Mill Esq / India House. *Subscription:* T B Macaulay *Extracts published:* Clive, *Macaulay*, pp. 365–6; 383; 384; 400.

Calcutta August 24. 1835

My dear Sir,

I have to thank you for a very friendly and interesting letter which Cameron delivered to me. He has arrived safe after a long voyage, and is now in my house which I am trying to make agreable to him till he can provide himself with one. All that I have seen of him satisfies me that the home authorities could not possibly have made a better choice. We agree perfectly as to all the general principles on which we ought to proceed, and differ less than I could have thought possible as to details.

We are now most vigorously at work on the criminal code. I entertain strong hopes that this great work will be finished in a few months, and finished in a manner useful, not only to India, but to England. When once the English people see the whole criminal law of a vast empire, both substantive and adjective, contained in a volume smaller than one of the hundred volumes of statutes and reports which a Templar must turn over to know whether a particular act be larceny or forgery, they will, I think, turn their minds to the subject of law-reform with a full determination to be at least as well off as their Hindoo vassals.

You are aware that Macnaghten declined the situation of Law Commissioner. I hardly know whether to rejoice or grieve at his determination. I have a great regard for him; and I think him a man of eminent abilities and information. But he is in the wrong on some very important fundamental points: and, wherever he is in the wrong, his talents, his high authority, his great local knowledge, and, above all, a certain mild and well-bred obstinacy which is the most striking feature of his character, render him a very mischievous person. There is a striking saying of Cæsar about Brutus which may be applied to Macnaghten. "Magna refert hic quid velit: nam quicquid vult, valde vult." Among those things which Macnaghten "valde vult," one is to keep up the whole of that vile system of institution fees and stamps in judicial proceedings which is my utter aversion. He does not at all like oral pleading, or the confrontation of parties. On these and many similar subjects he talks with considerable ability and with the greatest suavity and moderation. But he is firmly convinced that the country will be ruined if the philosophers get the upper hand; and would have differed from Cameron and me on general principles so widely that I fear we should have derived little benefit from his great knowledge and talents.

Macleod is a very acute man, with a mind fertile in objections. This is an invaluable quality in a law-commissioner. One such member of a Commission is enough. But there ought to be one such. He refines so much that he does nothing. He has not been able to produce a single definition which satisfies himself. But he is invaluable as a critic, or rather a hypercritic on all that others do. The real work of drawing up the Code will, as far as yet appears, be completely performed by Cameron and myself, under the constant checking of Macleod. Anderson is very willing to work but is utterly incompetent. He has absolutely no notion of any other jurisprudence than that which he has passed his life in administering: nor have we yet received from him even a single hint of the smallest value. – You see that I write to you quite freely. I do so because it is really important that you should know exactly how matters stand, and that, whenever a favourable opportunity may occur, you should do what may be in your power in order to procure good assistance for us. Personally I am on the best terms with my colleagues in the Law Commission.

I have laid before the Council of India a very extensive plan of reform in the civil procedure which is still under consideration. It embraces a new organization of the courts, – oral pleadings, – the confrontation of parties, – the abolition of all taxes on justice and of the suit in forma pauperis, – the use of the vernacular languages of the country in law-proceedings. It also contains a proposition for allowing one appeal in every case, and no more than one in any case. Ross is most vehement in favour of my propositions. Indeed he and I very seldom differ on any question: and I am not without hopes that the Governor General and a majority of the Councillors will agree to at least a large part of what I have recommended.

We hear that Lord Heytesbury's appointment is cancelled. I am truly glad of it; and quite content to see Metcalfe still at the head of affairs. I have a real personal regard for him. But, apart from that, I think that he has some of the best qualities of a Governor. He has indeed no reforming zeal. But he has not the smallest prejudice in favour of abuses. He would not take any great trouble to remove a defect from the laws. But he would not lift up his little finger to preserve an evil merely because it is ancient. I think him a Governor General decidedly above par. We cannot expect another Lord William.

There is a subject which seems to me of the highest importance, and with respect to which you may possibly be able to render a great service to India. I do not know whether the noise of our conflicts about education has yet reached you. It will infallibly reach you before long. Lord William appointed me last winter President of the Committee of Public Instruction. I found that body divided into two equal parties. All their proceedings were at a stand, and had been so for several months. The question was whether their funds which amount to a lac of rupees a year from the public treasury, and about as much more from other sources, should be employed in teaching the learned languages and the scientific systems of the East, or in communicating English knowledge. On the side of Sanscrit and Arabic were the most powerful of the old servants of the Company, Macnaghten, Prinsep, and Shakspeare, particularly. – On the other side were the cleverest and most rising young men – Colvin, for example, and Trevelyan, who is now my brother-in-law. We had a most obstinate conflict, and at last referred the case to the Government. Lord William, who placed a confidence in me for which I shall feel most grateful as long as I live, suffered me to draw the answer. It was determined that existing interests should be respected, but that all the funds, as they became available, should be employed in teaching English literature and science. Several of the old members of the Committee retired, and Lord William suffered me to nominate several new members. Cameron was among those whom I suggested; and, since his arrival, he has entered, apparently with hearty good will, on his functions. We have now fallen to work in good earnest. Instead of paying away our funds in jaghires to students of Mahometan and Hindoo theology, we have opened English schools at the principal towns in the two presidencies. The stir in the native mind is certainly very great. We have just learned that the resort of pupils to our school at Dacca is such that the masters whom we have sent are not sufficient, and that it has been found necessary to repel many applicants.

These measures have been most violently opposed. After Lord W[illiam]'s departure the Orientalists appealed to Sir Charles. Sir Charles acted like himself. He would never have taken so bold and decisive a measure as that of declaring for English education. But he is not at all a man to rescind such a measure when taken by another. He declared himself decidedly favourable to the new system. Even this declaration did not silence the opposition. The Asiatic society complained bitterly of the neglect with which we were treating the learned languages of the East, though they were themselves forced to admit that the Government could not find people to learn those languages without giving jaghires as motives to study, and could not sell a single copy of the oriental works which it was printing.

When the change of system took place twenty three thousand volumes, folios and quartos for the most part, choked up the rooms of the Government depository. These had all been printed at the public cost. Nobody ever bought or read them. Our outlay on books in the three years which ended last Christmas had been sixty thousand rupees; our receipts from the sale of books nine hundred rupees.

I dwell thus long on this subject, because I think it one of the greatest moment, and because I have no doubt that the struggle will be renewed at home. Indeed the Asiatic society have memorialized the Court. I need not impress on you the immense importance of introducing English literature into this country, – the absurdity of bribing people to learn Sanscrit and Arabic when they are willing to learn English gratis, – the absurdity of giving to error bounties and premiums of a sort which it would be objectionable to give even to sound and useful knowledge. There are very few things in my life on which I look back with so much satisfaction as on the part which I took in deciding this question. I am sure that we shall have your support at home if an attempt should be made to reverse that decision.

I have filled my letter with Indian politics; and I have left myself no room to discuss English politics. It is clear in which direction things are tending. The perfidy of the Court, the obstinacy of the Lords, the bigotry

157

of the Church and of the universities, will soon turn the great body of the Whigs into Radicals. I am not fond of violent changes when it is possible to avoid them. I like to see abuses die out quietly, as for example the old practice of fining and imprisoning refractory juries died out in the seventeenth century, – as the privilege of scandalum magnatum died out in the eighteenth century, – as the oppressive privileges of parliament have died out in our own time. I like to see good things come in as the practice of printing the debates of the houses came in, almost imperceptibly. Such revolutions produce no suffering to any human being. [They] excite no malignant passions: and, though slow, they are su[re. I] thought the Reform Bill absolutely necessary: and, having secured that, my wish was to leave the power of the aristocracy to its euthanasia. I was willing to trust to time, to reason, and to the vast power which the middle classes had obtained. I hoped that the Lords would find themselves in the situation in which the Patricians of Rome were when the plebeians had obtained equal political franchises, and that they would gradually melt into the mass, or that only the "nominis umbra" would remain. Ten, twenty, thirty years of delay are nothing in the existence of a nation. But one day of anarchy is a fearful evil. I was therefore inclined to say of the ballot, of the shortening of parliaments, of the abolition of the hereditary privileges of the peers – "Hæc cum nova sint, relinquo tempori maturanda." But I do not see that I have any choice. I must be governed on the principles of the Oxford Convocation and the Pitt Club, or I must join the Radicals. And, under these circumstances, my decision is speedily made. I believe that the great body of the Whigs will take the same course. Some fainthearted men will go back. But the impulse of the mass will be onward.

I ought to thank you for your kindness in sending me your publication relating to Mackintosh. Yet I cannot but regret that it should have appeared. I had a great regard for him. He was kind to me at a time when his kindness was valuable to me. I learned much from him: and, though I perceived weak parts in his character, they were not such as to deprive him of his claims to my respect and gratitude. He deserved to be treated with charity for he was himself singularly charitable. Considering him as an able man, an accomplished man, a man who was very kind to my self, a man whose life was singularly unfortunate, a man who had been most shamefully calumniated, a man whose worst faults were timidity and love of ease, and who was persecuted as if he had been an atrocious criminal, I could not but feel a great concern at seeing so keen an attack upon him by so formidable an adversary. I am sure that you have too much generosity to be displeased at the sincerity with which I speak what I think.

I have just learned with the greatest concern the death of my excellent friend Sharp. He was the best correspondent that I had in England. – I must close. / Believe me ever, my dear Sir,

Yours most faithfully

T B Macaulay

TO THOMAS FLOWER ELLIS, 30 DECEMBER 1835

MS: Trinity College. *Address:* T F Ellis Esq / 15 Bedford Place / London. *Subscription:* T B Macaulay. *Partly published:* Trevelyan, I, 441–4.

Calcutta December 30. 1835

Dear Ellis,

I have received a letter from you dated in the month of July last. It was accompanied by a copy of your answer to Palgrave. You have fairly won the victory. You have also, as you boast, kept your temper. Whether A be morally justified in keeping his temper for the purpose of making B lose his, is a question which will bear much discussion. In my opinion the most provoking thing in the world is meek, well-bred malice, – the malice of a Christian and a gentleman. You will make an excellent controversialist, I see. As Sir Dugald said to Montrose – "really, for a person that has seen so little service, you have a very pretty notion of war."

What the end of the Municipal reform-bill is to be I cannot conjecture. Our latest English intelligence is of the 15th of August. The Lords were then busy in rendering the only great service that I expect them ever to render to the nation – that is to say in hastening the day of reckoning. But I will not fill my paper with politics, – at least with English politics. Here we are going on as smoothly as possible. The criminal code is advancing, – not so quickly as I could wish, but very satisfactorily. All the people whose cooperation is of importance agree with me thoroughly as to general principles. We have one great advantage – an advantage beyond all hope. Ryan and Malkin go hand in hand with the government and the Law-Commission, and seem as much interested in the success of our work as if their own credit were at stake. This is most fortunate. For it was from this very quarter that we had most reason to expect opposition. The lawyers and attorneys of the Supreme Court, with Sir John Grant at their head, will no doubt give us all the trouble that they can. But our alliance with the Chief Justice and Malkin will enable us to set them at defiance.

I am in excellent health. So are my sister and my brother-in-law, and their little girl, whom I am always nursing, and of whom I am becoming fonder than a wise man, with half my experience, would chuse to be of anything except himself. I have but very lately begun to recover my spirits. The tremendous blow which fell on me at the beginning of this year has left marks behind it which I shall carry to my grave. Literature has saved my life and my reason. Even now I dare not, in the intervals of business, remain alone for a minute without a book in my hand. What my course of life will be when I return to England is very doubtful. But I am more than half determined to abandon politics, and to give myself wholly to letters – to undertake some great historical work which may be at once the business and the amusement of my life, and to leave the pleasures of pestiferous rooms, sleepless nights, aching heads, and diseased stomachs, to greater men, – to Roebuck and Praed. In England I might probably be of a very different opinion. But in the quiet of my own little grass-plot, when the moon, at its rising, finds me with the Philoctetes or the De Finibus in my hand, I often wonder what strange infatuation leads men who can do something better to squander their intellect, their health, their energy on such objects as those which most statesmen are engaged in pursuing. I comprehend perfectly how a man who can debate, but who would make a very indifferent figure as a contributor to an annual or a magazine – such a man as Stanley for example – should take the only line by which he can attain distinction. But that a man before whom the two paths of literature and politics lie open, and who might hope for eminence in either, should chuse politics and quit literature seems to me madness. On the one side is health, leisure, peace of mind, the search after truth, and all the enjoyments of friendship and conversation. On the other side is almost certain ruin to the constitution, constant labour, constant anxiety. Every friendship which a man may have becomes precarious as soon as he engages in politics. As to abuse, men soon become callous to it: but the discipline which makes them callous is very severe. And for what is it that a man who might, if he chose, rise and lie down at his own hour, engage in any study, enjoy any amusement, visit any place, travel to foreign countries, consents to make himself as much a prisoner as if he were within the rules of the Fleet, – to be tethered during eleven months of the year within a circle of half a mile round Charing Cross, – to sit, or stand, night after night, for ten or twelve hours, inhaling a noisome atmosphere and listening to harangues of which nine tenths are far below the level of a leading article in a newspaper? For what is it that he submits, day after day, to see the morning break over the Thames, and then totters home, with bursting temples, to his bed? Is it for fame? Who would compare the fame of Charles Townshend to that of Hume, that of Lord North to that of Gibbon, that of Lord Chatham to that of Johnson? – Who can look back on the Life of Burke, and not regret that the years which he passed in ruining his health and temper by political exertions were not passed in the composition of some great and durable work? Who can read the Letters to Atticus, and not feel that Cicero would have been an infinitely happier and better man, and a not less celebrated man, if he had left us fewer speeches and more Academic Questions and Tusculan disputations, if he had passed the time which he spent in brawling with Vatinius and Clodius in producing a history of Rome superior even to that of Livy. But these, as I said, are meditations in a quiet garden, situated far beyond the contagious influence of English faction. What I might feel if I again saw Downing Street and Palace Yard is another question. I tell you sincerely my present feelings.

I pass the three or four hours before breakfast in reading Greek and Latin. I really think that I am now in better training for an University Scholarship examination than when I was an undergraduate. I have cast up my reading account, and brought it to the end of the year 1835. It is as follows. It includes December 1834. For I came into my house and un-packed my books at the end of November 1834. During the last thirteen months then, I have read Æschylus twice, Sophocles twice, Euripides once, Pindar twice, Callimachus, Apollonius Rhodius, Quintus Calaber, Theocritus twice, Herodotus, Thucydides, almost all Xenophon's works, almost all Plato, Aristotle's politics, a good deal of his Organon, besides dipping elsewhere, the whole of Plutarch's Lives, about half of Lucian, two or three books of Athenæus, Plautus twice, Terence twice, Lucretius twice, Catullus, Tibullus, Propertius, Lucan, Statius, Silius Italicus, Livy, Velleius Paterculus, Sallust, Cæsar, and lastly Cicero. I have indeed still a little of Cicero left. I shall finish him in a few days. I am now deep in Aristophanes and Lucian. Of Aristophanes I think as I always thought. But Lucian has agreably surprised me. At school I read some of his dia-logues of the dead when I was thirteen; and, to my shame, I never, to the best of my belief, read a line of him since. I am charmed with him. His style seems to me to be superior to that of any extant writer who lived later than the age of Demosthenes and Theophrastus. He has a most peculiar and delicious vein of humour. It is not the humour of Aristophanes. It is not that of Plato. Yet it is akin to both, – not quite equal, I admit, to either, – but still exceedingly charming. I hardly know where to find an instance of a writer, in the decline of a literature, who has shewn an inven-tion so rich and a taste so pure. Nor is humour by any means his only merit. Some of the most brilliant and animated declamation that I know is to be found in his works. By the bye, it might amuse you to compare his excellent little piece περὶ τῶν ἐπὶ μισθῷ συνόντων* with Juvenal's Third Satire. The Case of Greek versus Roman is at least as well argued by Lucian

* 'On Salaried Posts in Great Houses'.

161

as that of Roman versus Greek by Juvenal. But if I get on these matters I shall fill sheet after sheet. They must wait till we take another long walk or another tavern dinner together, – that is till the Summer of 1838.

Malkin and his wife seem to be very well. He begins to like Calcutta, I think. He is as you may suppose, a very agreable addition to the society here: and I am certain that he will be infinitely more useful here than he could have been if he had remained at Penang.

I am delighted to hear of your professional success. I hope, when I return, to find you in the high road to the bench. I hope also to find that Frank is going on better with his Greek. He must not dare to look me in the face if he cannot pass a good examination.

Apropos of examinations, I have a long story to tell you about a classical examination here, which will make you die with laughing. But I have not time. I can only say that some of the competitors tried to read the Greek with the papers upside down, and that the great man of the examination – the Thirlwall of Calcutta – a graduate of Trinity College Dublin, translated the words of Theophrastus, ὄσας λειτουργίας λελειτούργηκε* *"how many times he has performed divine service"*. But I must stop. Remember me most kindly to Mrs. Ellis. Remember me also to our friends Adolphus and Drinkwater.

Ever yours affectionately

T B Macaulay

TO MACVEY NAPIER, 26 NOVEMBER 1836

MS: British Museum. *Address:* Professor Napier. *Subscription:* T B Macaulay. *Mostly published:* Napier, *Correspondence*, pp. 180–2.

Calcutta Nov 26. 1836

Dear Napier,

At last I send you an article of interminable length about Lord Bacon. I hardly know whether it is not too long for an article in a Review. But the subject is of such vast extent that I could easily have made the paper twice as long as it is.

About the historical and political part there is no great probability that we shall differ in opinion. But what I have said about Bacon's philosophy is widely at variance with what Dugald Stewart and Mackintosh have said on the same subject. I have not your Essay; nor have I ever read it since I read it at Cambridge, with very great pleasure, but without any knowledge of the subject. I have at present only a very faint and general recollection of its contents, and have in vain tried to procure a copy of it here. I fear however that, differing widely as I do from Stewart and Mackintosh, I shall hardly agree with you. My opinion is formed, not at

---

* 'He does not count any of the trierarchies or public services which he has performed' (Theophrastus: Jebb's translation).

second hand, like those of nine tenths of the people who talk about Bacon; but after several very attentive perusals of his greatest works, and after a good deal of thought. If I am in the wrong, my errors may set the minds of others at work, and may be the means of bringing both them and me to a knowledge of the truth. I never bestowed so much care on anything that I have written. There is not a sentence in the latter half of the article which has not been repeatedly recast. I have no expectation that the popularity of the article will bear any proportion to the trouble which I have expended on it. But the trouble has been so great a pleasure to me that I have already been very greatly overpaid. Pray look carefully to the printing.

In little more than a year I shall be embarking for England; and I have determined to employ the four months of my voyage in mastering the German language. I should be much obliged to you to send me out, as early as you can, so that they may be certain to arrive in time, the best grammar and the best dictionary that can be procured, – a German bible, Schiller's works, Goethe's works, and Niebuhr's History both in the original and in the translation. My way of learning a language is always to begin with the Bible, which I can read without a dictionary. After a few days passed in this way, I am master of all the common particles, the common rules of Syntax, and a pretty large vocabulary. Then I fall on some good classical work. It was in this way that I learned both Spanish and Portuguese; and I shall try the same course with German.

I have to thank you for the great care and punctuality with which you have attended to all my wishes about books. A box for me is now on board of a ship lying in the Hoogly; and I hope to get it through the Custom house in a day or two.

I have little or nothing to tell you about myself. My life has flowed away here with strange rapidity. It seems but yesterday since I left my country; and I am writing to beg you to hasten preparations for my return. I continue to enjoy perfect health. The little political squalls which I have had to weather here are mere cap-fulls of wind to a man who has gone through the great hurricanes of English faction. We have been most unfortunate in our work of codification. All the Law Commissioners have been so ill that none of them but myself has done a stroke of work for months; and one of them, Cameron, will, I think, go to the Cape immediately. I do what I can; and I still hope that I shall have the penal Code, with a commentary, ready for the press before the end of this Cold Season.

I shall send another copy of the article on Bacon by another ship. / Believe me ever, / Dear Napier,

Yours very truly
T B Macaulay

MS: University of London. *Address:* C Macaulay Esq. *Published:* W. Fraser Rae, 'Macaulay at Home,' *Temple Bar,* LXXXVI (May–August, 1889), 197–9.

Calcutta December 5 / 1836.

Dear Charles,

It is long since I wrote to you and long since I heard from you. But I do not attribute your silence, and I am sure that you do not attribute mine, to any want of affection. All that I hear of you gives me pleasure, and leads me to hope that you have a busy, useful, honorable, and prosperous life before you. To assist you at entering on it will be my duty, and not more my duty than my pleasure.

In another year my banishment will be over, and I shall be packing up for my voyage. I already begin to feel the pleasure of returning from exile. That pleasure ought to be very great to compensate for the bitter pain of so long and so complete a separation from home. And it is very great. For though England is not all that it once was to me yet I have no hopes or wishes but what point to England; and I would rather go home with the knowledge that I should die there next year than live here till seventy in the midst of whatever splendour or comfort India affords. I quite understand how it was that neither goddesses nor enchanted palaces nor royal matches nor immortality itself could bribe Ulysses to give up his rugged little Ithaca, and that he was willing to forego everything else to see once more the smoke going up from the cottages of his dear island.

Few people I believe have the feeling so strongly as I have it. Indeed the great majority of the members of the services here seem perfectly willing to pass their lives in India; and those who go home talk with very little pleasure of the prospect before them. This is not strange. For they generally come out at eighteen or nineteen. Their banishment is their emancipation. The separation from home is no doubt at first disagreeable to them. But the pain is compensated to a great extent by the pleasure of independence, – of finding themselves men, – and, if they are in the Civil Service, of finding themselves rich. A lad who six months before was under strict discipline, who could indulge in few pleasures for want of money, and who could not indulge in any excess without being soundly scolded by his father and his pedagogue, finds himself able to feast on snipes and drink as much champagne as he likes, to entertain guests, to buy horses, to keep a mistress or two, to maintain fifteen or twenty servants who bow to the ground every time that they meet him, and suffer him to kick and abuse them to his heart's content. He is surrounded by money lenders who are more desirous to supply him with funds than he is himself to procure them. Accordingly the coming out to India is quite as often an agreeable as a disagreeable event to a young fellow. If he does not take his furlough – and not one civil servant in three takes his furlough, – he remains in India till he is forty five or fifty, and is then almost unfit for England. He has outlived his parents. He is estranged from his early friends. His children who have been sent over to England at six or seven years old are estranged from him. He is a man of consequence in the East. In Europe he knows that he will be considered as an old, yellow-faced, bore, fit for nothing but to drink Cheltenham water and to ballot at the India House. He has acquired, it may be, a great deal of valuable information on Indian affairs, – is an excellent Oriental Scholar, – knows intimately all the interests of the native Courts, – is as well acquainted with the revenue-system of Bengal as Huskisson was with the revenue-system of England, – is as deeply read in Hindoo and Mahometan jurisprudence as Sugden in the law of England. He knows that these acquirements which make him an object of admiration at Calcutta will procure for him no applause – nay not the smallest notice – in London. He has probably acquired some lazy self-indulgent habits. He cannot dress without the help of two or three servants. He cannot dine without a great variety of dishes. He cannot go out without a carriage. Under such circumstances he finds England a wretched place. He was powerful. He was eminent. He was comfortable. He is utterly insignificant, and is forced to go without the attendance and the luxuries which habit have rendered necessary to him.

The case with me is very different. I have not yet become reconciled to the change from the English to Indian habits. I have not suffered the ordinary helplessness of my countrymen here to grow upon me. I never suffer anybody to assist me in dressing or in any of the thousand little offices which every man ought to be in the habit of performing for himself. My acquirements such as they are fit me far better for Europe than for Asia; – nor have I any reason to expect that I should be exposed to any mortifying neglect at home. I came hither at an age at which I had formed strict friendships; and I shall return before time has at all diminished the strength of those friendships. I shall leave nothing that I shall ever remember with regret.

I am exceedingly glad for the reasons which I have mentioned that Trevelyan is going to take his furlough. I really think it an inestimable advantage to a civil servant that he should, at about thirty, spend a couple of years in Europe. As a boy he can know nothing of English society. When he returns an old Nabob his tastes and character have taken their ply, and it is too late to think of giving them a different bent. But by visiting England while still young, with his mind in its full vigour, with his habits and feelings not yet unchangeably fixed, he becomes an Englishman, and looks forward with pleasure during the rest of his Indian career to his final return to England. I think that after an hour's talk with a civilian of forty I could guess nine times out of ten whether he had or had not taken his furlough. Some of the cleverest men and of the most valuable public servants in India have never seen England from sixteen to fifty. But, whatever their merit may be, there is always a certain peculiar narrowness and Orientalism about them. They hate the thought of going home: and they seldom enjoy themselves at home when they do go.

But I must not go on rambling in this way. – / Ever, dear Charles,

Yours most affectionately,

T B Macaulay

TO WILLIAM EMPSON, 19 JUNE 1837

Text: Copy (in Frances Macaulay's hand), Trinity College.

Calcutta June 19. 1837.

My dear Empson,

We are just at the close for which Heaven be praised of a tremendously severe and tremendously long hot season. The fury with which the sun has blazed upon us during the last 3 weeks is far beyond anything, not only in my short Indian experience, but in the recollection of the oldest English inhabitants of Calcutta. The tanks are dry; the earth is baked as if it had been in a furnace; the peasantry have begun to quit their villages and to assemble in crowds on the banks of the river. The natives themselves have not unfrequently died of mere heat. One groom dropped down a corpse yesterday while attending a buggy. Two soldiers died in the same way while on guard at Fort William. The Cholera Morbus which generally accompanies the hot weather has been raging among the lower classes. "Black fellow die much, master," said my barber to me.

. . . .

The impatience with which the rains have been expected you may imagine. They generally set in about the 5th or 6th of June. But this year they have been unusually delayed; and, to make the delay more painful, we have been frequently tantalized with dark masses of cloud which have yielded nothing but wind and thunder. At length yesterday evening some rain fell, enough to cool the air which was like a blast from a furnace, and soon after midnight we had a very heavy shower. I really do not think that I ever remember any public event which excited such general rejoicing. Indeed if the rain had been much longer delayed the heat would have been the least part of the evil. We should have had reason to apprehend famine.

I believe that no person in Calcutta, European or native, stood this terrible season better than I. It did not affect either my appetite or my sleep; nor did it for more than a day or two render me unwilling to exert myself vigorously. When it was at the worst I lay from 9 in the morning till 6 in the afternoon on my sofa under a punkah reading Voltaire and Plutarch, with all the windows and blinds of my library most carefully closed; for if the smallest cranny were left open, a blast like that from the mouth of hell rushed in. Twice a week I was forced to go to Council; and I really believe that the Council described in the 2nd book of Paradise Lost was a great deal cooler. As to Trevelyan who was forced to go daily to office, I was afraid that he would have a brain fever; and I believe that if he had not been copiously relieved by leeches he would not now have been alive. An old schoolfellow of mine, a brother of the present Lord Teignmouth, F. Shore, was carried off by the very first beginning of this raging heat. He was an honest, able, and public spirited man, though of very disagreeable manners, violent prejudices, and harsh temper. He came down from the Upper Provinces with a pulmonary complaint for which he was ordered to try the air of the other side of Bengal. But while he was waiting here for a ship the heat came on, and he sank at once under it.

Before the beginning of these heats our house had been made a sad one by the death of my younger niece, a little thing only 3 months old, but as engaging as a baby of that age can be. I did not feel the loss as I should have felt the loss of her sister who begins to prattle in a *lingua franca* made up of a dozen languages and is constantly pulling me to my book cases and saying "Tom, come picture." Still I was a very sincere mourner for the poor little creature, both on her mother's account and her own. Since I heard of the death of my sister Margaret, my spirits have never been what they once were, and a lighter domestic calamity than this would have been sufficient to depress them. The best thing that I know about myself, and it is some set-off against the many faults and weakness of which I am conscious, – is that, while I am more stoical than most of my acquaintance where my interests are concerned, I am more sensitive than most of them where my affections are concerned.

In all vexations the near prospect of return is a most powerful cordial to me. I believe that nobody ever loved his country as a place to live in with so exclusive a love as mine for England. I would not go again through what I have gone through for Lord Westminster's fortune. But that is all over. When you are reading this letter I shall probably be looking out for a ship and buying cabin furniture. As far as we can look forward, we have fixed the last week of January or the 1st week of February for our departure. By sailing at that time we may hope to get out of the Bay of Bengal with a fair wind, to be too late for the hurricanes of the Mauritius, and too early for the adverse North Westers of the Cape, and to reach England in the prime of the summer.

I do not pretend to say what I may do when I am there. But it must be some strong temptation that draws me again into political life. I have tried to weigh dispassionately the advantages and disadvantages of a parliamentary and of a literary career, and I am certain that I should be happier as a literary man than as a successful member of Parliament. The canvassing, the compromising, the subordination, which are absolutely necessary in politics do not suit my temper. Freedom is the best thing in the world, and great men, as Bacon says, are fourfold servants. If I engage in politics I may possibly be a Secretary of State, and enjoy all the contentment which Lord Londonderry and Mr. Canning enjoyed, till I end by cutting my carotid artery like the former, or die of anxiety, vexation and fatigue like the latter. But if I keep out of politics, I may speak my mind; and I have a good deal of Persius's feeling

"Hoc ridere meum, tam nil, nulla tibi vendo Iliade."

The comparison is really between freedom and slavery, toil and leisure, health and sickness. And as to fame I prefer the fame which is got by a good book, to "immense cheering prolonged for several minutes." Addison could not speak in Parliament; but what has become of all the eloquence of his noisy contemporaries? And Sir Roger de Coverley is as fresh as ever. Gibbon could not speak. The good orators, he said, filled him with despair, and the bad with terror. What has become of them all good and bad? Burke's publications have kept his fame alive and will always keep it alive; and the fame of Fox, though perceptibly decreasing, is not extinct. As to the rest, – Dunning, Barré, Lord North, Sir G. Saville, Dundas, Thurlow, Wedderburne – what remains of them? Who would give the worst chapter of the Decline and Fall for all that is extant of their eloquence? Would it be worth the while of a man who need not despair of equalling Gibbon to kill himself with bodily fatigue and mental anxiety at 55, when he might live in comfort, health and ease till 70, in order to leave a reputation like that of Col. Barré?

I say nothing of the present aspect of the political world, because everything may be changed before I reach England. Yet I must say that, as far as I can look forward, I see nothing in the prospect except separations of friends, coalitions with opponents, bitter enmities, questions which will stir up all the fiercest passions of men. This consideration has great weight with me. I doubt whether, if I took part in politics, I should not within a few years, be in strong opposition on most exciting questions to Rice, to Lord Lansdowne, to Lord Glenelg. Remember that the choice which I shall have to make is not a choice for a day. It is in my power to determine not to go into parliament. But it will not be in my power whenever a crisis comes which separates me from my most valued friends, to retire to private life. No public man has a right to steal off at the conjunctures which require vigorous exertion. But no man is bound to be a public man. A soldier is justly disgraced who quits the service on the morning of an engagement. But no man is bound to be a soldier. He is to consider before he embraces the profession whether he has courage for a day of battle. But when he has embraced the profession he must not abandon it in the hour of danger. I think that the rules of political life are very similar. It is a man's business before he engages in politics to consider whether he is prepared to make all the sacrifices of private feelings which are likely to be required by his public duty. I am certain that I am not so prepared. If I do engage in politics I hope that I shall have fortitude enough to act rightly at any cost. But the cost of acting rightly would probably be to a person of my opinions and feelings exceedingly great. I may change my mind. I profess to tell you only what I at this moment think. But my opinion has been unchanged or rather has been growing in strength during several years – and my judgment tells me that if I should swerve from my present resolution I shall bitterly repent my error.

I am ashamed to see what a quantity of paper I have filled with nothing but egotism. So I will leave off talking of myself and say a few words about my friends. A letter has arrived from Napier. The news which it contains about his health is a little and but a little better than what you sent. The article on Malthus is very good and interesting, – a little immoderate in eulogy perhaps; but that is a becoming fault in a funeral oration pronounced by a friend, particularly when that oration partakes of the nature of a defence against calumny and scurrility. You are quite right in falling on Coleridge. It is quite intolerable that a man on whose grave stone flattery could not venture to write the hackneyed praise of being a good husband and father, – a lazy sot, stupified by opium, – should, in the intervals between 'his drunken dozes' abuse the best men of his time, and that these Fescennine rants should be published as oracles. If I had not eaten in old times some grains of salt with Henry Coleridge and some bushels with Derwent I should be half inclined to try whether I could not say when sober some things which would [go] quite as deep as any that their kinsman said when he was tipsy.

MS: British Museum. *Mostly published:* Napier, *Correspondence*, pp. 256–8.

3 Clarges Street June 26. 1838

Dear Napier,

I assure you that I would willingly and even eagerly undertake the subject which you propose if I thought that I should serve you by doing so. But, depend upon it, you do not know what you are asking for. I have done my best to ascertain what I can and what I cannot do. There are extensive classes of subjects which I think my self able to treat as few people can treat them. After this you cannot suspect me of any affectation of modesty. And you will therefore believe that I tell you what I sincerely think when I say that I am not successful in analyzing the effect of works of genius. I have written several things on historical, political, and moral questions of which, on the fullest reconsideration, I am not ashamed, and by which I should be willing to be estimated. But I have never written a page of criticism on poetry or the fine arts which I would not burn if I had the power. I leave it to yourself to make the comparison. I am sure that on reflection you will agree with me. Hazlitt used to say of himself "I am nothing if not critical." The case with me is directly the reverse. I have a strong and acute enjoyment of great works of the imagination; but I have never habituated myself to dissect them. Perhaps I enjoy them the more keenly for that very reason. Such books as Lessing's Laocoön, – such passages as the criticism on Hamlet in Wilhelm Meister fill me with wonder and despair. Now a review of Lockhart's book ought to be a review of Sir Walter's literary performances. I enjoy many of them, – nobody, I believe, more keenly. But I am sure that there are hundreds who will criticize them far better. Trust to my knowledge of myself. I never in my life was more certain of anything than of what I tell you: and I am sure that Lord Jeffrey will tell you exactly the same.

There are other objections of less weight, but not quite unimportant. Surely it would be desirable that some person who knew Sir Walter, – who had at least seen him and spoken with him, – should be charged with this article. Many people are living who had a most intimate acquaintance with him. I know no more of him than I know of Dryden or Addison, – not a tenth part so much as I know of Swift, Cowper, or Johnson. Then again, I have not, from the little that I do know of him, formed so high an opinion of his character as most people seem to entertain and as it would be expedient for the Edinburgh Review to express. He seems to me to have been most carefully and successfully on his guard against the sins which most easily beset literary men. On that side he multiplied his precautions, and set double watch. Hardly any writer of note has been so free from the petty jealousies and morbid irritabilities of our caste. But I do not think that he kept himself equally pure from faults of a very different kind, – from the faults of a man of the world. In politics a bitter and unscrupulous partisan, – greedy of gain – profuse and ostentatious in expense, – agitated by the hopes and fears of a gambler, – perpetually sacrificing the perfection of his compositions and the durability of his fame to his eagerness for money, – writing with the slovenly haste of Dryden in order to satisfy wants which were not, like those of Dryden, caused by circumstances beyond his controul, but which were produced by his own extravagant waste or rapacious speculation; – this is the way in which he appears to me. I am sorry for it. For I sincerely admire the greater part of his works. But I cannot think him a high-minded man or a man of very strict principle. Now these are opinions which, however softened, it would be highly unpopular to publish, particularly in a Scotch Review.

But why cannot you prevail on Lord Jeffrey to furnish you with this article? No man could do it half so well. He knew and loved Scott; and would perform the critical part of the work – much the most important – incomparably. I have said a good deal in the hope of convincing you that it is not without reason that I decline a task which I see that you wish me to undertake.

I am quite unsettled. Breakfasts every morning – dinners every evening and calls all day prevent me from making any regular exertion. My books are at the baggage warehouse. My book-cases are in the hands of the cabinet-maker. Whatever I write at present I must, as Bacon somewhere says, spin like a spider, out of my own entrails. And I have hardly a minute in the week for such spinning. London is in a strange state of excitement. The western streets are in a constant ferment. The influx of foreigners and rustics has been prodigious, and the regular inhabitants are almost as idle and curious as the sojourners. Crowds assemble perpetually, nobody knows why, with a sort of vague expectation that there will be something to see, and after staring at each other, disperse without seeing any thing. This will last till the Coronation is over. The only quiet haunts are the streets of the city. For my part I am sick to death of the turmoil, and almost wish my self at Calcutta again, or becalmed on the Equator.

Empson is happy by this time. I shall not therefore trouble you with any kind remembrances to him. But give Jeffrey every sort of affectionate message from me.

Ever yours most truly
T B Macaulay

Text: Trevelyan, II, 33–4.

[Rome]

Rome was full enough of English when I arrived, but now the crowd is insupportable. I avoid society, as much as I can without being churlish; for it is boyish to come to Italy for the purpose of mixing with the set, and hearing the tattle, to which one is accustomed in Mayfair. The Government treats us very well. The Pope winks at a Protestant chapel, and indulges us in a reading-room, where the Times and Morning Chronicle make their appearance twelve days after they are published in London. It is a pleasant city for an English traveller. He is not harassed, or restrained. He lives as he likes, and reads what he likes, and suffers little from the vices of the administration; but I can conceive nothing more insupportable than the situation of a layman who should be a subject of the Pope. In this government there is no avenue to distinction for any but priests. Every office of importance, diplomatic, financial, and judicial, is held by the clergy. A prelate, armed with most formidable powers, superintends the police of the streets. The military department is directed by a Commission, over which a Cardinal presides. Some petty magistracy is the highest promotion to which a lawyer can look forward; and the greatest nobles of this singular State can expect nothing better than some place in the Pope's household, which may entitle them to walk in procession on the great festivals. Imagine what England would be if all the Members of Parliament, the Ministers, the Judges, the Ambassadors, the Governors of Colonies, the very Commanders-in-Chief and Lords of the Admiralty, were, without one exception, bishops or priests; and if the highest post open to the noblest, wealthiest, ablest, and most ambitious layman were a Lordship of the Bed chamber! And yet this would not come up to the truth, for our clergy can marry; but here every man who takes a wife cuts himself off for ever from all dignity and power, and puts himself into the same position as a Catholic in England before the Emancipation Bill. The Church is therefore filled with men who are led into it merely by ambition, and who, though they might have been useful and respectable as laymen, are hypocritical and immoral as churchmen; while on the other hand the State suffers greatly, for you may guess what sort of Secretaries at War, and Chancellors of the Exchequer, are likely to be found among bishops and canons. Corruption infects all the public offices. Old women above, liars and cheats below, – that is the Papal administration. The States of the Pope are, I suppose, the worst governed in the civilised world; and the imbecility of the police, the venality of the public servants, the desolation of the country, and the wretchedness of the people, force themselves on the observation of the most heedless traveller. It is hardly an exaggeration to say that the population seems to consist chiefly of foreigners, priests, and paupers. Indeed, whenever you meet a man who is neither in canonicals nor rags, you may bet two to one that he is an Englishman.

TO MRS CHARLES TREVELYAN, 20 MARCH 1839

Text: Copy, Trinity College. *Partly published:* Trevelyan, II, 51–2.

London March 20 1839

Dearest Hannah,

I have passed some very melancholy days since I wrote last. On Sunday afternoon I left Ellis tolerably cheerful. His wife's disorder was abating. The next day when I went to him I found the house shut up. I meant only to have asked after him: but he would see me. His sister who lost her own husband but a little while ago, told me that he was so strangely composed and firm that they were all very uneasy about him. I found him so. But it did not last. I was indeed myself very much touched when I went into the room, and thought how, only a month ago, she was there, the centre of such a happy circle, so amiable, so cheerful, so intelligent, so singularly cordial and graceful in her attentions to all his friends, so excellent a wife and mother, and still, though past her prime, a woman whom any man might love. He gave way to very violent emotion; but he soon collected himself, and talked to me about her for hours, sometimes convulsed by his feelings for a minute or two, but then recovering and going on again. They were married as soon as he left college, and had lived together eighteen years without, he said, a single cross word on either side. He supported himself on the whole wonderfully. He said that the reality was nothing to the suspense. While there was still some faint hope he was almost distracted. Poor fellow – he prayed bitterly to God to take him too. But he was quite calm when I was with him, and said that he had been wickedly impatient, and that it was most ungrateful, after having been during eighteen years happier than anybody whom he knew, to repine now. "Yet" he said "I was so proud of her. I loved so much to shew her to anybody that I valued. And now what good will it do me to be a Judge or to make ten thousand a year? I shall not have her to go home to with the good news." I could not speak, for I know what that feeling is as well as he. He talked much of the sources of happiness that were left to him, his children, his relations, and hers, and my friendship. –

He ought, he said, to be very grateful that I had not died in India, but was at home to comfort him. Comfort him I could not, except by hearing him talk of her with tears in my eyes. I staid till late. Yesterday I went again, and passed most of the day with him. He was composed, with occasional violent bursts of feeling. He talked of books and politics; but always came back to her. He talked also of his plans about his children which are not yet quite fixed. He has made me one of his executors. I shall go to him again today. For he says, and I see, that my company does him good. I would with pleasure give one of my fingers to get him back his wife, which is more than most widowers would give to get back their own.

I have had my proofs from Napier and am to have a revise. He magnifies the article prodigiously. In a letter to Empson he calls it exquisite and admirable, and to me he writes that it is the finest piece of logic that ever was printed. I do not think it is so. But I do think that I have disposed of all Gladstone's theories unanswerably; and I do 'not think that there is a line of [the] paper with which even so strict a judge as Sir Robert Inglis or my uncle Babington could quarrel as at all indecorous. I think that it will make some stir. I shall write no more till I am paid for it. I have just had Longman's account, by which I find that, if I were to be paid at the very lowest rate which is given for the worst articles, I ought to receive 180 £, and that, at the rate at which he used to pay me, I ought to receive 500 £. This is really too bad. But pray say nothing about it.

I am impatient for the 4th of April. I dine out on that day, and cannot help myself. For the party was made partly on my account. But I will certainly manage to see you. I am delighted to hear that my dear Baba plays at seeing Uncle waiting for her. Is she old enough to take care of a canary-bird or two? From her tenderness for the little fish, I think I may venture to trust her with live animals. – Here is a song for her.

> There was a little good Baba,
> And she said to her dear Papa,
> My dear Papa, I do so wish
> You would not catch the little fish.
> Then said Papa, "Why not my Jewel?"
> Then said Baba, "It is so cruel.
> If you were run through with a hook,
> And pulled along, and boiled by Cook,
> You would not think it nice at all,
> But you would kick and roar and squall.
> So let the little fishes play,
> Papa, and do not hurt them pray."

Love to Trevelyan and Baby Brother. When I talked of parties I forgot that Edward had a share in the house.

Ever yours

T B M

I have this instant a note from Lord Lansdowne who was in the Chair of *the* Club yesterday night to say that I am unanimously elected. Poor Ellis's loss had quite put it out of my head.

TO LADY HOLLAND, 3 MAY 1839

MS: British Museum. *Mostly published:* Sonia Keppel, *The Sovereign Lady,* 1974, p. 306.

Clarges Street / May 3. 1839

Dear Lady Holland,

Thank you for the loan of Eden's Book. It will, I have no doubt, be of great use to me. Lord Fitzwilliam was exceedingly friendly and cordial, and seemed greatly interested about my plan: and, as his faults are by no means those of a courtier, I am convinced that he was sincere. The assistance which he offers will be most valuable.

My present object is to collect as many facts as I can to illustrate the internal arrangements of private families towards the close of the seventeenth century. I have got the household books of an old Leicestershire family with which I am connected; and there I find full accounts of their income, their expenses, what they gave Lord Rutland's cook when they dined at Belvoir, what the son at Cambridge and the son at Westminster cost them, and so forth. Lord Fitzwilliam promises me similar information about his own family and some others in a much higher line of life. These are, in my opinion, the real materials of history. I have found more historical information in a small receipt-book than in a folio of diplomatic correspondence. I hope to get at the very ancient books of one or two of the oldest banks in London. They will no doubt contain much curious information.

Whether I shall succeed I cannot tell. But I shall do my best to place my readers in the England of the seventeenth century. I have had so many proofs of your kindness that I need not ask you to suggest to me any thing that may occur to you.

I certainly shall not forget Sunday. / Ever, dear Lady Holland,

Yours most faithfully,

T B Macaulay

MS: Trinity College. *Address:* Mrs. C. E. Trevelyan / 30 Nottingham Place / New Road. *Subscription:* T B Macaulay.

Oman's Hotel Edinburgh / Wednesday May 29. 1839

Dearest Hannah,

I got here on Monday evening, – harangued a great meeting of electors to day, – succeeded well – was most favourably received, – and am, I believe, as secure as if I were already returned. The Chartists have not twenty votes. The Radicals who stop short of Chartism have all joined me on the ground of the ballot though I have positively declared against descending below the 10 £ franchise. The Tories have not brought forward any candidate; and it is fully believed that they will bring forward none. If they do he has no chance at all. But a contest would make a considerable difference in the expence. As things stand I shall come in, I hope, for a mere trifle. I will send you a newspaper to morrow, if there should be one containing a good account of our proceedings.

I am in our old hotel ánd in our old rooms. Nothing is changed. The sight makes me sad whenever the incessant hurry of business allows me a moment to think.

When the election will take place is not yet fixed. But we hope that it will be on Tuesday next. If so I shall be in London again on Thursday afternoon. A fellow here – an ironmonger – tried to get up some stir about the Black Act; but sank under universal derision and contempt. The subject was not mentioned at the meeting to day.

Love to Selina, Fanny, Trevelyan, Edward, Charley etc. etc. – Does my dear Baba miss me? – Love to her and Baby Brother.

Ever yours

T B M

TO LORD MELBOURNE, 2 NOVEMBER 1840

MS: Royal Archives, Windsor Castle.

London November 2. 1840

Dear Lord Melbourne,

I have for some time been very desirous to call your attention to a matter personally interesting to myself. My brother, the Reverend John Macaulay, has for some years had the living of Loppington in Shropshire, worth about 250 £ a year. He has, I believe, established his character as a respectable parish priest. He is a good Whig, but very quiet and moderate as a clergyman should be; and I learn from several quarters that he has the good word of the Tory gentlemen in his neighbourhood. For his general character I might refer to the Bishop of Lichfield.

I do not think that my brother's tastes or qualifications are suited to a large town. But if it were in your power at any time to remove him to some country benefice of more value than that which he now holds, I really think that the appointment would be in itself a good one; and I should feel it as a great kindness. You will not suppose that I intend to dun you. I am quite sensible of the difficulties of your position; and shall not be in the least surprised or angry if you should not find it in your power to serve my brother. / Believe me

Yours very truly
T B Macaulay

TO THOMAS FLOWER ELLIS, [21 NOVEMBER 1840]

MS: Trinity College.

12 Gt. George St / Saturday
Dear Ellis,

I am just come back from council. All is as well as possible. The child is in excellent case; – the mother better than could be expected. She has had an hour's fine sleep since her delivery, and has taken refreshment. She behaved heroically. The great officers distinctly heard the cry of the child the moment that it was born; but the Queen never uttered a groan. Lord Albemarle told me that she only once asked whether it would soon be over. When she was told that it was a princess, she said "The next will be a boy." She desired Albert to go to the Council, saying that his appearance there would do more than anything to satisfy people about her health. Albert came to us in the highest spirits, and exulted (but do not mention this) over the poor King of Hanover.

Ever yours
T B Macaulay

TO LEIGH HUNT, 27 MARCH 1841

MS: British Museum. *Mostly published: The Correspondence of Leigh Hunt,* 1862, II, 9–10.

War Office March 27 / 1841
My dear Sir,

I have just had a long conversation with Lord Melbourne, on whom I have pressed your claims with as much urgency as I thought my self justified in using. I have not time to give you particulars, some of which would be curious and amusing. At last he told me that he feared a pension was out of the question, but that he would try to do something for you. This is less than I wished, but more, I own, than I expected.

I assure you that your letter has affected me much. I am sorry and ashamed for my country that a man of so much merit should have endured so much distress. I am far from rich. My office adds quite as much to my expenses as to my income; and I have several near relations dependent on me. I have however been sufficiently frugal to have the means of indulging now and then in an extraordinary luxury; and I am happy to say that I can at present spare without inconvenience the sum which I inclose. It will give me great pleasure to learn that it has enabled you to meet the pressure of immediate demands.

I heard the other day from one of poor Southey's nephews that he cannot live many weeks. I really do not see why you might not succeed him. The title of Poet Laureate is indeed ridiculous. But the salary ought to be left for the benefit of some man of letters. Should the present government be in office when a vacancy takes place, I really think that the matter might be managed. / Believe me, / My dear Sir,

Yours very faithfully

T B Macaulay

TO FRANCES MACAULAY, 28 JUNE 1841

MS: Trinity College. *Partly published:* Trevelyan, II, 92.

Edinburgh June 28. 1841

Dearest Fanny,

Things have been looking worse here. A non-intrusion opposition has been threatened. My language on Saturday displeased the violent churchmen, and they have been minded even to coalesce with the Tories against me. High Churchmen and Tories united could not, I believe, shake me. But it would have been a very unpleasant affair. The leading non-intrusionists however have had a conference with me, and, though we do not exactly agree, they own that they shall get more from me than from a Tory, and are now cordially on my side. I do not think that there is now any serious risk of a contest; – there is none at all of a defeat. But in the meantime I am surrounded by the din of a sort of controversy which is most distasteful to me. – "Yes, Mr. Macaulay; that is all very well for a statesman. But what becomes of the headship of our Lord Jesus Christ?" And I cannot answer a constituent quite as bluntly as I should answer any body else who might reason after such a fashion.

The account of the meeting of Saturday I have sent to Hannah, and begged her to forward it to you as soon as she has read it. I have no other copy at present. But I suppose that you will get the Scotch newspapers in town.

I have been vexed at hearing nothing about the little things, particularly as I left them not quite well; – vexed also at not hearing how Selina got over her exertion of Tuesday last. However if you have not written it is [. . . .]

TO THOMAS FLOWER ELLIS, 12 JULY 1841

MS: Trinity College. *Partly published:* Trevelyan, II, 92–4.

London July 12. 1841

Dear Ellis,

I cannot send you Virginia; for I have not a copy by me at present, and have not time to make one. When you return I hope to have finished another ballad on the Lake Regillus. I have no doubt that the author of the original ballad had Homer in his eye. All the legend of the Tarquins indeed has a touch of the Greek. The origin of the house is linked by the old tradition to the seditions of Corinth. The story of the pilgrimage of the Princes to Delphi is Greek all over. The œnigmatical oracles are quite Herodotean. The stratagem by which Gabii is taken, and the council given by Tarquin to Sextus are taken from Clio and Thalia, if I recollect right. The battle of the Lake Regillus is a purely Homeric battle. I am confident that the ballad maker had heard or read the fight over the body of Patroclus, or that over the body of Sarpedon. The whole is made up of single combats – quite in the style of Homer. There is a furious struggle for the corpse of Marcus Valerius – Homer again, and not exactly in the Roman fashion. Herninius strips Manilius of his rich arms, and is himself killed while doing so, – Homer to the life. Lastly the introduction of two Greek Gods who probably were hardly known much to the north of Tarentum in the age of the Tarquins confirms me in the opinion that this part of the legendary history of Rome was not purely national and Italian, but was fashioned on Greek models. We will talk more about this. I must think of writing a preface and a few notes. I may perhaps publish a small volume next spring. I am encouraged by the approbation of all who have seen these little pieces. – I find the unlearned quite as well satisfied as the learned.

I have taken a very comfortable little suite of chambers in the Albany; – and I hope to lead during some years a sort of life peculiarly to my taste – college life at the West end of London. I have an entrance-hall, two sitting rooms, a bed-room, a water-closet, a kitchen, cellars and two bed-rooms for servants, all for ninety guineas a year, and this in a situation which no younger son of a Duke need be ashamed to put on his card. Indeed there is a younger son of a Duke on my stair-case. We shall have, I hope, some very pleasant breakfasts there, to say nothing of dinners. My own housekeeper will do very well for a few plain dishes, and the Clarendon is within a hundred yards.

I own that I am quite delighted with our prospects. A strong opposition is the very thing that I wanted. I shall be heartily glad if it lasts till I can finish a history of England from the revolution to the accession of the House of Hanover. Then I shall be willing to go in again for a few years. It seems clear that we shall be just about 300. This is what I have always supposed.

Your ballads are delightful. I like that of "Ips, Gips, and Johnson" best. Napoleon is excellent, but hardly equal to the Donkey wot wouldn't go. Some of your poems were too loose for my modest collection.

I cannot lay my hand on our Edinburgh newspapers. There was nothing in them very particular. I got through very triumphantly and very cheap. I believe that I can say what no other man in the kingdom can say – I have been four times returned to parliament by cities of more than a hundred and forty thousand inhabitants; and all those four elections together have not cost me five hundred pounds.

Ever yours
T B Macaulay

TO MACVEY NAPIER, 27 JULY 1841

MS: British Museum. *Mostly published:* Trevelyan, II, 96.

London July 27. 1841

Dear Napier,

I am truly glad that you are satisfied. I do not know what Brougham means by objecting to what I have said of the first Lord Holland. I will engage to find Chapter and Verse for it all. Lady H[olland] told me that she could hardly conceive where I had got so correct a notion of him.

I really hope and expect to be able to send you an article on Hastings by the middle of September or soon after. Keep the latest place open. I will try to compress my matter within ninety pages. It is a noble subject. I have got to the Rohilla war already.

I am not at all disappointed by the elections. They have ended very nearly as I expected. Perhaps I counted on seven or eight votes more. And even those we may get on petition. I can truly say that I have not for many years been so happy as I am at present. Before I went to India I had no prospect, in event of a change of government, except that of living by my pen, and seeing my sisters governesses. In India I was an exile. When I came back, I was for a time at liberty. But I had before me the prospect of parting in a few months, probably for ever, with my dearest sister and her children. That misery was removed. But I found myself in office, a member of a government wretchedly weak and struggling for existence. Now I am free. I am independent. I am in parliament, as honorably seated as man can be. My family is comfortably off. I have leisure for literature. Yet I am not reduced to the necessity of writing for money. If I had to chuse a lot from all that there are in human life, I am not sure that I should prefer any to that which has fallen to me. I am sincerely and thoroughly contented.

But I must not run on talking about myself. I like Leigh Hunt's article and Senior's. My sister has carried away the Review, so that I have not read Stephen's, which every body praises to the skies, and, I have no doubt, with perfect justice.

Ever yours
T B Macaulay

Brougham is quite right about Charles Fox – quite. He was indeed *a* great orator. But then he was *the* great debater.

TO LEIGH HUNT, 29 OCTOBER 1841

MS: British Museum. *Published:* Hunt, *Correspondence,* II, 23–5.

Albany October 29. 1841

My dear Sir,

I do not wonder that you are hurt by Napier's letter. But I think that you a little misunderstand him. I am confident that he has not taken any part of your conduct ill, and equally confident that by the expression, *gentlemanlike,* which certainly he might have spared, he meant not the smallest reflection either on your character or manners. I am certain that he means merely a literary criticism. His taste in composition is what would commonly be called classical, – not so Catholic as mine, nor so tolerant of those mannerisms which are produced by the various tempers and trainings of men, and which, within certain limits, are, in my judgment, agreeable. Napier would thoroughly appretiate the merit of a writer like Bolingbroke or Robertson; but would, I think, be unpleasantly affected by the peculiarities of such a writer as Burton, Sterne, or Charles Lamb. He thinks your style too colloquial; and, no doubt, it has a very colloquial character. I wish it to retain that character, which to me is exceedingly pleasant. But I think that the danger against which you have to guard is excess in that direction. Napier is the very man to be startled by the smallest excess in that direction. Therefore I am not surprised that, when you proposed to send him a *chatty* article, he took fright, and recommended dignity and severity of style, and care to avoid what he calls vulgar expressions, such as *bit*. The question is purely one of taste. It has nothing to do with the morals or the honor.

As to the tone of Napier's criticism, you must remember that his position with regard to the Review and the habits of his life are such that he cannot be expected to pick his words very nicely. He has superintended more than one great literary undertaking – the Encyclopædia Britannica, for example. He has had to collect contributions from hundreds of men of letters, and has been answerable to the publishers and to the public for the whole. Of course he has been under the necessity of very frequently correcting, disapproving, and positively rejecting articles, and is now as little disturbed about such things as Sir Benjamin Brodie about performing a surgical operation. To my own personal knowledge, he has positively refused to accept papers even from so great a man as Lord Brougham. He only a few months ago received an article on foreign politics from an eminent diplomatist. The style was not to his taste; and he altered it to an extent which greatly irritated the author. Mr. Carlyle formerly wrote for the review, – a man of talents, though, in my opinion, absurdly overpraised by some of his admirers. I believe, though I do not know, that he ceased to write because the oddities of his diction and his new words compounded à la Teutonique drew such strong remonstrances from Napier. I could mention other instances. But these are sufficient to shew you what I mean. He is really a good, friendly, an honorable man. He wishes for your assistance. But he thinks your style too colloquial. He conceives that, as Editor of the Review, he ought to tell you what he thinks. And, having during many years been in the habit of speaking his whole mind on such matters almost weekly to all sorts of people, he expresses himself with more plainness than delicacy. I shall probably have occasion to write to him in a day or two. I will tell him that one or two of his phrases have hurt your feelings, and that, I think, he would have avoided them if he had taken time to consider.

If you ask my advice, it is this. Tell him that some of his expressions have given you pain; but that you feel that you have no right to resent a mere difference of literary taste; – that to attempt to unlearn a style already formed and to acquire one completely different would, as he must feel, be absurd, and that the result would be something intolerably stiff and unnatural; but that, as he thinks that a tone rather less colloquial would suit better with the general character of the review, you will, without quitting the easy and familiar manner which is natural to you, avoid whatever even an unreasonably fastidious taste could regard as vulgarity. This is my honest advice. You may easily imagine how disagreeable it is to me to say anything about a difference between two persons for both of whom I entertain a sincere regard. / Believe me, / Dear Sir,

Yours very truly

T B Macaulay

TO MACVEY NAPIER, 5 NOVEMBER 1841

MS: British Museum. *Mostly published:* Trevelyan, II, 103–4.

Albany London Nov 5. 1841

Dear Napier,

Leigh Hunt has sent me a most generous and amiable letter which he has received from you. He seems much touched by it, and more than satisfied, as he ought to be.

I have at last begun my historical labours, I can hardly say with how much interest and delight. I really do not think that there is in our literature so great a void as that which I am trying to supply. English history from 1688 to the French revolution is even to educated people almost a *terra incognita*. I will venture to say that it is quite an even chance whether even such a man as Empson or Senior can repeat accurately the names of the prime ministers of that time in order. The materials for an amusing narrative are immense. I shall not be satisfied unless I produce something which shall for a few days supersede the last fashionable novel on the tables of young ladies.

I should be very much obliged to you to tell me what are the best sources for information about the Scotch revolution in 1688, – the subsequent administration in William's reign, – the campaign of Dundee – the massacre of Glencoe, – and the Darien scheme. I mean to visit the scenes of all the principal events both in Great Britain and Ireland, and also on the continent.

Would it be worth my while to pass a fortnight in one of the Edinburgh libraries next summer? Or do you imagine that the necessary information is to be got at the British Museum?

By the bye a lively picture of the state of the Kirk at that time is indispensable.

Ever yours
T B Macaulay

TO LORD JOHN RUSSELL, [LATE FEBRUARY? 1842]

MS: Public Record Office. *Mostly published:* G. P. Gooch, ed., *The Later Correspondence of Lord John Russell, 1840–1878,* 2 vols., 1925, I, 55–6.

[London]

[. . .] as on the writer; and it is necessary to think of the effect of the plate by candle light as well as of the sense and style. If a continuous inscription is preferred, and yours can, without injurious mutilation, be brought within the proper dimensions, nothing can be better.

And now a word as to the very kind reproof which you have given me. In one point you are a little mistaken. Society has not seduced me from the House of Commons. I have been much more frequently occupied by my books than by either dinner parties or routs when you have missed me on the opposition bench. To say the truth, I am convinced, after full and calm consideration, that literature is my vocation and not politics. It was the same with Mackintosh. The fault of Mackintosh was that he halted between two opinions. He fell between two stools. He attended too much to politics for a man engaged in a great literary work, and too much to literature for a man who aimed at great influence in politics. Society too, as you justly say, stole away too much of his time both from parliament and from his study. I am six or seven years younger than he was when he first entered parliament, and am already weaned from that ambition which was the bane of his life. The part of a political leader is not one to which I aspire. I have had longings of that sort. But they are over; and hopes and schemes of a more reasonable kind have taken their place.

Do not suppose however that I will flinch from your side when I am wanted. There are some questions on which I think that I can be of use: and whenever those questions are brought forward you may command me. Indeed it is probable that I shall be more active during the remainder of the Session than I have hitherto been.

Ever yours most truly
T B Macaulay

MS: British Museum. *Mostly published:* Trevelyan, II, 106–9.

Albany London / April 18. 1842

My dear Napier,

I am much obliged to you for your criticisms. My copy of the Review I have lent, and therefore cannot refer to it. But I have thought over what you say, and should be disposed to admit part of it to be just. But I have several distinctions and limitations to suggest.

The charge to which I am most sensible is that of interlarding my sentences with French terms. I will not positively affirm that no such expression may have dropped from my pen in writing hurriedly on a subject so very French. It is however a practice to which I am extremely averse, and into which I could fall only by inadvertance. I do not really know to what you allude. For as to the words Abbé, and Parc-aux-cerfs, which I recollect, those are surely not open to objection. I remember that I carried my love of English in one or two places almost to the length of affectation. For example I called the *Place des Victoires* the Place of Victories, and the Fermier-Général D'Étioles a publican. I will look over the article again when I get it into my hands and try to discover to what you allude.

The other charge, I confess, does not appear to me to be equally serious. I certainly should not, in regular history, use some of the phrases which you censure. But I do not consider a review of this sort as regular history. And I really think that from the highest and most unquestionable authority I could vindicate my practice. Take Addison, the model of pure and graceful writing. In his Spectators I find "wench," "baggage," "queer old put," "prig," "fearing that they should smoke the Knight." All these expressions I met this morning in turning over two or three of his papers at breakfast. I would no more use the words *bore* or *awkward squad* in a composition meant to be uniformly serious and earnest than Addison would, in a state-paper, have called Louis an old put, or have described Shrewsbury and Argyle as smoking the design to bring in the Pretender. But I did not mean my article to be uniformly serious and earnest. If you judge of it as you would judge of a regular history your censure ought to go very much deeper than it does, and to be directed against the substance as well as against the diction. The tone of many passages, nay of whole pages, would justly be called flippant in a regular history. But I conceive that this sort of composition has its own character and its own laws. I do not claim the honor of having invented it. That praise belongs to Southey. But I may say that I have in some points improved upon his design. The manner of these little historical essays bears, I think, the same analogy to the manner of Tacitus or Gibbon which the manner of Ariosto bears to the manner of Tasso, or the manner of Shakspeare's historical plays to the manner of Sophocles. Ariosto, when he is grave and pathetic, is as grave and pathetic as Tasso. But he often takes a light fleering tone which suits him admirably, but which in Tasso would be quite out of place. The despair of Constance in Shakspeare is as lofty as that of Œdipus in Sophocles. But the levities of the bastard Falconbridge would be utterly out of place in Sophocles. Yet we feel that they are not out of place in Shakspeare. So with these historical articles. Where the subject requires it they may rise, if the author can manage it, to the highest altitudes of Thucydides. Then again they may without impropriety sink to the levity and colloquial ease of Horace Walpole's Letters. This is my theory. – Whether I have succeeded in the execution is quite another question. You will however perceive that I am in no danger of taking similar liberties in my history. I do indeed greatly disapprove of those notions which some writers have of the dignity of History. For fear of alluding to the vulgar concerns of private life, they take no notice of the circumstances which most deeply affect the happiness of nations. But I never thought of denying that the language of history ought to preserve a certain dignity. I would however no more attempt to preserve that dignity in a paper like this on Frederic, than I would exclude from such a poem as Don Juan slang terms because such terms would be out of place in Paradise Lost, or Hudibrastic rhymes because such rhymes would be shocking in Pope's Iliad.

As to the particular criticisms which you have made, I willingly submit my judgment to yours, though I think that I could say something on the other side. The first rule of all writing, that rule to which every other rule is subordinate, is that the words used by the writer shall be such as most fully and precisely convey his meaning to the great body of his readers. All considerations about the purity and dignity of style ought to bend to this consideration. To write what is not understood in its whole force, for fear of using some word which was unknown to Swift or Dryden, would be, I think, as absurd as to build an Observatory like that at Oxford, from which it is impossible to observe, only for the purpose of exactly preserving the proportions of the Temple of the Winds at Athens. That a word which is appropriated to a particular idea, which every body, high and low, uses to express that idea, and which expresses that idea with a completeness which is not equalled by any other single word, and scarcely by any circumlocution, should be banished from writing, seems to be a mere throwing away of power. Such a word as *talented* it is proper to avoid, first because it is not wanted, secondly because you never hear it from those who speak very good English. But the word *shirk* as applied to military duty is a word which every body uses, which is the word and the only word for the thing, which in every regiment and in every ship belonging to our country is employed ten times a day, which the Duke of Wellington or Admiral Stopford would use in reprimanding an officer. To interdict the use of it therefore in what is meant to be familiar and almost jocose narrative seems to me rather rigid.

But I will not go on. I will only repeat that I am truly grateful for your advice; and that if you will, on future occasions, mark with an asterisk any words in my proof-sheets which you think open to objection, I will try to meet your wishes, though it may sometimes be at the expence of my own.

The article is not ill printed. But there are two rather vexatious mistakes for one of which I am answerable. The other was in the part of the article which I did not see in the proofs. Count Bruhl is everywhere turned into Count Buhl. And the word Herrhholds, which will puzzle many readers, is substituted for Sternholds.

I think the first article in the new Number very clever and good in many parts. I should be glad to know who wrote it. He has committed one monstrous blunder, inexcusable in so knowing a person. He says that India is a loss to England in consequence of the great sums which we are forced to advance for her government. I know of no such advances. The first time that such a thing was ever hinted at was by Sir Robert Peel the other day. The truth is that India pays her own expences to a farthing, and remits to England a vast tribute in the form of civil and military pensions, dividends on India Stock, etc.

Who wrote the paper on Moore? I could not, I will fairly own, get through it. The budget I suppose to be Senior's.

Ever yours most truly

T B Macaulay

TO MACVEY NAPIER, 24 JUNE 1842

MS: British Museum. *Mostly published:* Trevelyan, II, 110–12.

Albany London June 24. 1842

Dear Napier,

I have lent the last number of the review to somebody or other, and therefore cannot at present search for errata. Nor does it much matter. When once such mistakes are made it is vain to correct them in a subsequent number.

I have thought a good deal about republishing my articles, and have made up my mind not to do so. It is rather provoking, to be sure, to learn that a third edition is coming out in America, and to meet constantly with smuggled copies. It is still more provoking to see trash of which I am perfectly guiltless inserted among my writings. But on the whole I think it best that things should remain as they are. The public judges, and ought to judge, indulgently of periodical works. They are not expected to be highly finished. Their natural life is only six weeks. Sometimes the writer is at a distance from the books to which he wants to refer. Sometimes he is forced to hurry through his task in order to catch the post. He may blunder; he may contradict himself; he may break off in the middle of a story; he may give an immoderate extension to one part of his subject, and dismiss an equally important part in a few words. All this is readily forgiven if there be a certain spirit and vivacity in his style. But as soon as he republishes, he challenges a comparison with all the most symmetrical and polished of human compositions. A painter who has a picture in the exhibition of the Royal Academy would act very unwisely if he took it down and carried it over to the National Gallery. Where it now hangs surrounded by a crowd of daubs which are only once seen and then forgotten, it may pass for a fine piece. He is a fool if he places it side by side with the master-pieces of Titian and Claude. My reviews are generally thought to be better written, and they certainly live longer, than the reviews of most other people. And this ought to content me. The moment that I come forward to demand a higher rank, I must expect to be judged by a more severe standard. Fonblanque may serve for a beacon. His leading articles in the Examiner were extolled to the skies; and not without reason while they were considered merely as leading articles: for they were in style and matter incomparably superior to any thing in the Courier or Globe, or Standard, – nay to any thing in the Times. People said that it was a pity that such admirable compositions should perish. So Fonblanque determined to republish them in a book. He never considered that, in that form, they would be compared, not with the rant and twaddle of the daily and weekly press, but with Burke's pamphlets, with Pascal's letters, with Addison's Spectators and Freeholders. They would not stand this new test a moment. I shall profit by the warning. What the Yankees may do I cannot help. But I will not found any pretensions to the rank of a classic on my reviews. I will remain, according to the excellent precept in the Gospel, at the lower end of the table where I am constantly accosted with "Friend, go up higher," – and not push my way to the top at the risk of being compelled with shame to take the lowest room. If I live twelve or fifteen years I may perhaps produce something which I may not be afraid to exhibit side by side with the performances of the old masters.

I hope that your judgment agrees with mine: and I rather infer from your expressions that such is the case.

Ever yours truly
T B Macaulay

You say nothing about your own health.

Rio's book is very good indeed, but hardly a subject for me. There is an article on it in the Quarterly. It is a lively and pathetic narrative of a Breton insurrection against Buonaparte during the 100 days. I had imagined that he was going to treat the great Vendean war: and, I believe, he still means to do so.

TO THOMAS FLOWER ELLIS, 29 SEPTEMBER 1842

MS: Trinity College. *Partly published:* Trevelyan, II, 118–19.

Albany Septr. 29. 1842

Dear Ellis,

Can you dine and take a bed at Clapham on Wednesday or Thursday next. I can promise you a haunch from a good buck of the Queen's, and Trevelyan and my sister beg hard for your company, and give you your choice between the days. I shall be glad to know as soon as possible.

Many thanks for the sheets. I am much obliged to Adolphus for the trouble which he has taken. Some of his criticisms are quite sound. I admit that the line about bringing Lucrece to shame is very bad, and the worse for coming over so often. I will try to mend it. I admit also that the inventory of spoils in the last poem is, as he says, too long. I will see what can be done with it. He is not, I think, in the right about the word *pilum*. Nor is he in the right about the "true client smile." The "true client smile" is not exactly in the style of our old ballads. But it would be dangerous to make those old ballads models, in all points, for satyrical poems which are supposed to have been produced in a great strife between two parties crowded together within the walls of a city and a republican city. And yet even in an old English ballad I should not be surprised to find an usurer described as having the "ryghte Jew grinne," or some such thing.

As to the quantity of interjection at the end of the Triumphal song, I rather think that Adolphus is right. And I will try to cut out a few exclamations. But the triumphal songs which have come down to us would lead me to think that this was the style of those compositions

189

> "Tuque dum procedis, Io triumphe,
> Non semel dicomus, Io triumphe
> Civitas omnis" –

And again.

> Io triumphe, tu moraris aureos
> Currus et intactoes boves.
> Io triumphe, nec Jugurthino parem
> Bello reportaste ducem.

I am more obliged to Adolphus than I can express for his interest in these trifles. As to you I need say nothing. But pray be easy. I am so, and shall be so. Every book settles its own place. I never did and never will directly or indirectly take any step for the purpose of obtaining praise or deprecating censure. Longman came to ask what I wished him to do before the volume appeared. I told him that I stipulated for nothing but that there should be no puffing of any sort. I have told Napier that I ask it as a personal favour that my name and writings may never be mentioned in the Edinburgh Review. And I shall certainly leave this volume as the ostrich leaves her eggs in the sand. By the bye tell me whether you will breakfast with me on Saturday morning. Au revoir at Miladi's.

T B Macaulay

TO MACVEY NAPIER, 19 OCTOBER 1842

MS: British Museum. *Partly published:* Napier, *Correspondence*, pp. 408–9.

Albany Octr. 19. 1842

Dear Napier,

This morning I received Dickens's book. I have now read it.

It is impossible for me to review it: nor do I think that you would wish me to do so. I cannot praise it; and I will not cut it up. I cannot praise it, though it contains a few lively dialogues and descriptions. For it seems to me to be, as a whole, a failure. It is written like the worst parts of Humphrey's Clock. What is meant to be easy and sprightly is vulgar and flippant, as in the first two pages. What is meant to be fine is a great deal too fine for me, as the description of the fall of Niagara. A reader who wants an amusing account of the United States had better go to Mrs. Trollope, coarse and malignant as she is. A reader who wants information about American politics, manners, and literature, had better go even to so poor a creature as Buckingham. In short I pronounce the book, in spite of some gleams of genius, at once frivolous and dull.

Therefore I will not praise it. Neither will I attack it, first because I have eaten salt with Dickens; secondly because he is a good man and a man of real talent, thirdly because he hates slavery as heartily as I do, and fourthly because I wish to see him inrolled in our blue and yellow corps, where he may do excellent service as a skirmisher and sharp-shooter.

I think that when you have read the book, you will be of my mind, that the less we say about it the better. If you think it necessary to have a review, you can have no difficulty in finding a reviewer. But I, you perceive, am out of the question.

What then shall I do for you? The only subject that occurs to me is Madame D'Arblay: and I will try my hand on that, if you can arrange matters properly with Leigh Hunt. In order that you may fully understand my feelings, I must tell you, what I earnestly beg that you will not mention to any body, that he has some obligations to me of a sort which would make it the basest thing in the world in me to use him ill or even indelicately. As you have made up your mind that he shall not review Madame, I do not use him ill in taking the subject. But I wish to treat him with all delicacy. I think that you might without impropriety tell him that, as the latter part of the Memoirs related so much to the trial of Hastings to which I had paid particular attention, you had thought it for the interest of the review to give the subject to me. And indeed it is possible that I may take this opportunity of adding a few touches to my view of Hastings' character and administration, and of Burke's conduct respecting the impeachment. If you approve of this suggestion, I will also write a few lines to Hunt, such as may sooth his self-love. God knows, he has few soothings of that kind, poor fellow!

His article on Madame de Sévigné is not profound, but very good and pleasant. The number generally is, as you say, readable. But my friend Mangles's Indian speculations seem to me to become heavier and heavier.

I cannot conceive that there can be any objection to the publication of Lord Holland's letter. There are many things indeed in the letter from which I dissent. But on the whole it does Lord Holland great honor. Nor can it be from regard for him that Brougham objects to the publication. For in all the doctrines of Lord Holland about the war of 1815, doctrines from which I dissent, Brougham notoriously concurred.

Ever yours truly

T B Macaulay

My little volume will be out, I think, in the course of the week. But all that I leave to Longman, – except that I have positively stipulated that there shall be no puffing.

MS: Christ Church, Oxford. *Published: Notes & Queries*, October, 1967, p. 369.

Albany October 28. 1842

My dear Hallam,

I am delighted to learn that you found any thing in my little volume to please you. I published it not without many misgivings. The plan occurred to me in the jungle at the foot of the Neilgherry hills; and most of the verses were made during a dreary sojourn at Ootacamund and a disagreeable voyage in the Bay of Bengal. My sister who had a copy of them shewed them last year to poor Arnold. He wrote to me about them with great kindness, and urged me to complete them. But for this encouragement I should hardly have ventured before the public, either as a poet or as a lecturer on points of classical learning.

I had very great pleasure in seeing your son at Cambridge, and in learning, as I did, that he had already made a most favourable impression on those whose good opinion will be of the greatest consequence to him.

I spoke to him about sitting for the University Scholarship. He had not thought about the matter. But I earnestly hope that he will, on no account, omit to do so. The honor, if he gets it, is the highest of its kind in either University. The examination, even if he fails, is the best preparation for all other classical examinations. It is not likely that he will succeed the first time. That Thirlwall succeeded the first time was thought marvellous. But the names of all who acquit themselves creditably are well known, and are not seldom published by authority. That he will acquit himself creditably I have not the smallest doubt.

Will you breakfast with me on Tuesday next at ten?

Ever yours truly

T B Macaulay

TO MACVEY NAPIER, 16 NOVEMBER 1842

MS: British Museum. *Mostly published:* Napier, *Correspondence*, pp. 409–11.

Albany London Nov 16. 1842

Dear Napier,

On my return from a short tour I found your letter on my table. I am glad that you like my lays, and the more glad because I know that, from good-will to me, you must have been anxious about their fate. I do not wonder at your misgivings. I should have felt similar misgivings if I had learned that any person, however distinguished by talents and knowledge, whom I knew, as a writer, only by prose works, was about to publish a volume of poetry. Had I seen advertised a poem by Mackintosh, by Dugald Stewart, or even by Burke, I should have augured nothing but failure; and I am far from putting my self on a level even with the least of the three. Almost all my friends, I believe, expected that I should produce something deserving only to be bound up with Lord John's unlucky Don Carlos. So much the better for me. Where people look for no merit, a little merit goes a great way: and, without the smallest affectation of modesty, I confess that the success of my little book has far exceeded its just claims. I shall be in no hurry to repeat the experiment. For I am well aware that a second attempt would be made under much less favourable circumstances. A far more severe test would now be applied to my verses. I shall therefore, like a wise gamester, leave off while I am a winner, and not cry Double or Quits.

As to Madame D'Arblay, I will fall to work on her immediately. I took her memoirs, her novels, and her reminiscences of her father with me on my travels last week, and read them again from beginning to end. She was certainly a woman of talents and of many good qualities. But she had so many foibles, and the style which she wrote, particularly in her later years, was so execrable, that I heartily congratulate my self on having refused to come under any engagements to her family. I need not say that I shall not follow Croker's example. But truth and a regard for my own character and that of the Review will compel me to mix a little delicate censure with the praise which I shall most cordially and sincerely bestow. Four sheets will be ample.

I shall certainly not visit Edinburgh while your meeting of fanatical priests is sitting. Indeed your advice and that of Sir James Craig have almost determined me not to go among you this year. Is there any chance that we may see you in the spring?

I agree with you about the last Number, which has had very fair success here. You do not say what you purpose to do respecting Dickens and his American Notes. As to poor Leigh Hunt, I wish that I could say with you that I heard nothing from him. I have a letter from him on my table asking me to lend him money and lamenting that my verses want the true poetical *aroma* which breathes from Spenser's Faery Queen. I am so much pleased with him for having the spirit to tell me, in a begging letter, how little he likes my poetry, that I shall send him a few guineas, which I would not have done if he had praised me: for, knowing his poetical creed as I do, I should have felt certain that his praises were insincere.

Ever yours
T B Macaulay

MS: British Museum. *Mostly published:* Myron F. Brightfield, *John Wilson Croker*, Berkeley, 1940, pp. 132–4; 359.

Albany London Jany. 3 / 1843

Dear Napier,

I made a slight alteration yesterday in the passage about Croker, but an alteration which in no respect diminished the severity to which you object. I must say that I only regret that my expressions were not stronger. Nobody detests lampoons on private character more than I, or has less offended in that way. But I conceive that when there stands recorded in public documents proof of immoral and infamous conduct against a public man, an allusion to such conduct is perfectly justifiable. It is clear from the journals of the House of Commons that Croker played the spy on Mrs. Clarke. It was sworn by himself, only the other day, that he was the most intimate confidant of Lord Hertford, at a time when Lord Hertford's House was as scandalous a nuisance as ever the Key in Chandos Street or the White House in Soho Square were. It was sworn by the girls of Lord Hertford's harem before Lord Abinger that Croker used to dine with them. By compliances of this sort he has obtained a legacy from an old debauchee whose name is held in as much abhorrence by the country as ever was that of Colonel Chartres. Add to this all the scandals of Croker's literary life, his ferocious insults to women, to Lady Morgan, Mrs. Austin and others, – his twitting Harriet Martineau with her deafness, – his trying to raise the London mob to hoot Marshal Soult at the Coronation. I might add a hundred other charges. These, observe, are things done by a privy-councillor, by a man who has a pension from the country of 2000 £ a year, by a man who affects to be a champion of order and religion. To shrink from expressing the sentiments with which such a scandal to letters and society must be regarded seems to me unworthy of the Review. I had written these words "It is merely a speck in the life of one who got a good place by playing the spy on a courtesan in his youth, and a good legacy by turning parasite to a whole seraglio of courtesans in his old age." And I should have printed these words if I had been going to publish with my own name. But it occurred to me that the fellow, dastard as he is, might show fight, and might address himself to you as Wallace did, and that some embarrassment might be the result. I have no apprehension that any such step can by possibility follow, if the passage be suffered to stand as I have left it.

If these considerations do not satisfy you, you can cut out all that follows the word "better books." Or you may substitute for the words which you wish to omit the following words. "We shall give him the highest gratification which a nature like his is capable of feeling, when we inform him that his attack was most acutely felt by Madame D'Arblay."

That Croker asked her for materials and got none was told me by Wilbraham late M.P. for Cheshire, who had it from Mme. D'Arblay's own sister. He told me this, not loosely as people sometimes tell things in conversation, but as a fact which he had ascertained, and which ought to be mentioned in the Review. It is also so probable that I wonder that I never guessed it to be the explanation of Croker's rancour. He went about to every body, as I know, for materials; and certainly was not likely to pass by such a person as Madame, – the last survivor of the Streatham parties. That he got nothing from her may be seen by a glance at his book. Wilbraham added, what is likely enough, that Croker's letter asking for information was exceedingly rude and imperious.

A happy New Year to you.

Ever yours

T B Macaulay

TO ADAM BLACK, 22 FEBRUARY 1843

Text: [Adam Black, ed.], *Biographies by Lord Macaulay*, Edinburgh, 1860, pp. xiii–xvii.

London, February 22, 1843.

My dear Sir,

I have delayed answering your kind letter till I received Mr. Wigham's communication. My mind is quite made up. I am certain that the only chance of our getting any mitigation of the existing evils is to act together cordially against the sliding scale. If the party of the Anti-Corn-Law League choose to separate themselves from the supporters of a moderate fixed duty, and to run down Lord John and those who agree with him, I am inclined to believe that we shall have to wait many years for any real improvement. The truth is, that the friends of perfectly free trade, of whom I am sincerely one, are in general quite mistaken as to their own strength. They live in towns; they herd together; they echo and re-echo each other's sentiments; they are accustomed to see large meetings collected, all animated by the same feeling; and they have got into a habit of repeating that public opinion is for free trade, that monopoly is detested by all except the aristocracy, and so forth. One would think, to hear them, that the United Kingdom had no rural population at all. Take such a county as Essex, with a population and a constituent body more than twice as large as that of Edinburgh; or Devonshire, with a population and a constituent body nearly four times as large as that of Edinburgh; and let any candidate for those counties talk Cobden's language on the hustings: nay, let him talk Lord John's, or even Gladstone's, and see how he will be received. He will be an object of as much detestation to the body of the farmers and yeomen as the Duke of Cleveland would be to our friends of the High Street. The Irish county members form, as you well know, a great part of the strength of the Liberal party in the House of Commons. There is hardly one of them who, whatever his opinion might be, would dare to vote for total repeal. He would infallibly lose his seat. It is to no purpose to say that this is ignorance and prejudice. I know it well; but I also know that you must work with such tools as you have. You are a minority of the people, told by the head. The higher and higher you go, the smaller is your minority. What, under such circumstances, is your clear policy? To consider all as with you who are not against you, to sink as much as possible all differences which exist between people sincerely desirous of extending the freedom of trade, and to supply, by prudence and union, the deficiency of strength. Instead of this, the members of the Anti-Corn-Law League seem to be determined to drive support from them. As if it were not enough to have against them the Government, the Church of England, the Peers, the House of Commons, the majority of the elective body – the majority, I firmly believe, of the people of the United Kingdom – they must attack the very persons by whose help alone they can hope to get any thing at all. Can any man seriously think that any improvement can be made in the Corn Law till some government shall take the question up? Now, what materials are there for a government among the total and immediate repealers? To imagine that we shall have a cabinet excluding Peel, the Duke, Stanley, Graham, Lord Aberdeen, on the one side; excluding Lord John, Lord Palmerston, Lord Lansdowne, on the other, and consisting of leading members of the Corn-Law League, is quite idle. From an appeal to physical force all good men shrink with horror, and all judicious men know that if such an appeal were made, the Anti-Corn-Law League would come by the worse. But if there is to be no appeal to physical force, you can obtain no part of what you have in view, except by the support of one at least of the parties in the state. One of these parties is much nearer to you in sentiment than the other; but your policy, I mean that of the League, seems to be to treat them both alike with every species of indignity and contumely. Some purposes this course may answer. It may fill the bellies of itinerant spouters; it may circulate reams of bad writing; it may very likely put Mr. Sharman Crawford or Colonel Thompson into my seat at Edinburgh; but it will not strike off a farthing from the price of the quartern loaf. These are my opinions. I express them to you without the reserve which might be proper in a letter intended for the public eye; but I have only one story for you, for Mr. Wigham, for the

Cabinet, for the hustings, and for the House of Commons, though I may vary the phrase according to time and place. You see that, in my opinion, you are all in the wrong – not because you think all protection bad, for I think so too; not even because you avow your opinion and attempt to propagate it, for I have always done and shall always do the same; but because, being in a situation where your only hope is in a compromise, you refuse to hear of compromise; because, being in a situation where every person who will go a step with you on the right road ought to be cordially welcomed, you drive from you those who are willing and desirous to go with you half way. To this policy I will be no party. I will not abandon those with whom I have hitherto acted, and without whose help I am confident that no great improvement can be effected, for an object purely selfish. How could I ever hold up my head, if I did? What change has taken place since last year, when I refused to vote with Villiers. The Corn Law has grown no worse; the arguments against it are the same. The only difference is, that the feeling at Edinburgh is stronger; and that I may hazard my seat. Be it so. I am quite resolved to run the hazard; and of this I am certain, that if, holding the opinions which I have expressed, I did not run the hazard, you would despise me heartily.

Ever yours,
[T B Macaulay]

TO LEIGH HUNT, 27 APRIL 1843

MS: British Museum.

Albany April 27 / 1843

Dear Sir,

I am glad to say that I am able without inconvenience to spare the sum which you were so good as to leave at my chambers this morning. I send a cheque for the amount, as I do not like to trust sovereigns to the post, and shall be truly happy if it proves useful to you.

I have not had time to read the last Number of the Edinburgh Review. But I expect much amusement from your paper.

Very truly yours
T B Macaulay

TO LEIGH HUNT, 28 APRIL 1843

MS: British Museum.

Albany April 28 / 1843

My dear Sir,

You must allow me to send back the cheque. I should not have done what I did if it had not been quite consistent with justice to my self and to all connected with me. I cannot indulge in these luxuries often. But when they are within my reach, I hope that you will not deny them to me. / Believe me, / Dear Sir,

Yours very truly
T B Macaulay

TO LEIGH HUNT, 1 MAY 1843

MS: British Museum.

Albany May 1. 1843

My dear Sir,

I will not contend with your scruples. But I trust that you will consider me as your banker to the extent of the sum which you have repaid, should you be again in difficulties. / Believe me

Yours very truly
T B Macaulay

TO MRS CHARLES TREVELYAN, 21 AUGUST 1843

MS: Trinity College. *Address:* Mrs. Trevelyan / Clapham Common / near London. *Subscription:* T B M. *Partly published:* Trevelyan, II, 141–3.

Paris August 21. 1843

Dearest Hannah,

What people travel for is a mystery. I have never during the last forty eight hours had any wish so strong as to be at home again. To be sure those forty eight hours have hardly been a fair specimen of a traveller's life. They have been filled with little miseries, such as made Mr. Testy roar and Mr. Sensitive sigh. I could very well add a chapter to Beresford's book. For example –

Groan 1. The Brighton railway; – a slow train –; a carriage crowded as full as it would hold; a sick lady smelling of æther; a healthy gentleman smelling of brandy; the thermometer at 102° in the shade, and I not in the shade but exposed to the full glare of the sun from noon till half after two, the effect of which is that my white trowsers have been scorched into a pair of very serviceable nankeens.

Groan 2 – and for this Fanny is answerable, who made me believe that the New Steyne Hotel at Brighton was a good one. A coffee-room ingeniously contrived on the principle of an oven, the windows not made to open; a dinner on yesterday's pease and the day before yesterday's cutlets; not an ounce of ice; and all beverages, wine, water, and beer, in exactly the state of the Church of Laodicea.

Groan 3. My passage to Dieppe. We had not got out of sight of the Beachy Head lights when it began to rain hard. I was therefore driven into the cabin, and compelled to endure the spectacle, and to hear the unutterable groans and gasps, of fifty sea-sick people. My stomach must be a pretty strong one to stand, not only the sea, but the sight of the effects which the sea produces on others. I went out when the rain ceased. But everything on deck was soaked. It was impossible to sit down, so that I walked up and down the vessel all night. The wind was in our faces, and the clear grey dawn was visible before we entered the harbour of Dieppe. Our baggage was to be examined at seven, so that it was too late to go to bed, and yet too early to find any shop open or any thing stirring. All our bags and boxes too were in the custody of the authorities, so that I had to pace sulkily about the pier for a long time without even the solace of a book.

Groan 4. The Custom house. I never had a dispute with custom house officers before, having found that honesty answered in England, France, and Belgium, and corruption in Italy. But the officer at Dieppe, finding among my baggage some cotton stockings which had not been yet worn, threatened to confiscate them, and exacted more than they were worth – between thirteen and fourteen franks – by way of duty. I had just bought these unlucky stockings to do honor to our country in the eyes of foreigners, – being unwilling that the washerwomen of Paris and Orléans should see an English member of parliament's stockings either in holes or darned. See what the fruits of patriotism are.

Groan 5. Mine inn at Dieppe. I need not describe it. For it was the very same at which we stopped for a night in 1840, and at which you ate of a gigot as memorable as Sam Johnson's shoulder of mutton. I did not discover where I was till too late. I had a cup of coffee worse than I thought any French cook could make for a wager. In the bed room where I dressed there was a sort of soap which I had half a mind to bring away that men of science might analyse it. It would be, I should think, an excellent substitute for Spanish flies in a blister. I shaved with it, and the consequence is that I look as if I had that complaint which our mother held in such horror. If I used such cosmetics often I should be forced to beg Queen Victoria to touch me.

Groan 6. My journey to Rouen. I would have posted if I could have found a vehicle on reasonable terms. But the rascal at the inn asked, for six hour's hire of the most miserable old thing that ever was made of rusty iron and rotten leather, about as much as would procure the handsomest chariot in London for a week. If he lets his cabriolet one day in the year on such terms, he must find it a valuable property. Indeed I doubt whether, if it were sold by auction, it would fetch as much as was demanded for a loan of a morning. As I was angry at the way in which I had been treated at the custom house, I refused with great vehemence – "Je suis étranger. Je suis Anglais. Je suis pressé. Et vous croyez que vous pouvez me voler sans difficulté. Non – j'irai dans la Rotonde de la Diligence." Then the scoundrel came down, – five franks, – ten franks – but I was too angry to give in, and went off in the vilest part of the Diligence – for the coupé was engaged – rather than give him a farthing for his britschka, as he called it. The journey was as uncomfortable as could be, except that the rain of the preceding night had laid the dust. But the jolting, the swinging, the confinement, the heat, were such as no English stage coach equals. However we went quick. In that respect the French diligences have greatly improved since I first knew them. We ran the thirty five miles in four hours. Twelve years ago we should not have done it in seven hours. How the improvement [has] been effected I do not well understand. For the car[riages] look much as they always did. The roads are as bad as ever; and the coaches are of the same clumsy construction which diverted me when first I saw France.

I might groan again for Rouen. For I was wretchedly lodged and fed there. But in truth I was quite out of sorts, having passed the whole of the preceding night in walking about the deck of the steamer, and having tasted nothing for twenty four hours and more but an execrable dish of coffee at Dieppe. I never felt so faint in my life. The ground seemed to roll beneath my feet like the vessel on which I had been pacing for hours, and all objects moved like the waves of the channel. However I made a sort of meal which a little revived me and went to bed at eight, fearing that I was going to be ill. I instantly fell sound asleep, and woke at six this morning as well as ever I was in my life.

You have seen Rouen – and yet you have not seen it. For the weather was too bad to allow you to judge of it. It is a noble city, and, as respects Gothic Churches, I really think, unequalled. For though there are finer Gothic Churches than the Cathedral, and a very few finer even than St Ouen, I am not aware that two such Churches as the Cathedral and St Ouen – I mean of course Gothic Churches – are to be found in any city in the world. I admired the Cathedral less, and St Ouen more than I ever did. But I was really too unwell to be very observant. At nine this morning I started for Paris and here I am, at Meurice's – for the name remains, though the man is dead. I have two small but comfortable rooms, not unreasonably high up – that is to say, not more than half as high as the Monument. Having written to you, I am going to try whether Very's partridges and Burgundy retain their flavour. Kindest love to all.

Ever yours

T B M

Direct to me at the Poste Restante here.

TO LADY HOLLAND, 7 SEPTEMBER 1843

MS: British Museum. *Address:* The / Lady Holland / 33 South Street / Grosvenor Square / London. *Subscription:* T B M. *Extract published:* Sonia Keppel, *The Sovereign Lady*, p. 370.

Nantes September 7. 1843

Dear Lady Holland,

I write to you because you charged me to write to you, though I have little or nothing to say but what you either know or would not care to know. But I would rather send you a dull letter than appear to have forgotten your request, or to be insensible to the kindness which induced you to make it.

I have wandered far since we parted. I have seen Chartres and have been a little disappointed. The Cathedral is fine, but hardly deserves to be placed, as it generally is, in the highest rank among Gothic Churches. I had expected too much, and was therefore perhaps unable to do justice to what I found. At Orleans the case was directly reversed. There I expected nothing. I knew that the Cathedral was begun in the seventeenth Century, when all taste for the architecture of the middle ages was extinct even in men of such capacity as Inigo and Wren. That any really fine Gothic Church should have been built in such an age seemed to me altogether impossible. I expected something like the Gothic building, as it is called, in the grounds at Stowe. I found, to my astonishment, a fine Church, worthy on the whole of the thirteenth Century, disfigured undoubtedly in one or two places by ornaments in the Italian style, but not more disfigured in that way than many fine Churches of the thirteenth Century have in the course of time been. If I had been placed in the interior and asked to guess without previous information in what age those fine arches were built, I should with confidence have assigned a date earlier than even 1500. I cannot help thinking that some picture or model of the old Church which was destroyed in the religious wars must have guided the architect. But I have no means of knowing how this was.

I have seen Bourges too, with a mixture of admiration, interest, and disgust. The Cathedral is indeed superb. The exterior has often been surpassed. But I am not sure that I ever saw so fine an interior in that style; and I have seen all the finest Gothic Churches in England and France except Rheims. But the town is the strangest old place. The Revolution seems to have never touched it. It lies on no great road. It is cut off by a dreary barren tract of several hours' journey from the Orleannois. I have heard several Parisians say that Berry is a Terra Incognita to the rest of France. And certainly Bourges seems to belong to the age of Louis XVI, or rather of Louis XIV. The streets are mean, narrow and crooked, the shops and inns a hundred years behind those of any large city that I have seen in France. There is, I understand, in the neighbourhood an unusually great number of old and noble families. They have been so lucky as to keep or to recover a large part of their ancestral estates. Bourges is their Paris. They come thither to pass the winter, and have mansions there which look like the hotels of the Fauxbourg St Germain on a smaller scale, and which have moreover an indescribable queerness of appearance, and a squalidity which seems to be caused, not by poverty, but by aversion to change and by ignorance of modern usages. I saw at the door of one of these hotels, in a street like those occupied by Jew clothesmen in Wapping, a carriage with a Count's coronet and a most ostentatious coat of arms. I half expected to see M. de Sotenville and his lady step out of it. These great gentry and the clergy of the Cathedral seem to bear rule in Bourges. The self-importance and the bigotry of the lowest hangers on of the priesthood surpasses anything that I saw in Flanders. I was at the best inn, and there was no want of courtesy or disposition to oblige. But the discomfort was almost insufferable. The only salon was filled with all the inmates of the house and all the comers and goers of the town, mine host casting up accounts, mine hostess looking over linen, the dogs from the street fighting for a bone, two hand-maidens stitching, a little girl learning to write, a little boy learning to read, a coxcomb with a long beard and a cigar in his mouth, an old pantaloon reading a paper three weeks old, a beggar who had poked in his head and a wen larger than his head at the window, and was whining his "Pour l'amour de Dieu, Messieurs." Lastly there was the Englishman, myself, trying to forget his ill humour in a very naughty but very amusing novel by Paul de Kock.

My observations on the beds at Bourges led me to think that, if I slept there, I should make acquaintance with a portion of the zoology of Berry about which I was not curious. The men and dogs had been quite enough for me. Accordingly I set off by a night coach for Orleans, resolving that not even the Cathedral should ever tempt me thither again, at least until the projected rail-road has introduced civilisation among the savage inhabitants.

I have said so much about Bourges that I have no time to say anything about my voyage down the Loire. It interested me greatly. I was much pleased with Chambord, still more by the castle of Blois. But on the whole the castle of Angers is the finest sight that I have looked on since I left Orleans. I am happy to say that this evening I begin my journey homeward. On Sunday I hope to be in Paris, and on the following Friday in London.

I have nothing to tell you in the way of news. You in London are indeed far better informed about the proceedings of her Majesty than we at Nantes. I confess that I think the visit to Eu ill-timed. My reason is this. I fear that Louis Philippe will find it impossible to pay to the Queen the respect due to her rank and sex without irritating his own subjects. A royal guest, particularly a woman, ought to be received with something like homage; and, in the present temper of the people here, any departure on the part of Louis Philippe from the punctilious assertion of equality is considered as a national humiliation. The Nantes papers are furious because a French band has been ordered on French ground to play "God save the Queen." They are furious because a tricolor flag has been cut down to the same dimensions with the English flag displayed before her Majesty. Every galanterie to her is construed into a degradation of France. I wish, for my own part, that she had never come hither, and I hope that she will soon take her leave. / Ever, dear Lady Holland,

Yours most truly

T B Macaulay

TO MACVEY NAPIER, 25 NOVEMBER 1843

MS: British Museum. *Published:* Napier, *Correspondence*, pp. 448–51.

Albany London / November 25. 1843

Dear Napier,

Many thanks for your excellent letter. I have considered it fully: and I am convinced that, by visiting Edinburgh at present, I should do unmixed harm.

The question respecting the Catholic clergy is precisely in that state in which a discussion at a public meeting can do no good and may do great mischief. It is in a state requiring the most painful attention of the ablest heads; nor is it by any means certain that any attention or any ability will produce a satisfactory solution of the problem.

My own view is this. I do not on principle object to the paying of the Irish Catholic priests. I regret that such a step was not taken in 1829. I would even now gladly support any well digested plan which might be likely to succeed. But I fear that the difficulties are insurmountable.

Against such a measure are all the zealots of the High Church and all the zealots of the Low Church, the Bishop of Exeter and Hugh Macneil, Oxford and Exeter Hall, all the champions of the voluntary system, all the English dissenters, all Scotland, all Ireland, both Orangemen and Papists. If you add together the mass which opposed the late government on the education question, the mass which opposed Sir James Graham's education-clauses last year, and the mass which is crying out for repeal in Ireland, you get something like a notion of the force which will be arrayed against a bill for paying the Irish Catholic clergy.

What have you on the other side? You have the statesmen, both Tory and Whig. But no combination of statesmen is a match for a general combination of fools. And even among the statesmen there is by no means perfect concord. The Tory statesmen are for paying the Catholic priests, but not for touching one farthing of the revenue of the Protestant Church. The liberal statesmen, – I, for one, if I may lay claim to the name, – would transfer a large part of the Irish Church revenues from the Protestants to the Catholics. For such a measure I should think it my duty to vote, though I were certain that my vote would cost me my seat in parliament. Whether I would vote for a measure which, leaving the Protestant Church of Ireland untouched, should add more than half a million to our public burdens for the maintenance of the Popish priesthood, is another question. I am not ashamed to say that I have not quite made up my mind, and that I should be glad, before I made it up, to hear the opinions of others.

As things stand, I do not believe that Sir Robert, or Lord John, or even Sir Robert and Lord John united, could induce one third part of the members of the House of Commons to vote for any plan whatever of which the object should be the direct payment of the Irish Catholic priests.

Thinking thus, I have turned my mind to the best indirect ways of effecting this object; and I have some notions which may possibly bear fruit. To explain them would take too much time. I shall probably take an opportunity of submitting them to the House of Commons.

Now I can conceive nothing more inexpedient than that, with these views, I should, at the present moment, go down to Edinburgh. If I did, I should certainly take the bull by the horns. I should positively refuse to give any promise. I should declare that I was not, on principle, opposed to the payment of Catholic priests: and I should reserve my judgment as to any particular mode of payment till the details were before me. The effect would be a violent explosion of public feeling. Other towns would follow the example of Edinburgh. Petitions would pour in by thousands as soon as parliament had assembled; and the difficulties with which we have to deal, and which are great enough as it is, would be doubled.

What I have written will serve as an answer to your question about Senior. You see what my view of the question is. Lord Lansdowne's is a little, and but a little different. He is most strongly for paying the Catholic priests, and is fully prepared to do so, without touching the Established Church, by laying on fresh taxes. He agrees with me in thinking that the revenues of the Established Church would be the proper fund for the purpose. But he reasons thus – "To pay the priests is matter of life and death. We cannot do it without the help of the Tories. The Tories will never consent to touch the Protestant Establishment. We must therefore compromise the matter, and take what is second best, since we cannot have what is best." This, as I have said, is not exactly my view.

I do not however think that the Edinburgh Review ought to be under the same restraints under which a Whig cabinet is necessarily placed. The Review has not to take the Queen's pleasure, to count votes in the Houses, or to keep powerful supporters in good humour. It should expound and defend the Whig theory of government, a theory from which we are forced sometimes to depart in practice. There can be no objection to Senior's arguing in the strongest manner for the paying of the Catholic priests. I should think it very injudicious to lay down the rule that the Whig Review should never plead for any reforms except such as a Whig ministry could prudently propose to the legislature.

I have a plan in my head which, I hope, you will not dislike. I think of reviewing the memoirs of Barrère. I really am persuaded that I could make something of that subject.

Ever yours

T B Macaulay

TO UNIDENTIFIED RECIPIENT, 21 FEBRUARY 1844

MS: Berg Collection, New York Public Library.

Albany London Feb 21 / 1844

Dear Sir,

I am much obliged to you for the little work which you have sent me. I have looked at the pages to which you refer me, and find there much from which I dissent, but certainly not a word of which I have the smallest reason to complain.

As to Archbishop Cranmer, let me only ask to what part of the narrative which I have given of his life you object. Is there a word which you can pronounce incorrect in my statement of the facts? If not, I really should be glad to know how such a course of conduct can be reconciled,

I do not say with the exalted piety of a father of the Church, but with the principles and feelings of an honest man.

As to the other passage to which you refer, I quite agree with you in thinking that the accumulation of wealth and the progress of civilisation would be no blessings if accompanied by intellectual and moral deterioration. But I dispute your facts. My habits and studies have been of such a nature that I think myself not ill qualified to compare the past state of our country with its present state. I am confident that I could prove that the ignorance of the populace of our time is knowledge and their vice virtue when compared with the ignorance and vice of their great grandfathers. I will venture to say that if only the London of 1744 could be called up before us, and if we were to take a Sunday walk through it from St James's Street to Moor-fields, the spectacle of irreligion, of bestial stupidity, of obscenity, of barbarity, would utterly appal us, and make us thankful for living in the age in which we live. On the other hand I am confident that if John Wesley could see London as it now is, he would say that he could not have imagined so great a change for the better. His own early journals furnish plenty of evidence of what I say. This is no reason for not exerting ourselves to improve the moral and spiritual condition of the labouring classes. God forbid. But it is fit that the truth should be known, and that we should not imagine that the world is becoming worse and worse, when in reality our standard of excellence is becoming higher and higher.

To go into the evidence on this subject would be a long, indeed an endless, business. I have said enough to shew that we differ, if I understand you rightly, as to a question of fact which can be determined only by much historical research.

With many thanks for your kind mention of my dear father believe me ever

Yours very faithfully
T B Macaulay

TO [MRS CHARLES TREVELYAN?, 18? JUNE 1844]

MS: Morgan Library.

[London]

Well, the ministry is saved, but at the expense of the house of Commons. A pretty figure we make. I voted without hesitation against rescinding on Monday what had been done on Friday. I am glad that there is not a change of administration. But I see that the Peel government has received a mortal wound. The agony will be long and lingering as ours was. But dissolution has commenced. I do not envy any of the ministers, and least of all Sir Robert and Gladstone.

There was one odd circumstance on Monday. There was Knatchbull voting, chatting and laughing, just after receiving the news that his brother had been hanged for murder in New South Wales. All the evening papers were full of the story. And observe – a legitimate brother, who had been a captain in the navy, and who, failing the elder, would have been baronet. Should Charles be hanged at Mauritius, I shall certainly shut my self up at least twenty four hours after the arrival of the intelligence.

So poor Tom Campbell is dead. His wits had long been drunk away. There is talk of Westminster Abbey. If so, his remains will be brought, I suppose, by Dover. It is melancholy to think that, having lived to be sixty-four, and having gone on multiplying volumes of verse and prose to the last, he has never written a line worth reading since he was twenty eight. Hohen-Linden, the Battle of the Baltic, the Seaman's song, Lochiel, Gertrude of Wyoming were all published more than five and thirty years ago. Since that time he has been doing nothing but writing down his early reputation, and at last very nearly succeeded, by the help of morning draughts of gin and water. I did not like him personally. He was vulgar, coarse and swaggering; and was the only man whom I ever heard talk against Christianity boisterously and indecently in a large mixed company, not one of whom answered him. Perhaps he was tipsy, though it was at breakfast. For the argument, "it is but the third hour of the day," however forcible when used by St Peter, was by no means decisive as to Tom Campbell's sobriety. Love to all.

Ever yours
T B M

TO FRANCES MACAULAY, 6 JULY 1844

MS: Huntington Library.

Albany London July 6. 1844

Dearest Fanny,

Stephen's paper, like all other human things, has its faults. But I like it much. So does Napier; and so does Jeffrey. The complaints of the Thorntons disgust me, but do not surprise me. What possible impropriety can there be in mentioning, as part of the description of their father's way of life, his oval saloon and his lawn? I am quite sure that, if you were left to your own taste and judgment, you would find no fault with these allusions. When I wrote that little eulogy on poor Lord

Holland, I brought in the library at Holland House; and the family did not think that I had done any thing indelicate or unfriendly. The widow and every one of the children thanked me with tears. Where, I should be glad to know, is the difference? If I were to write an account of Hannah More, should I not mention the root-houses and China roses of Barley Wood? If I were to write an account of my uncle Babington, should I be justly censured if I were to introduce something about the Temple, the old oak, the Chapel, and the family portraits? If there had been any sarcasm thrown on the taste of the villa at Battersea Rise, I could understand Miss Isabella's indignation. But to be angry because an old friend describing her father has, in the kindest spirit and most graceful manner, brought in the library and tulip-trees as a back ground to the portrait, would, in any other people, be an incredible instance of folly and perverseness. It does not however amaze me. There is a certain odd, shy, irritable fastidiousness about the Thorntons where their parents are concerned, which I never saw in any other people. The only safe course with them is absolute silence. Praise they spurn as an insult. All effusions of affection to the memory of either their father or their mother, are met with supercilious coldness, if not with resentment.

What right have they to complain of what is said about their father's fortune? Is it false? Is it discreditable to him? Can it possibly be injurious to them? Was it not necessary to the correct exhibition of his character? And was not his character public property? He was a Senator, a writer, a party-leader. He has been thirty years in his grave. Was it not fit that facts which strongly illustrated the vigour of his principles and the magnificence of his spirit, and which could do no harm to any living being, should be known?

But in fact you have yourself completely vindicated Stephen from the absurd charge of having acted indelicately towards the Thorntons. For you say; " *We* personally have nothing to complain of, though the Thorntons have;" and again; "The few pages about our dear father are the best and least objectionable." Now, I am certain of this, that, if the Thorntons have a right to complain, we have ten times as good a right. In the first place our father has been dead only six years. His circumstances therefore ought to have been spoken of with more reserve than the circumstances of a person who has been dead thirty years. Stephen says plainly that our father died poor. This, I am sure, is much beyond any thing that he says of Mr. Thornton's money-matters. Then he says that our father had an ungraceful figure and an ineloquent tongue. Now I really think that this is much worse than saying of a man that he has an oval saloon and massive tulip-trees. Yet you complain of his account of Mr. Henry Thornton, and do not complain of his account of our father.

The truth is that you look at his account of our father with your own eyes, and at his account of Henry Thornton with your friend Isabella's eyes. If you looked at the whole paper with your own eyes, you would see that neither the Thorntons nor we have the smallest reason to complain; but that, if the feeling of the Thorntons were justifiable, we should have far more reason to complain than they.

I hope that you will not encourage your friend's folly, though I do not in the least suppose that you can cure it. Remember what we owe to James Stephen. Remember that, but for him, Hannah and her children would now be fifteen thousand miles from us, if indeed they had escaped the tropical maladies. This is always present to my mind, and may perhaps make me partial. But weigh what I have said; and tell me whether I do him, on this occasion, more than bare justice.

I breakfasted with Sydney to day. There were Lord Lansdowne, the American and Belgian Ministers, Milman, Senior, and that bore Macculloch, who however held his tongue, the best thing that he could do.

Pray let me know whether you have heard from the travellers, and when they return. If they come from Rotterdam they must land in the Thames, I imagine. I cannot learn that there is any packet between Rotterdam and Dover. Perhaps therefore I may see them before they rejoin you. Kindest love to the dear children.

Ever yours
T B M

The railway disputes have been accommodated: and Birmingham shares have risen five or six per Cent at once. I am three hundred pounds richer than I was yesterday.

TO MRS CHARLES TREVELYAN, 9 OCTOBER 1844

MS: Trinity College. *Partly published:* Trevelyan, II, 153–5.

Rotterdam October 9. 1844

Dearest Hannah,

After a very pleasant day at Antwerp I started at seven yesterday morning by the steamer. I had, after much consideration, determined to take a servant with me. The landlord of the hotel St Antoine recommended one very strongly, and said that he would answer for the man's fidelity, that he was *père de famille*, and would be ruined if he misconducted himself. I liked the fellow's round, red, honest Flemish face, and was very desirous to have with me somebody who knew Holland and its language.

I therefore struck the bargain, and have hitherto had every reason to be satisfied with my attendant's honesty, intelligence, and respectful behaviour. I dare say that he will save me in one way or other as much as his board and wages will amount to. And if not four or five pounds are well expended in buying comfort. A Dutch gentleman on board of the steamer recognised my servant, and told me that he was a highly respectable man of his class.

But I had an odder conversation than this on board the steamer, and one which, I think, will amuse both you and Trevelyan. As we passed Dordrecht, which is, as you may remember, the first Dutch town of any consequence on the voyage, one of the passengers, an Englishman, said that he had never seen any thing like it. Parts of it reminded me of some parts of Cape Town; and I said so. An elderly gentleman immediately laid hold of me. "You have been at the Cape, Sir?" "Yes, Sir." "Perhaps you have been in India?" "Yes Sir." "My dear, here is a gentleman who has been in India." So I became an object of attention to an ill-looking vulgar woman, who appeared to be the wife of my questioner, and to his daughter, a pretty girl enough, but by no means lady like. "And how did you like India? Is it not the most delightful place in the world?" "It is well enough," I said "for a place of exile." "Exile," says the lady, "I think people are exiled when they come away from India." "I have never," said the old gentleman, "had a day's good health since I left India." A little chat followed about mangoes and mango-fish, punkahs and palanquins, white ants and cock roaches. I maintained, as I generally do on such occasions, that all the fruits of the tropics are not worth a pottle of Covent Garden strawberries, and that a lodging up three pair of stairs in London is better than a palace in a compound at Chowringhee. My gentleman was vehement in asserting that India was the only country to live in. "I went there," he said, "at sixteen in 1800, and staid till 1830, when I was superannuated. If the Company had not chosen to superannuate me, I should have been there still. I should like to end my days there." I could not conceive what he meant by being superannuated at a time when he could have been only forty six years old, and consequently younger than most of the field-officers in the Indian army and than half the Senior Merchants in the Civil Service. However I was too polite to interrogate him. That was a politeness, however, of which he had no notion. "How long," he asked, "were you in India"? "Between four and five years." "A clergyman, I suppose." Whether he drew this inference from the sanctity of my looks, or from my olive-coloured coat and shawl waistcoat, I do not pretend to guess. But I answered that I had not the honor to belong to so sacred a profession. "A mercantile gentleman, no doubt." "No." Then his curiosity got the better of all the laws of good breeding, and he went straight to the point. "May I ask, Sir, to whom I have the honor of talking?" I told him. "Oh, Sir," said he, you must often have heard of me. I am Mr. Ricketts. I was long at Lucknow." "Heard of you, – " thought I –, "yes, and a pretty account I have heard of you." I should have at once turned on my heel and walked away if his daughter had not been close to us, and, scoundrel as he is, I could not affront him in her presence. I merely said with the coldest tone and look "Certainly I have heard of Mr. Ricketts." "And doubtless you know my friend Mr. Turton." Like to like, thought I, – a well matched pair. "No, Sir," I said pretty scornfully, "I do not know Mr. Turton." He went on: "You are related, I think, to a civil servant who made a stir about Sir Edward Colebrook." It was just at my lips to say "Yes; – it was by my brother-in-law's means that Sir Edward was superannuated." But I commanded myself, and merely said that I was nearly related to Mr. Trevelyan; and then I called to the Steward, and pretended to be very anxious to settle with him about some coffee that I had taken. While he was changing me a gold William I got away from the old villain, went to the other end of the poop, took out my book, and avoided looking towards him during the rest of the passage. And yet I could not help thinking a little better of him for what had happened. For it reminded me of what poor Macnaghten once said to me at Ootacamund. "Ricketts," he said, "has excuses which Colebrook and others have not had. For he is really so great a fool that he can hardly be called a responsible agent." I certainly never knew such an instance of folly as that to which I had just been witness. Had he been a man of common sense and feeling he would have avoided all allusion to India; or at any rate would have talked about India only to people who were likely to be unacquainted with his history. If he knew anything about me, he must have known that I was Secretary to the Board of Control when that Board expressed its entire concurrence in the measures taken by the Company against him. Then too the senseless folly of his turning the conversation to the case of Sir Edward Colebrook. To do him justice however he seemed at last to understand what I thought of him, and kept out of my way as carefully as I kept out of his. A dirty dog! But he is not worth any expense of anger.

You have so recently been over the ground which I am now traversing that I shall not plague you with my travels. I am in the highest degree delighted with Holland. This afternoon I proceed to the Hague. Pray let me find a letter from you at Antwerp. I shall be there, I hope, this day week, and in London on the 21st.

Love to all.

Ever yours,
T B M

MS: Trinity College. *Published:* Hunt, *Correspondence*, II, 35–6.

Albany November 19 / 1844

My dear Sir,

Thanks for your note and for your very pleasing and interesting little volume.

I do not know that we differ in judgment about Spenser. But there is a liking which does not depend on the judgment. I see Rousseau's genius as clearly as any of his admirers. But he does not attract me. I read Gil Blas once a year: and I do not care if I never see Rousseau's novel again. It is the same with painting. I know that the Raising of Lazarus in the National Gallery is a great work; and I partly feel its merit. But I look at it with little or no pleasure, and should be very little concerned if I heard that it was burned. On the other hand there are pictures of much less fame and power which, if I could afford it, I would hang over my fire-place, and look at half an hour every day. So with female beauty. If a man were to say that Mrs. Siddons was not a fine woman, we should think that he must have no eyes. But a man might well say that, though a fine woman, she did not attract him, that she did not hit his taste, and that he liked Miss Foote's or Miss O'Neil's looks better. Just so I say about Spenser. To deny him the rank of a great poet would be to shew utter ignorance of all that belongs to the art. But his excellence is not the sort of excellence in which I take especial delight.

I shall be most happy to see you when you are passing by. I had heard of your windfall, and heartily rejoiced at the news.

Yours very truly

T B Macaulay

TO MACVEY NAPIER, 6 DECEMBER 1844

MS: British Museum. *Mostly published:* Napier, *Correspondence*, pp. 476–7.

Albany London / December 6. 1844

Dear Napier,

Thanks for your kind letter. I am glad that you have such an abundance of materials for the Review. By the bye I hope that you will make your arrangements for some three or four numbers without counting on me. I find it absolutely necessary to concentrate my attention for the present on my historical work. You cannot conceive how difficult I find it to do two things at a time. Men are differently made. Southey used to work regularly two hours a day on the history of Brazil, then an hour for the Quarterly Review, then an hour on the life of Wesley, then two hours on the Peninsular War, then an hour on the Book of the Church. I cannot do so. I get into the stream of my narrative and am going along as smoothly and quickly as possible. Then comes the necessity of writing for the Review. I lay my history aside; and when, after some weeks I resume it, I have the greatest difficulty in recovering the interrupted train of thought. But for the Review I should already have brought out two volumes at least. I must really make a resolute effort. Or my plan will end as our poor friend Mackintosh's ended.

My last article, as far as I can learn, has been generally liked here. Brougham, I see, has been abusing it and indeed the Review generally, in the Morning Herald. But he has found nothing worse to say of it than that the phrase "Pleasant boon-companion," is incorrect. For, says this great master of the language, *boon* is *bon*; and *bon* is pleasant; therefore a pleasant boon-companion is a pleasant pleasant companion, which is a pleonasm. To what degradation spite can reduce very considerable parts. There is however one of his criticisms, not on myself, to the truth of which I cannot help assenting. I was very sorry, I own, to see such a paper as that on storms within the blue and yellow cover. I hope that there is no danger of our having any more eloquence from the same quarter. Such execrable bombast taints every thing that comes near it. I agree with Lord Dunfermline and Stephen in thinking the first article excellent. I do not understand why the public does it so little justice.

As to the Lord Rectorship, I should of course not refuse it. But I shall take no step whatever relating to it. For God's sake let nothing be done which can in the smallest degree hurt Rutherfurd's feelings or compromise his interests.

I found the 110 £ at my banker's. All is quite right. –

Ever yours
T B Macaulay

TO MRS CHARLES TREVELYAN, 9 JANUARY 1845

MS: Trinity College. *Extracts published:* Trevelyan, II, 212–13; 306n.

Albany London Jany. 9. 1845
Dearest Hannah,
Fanny shewed me yesterday a letter from you. I was much vexed to learn that your head still plagues you. For God's sake take care of yourself; and have the best advice when you return. I am sorry also to find

that you are anxious about Georgy. I did not perceive that anything was the matter with him. Fanny brought him and Baba with Charley Cropper to the Albany at one yesterday. I gave them some dinner, fowl, ham, marrowbones, tarts, ice, olives, and Champagne. We have an odd companion at table; no other than Mohun Lal, who came just as we were going to sit down. The last ten years have changed him so much that I should not have known him in the least. He is positively ugly; and I used to think him good-looking for a Hindoo. He is also marked by small pox; and I did not recollect that he was so in old times. He ate the fowl and drank the Champagne in a way which, if he had any caste to lose, must most effectually have deprived him of every shred. I found it difficult to think of any sight for the children. It was growing dark indeed before we rose from table. However I took them to the National Gallery, and was excessively amused with the airs of connoisseurship which Charley and Baba gave themselves, and with poor Georgy's honestly avowed weariness. "Let us go. There is nothing here that I care for at all." When I put him into the carriage he said half sulkily. "I do not call this seeing sights. I have seen no sight to day." Many a man who has laid out thirty thousand pounds on paintings would, if he spoke the truth, own that he cared for the art as little as Georgy. Charley on the other hand was charmed. How ripe his judgment on such matters is you may judge from his pronouncing that the finest thing in the gallery beyond all comparison was a Canaletti of the grand canal at Venice. Baba shewed her historical knowledge by instantly making out the subject of Rubens's picture of the Romans carrying off the Sabine ladies. I owe poor Georgy another day of sight-seeing.

I had a great breakfast-party to day, Hallam, Rogers, Luttrell, Baron Rolfe, Mahon, Glenelg, Milman, etc. We did not break up till one. Then came a knock at the door, and in walked that miserable old charlatan, who, I hoped, had been hanged or guillotined years ago: – you must have heard of him, though I do not think that you ever saw him, – Leo, a hanger-on of Henry Drummond, a votary of Spurzheim, a compound of all the quackeries, physiological and theological, of half a century. I always detested the fellow; but I could not turn him out of the room. For he came up with, "Do you not remember me? You are so like the dear man, Zachary. It was just so that he used to look on me" (I looked, by the bye, as sulky as a bear). "I felt your dear scull when you was a child, and I prophesied that you should be minister of state. Paff! That is demonstration. I keep mine eye on you ever since. Paff! It come true." So I desired the man to sit down, and was as civil as I could be to one whom I knew to be a mere Dousterswivel. He then began a long story which I have quite forgot, except that he was in England for the purpose of making phrenological researches. "I hoped," he said, "for your great help. But this very morning, I have seen some phrenologists that told me that you would do me no good." "Pray who were they?" said I. "You shall forgive me. I shall not say the names. But they tell me you shall do me no good." I said with a very bitter smile that they were right, that I was a fixed unbeliever, and that he had nothing to expect from me in that line. Then he told me that he wished for my help in another way. I guessed what he meant, hesitated between five and ten pounds, and was looking for my cheque-book, when he pulled out an odd-looking packet. He had brought with him, he said, a most precious book to sell, an unique, Martin Luther's own psalter, with some notes by Martin's own hand. He had heard that there was some Duke who would give a great deal for it. Would I give him a letter to this Duke? I was glad to get off so cheap. I told him that I did not know to what Duke he alluded, that we had several Dukes bitten with Bibliomania, but that I would give him a letter to Panizzi at the British Museum, and that, if Panizzi did not buy the book, he would at least give a direction to some wealthy amateurs. To say the truth I am by no means satisfied that the book is genuine. Leo is a complete humbug, and is likely enough to have forged the devotional notes which he wants to sell as Luther's. However Panizzi will judge as to that matter. I sent Leo away with a letter of introduction, and hope, from the bottom of my soul, that I have seen the last of him.

How I run on. And I could run on an hour longer and over several more sheets. I have had a most curious correspondence with Palmerston; and I received to day a letter from him which, I think, gives a higher idea of his talents than anything that I ever heard or read of his. But this between ourselves – or as I suppose it must be, between you, me, and Trevelyan. Love to him. Kind and civil messages to all.

Ever yours

T B M

TO EDWARD EVERETT, 2 NOVEMBER 1845

MS: Massachusetts Historical Society. Extract published: P. R. Frothingham, Edward Everett, Boston, 1925, p. 308.

Albany London November 2 / 1845

My dear Everett,

I was truly glad to see your handwriting again, and to learn that you had not forgotten me. I have seen Holland twice or thrice and have talked much with him about you. There are many here who miss you as much as I do, and who are gratified by every mark of public respect which is paid you in your own country.

Holland has come back to us in a most grateful frame of mind. He tells me that he has been treated with constant kindness and courtesy. Of your jurists and men of Science he speaks very highly. He has also silenced some of your detractors by testifying that towels are multiplied and basons greatly enlarged since Stanley and Denison brought back their report. If he has any evil to tell, he keeps it to himself. The best proof that he has been well pleased is his intention to visit you again some years hence. I should much like to accompany him.

You will not expect much London news at this season. Our autumn has been a little animated by a visit from Thiers, who came apparently in order to make his peace with the Whigs. I paid him a compliment which I have paid to nobody else for a long time. I got up at seven in the morning to take a three hours' walk with him in the parks, and had the pleasure of hearing him relate, with wonderful spirit and clearness, a long history, important, if true, and, whether true or not, very entertaining. After conversing with him, I cannot wonder at his success in the tribune. For not only is his flow of language wonderful. But he has an extraordinary talent for arranging his thoughts on any subject, at a moment's notice, into a neat, plausible, system, which will not endure long or close inspection, but which, at the first glance, is not to be distinguished from a complete and deeply meditated theory. But, though this is the talent of a great debater, it is not the talent of a great historian. For my part I would much rather talk with Thiers than with Guizot. But I had much rather read a history of the Empire by Guizot than by Thiers.

Why should not you undertake to give us a history of the United States, such as might become classical, and be in every English as well as in every American library? In some way or other you will, I hope, keep us mindful of you, till we see you again, as surely we shall.

Pray remember me very kindly to Mrs. and Miss Everett. / Ever, my dear Everett,

Yours most truly

T B Macaulay

TO MRS CHARLES TREVELYAN, 19 DECEMBER 1845

MS: Trinity College. *Partly published:* Trevelyan, II, 166–7.

Albany Decr. 19. 1845

Dearest,

It is an odd thing to see a ministry making. I never witnessed the process before. Lord John has been all day in his inner library. His antechamber has been filled with comers and goers, some talking in knots, some writing notes at tables. Every five minutes somebody is called into the inner room. As the people who have been closeted come out, the cry of the whole body of expectants is "What are you?"

I was summoned almost as soon as I arrived, and found Lord Auckland and Lord Clarendon sitting with Lord John. After some talk about other matters Lord John told me that he had been trying to ascertain my wishes, and that he found that I wanted leisure and quiet more than salary and business. Labouchere had told him this. He therefore offered me the Pay Office, – one of the three places which, as I told you, I should prefer. I at once accepted it. The tenure by which I shall hold it is so precarious that it matters little what its advantages may be. But I shall have two thousand a year for the trouble of signing my name. I must indeed attend parliament more closely than I have of late done. But my mornings will be as much my own as if I were out of office. If I give to my history the time which I used to pass in transacting business when I was Secretary at War, I shall get on nearly as fast as when I was in opposition.

Some other arrangements are less satisfactory to me. Palmerston will hear of nothing but the Foreign Office. Lord Grey therefore declines taking any place. And I can see that all those who have been in the cabinet with him before are rather pleased than vexed at not having him among them. Clarendon said to me, "Before Lord Grey has been a fortnight in the House of Lords, he will be more hated than any peer who has sate there within the memory of men." Another appointment I and every body else who has heard of it must regret and condemn. Hobhouse is to go to the India Board again. I own that this makes me very angry. The best arrangement that has been made is that for the government of Ireland. The Lord Lieutenancy is to be offered to Lord Besborough. Labouchere has agreed to take the Secretaryship with the cabinet – a suggestion of mine by the bye. The Chancellor of Ireland is to be an Irish lawyer. This will be a most popular measure in Ireland. But I fear that Lord Campbell's resentment will be extreme, and not altogether unreasonable. He is to be offered the Duchy of Lancaster without the Cabinet, – a poor compensation. Fox Maule will be Secretary at War. I told Lord John that he was quite right to send a new man thither. Nobody will ever go twice. Lord Auckland will have the Admiralty. At least it is all but settled. Napier will be one of the Lords. Lord Clarendon will be President of the Board of Trade. The Vice-Presidentship will be offered to Cobden. Of course Cottenham will be Lord High Chancellor and Baring Chancellor of the Exchequer. I have now, I think, told you all that, as far as I am aware, is yet settled. You will therefore not be taken in by newspaper reports.

What a strange occurrence has just taken place. While we were wondering where Morpeth was to find a seat, Lord Wharncliffe unexpectedly dies. John Wortley goes to the House of Peers; and the West Riding – Morpeth's old seat, and his favourite object, – becomes vacant. We have no doubt of his carrying it with ease. It will be a fortunate circumstance for us that our administration will begin with elections of great importance in all of which we expect to be successful. Three in particular, that for the West Riding, that for the city of London, and that for Edinburgh, are likely to pass without even the shew of opposition. It will therefore be clear that we have a great mass of support in the country.

I am sorry that Fanny gave you a bad account of my looks. She saw me, I think, when I was really very uneasy, that is to say, while it was undecided that we should propose total and immediate repeal. From the moment that we determined that point rightly I have been as much at my ease as ever I was in my life.

Of course you will say nothing about the arrangements till they appear in the newspapers. It is possible that changes may still be made.

I hope that Lord John will give one of the Secretaryships of State to George Grey. It would be a great elevation. But I am sure that it is the right thing to do. I have told Grey that I look to him as our future leader in the Commons, and that no pretensions of mine shall ever interfere with his. Labouchere feels exactly as I do. Labouchere and Baring are at least as good men of business as Grey: and I may say without vanity that I have made speeches which were out of the reach of any of the three. But, taking the talent for business and the talent for speaking together, Grey is undoubtedly the best qualified among us for the lead: and we are perfectly sensible of this. Indeed I may say that I do not believe that there ever was a set of public men who had less jealousy of each other or who formed a more correct estimate of themselves than the younger members of this cabinet.

But I must have done. Love to Baba. Kind regards to all.

Ever yours
T B M

TO MRS CHARLES TREVELYAN, 9 JULY 1846

MS: Trinity College. *Partly published:* Trevelyan, II, 173–4.

Royal Hotel Edinburgh / July 9. 1846

Dearest Hannah,

I reached Edinburgh last night, and found the city in a storm. The lower dissenters and free churchmen have got up an opposition on the old ground of Maynooth, and have sent for Sir Culling Smith. He is to be here this evening. Comically enough, we shall be at the same inn. But the inn, – landlord, waiters, chambermaid, and boots – are all with me. About the result I have no doubt. We had to day a great meeting of electors. The Lord Provost presided. Near three thousand well dressed people, chiefly voters, were present. I spoke for an hour, as well, they tell me, as I ever spoke in my life, – certainly with considerable effect. There was immense cheering mingled with a little hissing. A shew of hands was called for. I had a perfect forest. The other side not fifty. To morrow the nomination takes place. It is probable that there will be no poll. If so, I shall probably be in town on Sunday morning before daybreak. If there is a poll, I shall hardly be able to be in London till Friday the 17th. For the votes will be taken on Tuesday: the result will be declared on Wednesday: and I shall not be able to start before Thursday. I rather wish – much as I dislike this detention – that these stupid fanatical brutes would go to a poll. They will never be quiet till they have tried their strength and been soundly beaten, and it is better to have the struggle now than at the general election when they may have organized themselves.

I am exceedingly well and in high spirits. I had become somewhat effeminate in literary repose and leisure. You would not know me again, now that my blood is up. I am such as when, twelve years ago, I fought the battle with Sadler at Leeds.

I dine to day at the new Lord Advocate's, – on Saturday, if I stay so long, at Napier's. The Sunday I shall probably pass at Riccarton. But it is impossible to make any arrangements definitively till we see [. . . .]

TO FRANCES MACAULAY, 14 OCTOBER 1846

MS: Trinity College. *Partly published:* Trevelyan, II, 176–7.

Albany Octr. 14. 1846

Dearest Fanny,

I am glad that you are so comfortable at Bovey Tracy. You half tempt me to run down for a day. When do you mean to come up to town?

I fear however that I shall not be able to go in that direction. I am to be at Edinburgh, and to spout at the opening of a public library in the beginning of November, and, till then, I think that I must confine myself to very short suburban excursions.

I think that you had better sell your new allotments. I have always thought so. I do not think that it would be wise in you to buy more London and North Western stock. Remember that you have staked every thing on that one venture. If I were you I would wait till it rises a little, as I hope that it will, and then I would sell largely. But you must judge for yourself. I inquired at the Bank about your deposits, and found that the needful had been done.

I have received the most disgusting letter by many degrees that I ever read in my life from old Mrs. Money. I can give you no idea of it but by transcribing it, and it is too long to transcribe. However, I will give you the opening. "My *dear friend,* Many years have past away, since my revered husband and your excellent father walked together as Xtn friends, and since I derived the sweetest comfort and pleasure from a close friendship with both your *blessed* parents." After a great deal more about various revered and blessed people she comes to the real object of her epistle, which is to ask for three livings and a bishoprick. I have been accustomed to unreasonable and importunate suitors. But I protest that this old hag's impudence fairly took away my breath. What am I to say to her? I cannot well tell her the truth, which is that of all crawling things, next to an Elliott and a cock roach, I detest a Money. In order to recommend her brats still more, she assures me that one of them has been curate to that blessed man Mr. Close. She is so moderate as to say that for her son James she will accept, nay very thankfully accept, even a living of five hundred a year. Another proof of her moderation is that, before she asks for a Bishoprick, she has the grace to say "I am now going to be very bold." Really the comedy of actual life is beyond all Comedy. Three things within the last month have tickled me more than anything on the stage – Henry's letter to Charles about Wilber's railway shares, Zachary's genealogical tree, and this application of Mrs. Money. Answer her however I must. – What can I say? Let me see – Huzza – I have done it. I am so proud of my performance that I will send you a copy. Is it not capital? –

Love to John, his wife, and his children.

Ever yours
T B M

TO MRS CHARLES TREVELYAN, 5 NOVEMBER 1846

MS: Huntington Library.

Edinburgh Nov 5. 1846

Dearest Hannah,

This letter and the writer of it will probably reach London together. I start by the mail at four to morrow. At five on Saturday morning I hope to be in my bed at the Albany. On Sunday I mean to see you again at Clapham.

Yesterday we held our meeting at seven in the evening. The Music Hall, a very fine room, not so large as Exeter Hall, but superior to any other similar place that I have seen in London, was crowded. I was on the left hand of the Lord Provost; the Archbishop of Dublin on the right. I spoke with immense applause, but without the least self-applause. For it was all poor debating-society stuff, a bad thing well done, a degree and but a degree better than Morpeth's trash. However the people hallooed, and waved their hats and handkerchiefs, and talked about my eloquence ringing in my ears, and told me that I was at once a legislator, a statesman, an orator, a wit, a critic, a philosopher and a poet, till I did not know which way to look. The Archbishop kept me in countenance. For he made a much greater fool of himself than I, and that without having my excuse. I was exhibiting in order to please my constituents, in order to secure my seat, in order to save my self the anxiety and the expense of a contest next summer. He was spouting for the mere pleasure of spouting. All his duties required his presence in his own province, suffering as it is from famine and from disturbances. What had he, at such a time, to do on a platform at Edinburgh? And such nonsense as he talked! – I was quite ashamed to see Macleod's face in the crowd. There he was, taking the gauge of our minds and regarding us all with unutterable contempt. When I came to my fine peroration I wished him from my soul as deaf as a post.

Just as I wrote these words in came two of my constituents, an artist, and a merchant. The merchant you have seen, Millar, the chairman of my Committee, a shrewd fellow, goodnatured and a staunch Whig, but a little too fond of his dinner and bottle, and much too fond of a job. "Oh Mr. Macaulay," cries the artist, "yere Gulliver was the finest thing that I ever heard." "Oh, Mr. Macaulay," responds the merchant, "but yon was a splendid harangue." Thought I, – My good friends you teach me a very useful lesson of economy. What a spend thrift I should be to go to the cost of diamonds for you, when paste serves the turn so well!

I am almost sorry that you could not make this trip with me. You would have been overwhelmed with kindness. You would also have found Edinburgh perfectly free from all political excitement, which is of course seldom the case during my visits. However it would have been impossible for you to travel two nights running.

I was amused by what I heard from Craig about Impey's book. One single copy is at Edinburgh. Several of my enemies borrowed it in the hope of finding something against me. But it has been too much for them. No person has held out beyond the twentieth page.

Mr. Park has brought my bust hither and is exhibiting it. Many people to go see it, and it is generally admired. It is not worth while to complain. But surely to carry about and to shew my property – for I have paid the whole price – without asking my permission is hardly an honest, and certainly not a delicate or gentlemanly proceeding. One of the orators yesterday night was declaiming about the progress of the arts in Scotland. "Have we not," said he, "produced a sculptor worthy to hand down to posterity the features of our honored representative?" I hope that this eulogium will make you value the bust more.

How I go on gossiping. I must stop. The waiter announces Jeffrey is below. Goodbye. Love to all.

Ever yours
T B M

TO MRS CHARLES TREVELYAN, 30 JULY 1847

MS: Trinity College. *Partly published:* Trevelyan, II, 187.

Edinburgh July 30. 1847

Dearest Hannah,

I hope that you will not be much vexed; for I am not vexed, but as cheerful as ever I was in my life. I have been completely beaten. The poll has not closed; but there is no chance that I shall retrieve the lost ground. Radicals, Tories, Dissenters, Voluntaries, Free Churchmen, spirit drinkers who are angry because I will not pledge myself to repeal all taxes on whiskey, and great numbers of persons who are jealous of my chief supporters here and think that the patronage of Edinburgh has been too exclusively distributed among a clique, have united to bear me down. I will make no hasty resolutions. But everything seems to indicate that I ought to take this opportunity of retiring from public life. Indeed many months must in all probability pass before I could get into parliament for any other place, even if I were so inclined: and it seems to me to be the most dignified course at once to retire, and finally. However I will take a few days for consideration.

To morrow I shall start by the express train at seven in the morning, and shall reach my chambers, I hope, between nine and ten in the evening. I am much more concerned about my dear Baba's eyes than about the loss of my election. I hope and trust that she will not be forced to forego the journey from which she promised herself so much pleasure. Thank her from me for her acrostic. Mr. Cowan's name will do very well for the blank space.

On Monday I shall run down to Cambridge and back again. Let me hear from you before you leave England. Love to all.

> Ever yours
> T B M

Thanks to Fanny for her kind letter. I shall write to her soon.

TO THOMAS FLOWER ELLIS, 30 JULY 1847

MS: Trinity College. *Partly published:* Trevelyan, II, 187

Edinburgh / July 30. 1847

Dear Ellis,

I am beaten, but not at all the less happy for being so. I will make no hasty resolutions. But I think that having once been manumitted, after the old fashion, by a slap in the face, I shall not take to bondage again. But there is time to consider that matter. I shall be in town to morrow night. On Monday I mean to go down to Cambridge and back again. Send a line to the Albany to let me know when I can see you.

> Ever yours
> T B Macaulay

TO MARGARET TREVELYAN, 21 AUGUST 1847

MS: Trinity College. *Partly published:* Trevelyan, II, 204–5.

Albany London / August 21. 1847

Dearest Margaret,

I must begin sooner or later to call you Margaret; and I am always making good resolutions to do so, and then breaking them. But I will procrastinate no longer. I will really be good.

> "Procrastination is the thief of time"

says Dr. Young. He also says

> "Be wise to day. 'Tis madness to defer"

and

> "Next day the fatal precedent will plead."

That is to say, I shall go on calling my darling Baba till she is as old as her mamma, and has a dozen Babas of her own. Therefore I will be wise to day, and call her Margaret.

I should very much like to see you and Aunty and Alice at Broadstairs, and to have a walk on the sands, and a talk about Mr. Elton and Miss Crawford. But I fear, I fear that it cannot be. Your Aunt Fanny asks me to shirk the Chelsea Board. I am staying in England chiefly in order to attend it; and I cannot with decency absent myself. When parliament is not sitting my duty there is all that I do for two thousand four hundred pounds a year. We must have some conscience. However it is not absolutely impossible that I may be able to run to Broadstairs between my arrival at Ramsgate and my embarkation for Ostend.

At any rate I shall soon be back. Michaelmas will, I hope, find us all at Clapham over a noble goose, or rather over two noble geese; – for one will hardly be enough. Do you know the beautiful Puseyite hymn on Michaelmas day. It is a great favourite with all the Tractarians. You and Alice should learn it. It begins.

> "Though Quakers scowl, though Baptists howl,
> "Though Plymouth Brethren rage,
> "We Churchmen gay will wallow to day
> "In apple sauce, onions, and sage.
> "Ply knife and fork, and draw the cork,
> "And have the bottle handy:
> "For each slice of goose will introduce
> "A thimblefull of brandy."

Is it not good? I wonder who the author can be. Not Newman, I think. It is above him. Perhaps it is Bishop Wilberforce. His good father taught him to like brandy: and that is one of the lessons which, when impressed on the young and ductile mind by parental precept and example, seldom fails to leave permanent traces. So we will suppose that it is the Bishop.

My dear little girl, I was so glad to hear from your Mamma how good you had been on your travels, and how much you were amused. I am impatient to hear all about them, and particularly about the funny little French miss that you travelled with. But we must wait patiently. In the meantime give my love to Aunt Fanny, and to George and to Alice. I expect to see George on Monday at Clapham.

Ever yours my love

T B Macaulay

TO [FRANCES? MACAULAY, LATE OCTOBER 1848]

MS: Trinity College. Partly published: Trevelyan, II, 231–2.

[London]

[. . .] time to miss any[thin]g, [for?] I am up at seven over proof sheets, and my work does not end till dinner time. My only recreations [. . .] concludes. I publish certainly on the 4th of December.

Longman seems content with his bargain. Jeffrey, Ellis, Macleod, and Hannah, all agree in predicting that the book will succeed. I ought to add Marian Ellis's judgment. For her father tells me that he cannot get the proof sheets out of her hand, and that she finds them as entertaining as a novel. These things keep up my spirits. Yet I see every day more and more clearly how far my performance is below excellence, and how much better I could make it if I took another year.

On Saturday Hannah comes back from Hastings. On Sunday I shall go to Clapham, my first holiday for many days. I shall be most happy to see you there again. Kindest love to John, his wife, and his children.

Ever yours
T B Macaulay

TO CHARLES MACAULAY, 27 NOVEMBER 1848

MS: University of London. *Published:* Rae, *Temple Bar*, LXXXVI, 199.

Albany London / November 27. 1848

My dear Charles,

I should have written to you more than once, if I had not apprehended that my letters might not reach Mauritius till you were on your voyage to England: and even now I write in doubt. We have all been much interested by your political and literary labours, and think them highly creditable to you and likely to be useful to the public. I have been working intensely during some months on my history, rising at day break, and sometimes sitting at my desk twelve hours at a stretch. This work is for the present over. On Friday next, the 1st of December, we publish. I hardly know what to anticipate. Every body who has seen the book, that is to say, Lord Jeffrey, Ellis, Trevelyan, Hannah, and Longman, predict complete success, and say that it is as entertaining as a novel. But the truth is that, in such a case, friends are not to be trusted, and booksellers, after they have struck a bargain, are even less to be trusted than friends. The partiality of an author for what he has written is nothing compared to the partiality of a publisher for what he has bought. However a few weeks will show. I am in doubt about sending you a copy, though I have ordered one to be reserved for you. You will probably see the book first in the Yankee edition. A New York house has given me £200 for early proof sheets. Longman is to pay me five hundred a year for five years in consideration of the privilege of printing six thousand copies. This is a very pleasant addition to my income: and, if the book succeeds, I shall probably find literature not only a more pleasant but a more gainful pursuit than politics.

We are all well – Hannah very much improved in health, I think – but she has been forced of late to play the nurse much more than does her good. I hope soon to meet your wife at Clapham, and to make acquaintance with the children. I could say a great deal about Edward Cropper and his marriage: but that may wait till we meet which I hope will be early in the summer. This strange and awful year is ending better than a few months ago there seemed reason to expect. England, Scotland, even Ireland, are quiet. In France and Germany the friends of order are getting the upper hand. In the United States the spectacle which Europe has lately presented seems to have strengthened the moderate party. We learn to day that Taylor has been elected President in opposition to the odious firebrand Cass. Peace, I hope, is now tolerably secure, and you may return without being afraid either of the stars and stripes or of the tricolor.

Ever yours affectionately

T B Macaulay

TO SIR EDWARD BULWER-LYTTON, 30 DECEMBER 1848

MS: Hertfordshire County Council.

Albany Dec 30. 1848

My dear Sir Edward,

Your praise is always delightful to me, and your censure always useful. I at once admit the justice of some of your criticisms, and should probably admit the justice of all, if, after hearing what I have to offer, you should still be of the same mind. I should much like to talk over with you some of the questions which you raise. For it is not easy to discuss them fully by letter. I will only say that the practice of repeating nouns, which you justly note as a peculiarity of my style, and which sometimes, I do not doubt, amounts to a vice, was adopted by me on principle. I repeat nouns that I may not misuse pronouns. There is no fault so common even in our best writers as that of putting *he* and *it* in wrong places. I have taken down Johnson's Lives of the Poets, and I transcribe absolutely at random, the very first paragraph on which I open.

"from this time Pope lived in the closest intimacy with his (Pope's) commentator, and amply rewarded his (Warburton's) kindness and zeal; for he (Pope) introduced him (Warburton) to Mr. Murray, by whose interest he (Warburton) became preacher at Lincoln's Inn, and to Mr. Allen who gave him (Warburton) his (Allen's) niece, and his (Allen's) estate, and by consequence a bishopric. When he (Pope) died, he (Pope) left him (Warburton) the property of his (Pope's) works."

The whole book, and nine tenths even of the good books in our language are written in this way. Only look at the last sentence. There is no reason whatever for connecting the *hes* and *hims* with Pope and Warburton rather than with Allen, except that the context guides the reader to the sense. I have a horror almost morbid of this fault. I could compose twice as fast as I do if it were not for the extreme scrupulosity with which I arrange my pronouns. I do not believe that in my two volumes, thick as they are, you will find one sentence resembling that which I have quoted. But it is not possible to avoid the abuse of pronouns except by a copious use of nouns. In the passage which I have quoted I should have repeated the names of Pope and Warburton; and you will, I think, allow that I should have been right in doing so.

I do not doubt that there is good ground for your criticism, and that I sometimes repeat nouns unnecessarily. But I cannot help thinking that I err on the right side. It seems to me that clearness and precision are the very first of all the graces of style. Rather than place words in such an order as to puzzle the reader I would copy the diction of an Act of Parliament or of a mortgage deed, and give you over and over again "the said Alexander Pope," "the said William Warburton, Clerk," and "the said Ralph Allen."

Excuse this garrulity. I wish to place my case fairly before so excellent a judge.

Ever yours truly
T B Macaulay

III · THE FINAL DECADE, 1849–1859

The enthusiastic reception of the first part of his *History*, in America and on the Continent as well as in England, could hardly fail to have greatly pleased and excited Macaulay, as it did. But he kept his head well, and only a few weeks after the publication of the first part settled down to work on the second. For this he continued his research in libraries and at the scenes of his story, visiting, for example, Ireland for local color (26 August 1849) and France for documents (26 September 1849).

Meantime, fresh honors continued to come to him; he was elected Lord Rector of the University of Glasgow, awarded a D.C.L. by Oxford, made Professor of Ancient Literature in the Royal Academy (2 March 1850), elected to the French Institute, and invested with the Prussian Order of Merit (13 December 1852), not to mention other major and minor distinctions. The most satisfying recognition, however, came when the electors of Edinburgh, penitent after their rejection of him in 1847, now came forward to beg him to sit again for the city in Parliament (19 June 1852). The pleasure of this triumph was at once undercut by a sudden crisis in his health: at the very moment of his election at Edinburgh Macaulay, weak and gasping for breath, was leading an invalid's life at Clifton (15 July 1852). He was never to know robust good health again, though he determinedly kept up his spirits and refused to make his own suffering a burden to others. In this condition he could take no active part in parliamentary life again, even supposing that he had cared much to do so. He attended irregularly, and spoke rarely. But he did good service in committees on such important matters as university reform, the Indian charter of 1853, and the introduction of competitive examinations for the Indian Civil Service (11 July 1854).

Work on the *History* remained the main business of his life. Ill health was a serious obstacle; parliamentary duties, however limited, cost him some time and trouble; another interruption occurred when a publisher brought out an unauthorized edition of his speeches, provoking Macaulay to devote a summer to preparing an edition of his own (4 August 1853). Still, he managed to produce two more volumes of the *History* at the end of 1855 (29 November 1855), and he scored a greater material success than he had even with the first volumes. The sales were so large that Longman, his publisher, was able to present him with a check for £20,000 only a few weeks after publication – 'a transaction quite unparalleled in the history of the book trade', as Macaulay was proud to write (11 March 1856).

The culmination of his honors came in 1857, when Lord Palmerston's government offered him a peerage, the first ever granted for literature (29 August 1857). But, though Macaulay was thus transformed into Baron Macaulay of Rothley, his life was not much changed. More and more in this decade he had settled into a fixed routine. London and the Albany were its center, from which he regularly ventured at Easter to visit the cathedrals of England with the Trevelyan family; in the summers he retreated to the country – to the Isle of Wight (3 September 1850), to Malvern (10 August 1851), to Clifton (15 July 1852), to Tunbridge Wells (1 August 1853), to Thames Ditton (11 July 1854), to Richmond (22 August 1855). In the autumn he might make a continental tour with Ellis, to Germany, perhaps (1 September 1853), or to Italy (8 September 1856). His personal interests remained unchanged. His domestic affections were entirely wrapped up in Hannah and her family. The children presented fresh points of interest as they grew up. George developed into a bright and promising schoolboy, with whom Macaulay took pleasure in discussing literature (1 August 1853); Margaret Trevelyan's engagement and marriage were notable events in his life (2 and 7 August 1858).

Public events appear less distinct and urgent. Macaulay was characteristically level-headed about such noisy outbursts as the furor over 'Catholic aggression' (15 November 1850); he shows the same style in his remarks on the missionary enterprises of a Miss Cunninghame in Italy (4 October 1853). The Crimean War hardly ripples the surface of his letters (29 November 1855); the Indian Mutiny creates more excitement (10 August 1857) but did not unsettle him as it did, for example, his brother-in-law Trevelyan.

Early in 1856 Macaulay left his chambers in the Albany, where he had gone some fifteen years earlier to live a 'college life at the West end of London', for a house on Campden Hill, Kensington. Here, in a comfortable house, attended by a full staff of servants and surrounded by his library of ten thousand volumes (25 February 1856), Macaulay could entertain his friends at dinner, or amuse his solitude by strolling on his lawn, among his flowers and trees. After the publication of the second part of the *History* he wrote little, and that little slowly (a final volume of the unfinished *History* was edited and published by his sister Hannah after Macaulay's death). Despite his ill health, Macaulay went on at ease, enjoying the world around him and, perhaps even more, the world of daydream within – 'the unreal world', as he admitted, 'in which I pass a large part of my life' (25 June 1858).

The end came not long after Macaulay learned that his beloved Hannah would, early in 1860, leave England to join her husband, who had gone out in the year before as Governor of Madras. The prospect of separation from her was, it would seem, almost more than he could bear (24 October 1859) and must have contributed to his death – though one need not seek farther than the medically certifiable reasons indicated by his prolonged ill health. He died, then, as he had once wished he might – alone, with 'nobody that I cared for near me. The parting is the dreadful thing' (13 December 1852). He was spared that. He now lies buried in Poets' Corner in Westminster Abbey.

MS: Cambridge University Library.

Albany London Feb 7. 1849

Dear Stephen,

I am suffering, not only with fortitude, but with great complacency, those inflictions which prove me to be an honest historian. The Bishop of Exeter thinks me unfair to the Church of England: Sam Gurney thinks me unfair to the Quakers: Dr. Vaughan thinks me unfair to the Puritans; and Lord Shrewsbury thinks me unfair to the Roman Catholics. I believe my position to be perfectly defensible on all the four sides: but if any side be more assuredly impregnable than the others, it is that which Lord Shrewsbury has attacked.

Will any person seriously deny that, since the time of Leo the Tenth and of Charles the Fifth, Italy and Spain have been going down politically and intellectually, and that England, Scotland, and Northern Germany have been rising? Spain to be sure produced a few eminent writers during the century which followed the Reformation. Then she became barren. Italy was not quite so barren. Yet what is the value of the Italian literature since 1600? And observe that the best Italian writers since 1600 were men emancipated from the yoke of the Church. Fra Paolo, my favourite historian, was, as Bossuet says, a Protestant in a friar's gown. What Alfieri, Parini, and other eminent Italians of the eighteenth century were it is unnecessary to say. I will venture to affirm that the single city of Edinburgh has done more for the human mind during the last hundred years than Italy, Spain and Portugal together during the last two hundred.

Lord Shrewsbury says that the whole literary glory of France is posterior to the Reformation. The truth is that the exception proves the rule which I have laid down. For, though France is called Roman Catholic, her literary glory is almost entirely derived from the two struggles which her great intellects maintained against the Church of Rome. Deduct all the writings of the Jansenist party and all the writings of the philosophers, and a pretty *caput mortuum* you will have left. It is amusing to see Rome claim the glory of the Port Royalists whom she persecuted. As to the Jesuits, what single great original work did any Jesuit ever produce? Bourdaloue's sermons and Fray Gerundio are the two best Jesuit books that I know of; and you will hardly place either very high. The Jesuits wrote good Latin. Of Greek they seem to have known but little. In no modern language has any member of the order produced any work which ranks above the third rate.

As to Germany little can be inferred from comparing together princi-palities and towns in which Catholics and Protestants are much intermixed. Look at the great line of separation; and say on which side of that line the intellectual glory of Germany is to be found. On which side of that line are Klopstock, Herder, Wieland, Goethe, Schiller, Lessing? Who would take the trouble to learn German, if it were not for what the Protestant part of Germany has produced?

Lord Shrewsbury asks how it is possible that a system which was favourable to civilisation up to the fifteenth century can then have become unfavourable to civilisation. I see no difficulty. In my opinion the part of the Roman Catholic system which has had the greatest effect on the well being of mankind is not the invocation of Saints, or the doctrine of purgatory, or the praying for the dead; but the authority given to the priesthood over the laity. Whether that authority be good or bad for the temporal interests of mankind must depend on this, whether the priesthood be or be not wiser than the laity. For it is on the whole desirable that intelligence should govern. Now up to the fifteenth century I believe that the priests were decidedly the most intelligent part of the community. Therefore the superstition – as I hold it to be – which induced the rest of the society to submit to their guidance, was a salutary superstition. In the sixteenth century the clergy had no intellectual superiority. From that time, therefore, I hold that the superstition which induced the rest of the society to submit to them was unmixedly noxious. This view may be erroneous: but surely it is not inconsistent. – But I must stop. Keep this letter to yourself. But you can use it as a brief for me, if Lord S. should harangue you again.

Ever yours
T B Macaulay

to Thomas Flower Ellis, 8 March 1849

MS: Trinity College. *Partly published:* Trevelyan, II, 253–4.

Albany March 8 / 1849

Dear Ellis,

Mr. Broderip's offer is most kind and liberal. I accept it with much gratitude. A collection made by Heber cannot but be highly valuable and curious. I should be able, probably in a few days, certainly in a few weeks, to make all the notes and extracts which I should require.

Do you think that it would be intrusive in me to write to Mr. Broderip or to call on him?

At last I have attained true glory. As I walked through Fleet Street the day before yesterday, I saw a copy of Hume at a bookseller's window with the following label. "Only £2 " 2 " o – Hume's History of England in eight volumes, highly valuable as an introduction to Macaulay." I laughed so convulsively that the other people who were staring at the books took me for a poor demented gentleman. Alas for poor David! As for me, only one height of renown yet remains to be attained. I am not yet in Madame Tussaud's Wax work. I live however in hope of seeing some day an advertisement of a new groupe of figures, Mr. Macaulay, in one of his own coats, conversing with Mr. Silk Buckingham in oriental costume, and Mr. Robert Montgomery in full canonicals.

I return Broderip's letter.

Ever yours

T B Macaulay

TO UNIDENTIFIED RECIPIENT, 25 MARCH 1849

MS: Buffalo Public Library. *Extract published: Catalogue of the Gluck Collection. . .*, Buffalo, N.Y., 1899, p. 74.

Albany London March 25. 1849

My dear Sir,

I have received a very kind and welcome letter from you which it would be ungrateful in me not promptly to acknowledge. What you tell me of the reception which my book has found in the United States gratifies me much, but at the same time surprises me. For it seems to me that very few books have in as high a degree the merit or demerit of being intensely English; and I should have thought that this peculiarity, which has conduced not a little to the success of my volumes here, would have made them seem dull to a people who have never seen anything resembling our Court, our Bishops, our country gentlemen, our country clergymen, to a people who are strangers to the feelings of loyalty to a family, respect for an aristocracy, zeal for the privileges of an established Church. I should have thought that our disputes about the patriarchal theory of government, the divine right of kings, regency, abdication, and so forth, would have been as uninteresting to you as the controversy between the followers of Omar and the followers of Ali. I am glad to find that I was mistaken.

I should greatly enjoy a trip to the United States if I could be sure that I should be as free and as obscure there as I am when I go to Paris or Brussels, that I should be at liberty to chuse my own associates, and that I should never be forced to make a show of myself at dinners and public meetings. But my dislike of exhibition, which was always strong, and which never yielded except to clear public duty, has, since I quitted politics, become almost morbid. And what I hear of the form in which your countrymen shew their kindness and esteem for men whose names are at all known deters me from visiting you. I need not tell you that I mean no national reflection. Perhaps the peculiarity to which I allude is honorable to the American character; but it must cause annoyance to sensitive and fastidious men. Brougham or O'Connell would have liked nothing better. But Cowper would have died or gone mad; Byron would have insulted his admirers, and have been shot or tarred and feathered; and, though I have stronger nerves than Cowper's, and, I hope, a better temper than Byron's, I should suffer much pain and give much offence.

I assure you that I and many others remember your visit to us with pleasure, and hope to see you here again. We have gone through rough times; but a quiet season seems to be before us. – But I must stop.

Ever yours truly
T B Macaulay

TO UNIDENTIFIED RECIPIENT, 31 MARCH 1849

MS: Cambridge University Library.

Albany March 31. 1849

My dear Sir,

I am grateful for your suggestions, though I am not convinced that I ought to adopt them. If I were conscious of having anywhere disgraced myself by trying to gratify prurient imaginations with licentious descriptions, I should, I hope, with shame and sorrow, hasten to repair so great an offence. I have always thought the indelicacy of Gibbon's great work a more serious blemish than even his uncandid hostility to the Christian religion. But I cannot admit that a book like mine is to be regarded as written for female boarding schools. I open a school for men: I teach the causes of national prosperity and decay: and the particular time about which I write is a time when profligacy, having been compelled during some years to wear the mask of hypocrisy, had just thrown that mask away, and stood forth with a brazen impudence of which there is scarcely any other example in any modern society. How is it possible to treat a subject like mine without inserting a few paragraphs, – perhaps there may be, in my two thick volumes, two pages, – which it would be better that a young lady should not read aloud? How many of the most instructive chapters in the Bible, Chapters of the highest value as illustrating the frailty of human nature, the tendency of crime to draw on crime, and the frightful effect of private vices on public affairs, are such as no parent would desire his daughter to read aloud? I am not aware that there is a single line in my work which can sully the imagination of anybody who is in the habit of listening to the morning and evening lessons at Church.

As to the other point to which you advert, I have done my best to tell truth, and have consequently been abused by High Churchmen, Low Churchmen, Papists, Quakers, Presbyterians and Voluntaries. I see no reason to retract a syllable. I have never denied that our Reformers, with one exception, were, in the main, honest men. The exception is Cranmer whom I believe, and can prove, to have had as little claim to the praise of honesty as old Talleyrand himself. / Believe me, / My dear Sir,

Yours very truly

T B Macaulay

TO LADY TREVELYAN, 26 AUGUST 1849

MS: University of London.

Cork August 26. 1849

Dearest Hannah,

Here I am comfortably rested in a very good hotel after wandering through a hundred and thirty miles of wild country, jolting on poneys up rugged mountain passes, and riding on Irish cars between places where there was neither poste chaise nor stage coach to be had. You know pretty well how little I like to be put out of my way, and how little horsemanship is in my way. You will therefore form a high notion of Killarney when I tell you that I think all my trouble overpaid. Even William's poetical feelings were aroused, and he declared that he had never seen anything so beautiful in his life. As a set off against the pleasure of seeing this most lovely of all spots I have had the pain of seeing a people, the most miserable that I ever fell in with in any part of the world. I passed scores, I may say hundreds of dwellings lying in ruin. My guide told me that the people had left their houses and gone to America. And yet there was nothing to be said against the landlords of that region. Lord Kenmare, the late Lord Headley, and the present Lady Headley are celebrated all over Ireland and beyond it for benevolence and judicious liberality. Then the clothes of the people: – you never saw a beggar in such things. And the endless mendicant whine which follows you mile after mile, – the dozens of children who run after you in every village and up every hill crying "Give me halfpenny – mother dead in workhouse – " Their strange appearance sometimes made me laugh, and I yet could hardly help crying. But what use is there in making oneself miserable? These things must not be thought on after this way.

So, it will make us mad.

I shall stay here to day and to morrow. On Tuesday I go back to Dublin. Wednesday I must pass in some researches at Dublin. On Thursday I run down to Londonderry. Friday I spend there. On Saturday I return to Dublin. On Monday I propose to come back to England, and on Wednesday or Thursday following (the 5th or 6th of September), I shall start with Ellis for Paris. Possibly I may just catch you before you set out for Enmore.

I have an invitation from the Archbishop to his villa. I am happy to say that I shall be able to excuse myself. I have also a very polite letter from Colonel Jones, offering me help at Athlone, where I shall not be. Possibly, if I should find it necessary, I may three years hence, make another short trip to Ireland for some finishing touches, and may then find a railway open to Athlone and Aughrim.

I have a letter from our brother Charles who seems delighted with your girls, especially with Baba. He talks of sending his boy immediately to school.

I suppose that Trevelyan's holiday is about to commence. It is high time. Everybody here talks with astonishment of the business which he gets through; and yet they can know only a part of what he has to do. Kindest love to him and to all. Tell Baba to send me a line. When shall you be in Westbourne Terrace. It makes me a little sad to think that I shall never again walk out to you at Clapham. But this is what the Scotch, I believe, call sinning my mercies.

Ever yours
T B Macaulay

TO MARGARET TREVELYAN, 26 SEPTEMBER 1849

MS: Trinity College.

Albany London / September 26. 1849

My dearest girl,

I am most thankful for your letter. You cannot think how often I have missed you and longed for you during the last week, which I have passed in solitude as complete as that of Robinson Crusoe before he fell in with Friday. Yet I was glad that you were enjoying yourself in the fresh air among the trees and not in streets that have been black with coffins and mourning coaches all day long. Now however the danger is all but over; and it will, I trust, be quite over before you return.

I saw hardly any change in Paris. Here or there was a miserable stunted poplar stuck in the pavement, and called a tree of liberty. On some of the public buildings are the words "Liberté. Egalité. Fraternité." In other things I saw no change. The shops, the galleries, the gardens of the Thuilleries, look just as they did. Véry's crawfish soup and partridges are just as good as ever. But every human being that I saw, high and low, was cursing the revolution, and breathing vengeance on the Red Party. I went to St Germains in company with a very intelligent and polished man, evidently a considerable proprietor. He had been in the fight last June year. "I am not young," he said, "I am the father of a family. I am a man of peace. Is it not cruel that I should have had to turn out, to take my fusil-de-chasse, and to fight in the streets to save my house and my children from those mad dogs. There we were, Sir, thousands of us, grey headed men, husbands and parents who had never drawn a trigger before except against a partridge." He described the fight at the point where he was. The first volley that he and his friends fired killed seven of the insurgents. "I had never seen a man die by violence before. I could not sleep for weeks without dreaming of their horrible faces." But there was no tenderness for them in his heart. "We have been too lenient with them. There should have been no prisoners made. They want to rob, to burn, to murder. They are as bad as ever. They will soon be up again. And then we will have no mercy. It shall be the last time. They shall be treated like dogs – like mad dogs." And he repeated this over and over. You may be shocked: but I quite sympathized with him. Had I been in Cavaignac's place at that time I would have made such an example of the rabble of the Faubourg St Antoine that the ears of all the world should have tingled. But how I run on to my darling about politics for which she does not care one straw. Love to Mamma and Papa and the Lady of the Castle; and tell her Ladyship how much I long to have a game of play with her. Pray remember me kindly to Grandmamma. M. Dumont wished me to present his homages to your uncle Otto. Pray convey them properly.

Ever yours dearest
T B Macaulay

TO FRANCES MACAULAY, 13 NOVEMBER 1849

MS: Trinity College.

Private

Albany Nov 13. 1849

Dearest Fanny,

I have not a line of Praed's writing. As to recollections, I will tell you, though I must beg you not to tell Moultrie or anybody else, that what I recollect I would much rather forget myself than publish to others. I hate public ruptures with friends. If they use me basely, – and Praed alone of all my friends ever used me basely, – my rule is

"Le bruit est pour le fat: la plainte est pour le sot:
L'honnête homme trompé s'éloigne et ne dit mot."

You had better merely tell Moultrie that I am afraid that I have no materials which can be of any use to him.

It is a very foolish thing, I think, to publish any biography or any remains of Praed. He was a wonderful boy at seventeen; and a wonderful boy he continued to be till he died at near forty. The best thing for his fame is that his early poetry should be read in the Etonian, where it appears as the work of a lad and is compared with the works of other lads. He never afterwards wrote better. I am not sure that he ever afterwards wrote so well. The proposed collection will, I am confident, do him no honour; and I have just so much kindness for him remaining as to wish that the plan were abandoned.

I hear nothing about the Rugby mastership. Malden was a candidate last time; and then he told me that he should not object, if elected, to go into the Church. I have heard nothing from him on this occasion. Remember me to Mr. and Mrs. Price.

Ever yours,
T B Macaulay

TO FRANCES MACAULAY, 2 MARCH 1850

MS: Huntington Library.

Albany London / March 2. 1850

Dearest Fanny,

Thanks for your letter. I am always delighted to hear from you and of you. Hannah and I have been planning a visit of a day to Brighton: but we must wait till the spring is further advanced.

I thought that I mentioned to you the change in my book cases. I have added two new rows of shelves; and am now pretty well able to accommodate my whole library. I have counted the books. There are more than seven thousand volumes, a tolerable collection, when you consider that only three or four hundred of them were our father's.

I am glad you like Campbell's Chancellors. It is a most amusing book. The life of Lord Mansfield is the best in his new work. You know probably that Denman has at last taken himself off, and that Lord C[ampbell] succeeds. It was high time.

It is generally believed that the Gorham case will be decided to day: but there have been so many postponements that I feel no confidence in reports. There is no doubt that the decision will be against the Bishop. Some people talk of a secession. My own belief is that it will be a very unimportant one, that no man eminent in learning or station will be among the seceders. Indeed if the Bishop himself, against whom the decision is, does not think himself bound to retire, why should others go?

I work quietly every morning, and get on, – not very fast, – but still I get on, and am tolerably satisfied. The difficulties are immense, chiefly because nobody has cleared the way for me. On the other hand I have the advantage of telling a story much of which will be quite new even to diligent students of history. I wrote a sheet yesterday about a landing of the French in Devonshire. I think it as interesting as any passage in my two first volumes: and it is my belief that the materials from which it is taken have never been examined by any person living except myself.

I have just been elected by the Royal Academy Professor of Ancient Literature, and approved by the Queen – fully approved Her Majesty was graciously pleased to declare. The Duke of Cambridge tells me that she speaks very handsomely of me. As to this Professorship it is purely honorary. The duties and the emoluments are identical and consist in dining with the Academy once a year at the opening of the Exhibition. Even speechmaking after dinner is not required. Dr. Johnson was my predecessor. The last professor was the Bishop of Llandaff. Hallam is my colleague as professor of Ancient History. He succeeds Goldsmith.

We all expect you here in little more than three weeks for our Easter tour. When the spring is further advanced I hope to see you and dear Selina at Brighton. My love to her.

Ever yours,
T B Macaulay

TO LORD MAHON, 2 AUGUST 1850

MS: Stanhope Papers, Chevening.

Albany London / August 2. 1850

Dear Lord Mahon,

I am sorry that I cannot go down to you. But, empty as London is, I am at present engaged daily.

As to the Museum, I should like Milman much. We thought of him before; and his present situation is of itself a sort of claim. The dean of the Cathedral of the Capital seems to be peculiarly fitted to be one of the superintendants of the great Museum and Library of the Capital.

I have the correspondence between Marlborough and Heinsius. I do not think that there is much in it. But I may hereafter find reason to change my opinion.

Have you seen Wordsworth's Prelude? – It is the Excursion, weaker and more tedious. Before I read the Prelude I was surprised that a man who had finished so long and elaborate a work should keep it near half a century in his desk, and leave it to be published by his executors. But, after I had read it, my astonishment was at an end. The plain truth is that he wrote it when he was a Jacobin and was ashamed to print it after he became an exciseman. He goes all the lengths of Thelwall or Tom Paine; and the poem ends with loud vauntings of his own incorruptible integrity, – vauntings which he might well shrink from publishing when he had become an electioneering agent of the Lowthers.

Kindest regards to Lady Mahon, and to my Valentine of whose favour I am not a little proud.

Ever yours truly
T B Macaulay

TO THOMAS FLOWER ELLIS, 3 SEPTEMBER 1850

MS: Trinity College. *Published:* Trevelyan, II, 280.

Madeira Hall / Ventnor / Septr. 3. 1850

Dear Ellis,

Here I am, lodged most delightfully. I look out on one side to the crags and myrtles of the Undercliff against which my house is built. On the other side I have a view of the sea which is at this moment as blue as the sky, and as calm as the Serpentine. My little garden is charming. I wish that I may not, like Will Honeycomb, forget the sin and seacoal of London for innocence and haycocks. To be sure, as Higman well knows, innocence and haycocks do not always go together.

When will you come? Take your own time: but I am rather anxious that you should not lose this delicious weather, and defer your trip till the equinoctial storms are setting in. The earlier therefore the better. I can promise you plenty of water and of towels, good wine, good tea, and good cheese from town, good eggs, butter and milk from the farm at my door, a beautiful prospect from your bedroom window, and, if the weather keeps us within doors, Plautus's comedies, Plutarch's lives, twenty or thirty comedies of Calderon, Fra Paolo's history, and a little library of novels, to say nothing of my own compositions which, like Ligurinus, I will read to you stanti, sedenti, cacanti, etc. etc.

I am just returned from a walk of near seven hours and of full fifteen miles, part of it as steep as the monument. Indeed I was so knocked up with climbing Black Gang Chine that I lay on the turf at the top for a quarter of an hour wheezing like a grampus.

Ever yours,
T B Macaulay

MS: Trinity College.

Ventnor Isle of Wight / September 9. 1850

Dearest Baba,

I begin to long for a letter from you. Tell me how you are, what you are doing, whom you see, what books you read. Give me the history of a day. I will set you the example. I am quite rural, a perfect Damon or Menalcas. I rise soon after six, and enjoy the fresh sea breeze of the morning. I breakfast before nine. Then I write a page or so. Then I take a book – generally a Greek book – in my pocket, and set out on a ramble. I stray hour after hour over crags and through thickets of laurels and myrtles. When I am tired, I sit down on the grass and read. My walks are prodigious. Yesterday I walked sixteen measured miles without stopping. When I come home, which is generally about four in the afternoon, I sit in my garden, an extremely pretty garden, and read Fra Paolo's History of the Council of Trent. When the sun sinks behind the Undercliff it becomes too cold to sit in the open air. So I go in, and read in my drawing room till seven. Then I dine, and amuse myself with a novel and with the Times which makes its appearance together with the peaches for my dessert. After dinner I stroll in my garden for an hour by starlight; and by ten I am in bed. I have no acquaintance here; nor have I, since I left you eight days ago at Westbourne Terrace, spoken a word except to give orders to servants. Yet I never found time pass quicker. On Saturday Ellis comes down to stay a week or ten days with me. I think I shall call him Saturday, as Robinson Crusoe, in his desert island, called his only companion Friday.

I hear the best accounts of our dear little Alice. I have heard nothing of or from Mamma yet. Perhaps you can give me news.

Kindest remembrances to Grandmamma. Write, and tell me whether you are happy and well, and above all whether I can be of any use to you.

Ever yours, dearest,

T B Macaulay

MS: Stanhope Papers, Chevening.

Albany Nov 11. 1850

Dear Lord Mahon,

I return poor Hallam's letter. It is a heartbreaking business. I wait in painful anxiety for further intelligence. If one could do anything – But what can one do? –

I have read Southey's Life; and a very stupid book it is. The chief materials are his own letters; and he was a bad letter writer. There was nothing light or playful about him. He did indeed sometimes try to gambol, but with miserable effect. That quaint silly conceit which you quote about the Guelphs and Ghibellines is a very fair sample of his pleasantry.

He was in the right as to the idle scheme of rewarding literary merit with stars and ribands. But it surely did not lie in his mouth to blame that scheme. For he was as proud of his laurel as any miss of a new gown, and was constantly perking in every body's face that most absurd of all distinctions. I dare say that he has boasted of it twenty times at least in his verses. Now every argument that can be urged against the instituting of a literary order of Knighthood may be urged against the Laureateship. Moreover the Laureateship is associated with so many contemptible names, Shadwell, Tate, Eusden, Cibber, Whitehead, Pye, that it at once moves laughter. It would be some time at least before a new order of Knighthood could fall so low. I hope and trust that the vacancy of that crown is to be perpetual.

Ever yours truly
T B Macaulay

TO FRANCES MACAULAY, 15 NOVEMBER 1850

MS: Trinity College. *Partly published:* Trevelyan, II, 196n.

Albany London / Nov 15. 1850
Dearest Fanny,

If I told you all that I think about these disputes I should write a volume. The Pope is a fool, and hates the English nation and government. He meant, I am convinced, to insult and annoy the Queen and her ministers. His whole conduct in Ireland has evidently been directed to that end. Nevertheless the reasons popularly urged against this Bull seem to me absurd. We always knew that the Pope claimed spiritual jurisdiction; and I do not see that he now claims temporal jurisdiction. I therefore cannot but despise the vulgar outcry which I hear wherever I turn. Yet I cannot help enjoying the rage and terror of the Puseyites, who are utterly prostrated by this outbreak of popular feeling.

I could wish that Lord John had written more guardedly; and that, I plainly see, is the wish of some of his colleagues: probably by this time it is also his own wish. He has got much applause in England: but, when he was writing, he should have remembered that he had to govern several millions of Roman Catholics in Ireland, that to govern them at all is no easy task, and that anything which looks like an affront to their religion is certain to call forth very dangerous passions. I see plainly that some of the ministers are uneasy; and I have reason to believe that Lord Clarendon is still more so.

In the meantime these things keep London all alive. Yesterday the ballad singers were entertaining a great crowd under my window with bawling.

"Now all the old women are crying for fear:
The Pope is a coming: oh dear! oh dear!"
The wall of Burlington Gardens is covered with "No Popery," – "No Wafer Gods," – "Down with the Pope," and so forth.

I am pretty well, and have not yet felt the change of weather much. I am glad that you give a better account of Selina. Kindest love to her.

Yours ever

T B Macaulay

I am much less disturbed about the Pope than about poor Hallam. He is expected in town to day or to morrow. What a cruel fate his has been. I could find it in my heart to cry for him.

TO SARAH GRANT FRANZ, 9 DECEMBER 1850

Text: Sarah Grant Franz, *Wild Flowers,* 1878, Preface.

Albany, London, December 9, 1850.

Madam,

I am gratified by hearing that my Essays have given you pleasure, but much more grieved by finding that my advice has given you pain. You quite misunderstood me if you thought that I meant to express a low opinion of your compositions. They are beyond the reach of many very clever and accomplished women. Four-fifths of Chalmers's Collection of the British Poets consists of verses far inferior to yours. But, if you ask me whether I think it likely that you will attain a place among those great masters of the art of whom no age or country produces many, of whom England cannot at this moment be said to possess one, of whom in all Christendom there are not six, I should be guilty of flattery if I encouraged you to hope for such success. I myself, when a young man, aspired to be one of those great masters. Reflection and observation convinced me that it was impossible. I relinquished all thought of rivalling them, and contentedly took my place at their feet. It is surely no calamity not to be one of so small a class. Nor do I see any reason to think that the few who attain that eminence are happier than those who do not aspire so high. I have myself had a happier life than any man of letters that I ever knew, and the explanation is this – that I loved letters purely for their own sake; that I considered the exercise of the intellect as its own reward; that, if fame did not come, I did not miss it; that, if it came, I reckoned it as a godsend, as clear gain over and above the ample recompense which I had already received in the act of thinking and composing. I ought to apologise for all this egotism, but I shall be quite willing to be thought by you an egotist if my experience can be of any use to you.

I should be very sorry if you were to acquiesce in my judgment without appeal. I am a very fastidious reader of poetry, and ought not to undertake to answer for the public. Let me advise you to take the opinion of some other critic. / I have the honour to be, Madam,

Your faithful servant,
T. B. Macaulay.

TO FRANCES MACAULAY, 24 MARCH 1851

MS: Huntington Library.

Albany London March 24 / 1851

Dearest Fanny,

I am pretty well at present, and indeed have had nothing to complain of except a cold which has spared nobody here. I do not expect to be able to leave town before Easter. If I do, I am afraid that I must go, not to Brighton, but to Oxford. I have a good deal of work to do in the Library of All Souls, for which Milman will give me credentials if they are needed.

By the bye Milman tells me that his son, who has just taken orders, thinks it necessary to dress after the present fashion of the young clergy. The lad went accordingly to a great maker of ecclesiastical garments, and ordered one of those long vests which are worn, as you have doubtless observed, by Puseyite parsons. "Oh, Sir," quoth the tailor, "I understand. An M. B. waistcoat. We make thousands of them." "An M. B. waistcoat!" said Milman the younger; "What does an M. B. waistcoat mean?" "Oh, Sir, all the trade know it by that name." "But what does it mean?" "The Mark of the Beast, Sir."

You are right about Drummond, but quite wrong about the Speaker. He acted admirably. The rule of debate is that you must abstain from personalities, but that you may be as severe on opinions, institutions, etc.

as you please. You must not say that Mr. John O'Connell is a traitor or a knave. But you may say that conventual institutions are seminaries of vice and madness; and, though the expression may be violent and reprehensibly coarse, it is quite within the limits of parliamentary language. Suppose that, in a debate on the Slave trade, Mr. Wilberforce or Mr. Fox had said that a slave ship was a hell on earth – would it have been competent to a Liverpool merchant who owned slave ships to call the orator to order for indecorum? Surely not. I think Drummond's language such as no man ought to use, but such, at the same time, as is not and ought not to be prohibited by the rules of parliament.

The general aspect of affairs is disagreeable – Lord John extremely unpopular and losing weight in the house, – the schism between the Whigs and the Peelites widening rather than closing, – the Irish absurd and profligate as usual. I comfort myself by thinking that, in this country, the excess of an evil scarcely ever fails to produce a remedy. I am heartily glad that I am out of the arena. I do not know what part I should have taken. My feelings and good wishes are with my old colleagues: but my judgment is with Lord Aberdeen and Sir James Graham. Graham ought not to have quoted me. I have published nothing on the subject. I have said nothing about it except in the security of private conversation, and it is not fair to bring before the parliament and the country what a man who has nothing to do with politics, says at a breakfast party or at a club.

Ever yours
T B Macaulay

I inclose a few lines for Selina.

TO SIR EDWARD BULWER-LYTTON, 17 MAY 1851

MS: Hertfordshire County Council. *Published:* Earl of Lytton, *Life of Edward Bulwer, First Lord Lytton*, 1913, II, 145–7.

Albany May 17. 1851

Dear Sir Edward,

Thanks for your pamphlet, which I have read, and for your play which I saw yesterday night. If the play amuses and interests me as much in the perusal as it did in the representation I shall rate it much higher than the pamphlet, though the pamphlet is what everything that you write must be.

As to your scheme, I am not aware that, except to four or five people in very small societies, I have expressed any opinion respecting it. But I certainly do believe that its tendency is to give encouragement not to good writers, but to bad, or, at best, middling writers. And I think that you would yourself feel some misgivings if you would try your plan by a simple practical test. Suppose that you succeed beyond your expectations as to pecuniary ways and means. Suppose ten or twelve charming cottages built on the land which you so munificently propose to bestow. Suppose funds to be provided for paying your Warden and ten or twelve fellows. And suppose that you then sit down to make your choice. Whom will you chuse? Form a list of the thirty best writers now living in the United Kingdom. Then strike off from this list first all who require no assistance, and secondly all who do indeed require assistance, but who actually receive from the state pensions as large as you propose to give. I believe that you will find that five or six and twenty, if not more, of your thirty, will fall into one or the other of these classes. I apprehend therefore that you will be driven to fill your Guild with, to use the mildest term, second rate writers; and this I say on the supposition that the selection is made with the greatest judgment and with an impartiality which the history of literary institutions hardly warrants us in expecting.

There is no analogy between the case of authors and the case of actors. A theatrical fund is a very good thing. For to the existence of the theatrical art it is necessary that there should be inferior performers. That Garrick may act Hamlet, he must have a Rosencrantz and Guildenstern. That Mrs. Siddons may perform Lady Macbeth, she must have a waiting woman. Nothing can be more reasonable than that those who derive pleasure from the exertions of genius should encourage that subordinate class of artist without whose help genius would be unable to exert itself. But there is no such connection between the great and the small writer as exists between the great and the small actor. In literature, I am afraid it will always be found that a bounty on mediocrity operates as a fine on excellence.

I could say a great deal more. But I have already plagued you too long. I need not say that I do justice to your motives, and to the motives of those who are joined with you in this undertaking: and you, I am sure, will not suspect me of wanting sympathy for men of merit in distress. If your project turns out well, I shall have real pleasure in taking to myself the shame of an erroneous prediction. Hitherto you have every reason to congratulate yourself. The success of yesterday night was complete. The principal criticism which occurred to me was that the scene in the coffee-room suffers from the crowding of the actors into so small a space. It seems hardly necessary to employ a spy for the purpose of watching conspirators who talk loud treason in so thick a press of people. It is not easy to set this right. Yet perhaps you might a little thin the room of company while the most important and secret things are said. In general the stage effect was admirable: and I was particularly delighted with Lord Wilmot.

Ever yours truly
T B Macaulay

TO MARGARET TREVELYAN, 10 AUGUST 1851

MS: Trinity College.

Malvern August 10 / 1851

My dearest Baba,

Another letter from my darling. I am much, very much obliged to you. It is a great happiness to me to think that you remember me; and nothing that interests you can be too trivial to interest me.

I live here in utter solitude, and enjoy it much. Yesterday indeed I was accosted by a man whose face I seemed to myself to recollect, but whose name had completely escaped me. He was very familiar, told me that he had been lamed by tumbling from a coach on the Allegany Mountains, gave me the history of his water cure, and asked permission to call. I could not refuse. But where or when I met him, at Calcutta or at Rome, – whether he is a member of parliament or an Edinburgh elector, a barrister on the Northern Circuit or a fellow of Trinity I have not the faintest notion. He will come, I hope, when I am out, and leave his card. He is the only acquaintance, if I can call him so, that I have seen.

I read and walk all day. Walking indeed is matter of choice with me. For there are vehicles without number; and, on the high roads, I am earnestly pressed to mount. Yesterday a hearse passed, returning from a funeral, and the driver, a most solemn looking being, asked me whether I would like a ride "There is plenty of room, Sir." I could not help laughing out. "All in good time," I said; "some day or other I shall want you; but I am not ready for you yet." He did not in the least relax his gravity. "I meant, Sir, that there was room on the box." I declined the privilege however of exhibiting myself to all Malvern on the box of a hearse, and pursued my ramble on foot.

To day I went to the Abbey Church – really a venerable and beautiful Church, and not a bad sermon. I think the Choir was under repair when we were here in 1846; for it did not then please me as it does now. You, I suppose, have forgotten all about that tour, – my rage at Spetchley and the imbecillity of the Worcester waiter excepted.

Love to all.

Ever yours
T B Macaulay

Just post time.

MS: Trinity College. *Partly published:* Trevelyan, II, 210–11.

Malvern August 19 / 1851

Dearest Baba,

I suppose that you are at Enmore again after your Plymouth trip. Pray give me an account of what you saw. My recollections of my only visit to Plymouth are very sad; and so should your mamma's be. I could cry to think of those times, though I managed not to cry then.

My days glide away here strangely fast. Except an occasional walk with Senior, I have no intercourse with anybody. He asked me to dinner. But he dines at two; and I cannot eat at that hour; so that I escaped. I have just now, on returning from a ramble of seven hours into the heart of Herefordshire, found on my table a card from Lord Gainsborough. I must return his call; and that will be, I hope, all that will pass between us. For he is the greatest fool and bore in the whole peerage.

No – no society for me, but the society of the hills and woods, of the flowers and streams, of the rapid Severn and the gentle Wye. Let me hold communion with nature, and avoid all fellowship with men. Towns, – who can bear the thought of those labyrinths of brick, overhung by clouds of smoke, and roaring like Niagara with the wheels of drays, chariots, flies, cabs, and omnibuses. Give me rural seclusion like this, especially when I can smell, as I now do, a leg of mutton on the spit for my dinner, – not your Middlesex mutton, fit only to make tallow candles of, but hill mutton, fed on the heath round the Worcestershire beacon. Truly judicious was the poet who sang –

> "Long live the mountain scenery!
> Long live the mountain mutton!
> Hyde Park, with all its Queenery,
> Lace, China, plate, machinery,
> Or Milman's City Deanery
> I prize not at a button."

"Queenery" – a word invented with bold but laudable poetical license: for, even in his boldness, our poet is always judicious. Àpropos of poets, I finished the Iliad to day. I had not read it through since the end of 1837, when I was at Calcutta, and when you often called me away from my studies to show you pictures and to feed the crows. I never admired the old fellow so much, or was so strongly moved by him. What a privilege genius like his enjoys. I could not tear myself away. I read the last five books at a stretch during my walk to day, and was at last forced to turn into a by path, lest the parties of walkers should see me blubbering for imaginary beings, the creations of a ballad-maker who has been dead two thousand seven hundred years. What is the power and glory of Cæsar and Alexander to that? – Think what it would be to be assured that the inhabitants of Monomotapa would weep over one's writings, Anno Domini 4551. – That is the parallel case. Loves and kind remembrances to all.

Ever yours,

T B Macaulay

TO MARGARET TREVELYAN, 18 SEPTEMBER 1851

MS: Trinity College. *Partly published:* Trevelyan, II, 205–6.

Malvern September 18. 1851

Dearest Baba,

I am extremely sorry to hear of your cold. However such things do not last. We have of late had as much fog here in the mornings as you can have had in London. The whole plain of the Severn, when I rise, is completely buried in mist on one side: the tops of the hills are capped with clouds on the other; and, instead of enjoying the most extensive prospect in England, I can but just distinguish the elms in my own grounds. The days continue to be dark and hazy till about one in the afternoon. Then the gloom disperses: the sky becomes blue: the sun shines out gloriously; and, from the top of the ridge all Herefordshire, Worcestershire and Gloucestershire lie spread out like a map before me. When I go to bed I see brilliant starlight: but when I wake again I again find everything covered with fog. This has been the regular course of every day since Sunday last. You, I am afraid from your account, have had our mornings, but not our afternoons.

I hope that you will be quite well on the 2nd of October, and that the weather will be fine. For I mean to take you on that day to the Exhibition. I am impatient to see the Swedish contributions; and I am not a little curious to know whether the resort of foreigners be really such as to give anything like a new character to the streets of London. Your sketches of the strangers are very droll.

Tell me how you like Schiller's Mary Stuart. It is not one of my favourite pieces. I should put it fourth among his plays. I arrange them thus – Wallenstein, William Tell, Don Carlos, Mary Stuart, the Maid of Orleans. At a great interval comes the Bride of Messina; and then at another great interval Fieschi. Cabal and Love I never could get through. The Robbers is a mere schoolboy rant below serious criticism, but not without indications of mental vigour which required to be disciplined by much thought and study. But though I do not put Mary Stuart very high among

249

Schiller's works, I think the Fotheringay scenes in the fifth Act equal to anything that he ever wrote, indeed equal to anything dramatic that has been produced in Europe since Shakspeare. I hope that you will feel the wonderful truth and beauty of that part of the play.

Sintram is trash – as unmeaning as the History of Jack and the Bean Stalk, and a great deal duller. Perhaps you may think otherwise. There is an age at which we are disposed to think that whatever is odd and extravagant is great. At that age we are liable to be taken in by such essayists as Carlyle, such orators as Irving, such painters as Fuseli, such plays as the Robbers, such romances as Sintram. A better time comes, when we would give all Fuseli's hobgoblins for one of Reynolds's little children, and all Sintram's dialogues with Death and the Devil for one speech of Mrs. Norris or Miss Bates. Tell me however, – as of course you will, – quite truly what you think of Sintram. By the bye the author's name is not Touché but I believe Fouqué. And àpropos of orthography, who taught you to spell Cohinoor in so queer a way? Is it one of your papa's odd forms of oriental words? I stick to the common practice, and continue to write *Mahomet,* though I see that the imposter figures as Mahommed, Mohammed, Mâhmet, Moûhmed, Mahômet, Mahmoud, and has in short as many aliases as one of the swell mob.

Love to Mamma and Papa and Alice.

Ever yours,
T B Macaulay

TO SIR CHARLES WOOD, 23 NOVEMBER 1851

MS: The Earl of Halifax.

Albany November 23 / 1851

My dear Wood,

You will not, I hope, think that I take an improper liberty with you if, emboldened by the recollection of our old political connection, and of the constant kindness which has existed between us, I venture to offer a suggestion about the Solicitorship of the Treasury.

I did not know till to day that the Solicitorship was vacant. I learned it from Trevelyan, on whom I called this afternoon; and we had some conversation about the importance of the office and the difficulty of finding a person perfectly qualified to fill it. The same thought struck us both at the same moment. I do not believe that there is at the bar any man fitter in any respect for such a post than Ellis, the Recorder of Leeds, and Attorney General of the Duchy of Lancaster. He has just been acting as Assessor to Lord Carlisle at Preston, and distinguished himself only last

Thursday by an argument in the Queen's Bench which was praised by the judges, and which every body describes as excellent, on the criminal information against Newman. He was in the Municipal Commission and in the Commission which went to the Channel Islands; and the reports which he drew up and which are among the blue books contain abundant proofs of research and ability. The report on the Channel Islands was commended by Guizot.

Ellis is one of my oldest and dearest friends, a friend of more than a quarter of a century. I lie under great obligations to him. A large part of the literary success which I have obtained I owe to the minute attention which he has bestowed on my writings, and to the kind severity of his criticism. But I should never think of recommending any man to such a place as the Solicitorship on personal grounds. Trevelyan, who is quite unbiassed, agrees with me. And I am confident that there is no Judge under whom Ellis has practised, no minister with whom he has done business, who will not confirm what I say. Lord Campbell, the Chancellor, Lord Carlisle, occur to me at once. If you are, as I collect from what Trevelyan said, looking out for a man of learning, of quick apprehension, of sure-footed judgment, I am certain that you cannot find a better.

Whether he would accept the place is a point about which I have some doubt. His professional income is larger than the salary: but a professional income is not a certainty; and his gains are as hardly earned as those of any man in the Inns of Court. Had he been in town, I would have seen him before writing to you. But he went into the country yesterday, and will not return till to morrow. In such cases every day is of importance. I have therefore determined to take the risk of being thought officious both by you and by him. / Ever, my dear Wood,

Yours very truly
T B Macaulay

TO SIR CHARLES WOOD, 25 NOVEMBER 1851

MS: The Earl of Halifax.

Albany November 25 / 1851

Dear Wood,

Thanks for the kind way in which you have taken my intermeddling.

I do not think that I can justly be accused of tardiness, at least by comparison with other historians. Robertson was ten years employed on the History of Charles the Fifth; and all Robertson's authorities were, I believe, in print. I do not remember that he consulted any M.S. I am confident that he made no journey to the scene of any event that he had to relate. I have to turn over thousands of pages of manuscript, French, Dutch and Spanish as well as English. I have been once to the Archives at Paris; and I must go again. I have visited Londonderry, the Boyne, Cork, Limerick, Killicrankie, Glencoe; and I shall probably visit Steenkirk, Landen and Namur. If in five or six years I can produce a tolerable history of William's reign I shall think that I have done my duty.

Ever yours truly
T B Macaulay

TO FRANCES MACAULAY, 19 JUNE 1852

MS: Huntington Library.

Albany June 19. 1852

Dearest Fanny,

I have not made and do not mean to make the smallest move towards the people of Edinburgh. But they, to my great surprise, have suddenly found out that they used me ill five years ago, and that they are paying the penalty of their injustice and unreasonableness. They could find nobody of whom they were not ashamed to stand for a place which had got so bad a character; and it seemed that they were in danger of having members who would have made them regret not only me, but Cowan. Then, without any communication with me, it was suggested by some of the most respectable citizens that the town might recover its character and put to flight the cliques which domineered over it, by electing me without asking me to go down or to give any pledge or even any opinion on political matters. The hint was eagerly taken up; and I am assured that the enthusiasm in my favour is great, and that I shall probably be at the head of the poll. All that I have been asked to do is to say that, if I am chosen on those terms, I will sit. On full consideration, I did not think that I could, consistently with my duty, refuse. To me personally the sacrifice is great, though I shall not make a drudge of myself, and though I shall certainly never, in any event, accept office. The appearance of my next volumes may be postponed a year or two. But it seems to me to be of the highest importance that great constituent bodies should learn to respect the conscience and the honor of their representatives, should not expect slavish obedience from men of spirit and ability, and should, instead of catechizing such men and cavilling at them, repose in them a large confidence. The way in which such bodies have of late behaved has driven many excellent persons from public life, and will, unless a remedy is found, drive away many more. The conduct of Edinburgh towards me was not worse than that of several other places to their members, but it attracted more notice, and has been often mentioned, in parliament and out of parliament, as a flagrant instance of the caprice and perverseness of even the most intelligent bodies of electors. It is therefore surely not an unimportant nor an undesirable thing that Edinburgh should, quite spontaneously, make a very signal, I may say, an unprecedented, reparation. The event will be the more remarkable because the whole island, but more especially Scotland, is Maynooth-mad. Almost every member who is chosen by Scotland will be pledged to vote at least for inquiry into the Maynooth system. Several good men who have refused to give that pledge, have been forced to retire. Now, if I am elected, I shall be elected unpledged; and that though every body knows that I am for the Maynooth endowment, and that I lost my seat in 1847 chiefly for supporting the Maynooth endowment. I cannot think that, in these circumstances, I should be justified in saying that I will not serve. If the parliament should be a long one, I shall probably take the Chiltern Hundreds before it ends. I shall certainly never consent to be reelected. Having nothing to hope or to fear from my constituents I shall be as independent as if I were a peer. So the matter stands. If they elect me, you may be assured that it will be without the smallest advance or concession on my part. If they do not elect me, I shall be more than content.

Do not talk about this matter more than you find absolutely necessary; but treat it lightly, as I do in all companies where I hear it mentioned. I have a vexatious cold in the head about which I think a great deal more. Six weeks ago I was longing for rain; and now I am longing for dry weather. These are the signs of advancing age. Love to John, his wife, and children.

Ever yours,
T B Macaulay

TO LADY TREVELYAN, 13 JULY [1852]

MS: Huntington Library. Envelope: Lady Trevelyan. Subscription: T B M.

Albany July 13

Dearest H,
 At twelve –

Macaulay	1275
Maclaren	1110
Cowan	1090
Bruce	793
Campbell	497 –

I think that there can now be no doubt of the result now. I have gained on every one of the other candidates steadily. At 10 I was 74 before Maclaren, at 11 I was 120 before him. At twelve I was 165 before him. I have also increased my distance from Cowan, though not much. There is now very little probability that either will pass me, and no chance at all of my being passed by both.

I have been in Bright's hands yesterday and to day. He tells me that it is all bile: and Holland who looked in as a friend to ask about the election told me, without a fee, exactly the same – "I see by your look that you are bilious." Bright has given me calomel enough to poison a gun elephant. To morrow I am off for Clifton. Unless I hear from you to the contrary I will call in Westbourne Terrace in the cool of the evening – say nine o'clock, and let you know the final result.

Ever yours,
T B Macaulay

TO LADY TREVELYAN, 15 JULY 1852

MS: Trinity College. *Envelope:* Lady Trevelyan / 20 Westbourne Terrace / Hyde Park Gardens / London. *Subscription:* TBM.

Royal Hotel / Clifton July 15 / 1852

Dearest Hannah,

I am here in tolerably comfortable rooms, but not as yet much better for the change of air. That was indeed hardly to be expected. I received to day kind letters from Craig, Rutherfurd and others; and I have been all the morning employed in writing answers. I intend to be extremely courteous and gracious to the Edinburgh electors now. It was proper to be reserved and high while the event was at all doubtful. But what then was dignity would now be insolence.

William has left me for Herefordshire. He is to make inquiries at Malvern, but to conclude nothing.

How many old recollections this place calls up. Yet how things are changed: or rather how I am changed. In this very house Selina and I in the summer of 1811 breakfasted with my uncle Colin. The Royal Hotel was then the boast of Clifton. It was considered as the first house of the kind in the kingdom. The splendour of the plate, china, and furniture astonished me. On every dish and saucer was a picture of the hotel. Now this palace seems to me a great, rambling, shabby, caravansery, in which I can just make shift to get my meals and my sleep. Hard by is a villa built by Sir William Draper with a cenotaph in the grounds. I well remember that the first time that I ever heard the word cenotaph was in 1811 from my uncle Colin when he showed me that monument. I did not know

Greek enough to discover the meaning and supposed that it had something to do with Senate, and was spelt with an S. But I thought house, grounds, and cenotaph, magnificent. Now – On the other hand the rocks and woods which then interested me not at all give me now the greatest delight.

Ask Selina whether she remembers our breakfast at the Royal Hotel when we lodged at a certain Mrs. Anderson's about a hundred yards from where I am now writing, – and made acquaintance with a certain Mrs. and Miss Elliot, – and got an abominable religious novel, then just published, and entitled Self Controul, – and saw my poor aunt Hannah very pale and weak in a great arm chair, and how we were shown a most extraordinary dwarf – a woman of forty, less than Alice, and how Uncle Colin took up Elements of Morality, and said that it was a Socinian book. These and hundreds of small events which happened here that summer I remember as if only a day, instead of forty one years, had passed since. Love to Trevelyan, Baba and Alice.

Ever yours,
T B M

TO THOMAS FLOWER ELLIS, 17 JULY 1852

MS: Trinity College. *Partly published:* Trevelyan, II, 322.

Royal Hotel Clifton / July 17. 1852

Dear Ellis,

I am a little better, and must soon think of going to Edinburgh and haranguing. The probability is that I shall leave London for the north just as you are coming back from the north to London. The earliest day on which I can make a public appearance is Saturday the 24th. Early in the following week I hope to see you in town, and to be able to concert plans for the summer, or rather for the autumn.

Rely on it that I shall never be in office again. Every motive is against it, – avarice and ambition as well as the love of ease and the love of liberty. I have been twice a cabinet minister, and never made a farthing by being so. I have now been four years out of office; and I have added ten thousand pounds to my capital. So much for avarice. Then for ambition, – I should be a far greater man as M.P. for Edinburgh, supporting a liberal government cordially, but not servilely, than as Chancellor of the Duchy or Paymaster of the Forces.

Tell Campbell that I am very sensible of his kindness. I receive congratulations from all quarters. The most fervent perhaps are from Graham. My own feelings are mixed. If I analyse them strictly I find that I am glad and sorry, glad to have been elected; sorry to have to sit. The election was a great honor. The sitting will be a great bore. I discriminate, you see, much more accurately than that pious old maid whose religious meditations are criticized in the Monthly Review. "For the sin of our first mother," says this lady, "our sex was justly punished with the cruel pains of conception."

I have a long story for you about my adventures with an apothecary here. They would furnish a good subject for a farce. But they must wait till we meet.

Ever yours
T B Macaulay

TO SIR WILLIAM GIBSON CRAIG, 24 JULY 1852

MS: Scottish Record Office. *Envelope:* Sir W Gibson Craig Bart. / etc. etc. etc. / Riccarton / Edinburgh. *Subscription:* TBM.

Albany London / July 24. 1852

Dear Craig,

I am sorry to say that, since I wrote to you last, I have been very unwell. To day Bright after a very long and close examination with the help of a mysterious looking tube, pronounced that the action of the heart was deranged, that quiet was absolutely necessary to me, and that it would be dangerous for me to make a long journey, and still more dangerous to make a long speech. He would hardly have prevented me from going to Edinburgh if my own sensations had not convinced me that the speech would be a matter of physical impossibility, and that I should be forced to sit down in five minutes. I shall remain a few days under his care, and then return by short journeys to Clifton. He encourages me to hope that some weeks of repose in that delicious air will set me up again. If I should want nurses my sister and niece will come down at an hour's notice.

I have no reason to doubt that this complaint will give way to proper treatment. But I feel that my health is giving way; and I look forward with much uneasiness to the late hours and bad air of the House of Commons. It is very probable that I shall, in no long time, be forced to apply to D'Israeli for the only place that I mean ever to take, the Stewardship of the Chiltern Hundreds. Of course I shall do nothing of the sort without consulting you. But it would be desirable that you and our friend Black should even now begin to consider what course, in such an event, it would be proper for you to take.

Before I leave town I will send you my address at Clifton.

Ever yours truly
T B Macaulay

MS: Trinity College. *Envelope:* Miss Macaulay / Temple House / Brighton. *Subscription:* TBM.

16 Caledonia Place / Clifton / August 8. 1852

Dearest Selina,

I am comfortably lodged here, and am getting better, in spite of the weather which prevents me from rambling all day as I did last year at Malvern and the year before at the Isle of Wight. Then I was never at home from ten in the morning till near six in the afternoon. Now I cannot venture out for half an hour without great risk of having to change everything when I come home. I have not had occasion to consult any physician here. Should I want one, I shall send for Dr. Symmonds.

The great evil of coming to a place like this is that all sorts of bores think themselves entitled to intrude on you and to kill the time by lounging in your drawing room. Yesterday while I was quietly reading, a Mr. Wightwick sent up his card. He told me that he had known John Macaulay at Plymouth I forget how many years ago; and on the strength of this connection he pestered me with his opinions about the weather, the waters, the scenery, and so forth. Scarcely was Mr. Wightwick gone when a Mr. Bruce enters, – a horrible old twaddle. He told me that he had seen my name in the subscription book of a reading room here; and that he thought that he might venture to call, because twelve years ago he had seen me at an evening party at old Mr. Longman's. Then he told me his pedigree – how he was great grandson of Sir Something Bruce of Kinross. Then he informed me that Mrs. Bruce was in weak health – that he had lately made a tour in the Isle of Wight – that he was pleased with the Undercliff – that Prince Albert had a farm at Osborne. I could have kicked him down stairs with the greatest pleasure. As soon as he was gone I ordered William to let nobody in whom he did not know, or who did not come on particular business. Nothing is so intolerable as a watering place idler who, because he is weary of his own company, pesters others with it.

The Harfords have been very civil; and I have a free admission to the grounds of Blaise Castle – a great favour. I intend to visit Barley Wood when the weather mends.

You are right about Miss Hay. I called her Miss Elliot in writing to Hannah. I confounded her with a Miss Elliot who, about the same time lodged at Clapham – at Rippens's or some such name.

Love to dear Fanny. It was very kind of her to offer to come and nurse me. But I hope that it will be long before I give so much trouble to anybody. Hannah is still at Enmore.

Ever yours
T B Macaulay

MS: Trinity College. *Extract published:* Trevelyan, II, 328.

Edinburgh October 31. / 1852

Dearest Hannah,

I arrived here at half after nine yesterday evening, rather tired, but pretty well. This is a fine day; and I feel quite equal to my work. I shall not dine out. I shall stay at home as much as I can during the day, and take a quiet walk in the evening when I shall not be seen. On Tuesday I am to harangue a great meeting. On Wednesday I go to York, and on Thursday to London. I may perhaps look in on you that evening.

I have just been to Guthrie's Church. It was Sacrament Sunday; and I saw the Presbyterian administration of the Eucharist which I had not seen for thirty five years. Guthrie is a man of considerable ability and energy; but, to be sure, if the question between forms of prayer and extemporaneous effusions were to be decided by comparing the English Communion service with his performance, there could be little doubt as to the decision. "Lord, if thou hadst invited us to nothing but crumbs and cold water we ought to have been thankful. How much more for bread like this, and wine to make us of a cheerful countenance!" This is not quite in the vein of "Therefore with Angels and Archangels." Loves.

Ever yours

T B M

The town is as still as if it were midnight. It is a Sunday – a Presbyterian Sunday – a Presbyterian Sacrament Sunday. A person who opposes himself to the fanatical humour on this subject runs a great risk of being affronted. There was one person whom Christians generally mention with respect who, I am sure, could not have walked Prince's Street in safety, and who would have said to some of my grave constituents "Ye Hypocrites!"

MS: Trinity College.

Edinburgh Nov 2. 1852

Dearest Hannah,

I have just returned from the meeting. I spoke an hour with immense applause. I found myself at last getting faint, partly with heat and partly with exertion, and ended rather abruptly. But the success was complete, and the enthusiasm of the audience such as I have hardly ever seen. I got better as soon as I was in the fresh air; and I now feel quite a load taken off my heart. I have entirely satisfied myself as to this – that my mental vigour, about which I care very much more than about my bodily health, has not been diminished by my illness. I wish that you and my dear Baba could have heard me. Love to all.

Ever yours
T B M

TO THOMAS FLOWER ELLIS, 13 DECEMBER 1852

MS: Trinity College. *Partly published:* Trevelyan, II, 354.

Albany December 13. 1852

Dear Ellis,

It is quite impossible that I can dine with you on Tuesday. If I venture out at all, it will be to the House of Commons. I have written to Hayter desiring him to pair me for this evening. I am better, but still unfit to face such weather as this.

The government, to my great relief, has decided that I cannot be permitted to become a Knight of the Prussian Order of Merit. To be sure I should not have had to carry my cross and ribband at my button hole more than once or twice a year: but that would have been once or twice too much. However I have written most politely to Humboldt, and have told him, with not less truth than civility, that his letter will be as much valued by me as the Insignia which I have been forced to decline.

Poor Empson died with admirable fortitude and cheerfulness. I find that his wife was lately brought to bed. I thought that she had been still expecting her accouchement. He spoke to her, to his friends, to his other children, with kindness, but with perfect firmness. But when the baby was put on his bed, he burst into tears. Poor fellow! – For my part, I feel that I should die best in the situation of Charles the First or Lewis the Sixteenth or Montrose. I mean quite alone – surrounded by enemies, and nobody that I cared for near me. The parting is the dreadful thing. I do not wonder at Russell's saying – "The bitterness of death is past."

Will you dine here on Friday? The debate cannot last so long, nor my Influenza. And then we will do justice to the Champagne.

[no signature]

MS: Trinity College. *Extract published:* Trevelyan, II, 323.

Albany March 14. 1853

Dearest Fanny,

I meant to vote for Mr. Alford, – that is, if I am able to vote at all. I have also written to Cornwall Lewis to advise him to do the same.

I hope to see you well on Monday. I am much easier since the weather became mild. But last July was a crisis in my life. I became twenty years older in a week, and shall never be young again. A mile is more to me now than ten miles a year ago. But it matters little if I can keep my faculties and my affections, and if my temper does not sour. I am not sure that I do not enjoy life more than I ever did. Though I am confined to my rooms except for two hours in the middle of the day when it is fine, I never feel the time heavy. I have been writing much. I have done with the national debt; and am pretty well satisfied.

I am taking the greatest care of myself that I may be able to go to Paris with you. The exertion of the first day is the only thing that I doubt about. I shall probably sleep the preceding night in Westbourne Terrace. Love to our friends at Rothley.

Ever yours
T B Macaulay

TO GEORGE OTTO TREVELYAN, 1 AUGUST 1853

MS: University of Newcastle. *Mostly published:* Trevelyan, II, 422–4.

Tunbridge Wells / August 1. / 1853

Dear George,

I am glad to hear that you are so pleasantly lodged, and that Mamma enjoys her palace and her park so much.

I am glad that you are working hard. Did you ever read Paradise Lost? If not, I would advise you to read it now. For it is the best commentary that I know on the Prometheus. There was a great resemblance between the genius of Æschylus and the genius of Milton; and this appears most strikingly in those two wonderful creations of the imagination, Prometheus and Satan. I do not believe that Milton borrowed Satan from the Greek drama. For, though he was an excellent scholar after the fashion of his time, Æschylus was, I suspect, a little beyond him. You cannot conceive how much the facilities for reading the Greek writers have increased within the last two hundred years, how much better the text is now printed, and how much light tne successive labours of learned men have thrown on obscure passages. I was greatly struck with this when at

Althorpe, I looked through Lord Spencer's magnificent collection of Aldine editions. Numerous passages which are now perfectly simple were mere heaps of nonsense. And no writer suffered more than Æschylus, for there is a lyrical obscurity, not only in his Odes, but even in his dialogue, as I dare say you have discovered.

Note particularly in the Prometheus the magnificent history of the origin of arts and sciences. That passage shows Æschylus to have been, not only a poet of the first order, but a great thinker. It is the fashion to call Euripides a philosophical poet: but I remember nothing in Euripides so philosophical as that rapid enumeration of all the discoveries and inventions which make the difference between savage and civilised man.

The latter part of the play is glorious. I know nothing finer than the whole from the lines

Σέβου προσεύχου, θῶπτε τὸν κρατοῦντ' ἀεί.
ἐμοὶ δ' ἔλασσον Ζηνὸς ἢ μηδὲν μέλει
δράτω κρατείτω τόνδε τὸν μικρον χρόνον
ὅπως θέλει· δαρὸν γὰρ οὐκ ἄρξει θεοῖς.*

Or is it βραχὺν χρόνον? I rather think βραχὺν is better.†

I am very busy here getting some of my speeches ready for the press; and during the day I get no reading except while I walk on the heath; and then I read Plato, one of the five first rate Athenians. The other four are your friends Æschylus and Thucydides, Sophocles, and Demosthenes. I know of no sixth Athenian who can be added to the list. Certainly not Euripides, nor Xenophon, nor Isocrates, nor Æschines. – But I forgot Aristophanes. More shame for me. He makes six. And I can certainly add nobody else to the six. How I go on gossiping about these old fellows when I should be thinking of other things. Love to Mamma and Papa and Baba and Alice.

Ever yours,
T B Macaulay

TO THOMAS FLOWER ELLIS, 4 AUGUST 1853

MS: Trinity College.

Tunbridge Wells / August 4. 1853

Dear Ellis,

I am sorry that I must give up the hope of seeing you here. But I hope that the days which you take away from your intended visit to Tunbridge

* 'Worship, adore, and fawn upon whoever is thy lord. But for Zeus I care less than naught. Let him do his will, let him hold his power for his little day – since not for long shall he bear sway over the gods' (Loeb translation).   † 'For a short time'; 'short'.

Wells you will add to your tour. I think that we shall probably find it more convenient to cross from Dover to Calais, and to go thence by railway, through Lille to Brussels. The boats to Calais always start at a fixed hour, as they carry the mails; and the voyage is not a third part of the voyage to Ostend, a matter which is of more importance to you than to me.

I write six or seven hours a day, and rather take to my work, and become partial to my speeches in their cleansed form. I walk on the heath two or three hours in the morning with Plato in my hand. I like the Theætetus much better than formerly, the Apology and the Phædon rather less. I have now begun the Republic. I think that I understand Greek better now than I ever did. Many passages which I could not make out in India now seem quite plain to me; and I have no more help in the way of notes here than there, indeed rather less.

I think of treating Vizitelly as Pope treated Curll; – the vagabond! – Craig wants me to attack him in an equity court. But I shall content myself with putting forth a ballad on his hanging himself. What do you say to this –

> Devil who erst didst play a tune
>   At midnight to Corelli,
> Scrape loud thy fiddle while I sing
>   The fate of Vizitelly.
>
> Beset by duns and bums enough
>   To puzzle Machiavelli,
> He climbed the stool, he tied the noose,
>   Poor Henry Vizitelly.
>
> A while he stood as pale as death,
>   And quaking like a jelly.
> "Ah me," he said, "I'm rightly named.
>   I soon shall *visit hell-I.*"
>
> After a minute's strife between
>   The *Nolle* and the *Velle*,
> He kicked the stool, and high in air
>   Swung Henry Vizitelly.
>
> But the rope broke; and down he fell;
>   And his guts burst out of his belly:
> So did this second Judas die
>   The pirate Vizitelly.

I leave Tunbridge Wells on the 19th for Hatfield where the Trevelyans are. On Tuesday the 23d I shall be at the Albany again. I shall probably hear from you before the 19th.

Ever yours,
T B Macaulay

Is not the pun in the third verse Σουιφτικώτατον.*

TO MARGARET TREVELYAN, 1 SEPTEMBER 1853

MS: Trinity College.

Heidelberg. September 1. / 1853

Dearest Baba,

I have not time to send you a history of my travels. But you will be glad to hear that they have been in the highest degree pleasant. We had one bad day, Monday; and that mattered little: for we only went from Cologne to Bonn through a country as flat as Lincolnshire. We have since had three glorious days. The first we spent in running up the Rhine by steam from Bonn to Mayence. At first I was a little disappointed: but after we had passed Coblentz and Ehrenbreitstein the scenery delighted me beyond description. I have gone down the Rhone, and both down and up the Loire; and neither deserves to be compared to the Rhine. From Mayence we went yesterday by railway to Frankfort, lounged about there during four hours, saw the house where Goëthe was born, the Cathedral where the Emperors were crowned, the cemetery with Thorwaldsen's sculptures, and, what interested me more than all, the Jewry – the Judengasse. In the afternoon we came hither by railway through a fine country. This morning we have passed near six hours in seeing the castle and roaming through the woods. We shall stay here to day, that our linen may be washed in the beautiful Neckar, and shall dine at seven on trout from the fishponds of the castle and on glorious hock marked with Prince Metternich's seal. To morrow we go to Strasburg, where I hope to find letters saying that you are all well. I know nothing about English matters. The Times of Saturday contained the last information that I possess. Perhaps the Queen is dead. Perhaps Lord Aberdeen is turned out. Perhaps there has been a Chartist insurrection; and the British republic has been proclaimed. God bless all at Hatfield.

Ever yours, dearest.
T B M

* 'Most Swift-like'.

MS: Huntington Library.

Albany London / October 4. 1853

Dearest Fanny,

I saw Palmerston's speech. It was very civil. I wish that it had been as true.

I do not very well know what to say about Miss Cunninghame. I should never think of trying to convert a Roman Catholic to Protestantism either in Tuscany or in England: for I think that, ten to one, I should make him an infidel, or, at least, unfix all his opinions. What I have seen of converted Roman Catholics has not made a favourable impression on me. But, I suppose, Miss Cunninghame thinks that the Pope is Antichrist, the Beast, the Man of Sin, and so forth; and, so thinking, she might, as it seems to me, defend her conduct by arguments which you would not find it easy to answer. The Laws of Tuscany forbid her to make converts, it is true: and the laws of Rome forbade the primitive Xtns to make converts; and the laws of England forbade our reformers to make converts. Why is she more bound to obey the Grand Duke than Peter was bound to obey Herod, or Lambert to obey Henry the Eighth? As I am unable to prove to her that she is in the wrong, so I must own myself quite unable to prove to the Grand Duke that he is in the wrong. He might say – "You in England punish people for circulating impious tracts. You punished the bookseller who sold Paine's Age of Reason. You sent Carlisle and Taylor, the Devil's chaplain, and a good many of their underlings to prison for distributing Atheistical and Deistical works. You cannot possibly think worse of the Age of Reason than I think of the Pilgrim's Progress. Paine's doctrines can do no more than send a man to Hell; and, in my opinion, Bunyan's doctrines will assuredly send a man there. I have as good a right to my opinion as you have to yours. Abolish therefore your own laws against blasphemy, before you blame me for inforcing my laws against blasphemy." I am clear as to this, that we have no right to interfere in the matter, except by expostulation. Nevertheless, my English blood is so much stirred that I should rejoice, though I should not approve, if the government were to act as Old Noll would certainly have acted, and to send a squadron to Leghorn. It is highly probable that, in a few years, Italy will be on fire and the Grand Duke an exile. I would not advise him to come to England. If he ventured into Exeter Hall, he would, I firmly believe, be torn in pieces.

The weather here is very variable. Yesterday and the day before were beautiful. It is now blowing and raining. I shall pass the day by my fire in correcting my speeches. I do not suppose that they will have any great success. But I do not think that they will lower my character. I am vexed to find how little I have improved in the course of twenty years. I spoke as well in 1831 as I could do now.

Ever yours,
T B Macaulay

Pray remember me kindly to your hostess.

A certain W. Money writes to me from France to ask me to get something for somebody. What is he? Is he a clergyman? Mrs. Evans has also written to ask me to get something for John Gisborne. I am afraid that the case is hopeless.

TO EDWARD EVERETT, 30 MAY 1854

MS: Massachusetts Historical Society. *Extract published: New York Ledger,* 25 February 1860.

Albany London / May 30. 1854

My dear Everett,

Your letter has given me much pleasure, and yet has made me very sad. I never imagined that you had forgotten or neglected me. I well know that the intermission of correspondence does not at all imply any intermission of friendly feeling.

I have nothing to complain of. My health is indeed not good. But I suffer no pain; and, though my pleasures are fewer than they were, I retain the great sources of happiness. My mind is as clear and my affections as warm as ever. Nothing can exceed the tenderness of those who are nearest and dearest to me. On the whole I find life quite as pleasant, now that I am confined, during many months every year, to my room, as when I was in the vigour of youth.

My book goes on. I hope in a few months to bring out two more volumes. I have not promised myself a great success. I know that the world punishes no offence so severely as that of having been overpraised; and, as my first two volumes were extravagantly overrated, I fully expect that my next two volumes will be underrated.

I say nothing of my parliamentary duties. In truth I never go down to the House except in a case of life and death. The late hours and the bad air would kill me in a week, if I attended as I used to do seven years ago. Why then, you will ask, continue to be a member? Solely because the people of Edinburgh wish me to do so. They think that they used me unjustly in 1847. They elected me, in my absence, without a farthing of expense, in 1852; and they now treat me with a delicacy and an indulgence hardly to be expected from gentlemen, and perfectly astonishing in a constituent body composed of six thousand ten pound householders.

In spite of the melancholy close of your letter, I will continue to cherish the hope that we shall meet here again. Till then let us occasionally, as you propose, exchange a few lines. God bless you.

Ever your affectionate
T B Macaulay

TO THOMAS FLOWER ELLIS, 11 JULY 1854

MS: Trinity College. *Partly published:* Trevelyan, II, 380.

Greenwood Lodge / Thames Ditton / July 11. 1854

Dear Ellis,

I have been working four or five days at my report on the Indian Civil Service, and have at last finished it. It is much longer than I anticipated that it would be, and has given me great trouble. I am just going to send it to John Lefevre, who will convey it to a private press of which the government has the command.

On the 22nd I am to be in town for the purpose of considering the report in company with my colleagues. Let me know whether, if I can get to the Temple on that day, I shall be likely to find you there.

To morrow I go vigorously to work on my history. I have been so busy here with my report that I have read nothing but comedies of Goldoni and novels of Eugene Sue.

The weather is very strange; sometimes gloriously fine; then nothing but clouds, rain and storm. On two successive days I have been ready to drop with the heat of the sun at three in the afternoon, and have been forced, at eight in the evening, to have a roaring fire. I walked yesterday to Hampton Court along the Middlesex bank of the Thames, and lounged among the avenues and flower beds about an hour. I wonder that no poet has thought of writing a descriptive poem on the Thames. Particular spots have been celebrated. But surely there is no finer subject of the sort than the whole course of the river from Oxford downward, – the noble University, – Clifden, – Windsor, – Chertsey, the retreat of Cowley, – St Anne's Hill, the retreat of Fox, – Hampton Court with all the recollections of Wolsey, Cromwell, William and Mary, Belinda's hair, the Cartoons, the Beauties; – then Strawberry Hill – then Twickenham and Pope's grotto – then Richmond, – and so on to the great City, – the forest of masts, – the Tower, – Greenwich Hospital, – Tilbury fort and the Armada. Is there any river in the world which, in so short a space, affords such subjects for poetry? Not the Tiber, I am sure, nor the Seine.

Do you know the river between Hampton Court and Richmond? If not we will make a voyage down, look at the ruins of poor Strawberry Hill, and at Pope's house and grotto, and dine at the Star and Garter. As to dining at the University Club, that would make it necessary for me to sleep in town, which I would gladly avoid. However we will discuss that matter when we meet.

Ever yours,
T B Macaulay

TO FRANCES MACAULAY, 14 OCTOBER 1854

MS: Trinity College.

Albany October 14 / 1854

Dearest Fanny,

We had a very pleasant visit to Aldingham. The house and grounds are most enviable and enviably situated. We saw Furness Abbey, and had a very handsome dinner at the inn there. I had not expected such a table in the wilderness. I liked what I saw of the children – especially of Arthur. Selina's suitor is a cross between a Lancashire clown and a Yankee pedlar. He has been much in the United States, and has brought home the genuine Connecticut twang of the nose to grace his utterance. However I dare say that he will make a good husband.

I do not understand what ground the Baptists have for complaining that Bunyan has no monument in the Abbey. I should never dream of complaining because Bishop Butler or Archbishop Leighton has not a monument in a Baptist meeting. The Abbey is a religious edifice. No man, however eminent, who has publicly separated himself from the Church, who denies the validity of the initiatory sacraments of the Church, who writes and preaches against the Church, has any claim to funeral honors in the Church. You might as well blame the Russians for not erecting monuments to our brave fellows who were killed at the Alma as blame the Dean and Chapter of Westminster for not erecting a monument to a man who was the enemy of the religious society to which they belonged. His place in heaven has nothing to do with the matter. You may as well say that his arms ought to be put up among the arms of the Knights of the Garter at Windsor because he is in heaven, or that a picture of him ought to be put among the pictures of the Scotch Kings at Holyrood because he is in heaven. A man in heaven has no right to have his arms at Windsor unless he was a Knight of the Garter. A man in heaven has no right to have his portrait at Holyrood unless he was a King of Scotland. And a man in heaven has no right to a monument in the transept of a Church, unless he was a Churchman.

William's niece is well again, except that she is very weak. I go to Woburn next Tuesday, and then I shall settle in town for some months. I shall meet the Chancellor at Woburn; and I am glad of it. For, though little in the habit of asking favours, I mean to ask him to do something [. . . .]

TO ADAM BLACK, 6 APRIL 1855

MS: National Library of Scotland. *Envelope:* Adam Black Esq / etc. etc. etc. / Edinburgh. *Subscription:* T B M. *Partly published:* [Black], *Biographies by Lord Macaulay*, pp. l–lii.

Albany London / April 6. 1855

My dear Sir,

I hope that you will not think me importunate if I again and very earnestly beg you to consider seriously the state of the representation of the City. I feel every day more and more that my public life is over. I am, not, thank God, in intellect or in affections, but in physical power, an older man by some years than I was last Easter. I see no chance of my being able again to take part in debate. By the bye, I hoped till lately that I might be able to go down to Edinburgh in the course of the summer and give a lecture at the Philosophical Institute. But the thing is impossible. My voice would not hold out a quarter of an hour. I have been forced to give up reading aloud to my sister; and I seldom pass an evening in animated conversation without suffering severely afterwards. The little that I can do for mankind must be done at my desk. I try to flatter myself with the hope that a sojourn at Palermo or Malaga may set me up again; and I shall probably try that experiment as soon as I have brought out the next part of my history. But in the meantime the feeling that I ought to be in the House of Commons preys upon my mind. I think that I am acting ungenerously and ungratefully to a constituent body which has been most indulgent to me. However, I will, as I have said, remain an M.P. till the end of this Session. But I must positively declare that I will, on the first day of next Session, at the very latest, take the Chiltern Hundreds. It would be a great relief to me if our excellent friend Craig would consent to stand at present. Pray let him know what I say.

I hope that I have managed Baillie Kay's affair to his satisfaction.

Ever yours truly,

T B Macaulay

MS: Trinity College.

Richmond Hill / August 22. 1855

Dearest Fanny,

I inclose a letter from Hannah which she wishes you to see. I am not quite easy about her husband.

I am very hard worked, but not the worse for it. In a few days the whole of my third Volume will be in print. I think it as good as either of the former two, whatever that praise may be worth. But we authors are said to be bad judges of our own compositions. About the fourth volume, which will not go to the printers for some time, I have great misgivings. I really do not know how it will look when the scattered scrawls are put together and printed fair. At present some of them are hardly legible. Connecting passages are wanting, – and the style requires much correction.

Love to Selina and Alice. I hope that you let the dear child have plenty of Miss Austen. All her lessons will not do her half so much good.

What do you think of a verse which I saw here over the shed of a man who lets out donkeys to the young ladies here.

"One angel came to Balaam's ass,
And met him by the way.
My asses do through Richmond pass
With angels every day."

I assure you that this is not the judicious poet's, though, I think, well worthy of him.

Ever yours
T B Macaulay

TO EDWARD EVERETT, 29 NOVEMBER 1855

MS: Massachusetts Historical Society. *Partly published: New York Ledger,* 25 February 1860.

Albany London November 29. 1855

Dear Everett,

Your letter of the 6th gave me pleasure and pain, pleasure because it is full of kindness, and pain because the writer does not seem to be happy. I hope that your sadness was merely the effect of temporary depression of spirits. I still look forward to the pleasure of seeing you again in the old country. You well know how gladly you will be welcomed by all that remains of the circle in which we passed so many agreeable hours together.

We shall hardly meet in the Albany. My lease expires in a few months; and, as I am a much more wealthy and a much less healthy man than when

I took up my abode here, I mean to change my quarters. I should like to settle very near London within an easy distance of the Clubs, of the British Museum, and, above all, of my sister and her children, and yet beyond the reach of the coalfog and riverfog which, during six months of the year, make it difficult for me to breathe. I must have room for near ten thousand volumes. I must have, if possible, an acre of green turf where I can walk up and down among lilacs and laburnums with a book in my hand. I must also have a spare bed for a friend; and I need not tell you that no friend will be more welcome to it than you.

Possibly, before I settle, I may visit Italy again. I shall vacate my seat in parliament on the first day of the approaching Session, and shall thus be freed from a tie which, though in my case singularly easy, nevertheless imposed some little restraint on my movements. I have corrected the last proof sheet of the second part of my History, and am fairly entitled to a holiday. You shall have a copy which will sometimes remind you of a very sincere friend. I have not promised myself that the book will be popular. The public has extravagantly overpraised me: it expects miracles: and it will probably punish me for its own folly. In the meantime I am enjoying my newly recovered liberty. I have been reading two very much better historians than myself, Herodotus and Thucydides. I ought not to forget our friend Prescott, over whose volumes I passed a very pleasant day by the fireside, while London was covered with one of our orange coloured fogs.

Thanks for your sketch of American politics. Our politics are not what you remember them. The ballot, free trade, Maynooth, the Irish Church, are scarcely mentioned. The only talk of the Clubs is about ports in the Euxine and fortresses on Mount Caucasus, the depth of the water in the sea of Azov, and the state of the roads between Sympherapol and Percop. A friend of ours said not long ago that my chambers were the only place where a man could pass a quarter of an hour in company without hearing the Crimea mentioned.

As to the great question of peace or war, there are few politicians here so peaceably disposed as myself; and yet I do not think the present moment a moment for making peace. But I will not inflict on you a dissertation in defence of my opinion. In truth I, like you, take little pleasure in contemporary politics. I am sometimes half afraid that I trouble myself about them less than a good citizen should. But my excuse is that the state of my health makes it impossible for me to take an active part. I am doomed to my desk and my fireside. I live much in the past; and I am therefore less violently excited than my neighbours about the present. But I must have done with this egotism. God bless you, my dear Everett: write to me a little oftener; and believe me always yours affectionately,

T B Macaulay

MS: The Earl of Halifax.

Albany London December 26 / 1855

Dear Wood,

I am truly gratified by your approbation. What you say of the public men of William's reign is too true. Many times I have wished that I had taken some subject more pleasing, some subject which I could treat without violating truth, and yet without disgusting and, I am afraid, sometimes wearying my readers by such a dreary, monotonous, spectacle of depravity. However, I have now got through the worst part of my task. If I should live seven or eight years longer, and should retain my faculties, I may hope to bring my narrative down to the accession of the House of Hanover. There I shall stop. In this way only I can now hope to be of use to my country. Every year I feel my bodily infirmities increasing. But while my intellect and my affections are spared to me, I shall not think myself unhappy.

All kind Christmas wishes to Lady Mary and to all in whom you and she are interested.

Ever yours truly
T B Macaulay

TO HENRY HART MILMAN, 29 DECEMBER 1855

MS: McGill University.

Albany December 29 / 1855

My dear Dean,

I did not till this day altogether give up the hope of meeting you next week at Bowood. But as Bright has just laid his final orders on me not to stir, I cannot any longer defer my thanks for your last three volumes. I think this quite your best work; and that is saying a great deal. That the History of Latin Christianity will have a high and permanent place in literature I have not the slightest doubt. I mean to read all the six volumes again with more attention than formerly; and I promise myself many happy evenings over them.

I have had a most pleasant month of mere literary idling and luxury. I have finished Photius, after digressing from him repeatedly to the authors whom he mentions, particularly Isocrates and Lysias. I have also read again Cicero's philosophical works, and think, as I thought at twenty two, when I read him under the chestnuts at Trinity, that the De Finibus is the best, that then comes the De Natura Deorum, and that the Tusculan

Disputations are the least valuable, – mere anointing for broken bones. A pleasant new year to you and Mrs. Milman.

Ever yours,
T B Macaulay

TO FRANCES MACAULAY, 13 JANUARY 1856

MS: Trinity College.

Albany London / January 13. 1856

Dearest Fanny,

Thanks for your letters. I am glad that you are so well pleased with my book. I am more than satisfied with the share of public favour that I enjoy. Against a little captious censure I have to set off an immense quantity of praise which is much beyond my desert. I sometimes think that I should very willingly barter some fame for a little better health, if such dealings were possible. Then I remember Addison's Mountain of Miseries, and ask myself whether I would consent to be thought a very middling writer on condition of breathing as freely as I did at twenty. There are moments when I might make such a bargain: but I should soon repent it, and long to change back again.

I shall not stir out till there is a change in the weather. In a few days I shall take the Chiltern Hundreds. But this is a secret. Pray keep it as such. Love to dear Selina.

Yours ever
T B Macaulay

TO EDWARD EVERETT, 25 FEBRUARY 1856

MS: Massachusetts Historical Society. *Mostly published: New York Ledger*, 25 February 1860.

Albany London February 25. 1856

My dear Everett,

I am in your debt for two letters. The second arrived this morning. Thanks for all your kindness, and for the two specimens of American typography, which had the good luck to elude the vigilance of our custom house officers.

I am much gratified by your approbation, though I know that your judgment, where I am concerned, is not quite impartial. The reception of my book here has been far more favourable than, in my most sanguine moments, I had expected. I have as yet heard little from the Continent: but the little that I have heard is encouraging. I attach great importance to the verdict of foreigners: for it indicates what the verdict of posterity is likely to be.

Thank God, I have done for ever with public business, and am free to enjoy letters and the society of those whom I love without any restraint. I have determined to fix my abode in a place which seems to have been made for me. On the same rising ground on which Holland House stands, and at the distance of perhaps two hundred yards from that dear old building is a villa with two acres of turf and flowerbed, called Holly Lodge. Even at this season it looks pretty; and in the summer I shall be able to hide myself among my rosebushes and to imagine that I am in a rural solitude, though in truth I shall be only two miles from Hyde Park Corner. I have ample room for ten thousand volumes, good air, a good gravel soil, and good water. I may add good neighbours: for the Duke and Duchess of Argyle, whose grounds are divided by a paling from mine, are excellent people. Here I hope to breathe more freely than in this great cloud of river fog and sea coal. How glad I shall be to have a walk with you on the grass before my library window; and I will not suffer myself to doubt that this pleasure is in store for me.

Ever affectionately yours,
T B Macaulay

TO THOMAS FLOWER ELLIS, 11 MARCH 1856

MS: Trinity College. *Extract published:* Trevelyan, II, 410.

Albany London March 11 / 1856

Dear Ellis,

I am still busy with upholsterers, linendrapers, silversmiths and dealers in China. My servants are all engaged. Hannah has chosen carpets and curtains for the rooms which require such articles, and has chosen, in my opinion, with great taste. I shall enter into possession on Monday next. Rawlinson has played me a pretty trick. After asking me to leave him my book cases, and thus inducing me to order a perfectly new set, he writes to say that he has changed his mind, and does not know that he shall take the chambers at all. He offers to pay for my new book cases: but that of course is an offer which it would not become me to accept; so that I shall be a loser of at least 200£ by his vacillation. However I shall now have a right to laugh at his theories about Nineveh and Ecbatana without restraint. Confound his winged bulls and cuneiform characters!

As some small set off against this loss, I am glad to tell you that on Thursday 20000£ are to be paid into my banker's hands by the Longmans. The payment need not have been made till December: but the

Longmans are flush of money, and thought that they could not invest it better than by clearing off a debt, and getting nine months' discount. The transaction is quite unparalleled in the history of the book trade; and both the people at Smith Payne and Smith's who are to pay the money and my friends who are to receive it have been much amused. I went into the City to day to give instructions, and was most warmly congratulated on being a great moneyed man. I said that I had some thoughts of going to the Chancellor of the Exchequer as a bidder for the next loan. In the meantime I have given orders for investing nineteen thousand pounds in a way which will bring up my certain income to three thousand a year, and leave a balance of two thousand five hundred at my banker's. My arms therefore are dangling in a most significant way; and, if the sight of them should affect you as the sight of Vellum's arms affected Tinsel, I hope that you will imitate Tinsel's frankness.

On Thursday week, if the weather be tolerable, I should make a short tour with the Trevelyans. We shall go first to Rochester, pass Good Friday there, go to Canterbury on the Saturday, attend the service in the Cathedral on Sunday, and return on Easter Monday.

I meditate a longer tour for the autumn. I mean to run across France to Marseilles, to go to Genoa by the cornice, and to see the principal cities of northern Italy which are accessible by railway. In a fortnight one can see Milan, Vicenza, Verona, Padua and Venice. Then I think of returning by the lake of Como, by the sublime pass of St Gothard, and by Zurich, to our old friend Basle. Thence there is railway to Boulogne. I shall be grievously disappointed and vexed if I have not your company in this expedition. Franz, of course, if he is to be had.

Ever yours
T B Macaulay

TO THOMAS FLOWER ELLIS, 16 MARCH 1856

MS: Trinity College.

Albany March 16. 1856
Dear Ellis,

I am not going to change my abode quite so soon as you seem to think. I come into possession of Holly Lodge to morrow. But near a month of whitewashing, bricklayer's work and carpenter's work must be done before I move. My new book cases will be up in little more than a week. All that I hear is greatly in favour of the place. The air, water, soil, are all pronounced excellent both by medical men and by the families which live on the spot; and my bargain is spoken of as a remarkably good one.

I was much amused by your account of Preston's achievements. He seems to be a perfect Satyr – Nympharum fugientum Amator.

I shall be sorry if you cannot go with me to Italy. If Walter really requires your tuition in the autumn, there is nothing more to be said. But I cannot admit the validity of your other reason. I am quite sure that you will yourself feel, on reflection, how unwise it would be, and how unworthy of a man of your abilities and principles, to sink into dejection, and to turn away with disgust from the beauties of nature, the master-pieces of art and the remains of antiquity, because every thing in this capricious lottery of life does not go as you could wish. You know how sincerely I feel for you. And you will not suspect me of speaking from any want of tenderness for your anxieties. But, for God's sake, do not make the evil ten times as great as it is by moping and pining and eating your heart. Remember how happy a man you are at the very worst – competence – security as to the prospects of your children – an attached family, affectionate friends who only wish to know how they can serve you, – an unsullied character, and all the enjoyments of the intellect – surely these are blessings of which you ought to think more. I forgot to mention health. But I assure you that I am much more inclined to envy you your lungs and limbs than to pity your misfortunes. Therefore *sursum corda.* Do not give those who love and value you the pain of thinking that your spirits are broken by a mishap which does not blemish your honor, which does not wound your affections, which leaves all your powers of body and mind unimpaired, and which does not deprive you of the means of living in the enjoyment of every comfort. The case is not one which requires the higher remedies of religion and philosophy. It is a case as Juvenal says

"Multis cognitus, et jam
Tritus, et e medio fortunae ductus acervo."

It would be unbecoming in a man like you not to meet ill luck of this sort with fortitude and even with cheerfulness. I am quite confident that I have not written a word on this subject which Marian would not subscribe. I only wish that you would speak to her with perfect frankness. I am certain that she would see the matter exactly as I do. / Ever my dear fellow

Yours affectionately

T B Macaulay

MS: Trinity College.

Albany London / March 29. 1856

Dear Ellis,

I shall be glad to see you again. Dinner shall be ready for you at half past seven next Thursday, unless I hear to the contrary from you. Our dinners here will be but few. I cannot fix the exact time of my migration. But I think that it will be about the 20th of next month. I find that I must have a dog, or rather a bitch, a little, sharp, yelping terrier, to deter those whom my old master Preston used, in his evening prayer, to describe as "the Sons of Violence and Plunder." Àpropos of dogs, I have just picked up a French novel by Paul Féval, in which there is a charming Englishwoman, Miladi Ophélie Dog. Àpropos again of dogs, I shall certainly not take any notice of Mr. Hepworth or Hebworth Dixon. He is a great fool. I should have thought that you must have heard of the two Penns – the Menæchmi. That point was raised five or six years ago. I still believe in my own twin. But I allow that there is something to be said on the other side. This is absolutely the only issue in the controversy which bears dispute. If people doubt, they doubt only because they will not take the trouble to examine with care the authorities to which I have referred them.

I am delighted with the tone of your letter. I most readily admit that you have had in one or two respects very bad luck. At Cambridge you are still mentioned as the best scholar that did not get a medal: and by lawyers you are mentioned as the ablest man in your profession who has not risen high. But, let the worst come to the worst, you are quite sure, I think, of a life income of two thousand a year. Your children are decently provided for. As to any extraordinary call, there are a thousand pounds, which I shall never miss, lying ready for you at a day's notice. My chief anxiety is about Walter. All that I hear of him is favourable. But I look forward with some trepidation to the Summer examination.

I have changed my mind about Denman, and shall not give a farthing. I find that he is very well off; and it seems to me quite monstrous that men like you, far his superiors in ability and learning, much his seniors, and not so rich as he is, should be expected to bear the charges of a foolish enterprise, about which you were never consulted, of which you have already borne much of the trouble, and of which, if it had succeeded, he would have had all the fruits. I repeat that I shall give nothing.

Ever yours

T B M

MS: Trinity College. *Address:* Miss Trevelyan / Oatlands / Esher / Inghilterra. *Extracts published:* Trevelyan, II, 247n; 434.

Venice September 8. 1856

Dearest Baba,

We arrived at Venice on Saturday afternoon; and I have hardly recovered, or rather have not recovered from the surprise caused by the first sight of this wonderful city. And yet I had been pretty well prepared by reading and conversation, and, above all, by Stanfield's and Canaletti's pictures for what I was to see. But the real streets and lanes of water, – the lofty mansions rising perpendicular from the brink of the water; – the great doors opening on the green sleeping canals, so that you make but one step from your boat to the marble staircase; – the absolute and entire want of horses, carts, carriages; – the strange silence of a city of a hundred and fifty thousand human beings among whom no wheel is ever heard to rattle; these things, though I knew them, I had never, as the Yankees say, been able to realise; and I have not yet, in forty eight hours, been able to become familiar with them.

The hotel where we are lodged was once the palace of a great Venetian noble. Our rooms are very handsome, and, at this season, pleasant. In December I can imagine that they would be very cold. The musquitoes with which we were threatened have done me little harm. Their buzz is worse than their bite. To be sure we sleep surrounded with curtains of musquito net, which resembles the musquito net of India, except that it is white and not green. My health is still good; and my sleep, which I had never, during some months, enjoyed in England, has during the last fortnight been as deep and sweet as when I was a boy.

I now see Galignani regularly, and am very well pleased with what I see. England seems to be profoundly quiet. God grant that she may long continue so, and that the history of the years which I may yet have to live may be the dullest portion of her history. It is sad work to live in times about which it is amusing to read.

As I was leaving Verona I received a letter from Mamma, for which I had just time to thank her. Pray give me a full account of Mrs. Becher Stowe's visit. There is nothing more pitiable than an ex lion or ex lioness. London, I have often thought, is like the sorceress in the Arabian Nights who, by some mysterious law, can love the same object only forty days. During forty days she is all fon[dness.] As soon [as] they are over, she [not] only discards the poor favourite, but turns hi[m] into some wretched shape, a mangy dog or a spavined horse. How many hundreds of victims have undergone this fate since I was born. The strongest instances, I think, have been Betty who was called the Young Roscius, Edward Irving, and Mrs. Becher Stowe. I feel so much pity for the poor woman that I would gladly show her some attention, though she ill deserves it of me. Has she brought her fanatical ass of a husband with her? He has been writing a book against Popery so absurd and abusive as to be a scandal to Protestantism. But I must have done. Lest, by any chance, my letter from Verona should have miscarried, I will repeat my directions, as far as they can now be of any use. From the time when you receive this till Wednesday the 17th inclusive, write to the Poste Restante, Marseilles. If you have occasion to write on the 18th, 19th, 20th or 21st, to the Hotel de Bristol Paris. I shall probably be in town on the 24th. Love to Mamma and Alice and to Papa and George if they are with you.

Ever yours

T B M

to Lady Trevelyan, 16 September 1856

MS: Trinity College. *Address:* Lady Trevelyan / Oatlands / Esher / Inghilterra. *Extract published*: Trevelyan, II, 408.

Genoa September 16. 1856

Dearest Hannah,

I found your letter and my little Alice's here. I had received my dear Baba's at Venice. You have all been very kind about writing. Our last day at Venice was a very fine one. In the evening the moon was at the full; the water like a sheet of plate glass reflecting the long rows of white palaces with green blinds. We had the gondola after dinner and were rowed the whole length of the Grand Canal and back, with some little deviation, to the Place of St Mark, where we strolled some time listening to the music. The place is strangely fascinating; and I left it with some pain when I thought that I may probably never see it again.

Two days of rapid travelling brought us hither. I am rather knocked up by the run, and must take two days to recruit. The first day of our journey was so cold and rainy that I was forced to wear my great coat. The second day was so hot that I could not walk ten yards in the sun without my umbrella. There have been several great and sudden changes of temperature within the last fortnight. When I posted from Novara to Milan on, I think, the first of September, the Alps, with the exception of Monte Rosa, were dark blue. Yesterday, when we posted from Milan to Novara, the whole ridge was white, Monte Rosa white half way down. These alternations, together with the exertion of travelling from seven in the morning till eight or nine at night, have brought back my difficulty of breathing. In the main however I am the better for my tour. We shall return a little more slowly than I had contemplated. I still expect to sleep at Holly Lodge on Friday the 26th, or, at latest, on Saturday the 27th.

Genoa I had seen before: but I find it prodigiously improved, prospering greatly, and far superior in all that indicates diligence and material wealth to any place in Italy. Yet the change, though doubtless a desirable one, is not altogether agreeable to my taste. A huge old palace, with flights of marble steps, long galleries, halls painted in fresco and gardens of orange trees is a grand sight while it is kept up nobly. It is a pathetic and interesting sight when it is falling into decay and shown by a superannuated family servant who has no wages but what he gets from the bounty of travellers. But the palaces of Genoa are turned into inns, academies, warehouses, manufactories, shops. A tailor is at work cross legged under the scutcheon of an illustrious house and in a court adorned with statues, surrounded by an Ionic arcade, and resounding, all through this hot day, with the noise of a cool fountain. And thus out of the death and corruption of the old and splendid Genoa, a new Genoa is springing which will perhaps surpass the old. In the meantime the process is not altogether pleasing.

I am not sure that I shall have time to write from Marseilles, except to William, to whom I must send a line to announce my return. At any rate, I will write to you from Paris. Love to the dear girls and their Papa. If I had time, I should tell Alice such a story about an adventure that I have had in the railway carriage – the lovely Giuseppa – handsome Englishman – etc. etc. She must not be surprised if I should present her, the week after next, with a Popish aunt, who will be able to assist her in her Italian studies. But perhaps the questions of religion and residence may be as hard to get over in the case of the Chevalier Macaulay as in that of the Chevalier Grandison; and I may be forced to leave the too charming Giuseppa here with a blister on her head and a strait waistcoat on her back.

Ever yours
T B Macaulay

TO WILLIAM WHEWELL, 1 DECEMBER 1856

MS: Trinity College. Published: D. A. Winstanley, Early Victorian Cambridge, Cambridge, 1940, pp. 437–8.

Holly Lodge Kensington / December 1. 1856

My dear Whewell,

Lord Lansdowne has shown me the letters which have passed between you, and has done me the honor to ask my opinion. I wish from the bottom of my soul that Milton had been a Trinity man. But, as his parents were so stupid and perverse as to send him to Christ's, I must admit that your arguments against putting up a statue of him in our Chapel are of great weight. I am glad, but not at all surprised, to find that Lord Lansdowne, though not quite convinced, is most amiably and generously desirous to do whatever may be pleasing to the College.

Then comes the question, – Who shall share the honors of Bacon and Newton in our ante chapel? An equal of Bacon and Newton it cannot be. In the registers of all the colleges of Cambridge and Oxford we shall find nobody, Milton excepted, who is worthy to be "terzo tra cotanto senno." We must chuse some second rate man to be the associate of our two first rate men. The choice is difficult. But I think that, if I had a voice, I should give it in favour of Bentley. I told Lord Lansdowne my reasons; and he begged me to write them to you, with whom the decision will rest. They are these.

Bentley is distinguished from all the other candidates mentioned in your letter, by one most important circumstance. He was decidedly the greatest man of his class. This cannot be said of Herbert or Pearson. It cannot be said even of Dryden or Barrow. Dryden's most enthusiastic admirers will hardly put him so high as third among our poets. Barrow did many things well, but nothing, I think, preeminently well. His fame rests chiefly on his sermons; and there are sermons of South, of Taylor, of Robert Hall, which I prefer to Barrow's best. But Bentley is the greatest man in his own department that has appeared in Europe since the revival of letters. That department, it may be said, is not the highest. I grant it. I do not rank the Phalaris or the Epistle to Mill with the Principia or the Novum Organum. Still, great reverence is due to the man who has done best what thousands of able and industrious men have, during four centuries, been trying to do well. And, surely, if there be in the world a place where honor ought to be paid to preeminence in classical learning, that place is our ante chapel. During several generations classical learning has been the peculiar glory of our college. In the sciences of which Bacon and Newton were the great masters we have been equalled, some may perhaps think, surpassed. But, in the studies from which Bentley derives his fame, we are, I believe, unrivalled. And this is to be attributed partly to the influence of his genius. To this day, unless I deceive myself, the scholarship of Trinity men has a peculiar character which may be called Bentleian, and which is not found in the scholarship of men who have gained the highest honors of Oxford. I am far from putting Bentley in the same rank with Newton. But in one respect the two men may fairly be classed together. They were the two intellectual founders of our college. Their minds have left an impress which is still plainly discernible. They may therefore, with peculiar propriety, appear together in our ante chapel.

There is another reason for preferring Bentley to Barrow. Barrow is buried in Westminster Abbey, and has a statue there. Bentley lies in our chapel, and has no statue, – not even, to the best of my recollection, a tablet. Now this I think really discreditable to us, – so discreditable that I would gladly subscribe a few guineas towards the removing of such a reproach. I shall be truly glad therefore if Lord Lansdowne's munificence repairs what seems to me a great neglect.

You say, I observe, in your letter to Lord Lansdowne – "Some have a moral blemish, as Bentley and Dryden." I agree with you as to Dryden. But surely you, to whom we owe that fine monument of Bacon, will, on reflection, admit that the faults of Bentley were not such as ought to be punished by permanent exclusion from public honors. Dryden was immoral as a poet, Bacon as a Judge, Bentley as Master of a College. I therefore would not set up any monument to Dryden in his character of poet, to Bacon in his character of Judge, or to Bentley in his character of Master of a College. But Dryden has no claim to a monument except as a poet. His licentiousness taints those very works on which alone his fame depends; and it is impossible to do honor to the writer without doing honor to the libertine. With Bacon and Bentley the case is quite different. You testified your respect for the great philosopher, although you knew that he had been a servile politician and a corrupt Chancellor. And Lord Lansdowne may surely testify in the same way respect for the great scholar, notwithstanding all the bad stories which are to be found in the pamphlets of Professor Colbatch and Serjeant Miller.

This is the substance of what I said to Lord Lansdowne yesterday evening. I shall be anxious to know how you decide. / Ever, my dear Whewell,

Yours very truly,
T B Macaulay

TO SIR CHARLES WOOD, 9 DECEMBER 1856

MS: Victoria Memorial Hall, Calcutta. Published: [N. K. Sinha], Bengal Past and Present, LXXXIII (1964), 154.

Holly Lodge Kensington / December 9. 1856

Dear Wood,

The time is at hand when the East India College at Hayleybury will cease to exist. I have no doubt that both you and I, in contributing to bring about this result, did our duty to England and to India. Nevertheless, I cannot but feel much pain when I think of the suffering which we have caused to several most respectable families; and I am most desirous to serve those whom I have been the means, not indeed of injuring, but, I am afraid, of ruining. I do hope that your influence will be exerted to obtain for the Professors a liberal compensation. I am sure that nothing facilitates reforms so much as liberality in compensating those who suffer by the abolition of abuses. If we really have succeeded in giving to India the inestimable blessing of a good civil service, we may well call on her to bear the charge of the few hundreds of pounds which will make all the difference between comfort and penury to those very deserving persons who have been the victims of our improved policy.

There is one who seems to me to have very peculiar claims, – Heaviside. Personal feeling about him I have none: for I never saw him in my life. But his merits have been strongly represented to me by men of the first distinction in science and literature. He has been nineteen years at the College. For the College he relinquished the fairest prospects at Cambridge. It is a hard thing on such a man, now no longer young, and unfitted by Academical habits for a stirring life, to have to begin the world again. It seems to me that a quiet stall in a Cathedral would be the very place for such a man. I really think that you, who carried through the last India Bill, who introduced the system of competition for civil appointments, and who, by doing so, really destroyed the College, might with peculiar propriety, bring this matter under Lord Palmerston's notice. At all events you will pardon me for writing to you on the subject. Our names will hereafter be mentioned together in connection with a great and beneficial reform; and you, I have no doubt, are as sorry as I am that it was not in our power to do our duty to the public without causing much distress to individuals.

Lefevre agrees with me entirely. I dare say that he will write to you about Heaviside. / Ever, my dear Wood,

Yours most truly,
T B Macaulay

TO FRANCES MACAULAY, 27 JANUARY 1857

MS: Trinity College.

Holly Lodge Kensington / January 27. 1857

Dearest Fanny,

Thanks for your letter. Three days ago I should hardly have been able to answer it with my own hand. But my rheumatism is gone, or nearly so: I have dismissed my physician; and I leave the completion of my cure to time.

I am sorry for Thackeray. He is a man of real genius, – the best, in my opinion, of living novellists, and quite capable of producing, with care and thought, works which might last as long as the language. But he wants money; and he gets it more rapidly and easily by lecturing than he could get it in any other way. His taste for fame is, I am afraid, not very delicate. He probably prefers it in the coarsest form. Huzzas and claps from crowded rooms give him, I dare say, more pleasure than the esteem of men who are qualified to judge. He should consider that of the sort of applause which he gets by turning mountebank, that wretched Spurgeon gets ten times as much as he.

Kindest love to Selina.

Ever yours,
T B Macaulay

TO THOMAS FLOWER ELLIS, 4 MARCH 1857

MS: Trinity College.

Holly Lodge Kensington / March 4. 1857

Dear Ellis,

I have had a miserable time of it since Monday. However starvation, calomel, mustard poultices, and, above all, the change of the wind, have revived me; and I can draw my breath with tolerable ease. But dining out is not at present to be thought of. I have sent excuses to the Stanhopes and Milmans.

I am vexed by the result of the division, more, however, for private than for public reasons. The country will thrive under any government that is likely to be formed.

What a strange thing! Perry – the scholar of Trinity of my year – has published a volume of Miscellanies in prose and verse. There is a poem to me in which he lays claim to a friendship which never existed between us, talks of having reclined by me on mossy banks in high converse while the river gently murmured by. I never reclined on a bank by him in my life, – never, to the best of my belief, ate any meal with him except in hall, never was in his rooms, never saw him in mine. I did not even know him to speak to till our third year; and he never resided after he had taken his degree. The difference between his recollections and mine reminds me irresistibly of a passage, not to be quoted, in the dialogue between Lacon and Comatas in Theocritus. The worst is that the book has been sent me from the author. What am I to say?

A line to tell me how you are? I will write as soon as I am in condition to dine with you.

Ever yours

T B Macaulay

TO HENRY STEPHENS RANDALL, 23 MAY 1857

MS: New York Public Library. *Envelope:* H. S. Randall Esq / etc. etc. etc. / Cortland Village / Cortland County / New York. *Subscription:* T B M. *Published: Harper's Magazine,* LIV (February 1877), 460–1.

Holly Lodge Kensington London / May 23. 1857

Dear Sir,

The four volumes of the Colonial History of New York reached me safely. I assure you that I shall value them highly. They contain much to interest an English as well as an American reader. Pray accept my thanks; and convey them to the Regents of the University.

You are surprised to learn that I have not a high opinion of Mr. Jefferson, and I am a little surprised at your surprise. I am certain that I never wrote a line, and that I never, in Parliament, in conversation, or even on the hustings, – a place where it is the fashion to court the populace, – uttered a word indicating an opinion that the supreme authority in a state ought to be entrusted to the majority of citizens told by the head, in other words, to the poorest and most ignorant part of society. I have long been convinced that institutions purely democratic must, sooner or later, destroy liberty, or civilisation, or both. In Europe, where the population is dense, the effect of such institutions would be almost instantaneous. What happened lately in France is an example. In 1848 a pure democracy was established there. During a short time there was reason to expect a general spoliation, a national bankruptcy, a new partition of the soil, a maximum of prices, a ruinous load of taxation laid on the rich for the purpose of supporting the poor in idleness. Such a system would, in twenty years, have made France as poor and barbarous as the France of the Carlovingians. Happily the danger was averted; and now there is a despotism, a silent tribune, an enslaved press. Liberty is gone: but civilisation has been saved. I have not the smallest doubt that, if we had a purely democratic government here, the effect would be the same. Either the poor would plunder the rich, and civilisation would perish; or order and property would be saved by a strong military government, and liberty would perish. You may think that your country enjoys an exemption from these evils. I will frankly own to you that I am of a very different opinion. Your fate I believe to be certain, though it is deferred by a physical cause. As long as you have a boundless extent of fertile and unoccupied land, your labouring population will be far more at ease than the labouring population of the old world; and, while that is the case, the Jeffersonian polity may continue to exist without causing any fatal calamity. But the time will come when New England will be as thickly peopled as old England. Wages will be as low, and will fluctuate as much with you as with us. You will have your Manchesters and Birminghams; and, in those Manchesters and Birminghams, hundreds of thousands of artisans will assuredly be sometimes out of work. Then your institutions will be fairly brought to the test. Distress every where makes the labourer mutinous and discontented, and inclines him to listen with eagerness to agitators who tell him that it is a monstrous iniquity that one man should have a million while another cannot get a full meal. In bad years there is plenty of grumbling here, and sometimes a little rioting. But it matters little. For here the sufferers are not the rulers. The supreme power is in the hands of a class, numerous indeed, but select, of an educated class, of a class which is, and knows itself to be, deeply interested in the security of property and the maintenance of order. Accordingly, the malecontents are firmly, yet gently, restrained. The bad time is got over without robbing the wealthy to relieve the indigent. The springs of national prosperity soon begin to flow again: work is plentiful: wages rise; and all is tranquillity and cheerfulness. I have seen England pass three or four times through such critical seasons as I have described. Through such seasons the United States will have to pass, in the course of the next century, if not of this. How will you pass through them. I heartily wish you a good deliverance. But my reason and my wishes are at war; and I cannot help foreboding the worst. It is quite plain that your government will never be able to restrain a distressed and discontented majority. For with you the majority is the government, and has the rich, who are always a minority, absolutely at its mercy. The day will come when, in the State of New York, a multitude of people, none of whom has had more than half a breakfast or expects to have more than half a dinner, will chuse a legislature. Is it possible to doubt what sort of legislature will be chosen? On one side is a statesman preaching patience, respect for vested rights, strict observances of public faith. On the other is a demagogue ranting about the tyranny of capitalists and usurers, and asking why anybody should be permitted to drink Champagne and to ride in a carriage, while thousands of honest folks are in want of necessaries. Which of the two candidates is likely to be preferred by a working man who hears his children cry for more bread? I seriously apprehend that you will, in some such season of adversity as I have described, do things which will prevent prosperity from returning; that you will act like people who should, in a year of scarcity, devour all the seed corn, and thus make the next year a year, not of scarcity, but of absolute famine. There will be, I fear, spoliation. The spoliation will increase the distress. The distress will produce fresh spoliation. There is nothing to stop you. Your constitution is all sail and no anchor. As I said before, when a society has entered on this downward progress, either civilisation or liberty must perish. Either some Cæsar or Napoleon will seize the reins of government with a strong hand; or your republic will be as fearfully plundered and laid waste by barbarians in the twentieth Century as the Roman Empire was in the fifth; – with this difference, that the Huns and Vandals who ravaged the Roman Empire came from without, and that your Huns and Vandals will have been engendered within your own country by your own institutions.

Thinking thus, of course, I cannot reckon Jefferson among the benefactors of mankind. I readily admit that his intentions were good and his abilities considerable. Odious stories have been circulated about his private life: but I do not know on what evidence those stories rest; and I think it probable that they are false, or monstrously exaggerated. I have no doubt that I shall derive both pleasure and information from your account of him. / I have the honor to be, / Dear Sir,

Your faithful Servant,
T B Macaulay

H. S. Randall Esq / etc. etc. etc.

TO LADY TREVELYAN, 10 AUGUST 1857

MS: Trinity College. *Partly published:* Trevelyan, II, 434–5.

Holly Lodge Kensington W. / August 10. 1857

Dearest Hannah,

I have just received a letter, half yours and half Baba's, from Frankfort; and glad I was to receive it. The weather at the beginning of last week was as hot here as it could be on the Rhine, as hot as I ever felt it out of the tropics, as hot, I think, as it was last summer at Turin and Milan. Then came a change. We had three days of sullen clouds, heavy showers, and chill breezes. I was forced to draw my blanket about me at night, and once seriously thought of having a fire in the library. Some people, – Lord Overstone among them, – began to fear that the harvest, which had promised so gloriously, would prove a failure. Happily yesterday afternoon the sky cleared. This morning there is not a cloud: the sun is blazing; and, no doubt, hundreds of thousands of acres will be reaped before night. Six or seven such days, and our bread is safe for the year.

No more news from India; that is to say, no later news than we had
before you started: but private letters are appearing daily in the newspapers, and details not found in those letters are reported in conversation.
The cruelties of the Sepoys, and, above all, the indignities which English
ladies have undergone, have inflamed the nation to a degree unprecedented
within my memory. All the philanthropic cant of Peace Societies, and
Aborigines Protection Societies, and Societies for the Reformation of
Criminals, is silenced. There is one terrible cry for revenge. The account
of that dreadful military execution at Peshawar – forty men blown at
once from the mouths of cannon, their heads, legs, arms flying in all
directions, – was read with delight by people who three weeks ago, were
against all capital punishment. Bright himself, Quaker as he is, declares
for the vigorous suppression of the mutiny. The almost universal feeling
is that not a single Sepoy, within the walls of Delhi, should be spared;
and I own that it is a feeling with which I cannot help sympathising.

I am reading Below the Surface. The book has merit. I wish the title
were less affected.

I went to the House of Lords on Thursday in the hope of hearing
Kelly on the great Shrewsbury case. But I heard only Roundell Palmer;
and very dull and feeble his speech was. I was so weary of it that I went
away in an hour, and have not ventured on another experiment. London
is emptying fast. On Wednesday the 12th, I shall dine with my neighbours
the Argylls; and that will probably be the last dinner of the season. Pray
let me be accurately informed about your movements. Love to Baba and
George, and Alice. I wrote to you last Monday, and to Baba on Thursday.

Ever yours
– T B M.

TO SELINA AND FRANCES MACAULAY, 29 AUGUST 1857

MS: Trinity College.

Holly Lodge Kensington / August 29. 1857

My dearest sisters,

What I am going to tell you must be for the present a strict secret.

I received yesterday a letter from Lord Palmerston informing me that
the Queen had permitted him to offer me a peerage. I was greatly surprised: but I did not hesitate one moment. I notified my respectful and
grateful acceptance; and, in a few days, I expect to be Lord Macaulay.
I must be Lord Macaulay of some place; and I find it difficult to make a
selection. I think I shall be Lord Macaulay of Rothley.

At my time of life and with my habits of mind, I am not likely to be much elated by such distinctions. But it is agreeable to me to think that I have never directly or indirectly solicited anything of the kind. Three years ago I should have doubted whether I could at all support the dignity of a peer. But I am now very far from being the poorest man of the honorable order.

Remember – strict secrecy. I shall write only to our brother Charles and to Trevelyan. Hannah I hope to see at Paris on Tuesday. If you have anything to say, direct to me at the Hotel du Louvre.

Ever yours
T B Macaulay

TO MARGARET TREVELYAN, 18 SEPTEMBER 1857

MS: Sir William Dugdale, Bt.

Holly Lodge Kensington / September 18. 1857
Dearest Baba,

I ought to have written before to you in answer to your two letters. It was not because you were not in my thoughts that I omitted to write. For indeed indeed you are very dear to me; and I am even weakly anxious for accounts of your health.

I am overwhelmed with letters of congratulation; and, empty as London is, plenty of people come to shake hands with me. I think I told your Mamma that I had written to Lord Belper for advice about my robes. He informs me that he, in the same situation, took the advice of Lord Overstone, and found it to be good. I have, accordingly, in reliance on the judgment of these very sensible and frugal patricians, sent for a certain Mr Hunter of Maddox Street, who had left a card here, and who is, it seems, robe maker to the Queen. This person, I am assured, will clothe me in scarlet, with the proper quantity of ermine and gold lace for £36.15.0. This I call moderate: for I was afraid that I might have had to pay £100.

On Tuesday I will take down with me to Malvern a heap of letters which I have received since I became a Lord. Some of them will interest you.

Your papa, your uncle Charles and Sir Edward Ryan, are to dine here quietly to day. I wish that I could flatter myself that anything will be talked about but India. The Indian news of to day is unpleasant, but does not at all affect the certainty of the result. Within a month from this time the tide will have completely turned; and another month will bring us news of the turn.

John and his son Charles called on me yesterday morning. Ellis was breakfasting with me. He had never seen either of them before. When they were gone, he said, "A fine young man, that nephew of yours. His mother must be a very handsome woman." A delicate compliment to John's appearance. Charles has been fitted out, and seems impatient for danger and distinction.

Love to Mamma and George.

Ever yours, my darling
TBM

TO THOMAS FLOWER ELLIS, 4 OCTOBER 1857

MS: Trinity College.

Holly Lodge Kensington / October 4. 1857

Dear Ellis,

I am sorry that I am under the necessity of being at the British Museum on Saturday afternoon. Panizzi has written to me pressingly. There is to be a meeting of Trustees after a longer interval than usual. There will be much to do. It is not easy in October to muster a Quorum; and I shall probably be in the Chair. I may not be able to escape till late; and I should not at all like to keep you waiting at chambers, in utter uncertainty as to the time of my coming.

We must give the plan up for this week; indeed, I fear, for this season. For I am already beginning to feel the approach of winter; and I doubt whether I shall accompany George to Cambridge. I wish to keep myself well in order that I may be able to take my seat on the first day of the Session.

Did you see an article about me in one of the papers of yesterday? I did not think that the splendour of my dress would ever have been a subject of remark in the public journals. It is related that a north country man was lately at a railway station, and that I was pointed out to him. "Look. That is Macaulay, the author." "Hoot man," was the answer; "That an author! Why he's vura weel dressed, that cheeld, and he has a vura gude hat. An author is as ragged as a potatoe bogle." Sir Edward Lytton will envy me this compliment more than any other that I ever received.

Ever yours
Macaulay

MS: Trinity College. *Extract published:* Trevelyan, II, 451n.

Holly Lodge June 25. 1858

Dear Ellis,

I am a little, and but a little, better. I have quite given up all thoughts of speaking to day. I should be forced to sit down in five minutes.

I went yesterday to Weybridge, passed a happy afternoon there, dined, and returned by a late train. We talked about the habit of building castles in the air, a habit in which Lady T and I indulge beyond any people that I ever knew. I mentioned to George what, as far as I know, no critic has observed, that the Greeks called this habit κενη μακαρια.* See Lucian's Hermotimus and his πλοιον.† Alice, who was some way off and did not hear distinctly, said "Kenneth Macaulay! What did the Greeks say about Kenneth Macaulay?" I shall always call the unreal world in which I pass a large part of my life my Kenneth Macaulay.

They have a very pleasant house, though a little too small, not for their own comfort, but for hospitality; and they are within two minutes' walk of the station, and yet are very little incommoded by the noise of the trains. I expect you on Tuesday.

Ever yours
Macaulay

MS: Trinity College.

Holly Lodge July 22. 1858

Dear Ellis,

I shall be glad to see you on Tuesday, since it cannot be earlier. We will then settle about Bromley.

Did not I point out to you a most absurd article on Metaphysics in the new edition of the Encyclopædia Britannica? The author is named Mansell. He has now got into a controversy with as great a fool as himself on the highly interesting and important question whether identity can properly be said to be a quality; – whether, for example, one of the qualities of Mr. Thomas Flower Ellis be his being the same person as Mr. Thomas Flower Ellis. Mr. Mansell contends strongly for the negative. He says that your being the same person as Mr. Thomas Flower Ellis is not one of your qualities, but the ground or substratum of your qualities. And these vagabonds pronounce it a desecration of philosophy to call Bacon and Newton philosophers.

* 'Empty happiness'.   † 'The Ship'.

I am just setting off for Weybridge. Poor Lady Parker is dead. She had long been hopelessly ill.

Ever yours,
Macaulay

TO HENRY THURSTAN HOLLAND, 2 AUGUST 1858

MS: The Viscount Knutsford.

Holly Lodge Kensington August 2 / 1858

My dear Holland,

I have this morning received a note from Lady Trevelyan, in which she tells me that my darling Margaret has consented to be your wife. When I say that this news has given me pleasure, I pay you no common compliment. For Margaret has been very dear to me from the day of her birth: I have watched, year after year, with the most tender interest, the development of her fine understanding and of her noble and amiable character; and it would make me miserable to see her united to any man, however rich and great, of whose principles and whose heart I had not a high opinion.

My pleasure is not without a large mixture of pain. Personally indeed I shall lose little by the change. But her father, her sister, and, above all, her mother, have much to suffer. I can wish you nothing better than that she may carry to the home to which she is going as much happiness as she has long diffused through the house which she must leave.

As for myself, the husband who possesses and deserves her affection will always be regarded by me as a most near and dear relation. / Ever, my dear Holland,

Yours very truly,
Macaulay

TO MARGARET TREVELYAN, 7 AUGUST 1858

MS: Trinity College.

Holly Lodge Kensington / August 7. 1858

My dear dear child,

Thanks for your sweet letter. I have read it with tears of pleasure and tenderness. I do indeed love you very much; and it is most gratifying to me to think that you love me, and will remember me kindly many years hence. As to the marks by which I try to show some part of the affection which I feel for you, you greatly overrate them. What have I to do with this opulence which has come too late for myself, except to employ it in promoting the happiness of others?

I have no doubt that we shall meet quite as often as formerly. And, now that I am going to have a good cook, I shall frequently give family dinners at which I shall hope to see both Mr. and Mrs. Holland. I assure you that I like him more than any young man that I know; and everybody has a good word for him.

By the bye, you cannot think how kindly and warmly Marian Ellis spoke to me about your prospects. She is exceedingly fond of you. Love to all. God bless you my dear Baba. I shall write to you at Calverton.

Yours ever
Macaulay

TO MRS HENRY THURSTAN HOLLAND, 7 DECEMBER 185[8]

MS: Trinity College.

Holly Lodge / December 7. 1856

Dearest Baba,

I am delighted to hear that you are so well and so happy. From your letter I judge that the weather is much finer at Fox Warren than here. I can hardly see the trees on my lawn; and the City is, no doubt, in Egyptian darkness. I have not stirred out since Thursday; and I had better have staid at home then. However I had the pleasure of seeing the children who are now objects of so much interest to us. Very engaging little things they are. I could with pleasure have spent a much longer time with them.

Lord Lansdowne, who has been in town under the care of a very clever aurist, called here two or three days ago, and talked most kindly about you and Holland. I really think that my dear old friend is less deaf than he was. He is much pleased by the general approbation which his present to Trinity College has obtained. I mean to see it next Easter; and I hope that you and your honest man, as Lady G. irreverently calls her husband, will be of the party.

Àpropos of Lady G. I applaud you for making poor Holland read Sir Charles Grandison right through. When we meet, your Mamma and I will examine him as severely as if he was a candidate for the Indian Civil Service. "What sum did Sir Charles present to each of the Danby family?" "How did Lord and Lady L. keep their money and draw it out?" "Of what religion was Mr. Bagenhall?" "In what square did Sir

Hargrave Pollexfen live?" "In what square Sir Charles Grandison, before his marriage?" "To what square did Sir Charles remove after his marriage?" "Where, and in what manner, did Lord G buy a town house?" "What became of Miss Cantillon?" Make Henry answer these in writing, without letting him see the book, and send me his answers that I may see whether he be worthy of a degree in Richardsonian learning. In the meantime give him my love. I am impatient to see you again, my darling. God bless you.

Ever yours,
Macaulay

TO MRS HENRY THURSTAN HOLLAND, 31 MARCH 1859

MS: Trinity College.

Holly Lodge Kensington / March 31. 1859

Dearest Baba,

I received your kind letter yesterday evening. Many thanks for it. I was forced to stay at home and to send an excuse to the Vernon Smiths. For the snow was half a foot deep, and was still falling; and it had begun to freeze. To day the thaw is proceeding rapidly. But my trees and flowers have suffered grievously. I breakfasted at the Duke of Argyll's, and met a small, but a very pleasant party. I have invited, for next Wednesday, the Duke, the Duchess, Dundas, Lord Glenelg, Lord Carlisle, Lord Grey, Labouchere, Charles Howard, Lady Trevelyan and Mrs. Holland. Mr. Holland and Lord Macaulay will make the company up to twelve exactly. Lord Grey I met this morning at Argyll Lodge, and found him extremely pleasant.

Whether Alice will come this afternoon I cannot tell. It is fine above, but dreadfully sloppy and dirty below; and the little Buxtons will be unable to have a run in the garden.

I am surprised to hear so bad an account of the St Leonard's circulating Library. You should go to Hastings for books. Love to Mamma.

Ever yours
Macaulay

I open my letter to tell you that your uncle John has just been here. I never was more surprised than by what he told me. I will never again flatter myself that I have the least insight into the character of any human being. What do you think is his reason – his principal reason at least –for running up to town at this season? He has not yet told Charles, and seemed to have some difficulty in telling me. But all the world will know it from the newspapers of next Monday. The people who have been busy of late in providing preachers for great congregations in London had heard, it seems, that a son of the pious and benevolent Z M, a brother of Lord M, and a brother in law of Sir C.E.T. was in the Church. They satisfied themselves that he was not a Puseyite; and they invited him to help them. He, who, I should have thought, would, of all men, have been the least likely to endure the thought of such an exhibition, is to preach in Exeter Hall, next Sunday, to three thousand people. I hardly knew what to say or which way to look. I asked him on what subject he meant to hold forth. He said that he thought that he could not use the opportunity better than by exposing the evils of Auricular Confession. He has chosen for his text "Cease ye from man whose breath is in his nostrils." Those words, he said, would be a good introduction to a discourse on the folly of trusting to the absolution of a frail fellow creature. In truth I hardly knew him. He seems to be possessed with the notion that now or never is the time for him to signalise himself as a pulpit orator, and that he may rise, nobody can tell how high, in his profession. He mentioned his son: but it was very slightly. Indeed I see that, till after next Sunday, it will be impossible for him to think of anything but the display which he is to make. You and Mamma will be amazed, I think, by all this, unless indeed you happen to remember that this is the first of April – April fools – April fools. Now was not that a good lie, well told? I have not seen John, and do not expect to see him till to morrow. Again ever yours

Macaulay

TO THOMAS FLOWER ELLIS, 1 APRIL 1859

MS: Trinity College. *Partly published:* G. M. Trevelyan, *Sir George Otto Trevelyan,* pp. 38–9.

Holly Lodge April 1, 1859

Dear Ellis,

How are you getting on? Does the case of Lord S——sbury come on or not? And when am I likely to have you here revelling in asparagus and young onions? I hope that last Wednesday has not been fatal to all the nurseries and kitchen gardens hereabouts. But such a change of weather I never saw. Tuesday was like a delicious day in May. Twenty four hours after the snow was falling in such thick large flakes that I could hardly see to the end of my little domain. Some of my trees have lost large boughs, which were unable to bear the double weight of their leaves and of the snow. Lilacs, thorns, willows, violets, wall flowers, almond blossoms, and apple blossoms all disappeared under one dead white covering. It was a most ghastly transformation. I never before saw a landscape in full leaf completely hidden by snow in the space of three hours. However yesterday the sun came out warm; and then the snow caught it. I never saw so rapid a thaw. But my flowerbeds look miserable. My gardener however encourages me to hope that no serious damage has been done. And indeed, as there was frost, it was rather an advantage that there was snow too. A few white patches are still lying on spots covered from the sun and open to the north wind. But, thank heaven, the wind has now changed. Had you anything of the sort? There was no snow at St Leonards as far as I can make out, though much wind and chill rain; and my brother John, who was travelling up from the north fell in with no snow till he got near town.

I hear every day from St Leonards, and sometimes twice a day. My dear child is well again, and expecting her husband, who, I believe, will join her this evening, and will take down little Alice with him. They all return next Monday. We have very good accounts of George from various quarters. He did very well at the University Scholarship examination. No Trinity man of his own year was near him. One man of his own year – a Johnian – was above him; and another – a Kingsman – close upon him. But this looks promising for a high place in the Classical Tripos. The examiners say too that he is very greatly improved. I cannot help feeling pleased that this improvement should have been the effect purely of his own unassisted studies, carried on from real love of ancient literature. He has had no cramming, but has gone in against the pupils of Donaldson and Shilleto with no other training than that which you and I had. I have half a mind to take the responsibility of advising him to go on in the same way during the next twenty months; and he would certainly take my advice: for he has struggled obstinately against the prevailing fashion, and had set his heart, as he owned to his mother, on being a scholar after the pattern of our generation and not after the new mode. His natural feeling about me has done him some harm, with, I hope, some good. His neglect of mathematics is to be ascribed to the bad example which I set him. It is owing to me too, I must say on the other side, that he lives in the very midst of an atmosphere reeking with Carlylism, Ruskinism, Browningism, and other equally noxious isms, without the slightest taint of the morbific virus. How I have run on – pouring out domestic tattle so copiously that I have left myself no room for politics. I could however add but little to what you will see in the papers.

Ever yours
Macaulay

MS: Trinity College.

Holly Lodge June 9. 1859

Dearest Hannah,

I do not know whether to give you joy of George's medal or not. He seems to be very ill satisfied. His epigram is certainly a good exercise, but far inferior to the poem which he wrote for the Camden prize.

Macleod was here yesterday, talking about Trevelyan much as he talked to you; and I answered much as you had done.

I am rather anxious to know what arrangement will be made about the Indian department, in the event of a change of ministry. Vernon, thank Heaven, is out of the question. I should prefer Lord Granville to anybody else. Next to Lord Granville I should like Charles Wood. I do not however think it by any means certain that the ministers will be in a minority; and, if they weather this storm, they are safe till 1860.

I have a story for you. Yesterday I breakfasted with the Stanhopes who had asked Mrs. Gaskell to meet me. I walked away, and was crossing the park, when a gentleman who was at some little distance called me by my name, and joined me. I did not know him, but, from the first words he said, I perceived that he had heard the debate in the Lords on the preceding evening. We chatted about it, till he said something which made me doubt whether I could safely continue the conversation. My companion might be a peer. He might be a gentleman of the press; and I might see my careless expressions in the Daily News or the Morning Post of the next day. "May I ask," I said, "with whom I have the honor of conversing?" The answer knocked me down. "The Duke of Cambridge." It was he. As you may suppose my hat was instantly off. "I beg your Royal Highness's pardon. You will not, I hope, suspect me of intentional disrespect." And I pleaded that odd infirmity of sight or memory, – I hardly know which to call it, – by which I have been led into so many scrapes. He was as good natured as possible, and we had a long talk about the war and the debate. We agreed very well. By the bye the speech in the debate which was most to my taste was Lord Ellenborough's. I agreed with almost every word of it. Lord Granville spoke well; but he did not, and indeed, situated as he was, could not say all that he thinks. He is, I am confident, of the same opinion with Lord Ellenborough and me.

I had a short walk with Thackeray yesterday and found that the literary world is in quite as unsatisfactory a state as the political worlds. Nothing but jealousies, enmities, cabal, detraction, knavery, ingratitude. Thank God, I have always, even when I was writing for bread, kept quite aloof from the whole race of hackney scribblers. I could hardly believe – even now I can hardly believe – some of Thackeray's anecdotes. I have left myself no room to relate them. Love to my little Alice. Tell me how you are accommodated, and how you spend your days.

Ever yours
Macaulay

TO FRANCES MACAULAY, 6 JULY 1859

MS: Huntington Library.

Holly Lodge Kensington / July 6. 1859

Dearest Fanny,

I am truly glad to have so good an account of your trip northwards. The weather is glorious here, hot, but not too hot, at least not too hot for those who like me can repose in the shade when the sun is high.

Yesterday poor Lord Ebrington called on me. I was extremely touched by his misfortunes and still more by the courage and cheerfulness with which he endures them. I am ashamed to think that I should ever suffer my complaints to make me querulous, when I see how he bears his. I have asked him to breakfast here on Friday where he will meet the Duke and Duchess of Argyle, Lord and Lady Belper, Baba, and, I hope, Dundas and the Milmans. Lord Ebrington gives a delightful account of Madeira. You teetotallers will be delighted to hear that, since the vines perished there, the condition of the common people has greatly improved.

Yesterday I dined at Lord Broughton's and sate next Lord Clarendon. We were talking about the difference between the young fellows of our generation and those of the rising generation. He denied that there had been any moral improvement. "The principal change" he said, "is that I used to call my father the Governor, and that now a youth calls his father the Relieving Officer." This name was quite new to me. Ask George if it is the established word for a father at Cambridge. If Lord Clarendon is right the deterioration is fearful. For the word Governor, irreverent as it is, implies authority. But a Relieving Officer exists merely to disburse money. A lad at home, I suppose, is said to be in the work house, – a lad at Cambridge to be receiving out door relief. By the bye why does not George write either to me or to his sister? "I am sorry to say it: but that young man is not the thing." Where is that?

Alice behaves much better. I had a delightful letter from her this morning which shall be answered in no long time. Love to Hannah, her good girl, and her naughty boy.

Ever yours,
Macaulay

MS: Trinity College. *Extracts published:* Trevelyan, II, 473; 474.

Holly Lodge Oct 24. 1859

Dear Ellis,

I shall be very glad if you can come here on Saturday or on Sunday morning. I have been very well in body since we parted. But in mind I have suffered much, and the more because I have had to put a force upon myself in order to appear cheerful. It is at last settled that Hannah and Alice are to go to Madras in February. I cannot deny that it is right; and my duty is to avoid whatever can add to the pain which they suffer. But I am very unhappy, so unhappy that I heartily wished when Stephenson's hearse passed through the Park on Friday that I could change places with him. You know what your feelings would be if Marian and Louise were both going to India in February; and you can sympathise with me.

However, I read, and write, and contrive to forget my sorrow during whole hours. But it recurs and will recur. I could almost wish that what is to be were to be immediately. I dread the next four months more than even the months which will follow the separation. This prolonged parting – this slow sipping of the vinegar and the gall – is terrible. It is something that my dear Margaret is left to me, though her grief adds to mine. She is at St Leonard's, getting on very well.

I am pleased to hear from George that he and young Everett are very great friends. Everett seems to be very clever and good hearted, though odd. His scholarship is of a different sort from ours. His composition, of which George sent me a specimen, would be thought very poor here. His quantities are right; and there is meaning and thought; but nothing can be more tuneless than the verse. On the other hand his reading is very extensive. His knowledge of the Latin authors, George says, is more than thrice that of the best men who go up from Eton and Harrow. This reminds me of the peculiar training which Pitt underwent. I am glad to hear that Everett takes to Cambridge, and still more to hear that he is grateful, warmly and affectionately grateful, for hints as to his deficiencies. George is raving about the seventh Book of Thucydides, and dying to visit Syracuse.

I have been studying Bentley's Horace, often dissenting, often doubting, always admiring. There is a wonderful note on that passage in the pretty hymn to Faunus

"Ludit herboso pecus omne campo
Cum tibi Nonæ redeunt Decembres;

Festus in pratis vacat otiosus
      Cum bove *pagus*.
   Inter audaces lupus errat agnos etc."

I do not know whether you are aware that all the M.S.S. of the greatest celebrity have *pardus* instead of *pagus*. It required, one would think, no great sagacity to see that *pardus* could not be right. For there were no pards in Italy except in the dens under the amphitheatres. But how did the mistake originate? And how did it spread so as to corrupt almost all the M.S.S.? Bentley's solution of this problem is admirable. The transcribers in the middle ages were generally monks. Some good Benedictine had in his head the verse of Isaiah, "Habitabit lupus cum agno; et pardus cum hædo accubabit." He saw that Horace made the wolf live peaceably with the lamb, and was struck by the wonderful coincidence between this profane poem and holy writ. So, knowing nothing about zoology, he brought in the pard too, by the alteration of a letter, and thought, no doubt, that he had done a great feat. This reading, once introduced, was so exactly suited to the taste and the erudition which then flourished in monasteries that it was generally adopted. Does not this strike you as a most ingenious and satisfactory explanation?

But I must stop. Let me know when I shall see you, as soon as you are able to fix a time.

Ever yours
Macaulay

TO GEORGE OTTO TREVELYAN, 24 OCTOBER 1859

MS: Trinity College. *Published: Times Literary Supplement,* 9 March 1916, p. 115.

Holly Lodge Kensington / October 24. 1859

Dear George,

Thanks for your letters. I am truly glad to find that you are on a friendly footing with Everett. I have a great value for his father. Pray bring the young fellow to call on me when you are next in town, if he should be in town too; and tell him that I should be most happy to be able to serve him in any way.

I hope that you, like him, will be more grateful for good advice than for praise. I therefore take the liberty to point out to you a false spelling of which you are guilty, a false spelling too particularly censurable in a scholar – "to *pander* to the insatiable love of rhetoric." Now you are surely aware that the word *pandar* is simply the proper name of the warrior whom Homer calls Pandarus, and who is prompted by Minerva to break the treaty between the Greeks and Trojans. The poets and romancers of the middle ages, knowing generally that he had been represented by Homer as a faithless and dishonorable man, made him connive, and more than connive, at the gallantries of his niece Cressida. Thence the name of Pandarus and Pandar was given to pimps. When Falstaff wishes Pistol to carry a love letter to a married woman, Pistol exclaims

"Shall I Sir Pandarus of Troy become?"

It is therefore most incorrect to spell the word *pander*. In fact this spelling, like *Syren*, like *Sybil*, like *pigmy*, and some other spellings which might be mentioned, raises a strong presumption that the person who is guilty of it does not know Greek.

I am glad that you are properly interested about the siege of Syracuse. The seventh book of Thucydides is the finest piece of history in the world. Livy, Tacitus, Sallust, Xenophon, vanish before it. It is absolutely perfect. I have often wished to visit Syracuse. But I believe that the coast has undergone considerable changes. The quarries in which the prisoners were confined remain; and, to judge by the pictures which I have seen, must be well worth visiting.

I wonder that you should carry away from the De Natura Deorum no impression but that of the style. Surely the Academic philosopher makes minced meat of the Epicurean. The first book I think the best. But on the whole I prefer the argument against the Epicurean in the De Finibus. The De Fato and the De Divinatione are also, I think, excellently reasoned.

I have of late been reading Bentley's Horace again, with frequent dissent, with frequent doubt, and with constant admiration. I am meditating an attack on Athenæus, of whom I know less than I could wish. I must begin by getting a better edition than the old folio which I now possess.

Mamma came back on Thursday. On Friday she and Alice dined with me; and to morrow I am to dine with them. Yesterday Sir Henry Holland called here. He spoke most kindly about you. In another week, I suppose, Baba will be returning to Chester Square. I am well enough in body – very much otherwise, as you may suppose, in mind – but I put a force on myself, and plague other people with my feelings as little as I can.

Ever yours
Macaulay

MS: Trinity College.

Holly Lodge November 15 / 1859

Dearest Fanny,

The reports which you mention are quite absurd. Do you imagine that, if Lord Palmerston expected an invasion in a fortnight, the whole nation would not be called to arms? He does not warn the country. He does not, as I think that I can venture to affirm, hint any such apprehension to the Secretaries of State and to the Lord Privy Seal. And am I to believe that he keeps this tremendous secret from his colleagues, only in order to tell it to the gossips of Brighton? These stories are just as idle as the trash of Cumming and Elliot about the prophecies. If you were well acquainted with that subject, you would know that there has never been a generation since the first establishment of Christianity in which it has not been confidently asserted that the prophecies plainly referred to contemporary events, and that the end of the present dispensation was at hand. The taking of Jerusalem in the first Century, the dissolution of the Western Empire in the fifth century, the Crusades in the eleventh Century, the Thirty Years' war, the war of the Spanish Succession, the French Revolution, the conquests of Buonaparte, all have been supposed to indicate the approach of the last scene of the great drama. A hundred and thirty seven years ago Bishop Lloyd of Worcester, a very learned and pious man, not less pious and much more learned than either Elliot or Cumming, proved to Queen Anne out of Daniel and the Revelations that a great and decisive crisis in human affairs was at hand. Lord Treasurer Oxford raised some objections. "Madam," said the Bishop. "I speak according to the word of God, which will be fulfilled, whether your Majesty's Treasurer likes it or not." When I was a boy, no human being doubted that Buonaparte was a principal subject of the prophecies of the old Testament. I was not born when he went to Egypt. But I have heard my father say that the prophets were then wilder than ever he remembered them. They fully expected the battle in the Valley of Jehosaphat and the restoration of the Jews within a year. The truth is that every generation is of more importance to itself than all preceding and all future generations. Every generation therefore imagines that it is of special importance in the great scheme of divine government which goes on slowly unrolling itself through thousands upon thousands of years. Our self love makes us think that visions seen in Assyria two thousand five hundred years ago must have related to us rather than to any of those who have lived before us or who are to come after us. We laugh at Bishop Lloyd who thought that these visions prefigured the French King of his time and the Sultan of his time; and we confidently maintain that they prefigure the troubles of our time. Our grandchildren will laugh at us, and will find in the Bible clear predictions of the wars which will in their time rage between South America and Australasia. Cumming and Elliot are in their calling. But I am sorry that Lord Carlisle should make such a fool of himself.

Ever yours,
Macaulay

TO GEORGE OTTO TREVELYAN, 22 NOVEMBER 1859

MS: Fitzwilliam Museum. *Published: Times Literary Supplement,* 9 March 1916, p. 115.

Holly Lodge Nov 22. 1859

Dear George,

Thanks for your letter. This is the day of the Christening, and the hour of the Christening; and I am writing to you instead of doing my duty at the font. The reason is that the ninth plague of Egypt is upon us. The fog is such that I cannot see one tree in my garden; and, bad as things are here, the postman reports that they are worse still at Knightsbridge. If I were to venture out, we should probably have a burial in the family, as well as a christening. I therefore stay, very disconsolately, by my fire side, and wait for my footman whom I have sent to Belgravia for news, and who may perhaps find his way back through the darkness in the course of a few hours.

I am glad that you mean to pass the Christmas Vacation at home. But you must read resolutely. There is no chance of my visiting Cambridge at present. The story about my two volumes is a newspaper lie. One Volume may perhaps appear two years hence.

I sympathise with the grievances of your rifle corps. But there is nothing new under the sun. The young volunteers of 1803, of whom few are now left, and those few Law Lords, Archdeacons, and Professors, were treated in just the same way. My old master Preston was one of them, and retained many years a bitter sense of the injustice and incivility which they had to endure. By the bye, one of the most eager and warlike among them was Garratt, the second wrangler and first Smith's prize man of 1804. This always amused me: for Garratt was quite a dwarf, – the very smallest man that I ever saw gratis.

I was delighted by Butler's success; and the more so because it was unexpected. I suppose that he will be made a Doctor of Divinity without delay. My kind regards to him if he is at Cambridge, and my warm congratulations.

Sir Charles Wood, the Secretary of State for India, dined here on Saturday. I was glad to learn from him that your father is going on as well as possible, and giving the highest satisfaction to the home authorities.

Ellis told me that he had heard from you. I am of his mind about the Parmenides and about the two dialogues which cannot be separated from the Parmenides, the Politicus and the Sophista. Here Whewell agrees with us. But he thinks the Laches genuine; and I am sure that it is spurious. I will give you my reasons at Christmas if you care to hear them.

If you are asked to write the tripos verse of 1860, you may make an excellent eclogue on the Cambridge Rifle Corps. Menalcas, with his bow and quiver, comes to the mouth of a cave overhung with ivy and wild vines, where Daphnis and Alexis are contending in verse, with Damœtas for judge. Menalcas indignantly bids them throw away their pipes, and take to their arms. "Have you not heard that the tyrant who calls himself a Heracleid, threatens Arcadia with invasion and subjugation? All the shepherds are mustering from Cyllene to Phigalia. The beacons are ready to be lighted on the tops of Mænalus and Parthenius. The women and children are taking refuge behind the walls of Tegea and Orchomenus. There are mighty gatherings of archers and spearmen in the valleys of Ladon and Erymanthus. And you sit here disputing the prize of singing (i e the Craven scholarship) as if all were quiet." Perhaps you might bring in a fling at the Lord Lieutenant.

Ever yours,
Macaulay

TO LORD PALMERSTON, 2 DECEMBER 1859

MS: National Register of Archives.

Holly Lodge Kensington December 2. 1859
Dear Lord Palmerston,

I have considered the question which you put to me last Saturday; and I will now tell you my opinion with perfect sincerity.

There may be candidates for the Chair of Modern History at Cambridge of whom I have not heard. Of those whose names have reached me the two of most note are Dr. Latham and Mr. Helps. My acquaintance with those gentlemen is the slightest possible. I have no bias towards either, except that I know Dr. Latham to be very poor, and that, for that reason, I should, if the question were one of mere private feeling, be inclined to give my voice in his favour. But private feeling has nothing to do here; and, as you have done me the honor to ask my advice, I am

303

bound to give it you with a single view to your credit and to the public interest, which are identical.

Both these gentlemen have considerable merit. If I were asked which of them was the superior in abilities and attainments, I should find it difficult to decide. But each of them has his own proper field. If you were looking out for a Professor of Ethnology, I should say that Dr. Latham was your man. But the part of history which has chiefly engaged his attention is so far from being modern history that it is more ancient than what we commonly call ancient history. The Romans and Greeks are to him people of yesterday. His researches go back to times before Nineveh and Memphis were built, nay, before the negro race, and the copper coloured race, and the white race, had branched off from the common stock. He will prove to you that the Magyars and the Laplanders are near of kin, and that the tribes which inhabited the Spanish peninsula, when the first Carthaginian factories were formed there, were not Celtic. As to the history of our own country, he would, I doubt not, have much that would be interesting to say about the early part of it, about the Druidical institutions and monuments, about the fusion of British, Roman, German, and Scandinavian elements in our language and in our blood. But I do not apprehend that he has made a particular study of the events of the last five centuries. Nevertheless, if you should give him this Professorship, I have no doubt that a vigorous mind like his, accustomed to close application and to historical research, would produce much that would be valuable on the subjects to which it would then be his duty to direct his attention. But the attention of Mr. Helps has long been specially directed to some very interesting and important portions of modern history. He has treated those portions of history ably and popularly. Without, therefore, pronouncing him the superior man of the two, I am forced to say that I think him the fitter of the two for the vacant Chair; and all that I hear leads me to think that, if you make choice of him, your choice will be applauded by the public.

Having thus discharged my conscience, at some cost of private feeling, I cannot help adding that I am greatly concerned for poor Latham. His talents and learning are held in high estimation both here and in foreign countries; and yet he is, I am afraid, in extreme penury. I do not wish to see pensions lavished on poets, novellists, and historians. If they write well, they can scarcely fail to find readers in plenty, and will want no other Mæcenas than Longman or Murray. But there are walks of literature and science in which a man may toil long, and diligently, and usefully, and honorably, without earning even a bare subsistence. He may display such powers and make such discoveries that his name shall be mentioned with respect in every Academy from Petersburg to Madrid; and yet he may make less by the labour of his whole life than the booksellers are willing to give for some showy articles in a Review. The case of such a man seems to me to be peculiarly entitled to the attention of such a minister as your friends are proud to believe you to be. Latham seems to me to be exactly the man on whom a pension would be with propriety bestowed. Excuse me for offering this suggestion. I could not help it. Having myself been one of the most fortunate of literary men, one of the very few literary men whom the favour of the public has raised to opulence, I cannot but feel great compassion for writers, who, with perhaps more merit than mine, have had less popularity; and for Dr. Latham I feel peculiar compassion, because I have been compelled by a sense of duty to give, on the present occasion, an opinion adverse to his wishes. / Ever, my dear Lord Palmerston,

Yours most faithfully,
Macaulay

The / Viscount Palmerston / etc. etc. etc.

TO EDWARD EVERETT, 21 DECEMBER 1859

MS: Massachusetts Historical Society. *Extract published: New York Ledger,* 25 February 1860.

Holly Lodge Kensington / December 21. 1859

My dear Everett,

Last week I received your letter of the 29th of November; and scarcely had I read it, when your son was announced. He found me at a bad time. For a severe frost had just set in. My blood was frozen in my veins; and I could hardly speak for coughing. I was however truly glad to see him; and I hope that, whenever he stays a week or two in London, I shall see much more of him. He was just on the wing for the Speaker's. Thence he meant to go to Lord Hatherton's; and thence to Cambridge. I am assured that he has already made himself liked and esteemed among the undergraduates; and, from the short glimpse which I caught of him, I can well believe it.

There was nothing that the most austere censor could blame in his writing to me. He did not write till I had sent him, through his friend George Trevelyan, a message which it would have been unkind and ungraceful not to acknowledge.

I am truly glad that your son and George are intimate. Originally, I believe, George's motive was to please me. But he very soon found that his new friend, though not, in all points, trained according to the English pattern, was, in parts and character, one of the first young men in the University. [. . .]

MS: Trinity College. *Mostly published:* Trevelyan, II, 477.

Holly Lodge Xmas Day 1859

Dear Ellis,

I send a line, as you desired, though it will tell you only that I am much as I was. The physicians think me better; but there is little change in my sensations. The day before yesterday I had a regular fainting fit, and lay quite insensible. I wish that I had continued to lie so. For if death be no more – Up I got however; and the Doctors agree that the circumstance is altogether unimportant.

I hope that you will be able to come next Saturday. At all events, write from Leeds.

Ever yours
Macaulay

INDEX

Russell, Lord John, afterwards 1st Earl, Whig prime minister, 49, 65, 66, 67, 71, 91, 94, 134, 193, 195, 196, 204, 216–18, 242–3, 245
Letter to: 184
Russell, Lady Louisa, 81
Russell, William, Lord, afterwards 8th Duke of Bedford, 52, 54, 55
Russell, Lord William (1639–83), 106, 259
Rutherfurd, Andrew, 213, 254
Ryan, Sir Edward, 159, 288

Sadler, Michael Thomas, TBM's opponent at Leeds, 47, 83, 84, 219
St Aulaire, Comte de, 67
Sallust, 161, 300
Saville, Sir George, 168
Scarlett, James: see Lord Abinger
Schiller, Johann Christian Friedrich, 163, 232, 249
Scholefield, James, 15
Scott, Sir Walter, 21, 25, 39, 58, 78, 124, 170–1
Senior, Nassau, contributor to *Edinburgh Review*, 181, 183, 187, 205, 209, 248
Seward, Anna, 37
Seymour, Lady, 87
Shadwell, Thomas, 242
Shakespear, Henry, 156
Shakespeare, William, 25, 122, 124, 126, 186, 250
Sharp, Granville, 9
Sharp, Richard, merchant and man of letters, 58, 68, 106, 110–11, 121, 159
Shaw-Lefevre, Sir John, 266, 282
Sheil, Richard Lalor, M.P., 51, 63
Shepherd, William, 44
Sheridan, Richard Brinsley, 53
Shilleto, Richard, private tutor, 295
Shore, Frederick John, 167
Shrewsbury, 16th Earl of, 231–2
Sibthorpe, Richard Waldo, 34
Siddons, Mrs Sarah, 212, 246
Sidney, Algernon, 106
Sierra Leone, 13
Silius Italicus, 161
Simeon, Charles, 5
Simonides, 151
Sismondi, J. C. L. Simonde de, 14, 124
Smith, Sir Culling Eardley, 219
Smith, John, 65
Smith, Robert Vernon, afterwards Lord Lyveden, 293, 296
Smith, Sydney, clergyman and wit, the Smith of Smiths, 32–3, 58–9, 60, 61, 77, 91, 110, 209

Smith, Mrs Sydney, 32
Smith Payne and Smith's, bankers, 274
Smollett, Tobias, 12
Smyth, William, 37
Sophocles, 161, 186, 261
Sotheby, William, 37
Soufflot, Jacques Germain, 47
Soult, Marshal, 194
South, Robert, 280
Southey, Robert, 21, 178, 185, 213, 242
Spencer, 2nd Earl, 52
Spencer, 3rd Earl: see Lord Althorp
Spencer, Captain Frederick, 4th Earl, 69, 261
Spenser, Edmund, 212
Spring-Rice: see Rice, Thomas Spring-
Spurgeon, Charles Haddon, evangelical preacher, 283
Spurzheim, Johann Kaspar, 214
Stainforth, George, 7, 8, 16, 26
Stanfield, Clarkson, 277
Stanhope, Philip Henry Stanhope (styled Lord Mahon), afterwards 5th Earl, Tory politician and historian, 53, 72, 214, 283, 296
Letters to: 239, 241
Stanley, Edward George: see 14th Earl of Derby
Statius, 161
Stephen, Sir James, 79, 81, 100, 181, 207–9, 213
Letters to: 119, 231
Stephenson, Robert, engineer, 298
Sterne, Laurence, 182
Stewart, Dugald, 162, 193
Stewart-Mackenzie, James Alexander, M.P., 87, 99, 101, 121
Stopford, Admiral Sir Robert, 187
Stowe, Calvin, 278
Stowe, Harriet Beecher, 277–8
Strutt, Edward: see Lord Belper
Sue, Eugène, 266
Sugden, Edward, later 1st Baron St Leonards, Lord Chancellor, 165
Sutherland, James Charles Colebrooke, letter to, 154
Swift, Jonathan, 170, 186
Swinburne, Lady, 33
Sylla, 9
Symonds, Dr John Addington, 257

Tacitus, 13, 19, 23, 186, 300
Tait's Edinburgh Magazine, 119
Talleyrand, Charles, Prince de, 66–7, 73, 235
Tasso, Torquato, 124, 186